MYTH
AMERICA

MYTH AMERICA

HISTORIANS TAKE ON THE BIGGEST LEGENDS AND LIES ABOUT OUR PAST

EDITED BY
KEVIN M. KRUSE AND
JULIAN E. ZELIZER

BASIC BOOKS

New York

Basic Books

Hachette Book Group

1290 Avenue of the Americas, New York, NY 10104

www.basicbooks.com

Printed in the United States of America

First Edition: October 2022

Published by Basic Books, an imprint of Perseus Books, LLC, a subsidiary of Hachette Book Group, Inc. The Basic Books name and logo is a trademark of the Hachette Book Group.

The Hachette Speakers Bureau provides a wide range of authors for speaking events. To find out more, go to www.hachettespeakersbureau.com or call (866) 376-6591.

The publisher is not responsible for websites (or their content) that are not owned by the publisher.

Print book interior design by Amy Quinn.

Library of Congress Cataloging-in-Publication Data

Names: Kruse, Kevin Michael, 1972– editor. | Zelizer, Julian E., editor.

Title: Myth America : historians take on the biggest legends and lies about our past / edited by Kevin M. Kruse, Julian E. Zelizer.

Description: First edition. | New York : Basic Books, 2022. | Includes bibliographical references and index.

Identifiers: LCCN 2022001566 | ISBN 9781541601390 (hardcover) | ISBN 9781541601406 (ebook)

Subjects: LCSH: United States—History—Errors, inventions, etc. | United States—Historiography.

Classification: LCC E179 .M993 2022 | DDC 973—dc23/eng/20220519

LC record available at https://lccn.loc.gov/2022001566

ISBNs: 9781541601390 (hardcover), 9781541601406 (ebook)

LSC-C

Printing 1, 2022

To the archivists, librarians, teachers, and fellow historians who give us a better, and more accurate, understanding of our nation's past.

CONTENTS

INTRODUCTION

Kevin M. Kruse and Julian E. Zelizer

W E LIVE IN THE AGE OF DISINFORMATION.
To be sure, there have always been lies in our public discourse. But in the last few years the floodgates have opened wide, and the line between fact and fiction has become increasingly blurred if not completely erased. Unlike past eras in which myths and misunderstandings have clouded our national debate, the current crisis stands apart both for the degree of disinformation and for the deliberateness with which it has been spread.

Crises never have a single cause, but in this instance a good deal of blame can be attributed to the political campaigns and presidency of Donald Trump. His administration thrived on deceptions and distortions, reframing its own lies as "alternative facts." The fire hose of falsehoods coming from the Trump White House was so pronounced that the *Washington Post* launched a database tracking them all, accounting for more than thirty thousand instances in the end.[1] Whereas previous presidencies might have been embarrassed by such fact-checking, Trump and his aides simply waved away these corrections as "fake news."[2] Even when watchdogs inside the administration pushed back against the president's statements, they too were ignored or, in the case of five inspector generals, simply dismissed.[3] This consistent embrace of disinformation could, at times, turn deadly. As the COVID-19 pandemic swept the nation, the administration effectively went to war with scientists and medical experts, engaging in what the Union for Concerned Scientists called "an egregious pattern of ignoring, sidelining, and censoring the voices of scientists and their research." Refusing to face facts, President Trump insisted in February 2020 that the number of coronavirus cases in the nation would "within a couple of days . . . be down to close to zero."[4] When he left office less than a year later, however, the country had experienced tens of millions of cases and four hundred thousand deaths from the virus.[5] The Trump administration's long-running war on the truth culminated with a massive campaign to discredit the 2020 election and a violent insurrection at the United States Capitol designed to stop the certification of the results. This may have been, as critics charged, "the big lie," but it was only one of many.

The Trump presidency pushed the country to this crisis point, but it was able to do so only because of two large-scale changes that have in recent years given right-wing myths a huge platform and an accordingly large impact on American life.

The first major development was the creation of the conservative media ecosystem, which ranges today from cable news networks such as Fox News, Newsmax, and One America News to websites such as Breitbart. Unlike the network news programs of the so-called mainstream media, which placed great emphasis on an evenhanded approach that hewed to objective facts and eschewed editorializing, these new outlets have taken a different tack. Abandoning the old broadcast television approach of the post–World War II era, they instead embraced a "narrowcast" model of the cable age, one that seeks to echo the partisan point of view of a carefully cultivated target audience and to amplify their assumptions back to them. Engaging and enraging viewers became the primary aim, it seems, not any conventional journalistic commitment to the truth. (Indeed, when its popular host Tucker Carlson was sued for slander, Fox News, own lawyers argued that Carlson's on-air statements "cannot reasonably be interpreted as facts" because the show clearly engages in "exaggeration" and "non-literal commentary.")[6] Importantly, the conservative media ecosystem was augmented by the even more wide-open world of social media, especially Facebook, Twitter, and Reddit, where the tendency to find like-minded partisans and the freedom from fact-checkers took disinformation to new depths. Taken together, these venues have given far-right lies unprecedented access to significant numbers of Americans and, just as important, let ordinary Americans spread lies to one another as well. As a result, misinformation and disinformation have infused our debates about almost every pertinent political question.

The second significant change, related to the first, is the devolution of the Republican Party's commitment to truth. All political parties, by their very need to pull in voters and push them to the polls, have long engaged in various versions of political spin, privileging selective evidence and occasional outright lies. But, until recently, Republicans fashioned themselves as realists who would keep the irrational idealism of Democrats in check. Despite his own record of drifting away from facts in ways big and small, President Ronald Reagan took pride in presenting his brand of conservatism as one committed to clear-eyed truths. "It isn't so much that liberals are ignorant," he liked to say. "It's just that they know so many things that aren't so."[7]

Within a generation of the Reagan era, however, Republicans' self-image as realists respecting hard facts had taken a beating. "Remember Republicans?" the screenwriter and Bush-era blogger John Rogers asked in 2004. "Sober men in suits, pipes, who'd nod thoughtfully over their latest tract on market-driven fiscal conservatism while grinding out the numbers on rocket science. . . . How did they become the party of fairy dust and make believe? How did they become the anti-science guys? The anti-fact guys? The *anti-logic guys*?"[8] Surprisingly, Republicans largely did it to themselves. In 2004 a top aide to President George W. Bush famously scoffed at what he called "the reality-based community."[9] In foreign affairs and domestic policies alike, the administration engaged in a running battle with experts and the facts they carried with them.[10] By 2008, the shift had become clear, with prominent politicians like Alaska governor Sarah Palin, the party's vice-presidential candidate, positioning themselves against intellectuals, universities, the media, and other sources of valid information.[11]

During the Obama era, out-of-power Republicans felt freer to criticize what the administration was doing and craft fantastical complaints about what it was not. They propagated wild conspiracies about the existence of "death panels" in the Affordable Care Act and spread claims that the program would provide coverage to undocumented immigrants.[12] When Obama pushed back against the latter falsehood in a formal address to a joint session of Congress, Republican congressman Joe Wilson yelled out "You lie!" Even after fact-checkers proved that the president had not, in fact, lied, Wilson remained undeterred, promoting his outburst in a fund-raising pitch that quickly raked in a million dollars.[13] During the 2012 presidential campaign, Republicans devoted themselves to similar attacks on facts, ranging from "unskewing" poll numbers they didn't like to dismissing employment statistics they found "suspicious."[14] Notably, as the party drifted further and further from the facts, Donald Trump gained a foothold in conservative circles by spreading the "birther" conspiracy that Barack Obama had not been born in the United States and was therefore ineligible to be president.[15] With Trump's own run for president four years later and the ascendancy of the QAnon conspiracy on the far-right fringes, the transformation was complete.[16]

The current war on truth has unfolded along multiple fronts. The fields of science, medicine, law, and public policy, among others, have been the subject of sustained assaults. But history too has come under attack, and for obvious reasons. As George Orwell famously observed in his dystopian novel *1984*, "Who controls the past controls the future."[17]

Claims about what happened before are, in some sense, claims about what can or cannot happen again. But such claims can be misleading and even malignant. In their classic work *Thinking in Time*, Ernest May and Richard Neustadt explored the ways in which clumsy misapplications of history can create catastrophes in public policy as the "lessons" of the past become limitations on the present, or worse.[18] As Sarah Maza has echoed in her own work, "Trying to fit a scenario from the past onto one in the present can be disastrous: 'We will liberate Iraq, as we did Europe!' 'Don't go for a diplomatic solution—remember Munich!'"[19]

Narratives about the past can distort the present in less obvious ways as well. If people allow themselves to become "complaisant hostages of the pasts they create," in the words of Michel-Rolph Trouillot, they find it impossible to imagine futures that are substantially different.[20] The recent controversies over Confederate monuments are a prominent case in point. Largely constructed in the early twentieth century, these statues and memorials were part of a campaign to promote the Lost Cause of the Confederacy, an alternate version of the past that whitewashed the role of slavery in the rebellion and recast traitors who warred against the United States as American patriots. Generations raised under this consciously crafted mythology came to believe that act of spin was "history," and they have naturally seen efforts to undo the damage of the Lost Cause mythos—to restore the real historical record—as a devious attempt to "rewrite history."

Efforts to reshape narratives about the US past thus became a central theme of the conservative movement in general and the Trump administration in particular. From its very first hours, when White House Press Secretary Sean Spicer lied that the new president had "the largest audience ever to witness an inauguration, period," the Trump White House repeatedly made outlandish claims about its "unprecedented" place in history—how Trump's approval ratings were the highest ever, how he was the first to do this or the best to do that, how past presidents like Jackson and Lincoln and Reagan were mere forerunners of his greatness, etc. With the Republican Party echoing its claims and right-wing media voices amplifying them, the Trump White House represented a concerted effort to rewrite history in real time.[21]

These efforts culminated in the closing months of the administration with the creation of the President's Advisory 1776 Commission. The commission would provide, the president promised, a version of history that would enable "patriotic education," but that goal is inherently at odds with the study of history. A history that seeks to exalt a nation's strengths without examining its shortcomings, that values feeling good over thinking hard, that embraces simplistic celebration over complex understanding, isn't history; it's propaganda. To that end, the "1776 Report"—whose authors notably included *no* American historians—was rushed into print in the very final days of the Trump presidency, one final effort to twist the record. Among other distortions, the report compared nineteenth-century supporters of slavery to contemporary proponents of "identity politics" and equated early twentieth-century progressivism with fascism.[22] When Trump finally left office, Republicans in Congress and in state legislatures picked up his "history war" as their own. They have worked to block the teaching of popular histories such as the *New York Times'* 1619 Project and turned the advanced legal field of critical race theory into a threat that is allegedly menacing elementary school-children.[23] William F. Buckley famously defined a conservative as some-one who "stands athwart history, yelling Stop," but conservatives in our era have increasingly focused on thwarting history, full stop.

To be sure, political debates about history are nothing new. But a brief look at the most recent one—the so-called history wars that unfolded in the mid-1990s—shows the ways in which our current debate is different from what's come before.

First, there was a controversy over a proposal for a set of national history standards. The idea, launched as a joint program by George H. W. Bush's Department of Education and the National Endowment for the Humanities, seemed to have a thoroughly conservative lineage. NEH Chair Lynne Cheney, wife of then secretary of defense and future vice president Dick Cheney, said the standards were needed to strengthen Americans' mastery of basic historical facts. Yet she acknowledged that interpretations of those facts might well vary. "History," she noted in 1991, "is contentious." The draft of the standards revealed that admission to be an understatement. Reflecting the ways the historical profession had shifted away from conventional tropes of Western civilization and "Great Man history" over the previous decades and broadened the ana-lytical lens to account for the experiences of working-class people, racial and religious minorities, women, gays and lesbians, and other previously overlooked groups, the standards proposed by the academics and admin-istrators recruited for the project quickly became a new front in the cul-ture wars of the early 1990s. In an op-ed for the *Wall Street Journal*, Lynne

Cheney denounced them for providing an overly "grim and gloomy" interpretation of US history. Other conservatives washed their hands of the project as well, but so did the whole political establishment. In a stunning rebuke, ninety-nine US senators voted to condemn the standards. The project was abandoned.[24]

In 1995 a similarly fierce controversy unfolded over the Smithsonian Institution's plan to commemorate the fiftieth anniversary of the atomic bombing of Hiroshima. The centerpiece of the exhibit would be the *Enola Gay*, the B-29 bomber that carried out the mission; the controversy came over how to contextualize the display. Curators insisted that they sought only to provide an "honest and balanced" narrative of the event, but opponents—including military and veterans' organizations—criticized the exhibit for providing what they saw as a forced false equivalence between the United States and Japan. Republican congressman Tom Lewis summed up the feeling of many on the right when he said the Smithsonian's job was "to tell history, not rewrite it." The director of the museum redid the display to avoid any controversy and, indeed, virtually even any commentary, displaying the plane on its own as a "fact" devoid of "interpretation." And that, in turn, led to protests from historians. The Organization of American Historians formally condemned "revisions of interpretations of history" that came about not from scholarly motives but rather from patriotic demands or political considerations. Despite the controversy, historians resolved to maintain their public engagement. "The only alternative to learning from this tragedy," David Thelen wrote in a roundtable for the *Journal of American History*, "is to retreat into safe professional harbors where we talk only 'with' ourselves."[25]

Although those debates remind us how common it has been for history to become politicized, the tumult of the 1990s represented a crisis that was qualitatively different from the one we now face. As Joyce Appleby, Margaret Jacob, and Lynn Hunt wrote in *Telling the Truth About History*, it is one thing to acknowledge how historians were influenced by their particular context and could therefore disagree about how to interpret certain facts; it is quite another thing to ignore the facts altogether.[26] In the past, Americans have argued about which facts were more important in their explanatory power or causal emphasis; in the present, we are often reduced to arguing about which facts are even facts. Unmooring our debates from some shared understanding of facts inevitably makes constructive dialogue impossible because there is no shared starting point.

This shift has been driven by the rise of a new generation of amateur historians who, lacking any training in the field or familiarity with its norms, have felt freer to write a history that begins with its conclusions and works backward to find—or invent, if need be—some sort of evidence that will seem to support it. A cottage industry on the right, in particular, has flourished with partisan authors producing a partisan version of the past to please partisan audiences, effectively replicating the "narrowcasting" approach of conservative cable news. Often, these arguments are based on "facts" that simply aren't facts or on narratives that fundamentally misconstrue what we know from the archives. Decades of well-regarded research have been simply disregarded for the sake of convenience; academic consensus built painstakingly over time has been waved away as more "fake news." The public, as a result, is inundated with wild claims about history that don't match what any legitimate historian—on the right, left, or center—would deem to be true.

For historians, this assault on history represents a new front in a long-standing campaign to engage and educate the general public about our shared history. For all the clichés about academics being shut off from the real world in ivory towers, American historians have long worked to bring their expertise about the past into their present. In 1931 Carl Becker used his presidential address to the American Historical Association to remind his colleagues that their archival research and scholarly work was only the start. "The history that lies inert in unread books," he chided, "does no work in the world."[27] Becker's call for historians to share their insights and illuminate public debate has been answered time and time again. In the early days of the civil rights movement, for instance, John Hope Franklin and C. Vann Woodward confronted then-commonplace myths about the origins and operations of segregation. During the Vietnam War, a new generation of scholars such as William Appleman Williams and Gabriel Kolko challenged long-standing legends about the workings of US foreign policy. Social and cultural historians in the 1970s and 1980s wrote new histories of the nation from the bottom up, expanding our view to include long-overlooked perspectives on gender, race, and ethnic identities and, in the process, showing that narrow narratives focused solely on political leaders at the top obscured more than they revealed. Despite the fact that the term *revisionist history* is often thrown around by nonhistorians as an insult, in truth all good historical work is at heart "revisionist" in that it uses new findings from the archives or new perspectives from historians to improve, to perfect— and, yes, to *revise*—our understanding of the past.

Today, yet another generation of historians is working once again to bring historical scholarship out of academic circles, this time to push back against misinformation in the public sphere. Writing op-eds and essays for general audiences; engaging the public through appearances on television, radio, and podcasts; and being active on social media sites such as Facebook, Twitter, and Substack, hundreds if not thousands of historians have been working to provide a counterbalance and corrections to the misinformation distorting our national dialogue. Such work has incredible value, yet historians still do their best work in the longer written forms of books, articles, and edited collections that allow us both to express our thoughts with precision in the text and provide ample evidence in the endnotes. This volume has brought together historians who have been actively engaging the general public through the short forms of modern media and has provided them a platform where they might expand those engagements into fuller essays that reflect the best scholarly traditions of the profession.

The lies and legends addressed in the twenty essays in this edited collection are by no means the only ones prevalent in public discourse today, but they represent some of the most pressing distortions of the past in the present moment. Because there has been such a robust debate over the role of slavery in America's political development by contributors and supporters of the 1619 Project as well as by its critics, we decided to focus our limited space here on other issues that have not received as much attention.

Many of the lies and legends in this collection, as we have already noted, stem from a deliberate campaign of disinformation from the political Right. Some of these have obvious partisan motives, such as the efforts to portray Democratic programs such as the New Deal or Great Society as misguided failures or the campaign to present the "Reagan Revolution" as an unbridled success. Others have worked to bolster broad ideological stances that reinforce the modern Right, framing the free market as wholly good or democratic socialism as wholly bad, for instance, or characterizing feminism as a deliberate plot against the family.

Whereas those distortions embody the kind of predictable spin that has long been a part of US party politics, a more ominous strand of disinformation—focused on racial issues and stoking racial resentment—has surged to the forefront in recent years, driven in large part by the rise of white nationalism and the inroads it has made in Republican politics. Not long ago, during the time of George H. W. Bush, the GOP worked aggressively to confront past incidents of racism, with its leaders even going so far as to offer formal apologies for past practices like the "southern strategy." However, that push for reckoning and reconciliation was abruptly abandoned in the Trump era and replaced by outright denialism. Rather than apologize for the southern strategy, new voices on the right simply asserted that there had never *been* a southern strategy and that, as a result, there was nothing to apologize for. Seeking to paper over proof of racism in the movement's past and present, they have tried to rewrite the history of a range of issues: immigration and the border, civil rights protests and white backlash, police violence and voter fraud. These efforts have sought to retrofit history as a rationale for present policies and programs.

Although partisan motives animate much of the current crisis of misinformation, this volume also addresses a number of lies and legends that were born long before this moment and spread well beyond a single political party or ideology. These "bipartisan" myths, without any overt motive behind them, have proved more stubborn than the partisan ones. Some of these misunderstandings are rooted in a persistent belief in American exceptionalism, expressed both generally and also in the particulars, as in claims that America has never been an empire or that Americans have not previously engaged in insurrections. Other myths have invented false pasts—about "vanishing" Native Americans or a virtuous policy of "America First"—to undergird the same claims of

American exceptionalism. Americans across the political spectrum have embraced these arguments, but such widespread acceptance of a myth still doesn't make it true. Misinformation is wrong, no matter how narrowly or widely it is held.

This collection is by no means exhaustive in its coverage. There are other significant myths and misunderstandings we haven't addressed in this limited space, and there will surely be new lies and legends created in the coming years. But we hope that this intervention by some of the most prominent historians in the United States can serve as a model of sorts, both for the broader work done by historians engaged in the public sphere and for the broader debates that Americans outside the historical profession can and should have with one another. We need to see the past clearly in order to understand where we stand now and where we might go in the future.

1

AMERICAN EXCEPTIONALISM

David A. Bell

"AMERICAN EXCEPTIONALISM" HAS A DOUBLE MEANING. IT FIRST arose as an analytical term, referring to the proposition that the social and economic structures of the United States represent an exception to normal laws of historical development. To the extent that the analysis came with a value judgment attached, that judgment was negative. The United States was a historical aberration—a country that was failing to evolve in the proper, desired direction. More recently, though, the analytical meaning has been overshadowed, in the political sphere, by a prescriptive, moralizing one that refers less to American difference than to American superiority. When politicians today invoke "American exceptionalism," they almost always mean that the United States has desirable qualities that other nations lack and has a special, chosen, superior role in human history.[1]

This essay will first look briefly at the question of whether it makes sense to call America "exceptional." It will then turn at greater length to the strange history of the term *American exceptionalism* itself, explaining why it has acquired such prominence and what has been at stake for those who have used it. In the process the essay will call attention to the two most important actors in that history: the man initially responsible for promoting the term in the 1920s and the man who did the most to introduce it to the US political mainstream seventy years later. They were both ardent radicals, albeit of rather different sorts: Joseph Stalin and Newt Gingrich.

Is America in fact "exceptional"? To address the question concisely, consider these three propositions. First, most nations can be considered exceptional in one sense or another. After all, the word refers to deviation from a norm—but which norm? Can we group together all aspects of a nation's development—social, economic, political, cultural—into a single framework? Marxists have very often answered this question in the affirmative, and it is therefore not entirely surprising that the term *American exceptionalism* originated in the international communist movement. But for those who don't subscribe to such all-embracing theories, the situation is murkier. A nation may look exceptional with respect to one criterion and entirely typical with respect to another. In fact, scholars have managed to demonstrate that nearly every nation on the planet represents an exception to the planetary norm. They speak of the "exception française" and the "deutsche Sonderweg," or special path. A sizable literature exists not only on "Chinese exceptionalism" but also on "Serbian exceptionalism." Tunisia's relative success in navigating the Arab Spring led some to speak of "Tunisian exceptionalism."[2] The relative paucity of references to British and Japanese exceptionalisms may derive simply from the fact that scholars of both countries take the exceptional status of each so utterly for granted.

Second, very few of the copious contemporary discussions of "American exceptionalism" have come close to showing that America really does represent a deviation from a significant international norm. Doing so in a serious way would require paying attention not just to America itself but also to the countries from which America supposedly differs—something that might even involve speaking a language other than English. Yet virtually none of the politicians who speak so readily about "American exceptionalism" even mention other countries, except in the vaguest sense, and surprisingly few of the scholars who use the term discuss other countries in a systematic way.[3]

Finally, modern nationalism by its nature has led virtually every nation to strive to distinguish itself from others: to highlight and even to exaggerate its own unique qualities and to proclaim its own unique destiny. French nationalists tout the elegance and sophistication of their "civilization." Serbians have traditionally considered themselves the shield of Christianity. Haitians take pride in being the first country whose people freed themselves from slavery. China has its uniquely harmonious, rational Confucian culture.[4] The idea of "American exceptionalism," in other words, falls squarely into an entirely common pattern. There is nothing exceptional about it.

Taken together, these three propositions strongly suggest that the term *American exceptionalism* makes very little analytical sense. Whereas scholars have found it useful to look at specific ways in which US national development differs from that of other countries (for instance, America's failure to develop a robust socialist movement or a Western European–style welfare state), these differences do not justify calling America an exception to a comprehensive planetary rule.

On the other hand, the idea itself has had a fascinating if also dispiriting history. Before the term entered political life in the late twentieth century, political narratives about America's exceptional character served to justify various projects of national aggression against both Native and foreign peoples, but they also highlighted what Americans saw as their best qualities and their moral duties, giving them a standard to live up to. The term *American exceptionalism* has done much not only to displace these earlier narratives but also to erase their aspirational moral content. Today, the term most often serves as an empty symbol, a mere marker of difference and superiority and a convenient rhetorical cudgel in the country's unending, vicious political combat. As such, somewhat ironically, the rise of the term illustrates the decline of American idealism.

Historians have sketched out parts of this story very well, but this last piece of it in particular, and therefore the overall arc, have so far attracted less attention.⁵

From the moment Europeans arrived on American shores, they crafted stories about their special destiny, and in the early-modern Western world, such stories usually invoked ancient models. First, there was ancient Israel: "For thou art an holy people unto the Lord thy God, and the Lord hath chosen thee to be a peculiar people unto himself, above all the nations that are upon the earth" (Deuteronomy 14:2). Not only did the God of the Old Testament select Israel from above other nations, and not only did he bind it to him by a covenant; in doing so, he also bound its people to one another in a tight web of commandments and ritual practices, giving their community exceptional homogeneity, cohesion, and endurance. Of course, in the eyes of medieval and early-modern European Christians, the covenant was less a gift than an obligation, and one at which ancient Israel had woefully failed. The other model was Rome, the most powerful empire in all history, one whose institutions, laws, and language still marked Europe centuries after its fall and whose history and literature remained the foundation of formal education until deep into modern times. Fables of national origin spun by medieval and early-modern European poets tended to copy the epic story of Rome's founding imagined by Virgil in the *Aeneid*.⁶

The first of these models in particular is often seen as having special importance for American history and for the story of "American exceptionalism." Early-modern Protestants, in their fervent and fearful belief that God had predetermined only a small elect for salvation and consigned the rest of the human race to damnation, found comfort in imagining themselves part of a new chosen people: a new Israel. The idea found purchase in England, Scotland, Sweden, the Netherlands, Dutch South Africa—and also in New England. Indeed, the idea of an "American Zion" retained a powerful hold on the national imagination until well into the nineteenth century, if not beyond. Out of this history has come the idea, shared well beyond the walls of the academy, that America's sense of itself flows directly from that foundational moment when Puritan settlers, imagining themselves a new chosen people, alighted in the Western Hemisphere. Historians and politicians alike have highlighted one text in particular: John Winthrop's lay sermon "Model of Christian Charity," supposedly delivered on board the Puritans' ship *Arbella* in 1630, containing the words "we shall be as a city upon a hill" (Ronald Reagan later embellished it into "a shining city upon a hill").[7]

But Americans' sense of themselves and their character was never so unitary. The insistent attention to the Puritans of New England tends to eclipse the fact that the inhabitants of all the British colonies, and their successor states, imagined themselves as Romans at least as often as they saw themselves as Israelites.[8] Puritan rhetoric might have been resonant, but as Daniel Rodgers has demonstrated, Winthrop's sermon itself remained virtually unknown until the nineteenth century, and its text, far from expressing confidence in some sort of grand new national mission, breathed with agonized doubt regarding whether the colonists could uphold the obligations of the covenant. To be as a city on a hill meant above all exposing one's conduct to the world's judgment.

The stories that nations tell about themselves also change over time, and America has had a bewildering and contradictory plethora of them. John Winthrop accepted inequality as a basic premise of human existence, valued subjection to God above political freedom, and expected happiness only in the world to come. His vision for an American community had little in common with that of the Americans of the revolutionary generation who championed life, liberty, and the pursuit of happiness in this world and took pride in seeing their republican experiment copied across the globe. In the nineteenth century a powerful and fundamentally new American myth arose: that of the endless frontier. For its proponents, the essence of the American spirit lay in restless movement westward. As the Mexican writer Octavio Paz later summed up the idea, "America was, if it was anything, geography, pure space, open to human action." In much the same period, those Americans who considered slavery the "sole cause" of civilization (William Harper) identified the country with this horrific institution and believed that America had a special mission to promote human bondage throughout the world.[9]

In the later nineteenth century, yet more material flooded into the already-crowded canon of stories that supposedly defined America's essence. On the one hand, there was the vision of the country as a land of immigration, with a "golden door" open to people from around the world seeking freedom and opportunity. Yet just two years after Emma Lazarus composed those words in her poem about the Statue of Liberty, the influential clergyman Josiah Strong published a best-seller, *Our Country*, which identified America with the "Anglo-Saxon race" and its struggle for Darwinian supremacy in the world. By the end of the century, men like Senator Albert J. Beveridge were championing America's acquisition of an overseas empire as "the mission of our race, trustee, under God, of the civilization of the world." The twentieth century added further stories: that of the United States as an active apostle of democracy, spreading it not just by example but also by persuasion and if necessary by force, or somewhat differently as what Madeleine Albright called "the indispensable nation," guaranteeing global peace and security.[10] Yet another set of stories identified America above all with the spirit of free enterprise, generating exceptional wealth and prosperity.

Among all these stories, and all these definitions of an American spirit, character, or mission, it is hard to find a common ideological thread, let alone to unwind that thread back to a single moment in the year 1630. Some expressions of what makes America exceptional have put strong emphasis on one vision or another of "freedom," but not all of them (not John Winthrop's or William Harper's or Josiah Strong's). Some of them still have resonance today, but not all. They arose at different moments and for different reasons, serving the needs of different constituencies. Some of them justified the expropriation of native land; others legitimized military adventurism from the Philippines War to the Iraq War. But many of them also served to promote a moral ideal: to be God-fearing, or self-reliant, or welcoming of strangers, or promoting of peace throughout the world.

The term *American exceptionalism* itself did not originally have much connection to these patriotic narratives. Indeed, the first people to use it, as members in good standing of the international communist movement, considered such narratives to be little more than bourgeois mystification. For them, anything that made America exceptional was, by definition, not a virtue but a problem.

How and where did the term first appear? In the 1920s an American communist named Jay Lovestone tried to explain, nervously, to Joseph Stalin's Comintern why communism had made such little progress in the United States. The reason, he suggested, was that the path followed by American capitalism represented an "exception" to the normal laws of historical development. But Stalin would have none of it. He knew the danger of allowing Communist parties around the world to craft distinct, independent paths for themselves, in line with what they claimed to be particular national circumstances. In 1929 he blasted Lovestone as a "deviationist" and condemned the very idea of "American exceptionalism" as a species of ideological heresy. American Communists loyally repeated his point in their own publications.[11]

The term might easily have died a natural death then and there, in the sectarian debates of the Depression. But American intellectuals of the mid-century, usually from a socialist background, picked it up again as they sought to explain why a strong socialist movement had never arisen in the United States. Following from their inquiries, a broader academic discourse gradually took shape around the different ways that America represented an exception to general rules of historical evolution, for instance because it had avoided the "feudal" stage of history. In an era of vibrant social-scientific inquiries into comparative social and economic development, lavishly funded by foundations and government agencies eager to understand why some nations *did* turn toward socialism, the topic of "American exceptionalism" flourished. But into the 1980s these discussions remained essentially scholarly. The figure most associated with the term was probably the sociologist Seymour Martin Lipset. Vigorous debates also took place among historians about the exceptional nature of American labor politics and America's failure to create a full-fledged welfare state.[12]

But then "American exceptionalism" jumped from the seminar rooms to the culture at large. The frequency of its appearance in the Google Books database rose nearly twelve-fold between 1985 and 2019. In the

LexisNexis periodical database it rose nearly twenty-five-fold just between 2000 and 2010.[13] What had previously been an academic term of
art became a rhetorical weapon in the increasingly polarized US political
landscape.

Many figures helped the term make this transition, but Newt
Gingrich—a history PhD who considers himself an intellectual and likes
to show off his command of scholarly language—was the most important.
In the 1994 election, in which Republicans took control of the House of
Representatives for the first time in forty years, the then minority whip
was already making the term a centerpiece of his stump speeches:

> We have to recognize that American exceptionalism is real, that Amer-
> ican civilization is the most unique civilization in history, that we bring
> more people of more ethnic backgrounds together to pursue happiness
> with greater opportunity than any civilization in the history of the world.
> And we just don't say that anymore. Let me be candid. Haitians have more
> to learn from America than Americans have to learn from Haitians. The
> same is true of Bosnia. As far as I'm concerned, this counterculture notion,
> this politically correct notion that, "Oh, gee, we shouldn't make any value
> judgments," that's silly.

Gingrich has since returned to "American exceptionalism" at every possible opportunity. It is arguably his Big Idea. He has taught college courses
on the subject, some of them available online.[14] With help from a ghost-
writer he has produced a book titled *A Nation Like No Other: Why American Exceptionalism Matters*. And with his wife, Callista, he has turned
the book into a film titled *A City upon a Hill: The Spirit of American Exceptionalism* (a Citizens United production).[15] He presents America as pos-
sessing more freedom, more opportunity, more faith, and more moral
strength than any other nation on Earth (although his discussion of these
other nations is cursory in the extreme) and as having a unique mission to
transmit its values to others.

Gingrich's passion for American exceptionalism was not, of course,
motivated by abstract intellectual curiosity. With his unerring instinct for
the political jugular, he recognized that the term could provide a highly

effective political weapon against the Democratic Party and "the Left." By the 1990s, with international communism vanquished and McCarthyism long largely discredited, accusations of treason no longer served the Republican cause well. But the charge of not believing in "American exceptionalism" could accomplish the same purpose in a more subtle manner by casting Democrats and leftists as unpatriotic, countercultural cosmopolitans who, in an age of globalization, preferred other countries to their own and who despised the values of ordinary Americans. For Gingrich, demonstrating America's exceptionality has always mattered less than denouncing the Left for not believing in it. Other conservatives—notably William Kristol and David Brooks, whose "American Greatness" project was grounded in the idea of America as "an exceptional nation founded on a universal principle"—arguably took the term more seriously. But they had less influence than the Georgia congressman.[16]

In a basic sense, of course, Gingrich was right about at least one set of his ideological opponents. Very few Americans who describe themselves as "progressive"—and almost no academics in this category—would subscribe to Gingrich's version of American exceptionalism. The more progressive that Americans are in their politics, the more likely they are to see America as exceptional, if at all, in large part because of the harm it has done: the treatment of indigenous peoples, slavery, US foreign policy in the twentieth century, and contemporary inequality and racism. In a 2011 Pew Research poll, 67 percent of "staunch conservatives" agreed with the statement "The U.S. stands above all other countries," whereas just 19 percent of "solid liberals" did.[17]

Mainstream Democratic politicians, though, were not so squeamish, especially after September 11, 2001. As the LexisNexis statistic suggests, the use of the term *American exceptionalism*, already on the rise, accelerated significantly after the terrorist attacks. To many, the term offered a ready explanation for why the attacks had occurred: Al-Qaeda struck at us because it hated our exceptional values and positive role in the world. The idea of "American exceptionalism" also served as a source of pride in a country badly shaken by the catastrophic events. And the idea justified subsequent actions, including especially the invasion of Iraq, as natural extensions of America's historic, exceptional mission to spread democracy throughout the world.[18] Mainstream Democrats not only embraced the term but also found that its very emptiness made it strategically useful. They could happily profess their belief in American exceptionalism in the hope of winning over, or at least appeasing, voters who had very different ideas about what made America "exceptional." In the early 2000s the journalist Charlie Rose made a habit of asking interviewees if they believed in American exceptionalism, and mainstream Democrats almost always answered in the affirmative. In 2007 Barack Obama's campaign strategist David Axelrod told Rose that "I really do. I think that, you know, we are a remarkable experiment, an ongoing project in self-governance . . . we are and should be a beacon to the world."[19]

But throughout the early twenty-first century the term continued to serve the purposes of the Right especially well, never more so than when Obama himself burst upon the political scene. The son of a foreign, Black, Muslim father and a white American mother widely described as a hippie, and with a cool, professorial mien, Obama could easily be caricatured as the embodiment of cosmopolitan, countercultural, "un-American" values. At a 2009 press conference, Edward Luce of the *Financial Times* asked Obama if he believed in American exceptionalism. Obama replied: "I believe in American exceptionalism, just as I suspect that the Brits believe in British exceptionalism and the Greeks believe in Greek exceptionalism." Obama went on to offer a warm appreciation of America's special place in world history, but Republicans gleefully quoted him out of this context and fell over themselves to pillory him for the remarks. Obama himself, recognizing the power of the attacks, quickly began inserting even more fulsome praise for American exceptionalism into his speeches, but the Republicans continued to highlight the original remarks. Gingrich, in his 2011 book, called Obama "outright contemptuous of American exceptionalism."[20]

The strange story of "American exceptionalism" did not end with the Obama presidency. Donald Trump took it in yet another strange new direction. Trump detests as elitist and phony the sort of pseudo-intellectual lucubrations that Gingrich adores. He prefers the blunt language of "making America great" and "winning" to the multisyllabic complexities of "exceptionalism." He has, on occasion, read speeches that incorporate the concept, as in his acceptance of the Republican presidential nomination in 2020.[21] But as he made clear in a 2015 interview, and amply confirmed in his actions as president, he does not in fact see America as an "exception" to any sort of worldwide pattern. Trump's vision of history and of international affairs is one of brute competition between nation-states that differ principally in their degree of toughness and strength, not in their essential qualities. When asked directly about "American exceptionalism" in the interview, Trump responded:

> I never liked the term. And perhaps that's because I don't have a very big ego [*sic*] and I don't need terms like that . . . I want to take everything back from the world that we've given them. We've given them so much. On top of taking it back, I don't want to say, "We're exceptional. We're more exceptional." Because essentially we're saying, "We're more outstanding than you. By the way, you've been eating our lunch for the last 20 years, but we're more exceptional than you." I don't like the term. I never liked it.[22]

Gingrich and other conservatives, who would have spontaneously combusted if Barack Obama had spoken these words, largely acquiesced to Trump on this issue. In the 2016 presidential campaign, it was the mainstream Democrat Hillary Clinton, not her opponent, who repeatedly invoked American exceptionalism. ("If there's one core belief that has guided and inspired me every step of the way, it is this. The United States is an exceptional nation. I believe we are still Lincoln's last, best hope of Earth. We're still Reagan's shining city on a hill.")[23]

With Trump, did we reach the end of "American exceptionalism" as a salient political concept? Between him and those on the other side of the aisle who (for very different reasons) share his dislike for the term, the fraction of Americans who see it as having real meaning and serving a real purpose is almost certainly shrinking. Some on the left may continue to see America as having played an exceptionally destructive role in world history, but this version of the concept does not exactly have much potential as an electoral slogan. The sad experience of the United States in the COVID-19 pandemic, when the country proved "exceptional" only in the incompetence of its government on many levels and the bizarre resistance of much of the population to basic public health measures, made the myth harder to sustain than ever. As one much-cited article put it in August of 2020, "In a dark season of pestilence, Covid has reduced to tatters the illusion of American exceptionalism."[24]

Yet we have been here before. In 1975, well before Gingrich came on the scene, the sociologist Daniel Bell wrote an article titled "The End of American Exceptionalism." Reflecting the grim mood of the post-Vietnam moment, he commented: "Today, the belief in American exceptionalism has vanished with the end of empire, the weakening of power, the loss of faith in the nation's future."[25] The diagnosis was understandable, but the obituary was premature. The notion of America having a unique role among all nations and the specific term *American exceptionalism* proved far too useful to pass away in that earlier season of national despair. The very vacuity of the notion has been its strength, for it can be filled with whatever content is desired, even as it flatters US audiences by assuring them of their membership in the elect. There is little reason, then, to think that it will pass away in the new season of despair that we are living through today. But the mere notion of being exceptional can do very little to inspire Americans actually to *be* exceptional and to aspire to become a better people.

2

FOUNDING MYTHS

Akhil Reed Amar

T HOSE WHO MISUNDERSTAND THE FOUNDING ARE APT TO MISREAD the Constitution. Alas, Americans from all educational strata and all points on the political compass routinely misinterpret this critical era and in the process muddy the letter and spirit of the supreme law of our land. Here are five especially widespread and interrelated misunderstandings, each followed (in parentheses and italics) by a brief statement of the myth-busting truth of the matter:

Myth 1: James Madison was the father of the Constitution. *(No, that would be George Washington—and paternity matters.)*

Myth 2: The key *Federalist* essay is Madison's *Federalist* No. 10. *(No, almost no one read that Madison essay in the 1780s or indeed in the ensuing century. The key* Federalist *essays in the ratification era were*

John Jay's and Alexander Hamilton's nos. 2–8, explaining the Washingtonian and geostrategic essence of the Federalists' plan.)

Myth 3: The framers believed in "republics" but disdained "democracy." *(No, despite certain language that appeared in Madison's* Federalist *No. 10, these two words were more synonymous than oppositional in general 1780s discourse. Regardless of the label we now choose to use, the framers believed in and practiced popular self-government.)*

Myth 4: The Constitution was indeterminate on (and perhaps even supportive of) secession. *(Ridiculous. Washington's geostrategic Constitution categorically repudiated unilateral state secession.)*

Myth 5: The Constitution was designed by the rich for the rich. *(Not really. The document was just what it said it was—a text ordained by the People, not by the Property. Beard is bunk.)*

Let's begin by popping a trio of interrelated bubbles about James Madison, *The Federalist* No. 10, and the linguistic innovation that Madison introduced in that now-famous ratification essay, which sharply contradistinguished *republics* from *democracies.*

Many today view Madison as the father of the Constitution. But when the grand Philadelphia Convention met in the summer of 1787 to propose a solution to the myriad and interlocking failures of America's first continental legal system—the sagging Articles of Confederation—few Americans had even heard of the diminutive Confederation congressman. By contrast, everyone knew of George Washington, the legendary commander in chief who had won the Revolutionary War and then disbanded his army rather than trying to make himself king (as had William the Conqueror) or lord protector (as had Oliver Cromwell) or emperor (as had Augustus Caesar and as would Napoleon). Washington's thrilling act of republican renunciation and self-restraint had inspired contemporaries high and low the world over. The Philadelphia Convention had broad popular credibility in America mainly because Washington, bowing to public opinion, reluctantly agreed to suspend his retirement to attend the grand gathering.

The convention that ensued was Washington's convention, not Madison's; likewise, the proposed Constitution that emerged was emphatically Washington's. At the conclave's outset, the delegates unanimously made Washington their presiding officer. (His title at Philadelphia—Mr. President—would poetically become his title under the Constitution itself.) Most of the delegates had borne arms in the war, a third were veterans of Washington's Continental Army, and five of the fifty-five delegates—one from each of five distinct states out of the twelve that met in Philadelphia (Rhode Island boycotted the event)—had personally served as Washington's aides-de-camp. These former aides were obviously Washington's men, not Madison's: New York's Alexander Hamilton, Pennsylvania's Thomas Mifflin, Maryland's James McHenry, Virginia's Edmund Randolph, and South Carolina's Charles Cotesworth Pinckney.

The document that emerged from this conclave was also obviously Washington's. The Philadelphia Constitution's primary goal was geostrategic: the fledgling American regime needed to create a strong and indivisible union able to defend itself against Europe's Great Powers—England, France, and Spain, each of which still coveted New World land and thus posed a potentially existential threat. Long before he even knew Madison, Washington had emphasized the need for such an indivisible union—most dramatically in his initial farewell address, a world-famous circular letter to America's governors in 1783.

Compared to Revolution-era state constitutions, which provided the basic template for the Philadelphia plan's bicameral and tripartite federal system, the most distinctive element of the proposed new federal constitution was its astonishingly powerful chief executive. America's newly minted president could win election independently of Congress and thereafter win infinite and independent reelection, would enjoy a long (by 1787 gubernatorial standards) term of office, would wield a remarkably powerful pair of veto and pardon pens, would command a continental army and navy, and would also stand atop all the other executive departments that would eventually emerge. The Philadelphia delegates undeniably designed this office for the trusted Washington, who would ultimately win unanimous election and reelection as America's first president. (Madison, by contrast, would fail to win the US Senate seat he coveted and would struggle even to secure a House seat.) Prior to Philadelphia, Madison had given no real thought to how federal executive power should be structured, as he candidly admitted in a mid-April 1787 letter to Washington.

True, in the run-up to Philadelphia, Madison had pondered certain other features of his hoped-for Constitution. He favored a bicameral federal legislature flanked by an independent executive and an independent judiciary. But this was old hat in 1787. Most revolutionary state constitutions followed some version of this basic template, a template endorsed by both New York's John Jay and Massachusetts's Henry Knox in early 1787 letters that reached Washington well before Madison sent the general his own preferred plan. (Note that all three men were advising Washington, not vice versa. Well before Philadelphia, everyone understood that Washington was, in modern parlance, the man.) Another defining element of the eventual Constitution—its ratification by the American people—was foreshadowed by Washington himself no later than mid-1783, when he barely knew Madison.[1]

Although Madison did bring some original ideas to the Philadelphia conclave, most of his pet projects fell by the wayside. Madison argued relentlessly for a Senate that, like the House, would be apportioned by population. He lost. He argued tirelessly for a congressional "negative" (that is, a veto) over state law. He lost again. He wanted leading judges to join the president in wielding the veto power. Here, too, he lost. He pleaded for broad federal power to tax exports. Yet again he lost. Prior to the ratification process, his biggest achievement was, in a word, *Washingtonian*: along with others, he had played a key role in cajoling Washington to suspend retirement and attend the Philadelphia conclave.

When the Convention adjourned and its plan became public, an epic challenge loomed ahead. Americans up and down the continent would need to ratify the plan in specially elected conventions chosen by uniquely inclusive electorates. What the framers envisioned in late 1787 and what in fact unfolded over the ensuing year was nothing less than the most democratic deed that had ever occurred up to that point in the planet's history. Never before had so many persons over so large a landmass been invited to assent so explicitly to the basic ground rules that would govern themselves and their posterity. Once done, this explosive deed would change the world in a big bang that would radiate out across both centuries and oceans—leading to many later and even more democratic American amendments and eventually giving rise to today's world, in which democracies govern most of the planet's inhabitants.

In the year that changed everything, this hinge of human history, it was Washington's world-famous name that loomed the largest and carried the Philadelphia plan to victory. The fact that Washington endorsed the plan and the expectation that he would lead the new government counted for more than all the other speeches and writings of all the other backers of the plan put together.

In a brief letter to the Confederation Congress summarizing the proposed plan on behalf of the Convention—a letter later reprinted alongside the envisioned Constitution in tens of thousands of copies circulated among the citizenry—Washington explained the main lines and aims of the new system. This key letter made clear that the proposed Constitution, if ratified, would end state sovereignty and unite America into a strong union necessary to solve the basic problems of continental government that threatened the very survival of independent America. "The friends of our country," wrote Washington, "have long seen and desired, that the power of making war, peace and treaties, that of levying money and regulating commerce, and the correspondent executive and judicial authorities should be fully and effectually vested in the general government of the Union." But, he noted, it would obviously be improper to "delegat[e] such extensive trust to one body of men"—that is, a unicameral Congress combining legislative, executive, and judicial power. "Hence results the necessity of a different organization"—namely, a newly modeled bicameral and tripartite system at the federal level akin to the governments of each individual state. "It is obviously impracticable in the foederal government of these States, to secure all rights of independent sovereignty to each, and yet provide for the interest and safety of all." In other words, individual state sovereignty—the bedrock principle of the Declaration of Independence and the Articles of Confederation—now needed to yield. "In all our deliberations on this subject we kept steadily in our view, that which appears to us the greatest interest of every true American, the *consolidation* of our Union, in which is involved our prosperity, felicity, safety, *perhaps our national existence.*"[2]

For years, Washington had been preaching precursors of this sermon to any who would listen. This was also the basic message of a series of newspaper essays that first appeared in New York under the pen name "Publius." Eventually numbering eighty-five essays and repackaged into a two-volume book published in the spring of 1788, *The Federalist* was the brainchild of Alexander Hamilton, who enlisted John Jay and Madison to join him under the joint pseudonym.

Seven of the first eight essays—*The Federalist* nos. 2 through 8, authored by Hamilton and Jay—explained in vivid detail the key geostrategic argument for a newly minted and indivisible union, along the lines that Washington and Hamilton in particular had been advocating for many years.

As Jay/Publius explained in *The Federalist* No. 5, this union was expressly modeled on the indissoluble geostrategic "entire and perfect union" of Scotland and England four score years earlier. Britain was free and strong, Hamilton/Publius explained in the climactic *Federalist* No. 8, because it was a defensible island protected by the English Channel. By uniting indissolubly, America could likewise be free and strong, protected by the Atlantic Ocean. Land borders between continental European nation-states had led to standing armies, military dictators, and horrific bloodshed on the continent itself. International land borders between thirteen sovereign American states or between several regional confederacies or nation-states would ultimately lead to the same fate in the New World. The states thus needed to merge into one indivisible and continental nation-state, as Scotland and England had merged in 1707 to form the mighty British nation.

This was the main argument that persuaded open-minded, fence-sitting Americans in 1787–1788. It was an argument that a farmer or tradesman could understand in response to his obvious questions: *Why do we need to go beyond sovereign states and try to create a continental republic the likes of which have never been seen in human history? Given that most of history's successful republics have been small (a point popularized by the cele-brated French writer Montesquieu)—and given that until now our sovereign state has never been indissolubly linked to any other sovereign state—why must we become continental?*

Madison/Publius had his own answer to these questions in *The Federalist* No. 10—the masked Virginian's first contribution to the collaborative project. This answer was not geostrategic. It did not fit within the main outlines of the Washington-Hamilton-Jay solution to the confederation crisis but rather aimed to offer a *different* reason to vote yes on the proposed Constitution. Madison's essay built on the most original ideas that he had pitched at Philadelphia, and in college courses today this essay is widely taught for its intriguing claims about democracy, demography, representation, majority rule, minority rights, property rights, factionalism, and governmental economies of scale. Arguing that the new federal government would likely protect minority rights better than would individual states—because majority tyranny would be harder to pull off in a large and diverse democracy, and because continental lawmakers would likely be men of greater wisdom than would state legislators—the essay foreshadowed much of post–Civil War American history.

But in 1787–1788, almost no one paid attention to Madison's masterpiece. The early geostrategic *Federalist* essays were widely reprinted; *The Federalist* No. 10 was not. Unlike the main ideas of *The Federalist* nos. 2–8, Madison's concepts in No. 10 were not echoed in other newspaper pieces by other authors or by speakers in ratifying conventions. Number 10 failed to make a deep impression in American coffeehouses and taverns where patrons read aloud and discussed both local and out-of-town newspapers.[3] (If Publius had a great answer to the farmer/tradesman's basic question—*why a truly continental nation-state?*—the best place to give that answer in a newspaper would be in the first few essays, not the tenth.) The only Madison essay that was widely reprinted in 1787–1788, *The Federalist* No. 14, opened with a nice recapitulation of the geostrategic argument, an argument that Madison plainly endorsed even though he had some other, more original ideas that he had to get off his chest.

One of these ideas was that popular governments based on the concept of representation could operate over much larger areas and populations than could systems of direct democracy in which voters met in person to legislate—most notably ancient Athenian assemblies and New England town meetings. Aiming to blunt Montesquieu's famous claim, emphasized at every turn by Anti-Federalist skeptics of the Philadelphia plan, that truly self-governing societies could work only over small areas, Madison introduced his now-famous distinction between "republics" and "democracies." The latter relied on direct and daily citizen participation, and as to them, said Madison, Montesquieu had a point. But "republics" based on smaller representative assemblies could span large distances and encompass large populations, Madison argued.[4]

The distinction between small representative assemblies and large citizen assemblies was then and remains now a powerful one. Indeed, this point was hardly unique to Madison in 1787. But others at the time did not routinely equate "republics" with representation or "democracy" with pure populism. On the contrary, many other Americans at the time tended to treat the words *republic* and *democracy* as broadly synonymous. A democracy could be either direct or indirect. Perhaps the word *democracy* was slightly edgier—much as it is edgier today to call someone a "left-winger" rather than a "liberal." But Madison's sharp distinction between "republics" and "democracies" was his own innovation, and it was not widely embraced.

Madison himself knew this. In No. 10 he referred to "a republic, by which *I mean*" not "a republic, by which is *generally meant*." In No. 14 he confessed that the "prevalen[t]" understanding "confound[s] a republic with a democracy." Sure enough, Madison's contemporaries often referred casually to England's House of Commons and state lower houses—all of which rested on principles of representation—as particularly "democratic" or "democratical" elements of their respective constitutions. Conversely, late eighteenth-century "republics" could indeed make use of certain forms of direct political participation—as had, for example, Massachusetts in ratifying its state constitution in 1780 and in its general tradition of town meetings. Ancient Greek governments, which had practiced various forms of direct democracy, were also commonly described as "republics"—a description that appeared in three of the four *Federalist* essays immediately preceding Madison's stipulated definition in No. 10.

At the same time that Madison was drawing his fine linguistic distinction, other leading Federalists were obliterating it, proclaiming that a "republican" government could be either directly or indirectly democratic. In the Pennsylvania ratifying convention, the brilliant James Wilson, a Philadelphia alumnus widely viewed as America's ablest lawyer, explicitly equated a "republic" with a "democracy." Wilson went on, repeatedly and proudly, to pronounce the Constitution "democratic" and "democratical." In a proper republic/democracy, "the people at large retain the supreme power, and act *either* collectively *or* by representation." The Constitution met this test, Wilson declared: "All authority, of every kind, is derived by REPRESENTATION from the PEOPLE, and the DEMOCRATIC principle is carried into every part of the government." Similarly, South Carolina's Charles Pinckney described a republican government as one in which "the people at large, *either* collectively *or* by representation, form the legislature." Echoing Wilson, future chief justice John Marshall repeatedly sang the praises of democracy in the Virginia ratifying convention: "Supporters of the Constitution [are] firm friends of the liberty and the rights of mankind. . . . *We, sir, idolize democracy.* . . . We admire it [the proposed Constitution], because we think it a well-regulated democracy. . . . We contend for a well-regulated democracy."[5]

When the word *democracy* appeared in the Founding era, it was often associated with, rather than defined against, republicanism—even by Madison himself. Madison's preferred system of filtered representation over an extended geographic sphere, which *The Federalist* No. 10 proudly labeled "the *republican* remedy for the disease most incident to *republican* government," had earlier been described by Madison at Philadelphia as "the only defence agst. the inconveniences of *democracy* consistent with the *democratic* form of Govt."[6] In the 1790s, when various pro-Madison groups sprang up, some called themselves "Republican societies," others "Democratic societies," and still others "Democratic-Republican societies." The political party that Madison and Thomas Jefferson created in this decade was variously described as the "Republican" party and the

"Democratic-Republican" party. Thus, today's Democratic Party claims the "Republican" Jefferson as one of its founders.

With the foregoing myth-busting account in mind, we can now quickly pop a pair of related myths about secession and plutocracy.

On secession, recall that the key *Federalist* essays—the ones that were widely reprinted and loudly echoed in the several state ratification debates—were the essays that preceded and immediately followed No. 10, not No. 10 itself, which veered off on a tangent. The main *Federalist* argument in these influential essays was a Washingtonian geostrategic one that emphatically repudiated the idea that any individual state, post-ratification, could unilaterally leave the Union.

The Federalist No. 5 thus made clear that the model for USA 2.0 was the indissoluble union of England and Scotland. (Today, there is talk of Scottish secession, but it is basic British law that secession cannot be *unilateral*: Britain as a whole must agree to any breakup.) Post-1707 Britain was free and strong, argued Publius in the early *Federalist* essays, precisely because Britons had eliminated internal land borders and internal armies. America needed to follow the same model for the same reason, explained *The Federalist* No. 8. Thus, *The Federalist* No. 11 expressly described the new plan as one for a "strict and indissoluble" union. Were unilateral state secession legally permissible, any state could at any future date ally with any foreign European monarchy of its choosing and thereby threaten its land-bordering neighbors with an army buttressed by European monarchs, murderers, and mercenaries. Any such alliance would obviously imperil the entire Washingtonian project, which envisioned a largely demilitarized America in which Americans would never need a large army to guard, say, Maryland and points north from Virginia, or Virginia from the Carolinas.

The text of the Constitution and its ratification history were utterly clear on this point. Article VI proclaimed the Constitution the supreme law of the land, regardless of what any state in the future might say or do unilaterally—no ifs, ands, or buts. Anyone who took up arms against America, even if backed by his home state, would be committing treason, said Article III. The Constitution pointedly dropped the emphatic language of the Articles of Confederation proclaiming that each state was sovereign—an enormously consequential omission duly noted by all leading Anti-Federalists. In the same spirit, the Constitution's Article V dropped the Confederation rule that future amendments would require state unanimity. Such a rule made sense for a pure league of sovereign states—the Confederation—but made no sense for a newly modeled Washingtonian system in which states would no longer be sovereign as they once had been. The new plan was exactly what it said it was—not a *league*, not a *confederation*, not a *treaty* of *sovereign* states, but a true and indivisible *Constitution* obviously modeled on contemporaneous state constitutions. (In turn, these constitutions were universally understood as internally indivisible. No one thought in 1787 that Boston could unilaterally secede from Massachusetts or that Charleston could unilaterally exit from South Carolina.)

In the ratification process, Anti-Federalists everywhere highlighted the proposed Constitution's indivisibility and urged Americans to think twice, and then thrice more, before agreeing to such an audacious and unilaterally irreversible plan. In response, leading Federalists across the continent in both speech and print expressly avowed indivisibility and routinely highlighted the analogy to the indivisible union of Scotland and England some four score years earlier. *Never, in the entire year of ratification, did any leading Federalist suggest that a state could unilaterally leave the new Union*—even though such an assurance would doubtless have made it much easier for states' rights men to say yes.[7]

In the New York ratifying convention, compromise-minded Anti-Federalists offered to vote yes so long as the state could reserve a right to withdraw from the union over the next few years if no federal Bill of Rights materialized. Federalists flatly rejected the proffered compromise. At the risk of losing the entire state, Federalists insisted that the state convention must ratify cleanly, with no attempted reservation of a secession right. Hamilton read aloud a letter from Madison on this key point: "The Constitution requires an adoption *in toto*, and *for ever*. It has been so adopted by the other States" (including Madison's Virginia). Hamilton and Jay went on to elaborate the key point in their own words. The

Constitution's required oath to the document itself as the supreme law of the land "stands in the way" of any purported secession right. "A reservation of a right to withdraw . . . was inconsistent with the Constitution, and was no ratification."[8]

As Hamilton, Jay, and Madison made these points unequivocally clear, all America was watching breathlessly. Would the Federalists' insistence on this bedrock nonnegotiable point doom the deal?

In the end, the New York ratifying convention said yes by the narrowest of margins. Newspapers in virtually every state—including, notably, Virginia and both Carolinas—covered the cliff-hanger in detail. Americans everywhere in 1787–1788—the hinge of human history, the year that changed everything—understood exactly what they were agreeing to, and why.[9]

How can it be that so many Americans today miss the central argument of the key *Federalist* essays and the key Federalists? Much of the blame lies with Charles Beard, who in 1913 wrote the single most influential twentieth-century book on the Constitution. Beard's ambitious and widely read *Economic Interpretation of the Constitution* argued in effect that the Constitution was an undemocratic quasi-coup foisted on America by a wealthy elite—a document by and for the one-percenters, so to speak. Modern neo-Beardians of various stripes tell a dark Founding story that goes something like this:

> Well-heeled delegates met in secret and exceeded their limited instructions (to modify the Articles of Confederation, not scrap them entirely). These plotters then pressured/bamboozled America into accepting a document designed mainly to protect private property and fatcat creditors, and to suppress incipient movements for economic justice—for debtor relief laws, paper money laws, and the like, movements that were beginning to gain traction in state governments that were, in Federalist eyes, unduly democratic.

Madison's *Federalist* No. 10 was Exhibit A for Beard and his legions of followers. On the Beardian reading, Madison's No. 10 dissed democracy and stressed property rights and incipient class conflict. Madison was a kind of Marxian analyst *avant la lettre* (although, of course, he was on the side of the ruling class contra the emerging proletariat). States, in this reading, were more threatening to minority rights than the larger, wider-ranging federal government would be, and the all-important representation principle would likely lead to an elite federal Congress that would be less vulnerable to mass pressure for economic redistribution than were the more numerous, less refined, more democratic and demagogic state lawmakers.

There is a touch of truth in this dark Beardian tale, but also massive mythmaking. Recall that no one at the time paid much attention to No. 10. Indeed, almost no leading politician or scholar paid much heed to No. 10 in the ensuing century and a quarter, even as many other Federalist essays did feature prominently in America's ongoing constitutional conversation. Beard almost single-handedly vaulted Madison's intriguing essay to the forefront of American constitutional discourse.[10]

Aside from the details of who read which *Federalist* essay when, a much larger question looms: Was the Constitution itself, as Beard and neo-Beardians claim, fundamentally antidemocratic?

Hardly. The Constitution did not say "We the Property," nor did it do "We the Property." The original document itself mentioned property only once—in Article IV's reference to government property, not private property. More important, the Constitution was put to an epic "We the People" vote with specially democratic procedures and protocols. In eight of the thirteen states, ordinary property qualifications (either to vote for convention delegates or to run as a delegate or both) were lowered or eliminated. In no state were property qualifications raised for this special once-in-a-lifetime ratification experience. In New York, for example, all adult free male citizens could vote for convention delegates—no race tests, no property tests, no religious tests, no literacy tests. These were not the rules for ordinary New York elections. Rather, they were special rules—especially democratic rules—designed for an especially democratic ratification process. We the People, indeed. That is, in deed.

Beard knew these facts and hid them from his readers. Later Beardians either did not know these facts or did not care. The facts came to light only in 2005, in another ambitious and widely read academic tome, *America's Constitution: A Biography.*[11]

True, the Convention met in secret, but secrecy lapsed on the conclave's last day. Secrecy aimed to promote candid initial deliberation, not to suppress sordid delegate motivation. In the ensuing ratification process, many delegates openly discussed details of their earlier deliberations.[12] (This too is a fact that neo-Beardians either do not know or choose not to mention.) True, the delegates went beyond their strict instructions, but diplomats and lawmakers back then did this routinely when exciting negotiating possibilities unexpectedly materialized at the bargaining table. Washington and company exceeded the *letter* of their instructions to fulfill the *spirit* of their instructions: please fix the broken Confederation! Their proposal became law only after the Confederation Congress unanimously forwarded their plan to the several states, and only after the American people in state convention after state convention said yes, we do.

If the document was truly antidemocratic, why did the People vote for it? Why did tens of thousands of ordinary working men enthusiastically join massive pro-constitutional rallies in Philadelphia and Manhattan? Why did America's Electoral College vote unanimously, twice, to make the Constitution's father, George Washington, the renewed union's first president? Why did voters vote overwhelmingly for Federalists in the first set of national elections?

Here's why: because, contra Beard, the document was remarkably democratic for its time, if we bracket for a moment the slavery issue. (We shall shortly return to the slavery issue—an issue that Beard, interestingly, all but ignored.)

Unlike the Articles of Confederation, the Constitution featured a new institution—the House of Representatives—elected directly by the people. The 1787 plan rejected property qualifications for House service, Senate service, and the presidency. No contemporaneous state did anything truly analogous. The Philadelphia plan also provided for a regular census and a regular reapportionment, unlike most states. The new document additionally promised that federal lawmakers would draw salaries, so that even middling men, and not merely the idle rich, could serve.

Most states did nothing like this. In sharp contrast to the rules in most states, the new Constitution promised to open government service to persons of every creed, even agnostics and atheists. Also, the Philadelphia Constitution's age rules aimed to blunt dynastic power by prohibiting the early election of famous favorite sons while giving lowborn men a chance to rise and show their stuff. This, too, was more democratic than most state constitutions.

If the Constitution was fundamentally democratic for its time, does this mean it was also fundamentally antislavery?

No. Democracy (for a given people/citizenry) and enslavement (of other peoples/nationalities) could conceptually coexist and indeed did famously coexist for centuries in the most notable ancient democracies/ republics, namely Periclean Athens and the Roman Republic.

In fact, America's pro-democracy Constitution of 1787 was, sadly, also pro-slavery in its basic structure and foreseeable effects, even though not everyone at the time, especially in the North, foresaw the foreseeable during the drafting and ratification process. The Three Fifths Clause gave slave states a massive advantage in the House and in the Electoral College—an advantage that in turn would ultimately warp the antebellum presidency, the federal judiciary (whose members were nominated by presidents), state legislative apportionment, Senate selection, western expansion policy, and much more.[13]

The pro-democracy and pro-slavery Constitution that emerged under the republican plantation owner George Washington was thus, in a word, *proto-Jacksonian*. In various ways, Andrew Jackson called to mind George Washington himself. Both men were deep believers in American self-government (though Jackson was not merely democratic but also often demagogic). Both men famously bested the British on the battlefield (Jackson even more decisively than Washington). And both men were also, alas, southern slaveholders. (Washington was increasingly embarrassed by this fact and in his last act freed his slaves; Jackson was not and did not.)

On reflection, we should not be surprised that Jackson—a strong pro-democracy and pro-slavery president who also embodied fierce anti-secessionism and a muscular attitude toward European monarchs—would ultimately become the dominant political figure in antebellum America. After all, Jackson personified some of the Constitution's most striking structural elements: its populism, its military resilience, and also, alas, its special accommodation of slavocracy.

In sum, America's Constitution was far more democratic and geostrategic than we have been taught by twentieth-century neo-Beardian and neo-Madisonian mythmakers. The document's deep power structure was also, sadly, more skewed toward slavery than many mainstream scholars have been willing to admit. America's Constitution was not truly Madisonian; it was Washingtonian and proto-Jacksonian.

3

VANISHING INDIANS

Ari Kelman

IN APRIL 2021, RICK SANTORUM, A FORMER REPUBLICAN SENATOR and failed presidential candidate, spoke before the Young America's Foundation, an organization devoted to inculcating conservative values—including the importance of "individual freedom, a strong national defense, [and] free enterprise"—in its members. Santorum, in the decade and a half since losing his Senate seat, had fashioned himself into a political pundit and commentator, someone media outlets and movement conservatives could reliably count on to serve up hard-right rhetoric in print and in person. In his speech about the sanctity of religious liberty, Santorum looked back to the nation's origins, suggesting that when European colonists arrived in what would become the United States, they found only a "blank slate." There was "nothing here," he insisted. Drawing an unbroken line between colonial pioneers and practitioners of modern conservatism, he noted that "we birthed a nation from nothing."

Santorum, catching himself, allowed that "yes, we have Native Americans." But of their contributions to the nation's development, "Candidly there isn't much Native American culture in American culture." In just a few sentences, Santorum had erased the history and culture of Indigenous Americans; Native peoples, if they had played any role in the nation's development, had long since departed the stage, leaving behind little of substance.[1]

Although Santorum later insisted that he had been misunderstood, his remarks echoed and amplified persistent misconceptions about the mechanisms and consequences of American imperialism: the myth of the vanishing Indian. The notion that Native peoples would sink whenever they found themselves awash in a flood tide of settlers predated the founding of the republic. Colonists in New England systematically erased evidence of long-standing Indigenous cultures and societies as a way of legitimating Euro-American land claims. The presence of so-called Indians in the region, newcomers insisted, had been only fleeting, an ephemeral curiosity whose time had come and gone. By the mid-nineteenth century, pseudoscience propped up such claims. God and nature, racial theorists insisted, had destined savage Indians to disappear when confronted by white civilization. As time passed, an equally crude cultural explanation emerged to supplement that sort of environmental determinism: Indians were always and everywhere premodern people; they were incapable of adapting and surviving in a fast-changing world. In the years after the Civil War, onlookers nationwide kept waiting for these primitives to disappear, even as warfare between federal and Indigenous soldiers bathed the American West in blood.

At the dawn of the twentieth century, tribal nations were often confined to reservations. Many Native homelands, ostensibly guaranteed to their inhabitants in perpetuity, were being privatized and sold at market. In the coming years, the independent political standing of some tribes would be terminated by federal authorities. Across the 1920s and 1930s, even as Indigenous people gained the prerogatives of citizenship, audiences consumed films, photographs, and books that depicted Indians as endangered or extinct. Through the 1960s, with wars abroad and struggles for civil rights at home shifting the cultural context, the myth of the vanishing Indian persisted. In 1970, Dee Brown published *Bury My Heart at Wounded Knee: An Indian History of the American West*. An account of the continent's conquest and colonization, Brown's book allowed Native people to speak for themselves. But he still concluded that by the end of the nineteenth century, the "culture and civilization of the American Indian was destroyed." A hugely popular work of revisionist history intended to document a vibrant Indian past, *Bury My Heart at Wounded Knee* instead reduced Indigenous history to declension, destruction, and disappearance. Brown's work, no matter the author's intentions, seeded the ground for a speech like Santorum's.[2]

By the time that Rick Santorum spoke before the Young America's Foundation, the erasure of Native peoples, whether from literature or the landscape, had a long history. Jean O'Brien, a renowned White Earth Ojibwe scholar, has written about British colonists in New England first dispossessing and then displacing Native Americans. Settlers, she demonstrates, claimed to have created the region's enduring institutions— to have ushered in the foundations of civilization and modernity—and then began casting Indians as immutably premodern. Indians facing a changing world could not adapt, New Englanders insisted. Instead, overmatched and unfit, tribal peoples would vanish from the scene. In this way, settlers absolved themselves of guilt for the cruelty they visited upon Native nations; they turned imperial violence into innocent virtue. Constructed narratives of regional progress hinged on episodes in which colonists confronted and overcame savages, replacing them with white settlements. What had been a time without history gave way to an era of colonial primacy and progress. The disappearance of Indians became a mile marker on the road to transforming a hideous and desolate wilderness into a congenial settler homeland.[3]

Many leading figures within the founding generation believed that Indians would eventually vanish, their disappearance clearing the way for the young United States to thrive. Supreme Court Justice Joseph Story, looking back on the consequences of the conquest and colonization of Massachusetts for Native peoples, asked, "What can be more melancholy than their history?" Pointing to an emerging racial explanation for the transition from Native to non-Native control of the Atlantic coast, he observed, "By a law of their nature, they seem destined to a slow, but sure extinction." Encapsulating the myth of the vanishing Indian, he concluded: "Everywhere, at the approach of the white man, they fade away. We hear the rustling of their footsteps, like that of the withered leaves of autumn, and they are gone forever." Some of Story's contemporaries, including Thomas Jefferson, held more nuanced views of Indigenous people. Jefferson theorized that Indians were likely capable of improving their race. So long as they embraced Christianity and adapted to sedentary agriculture, he believed that Native people could assimilate and perhaps even become productive Americans, yeoman farmers capable of republican virtue. But Jefferson, Story, and their peers elided episodes of settler violence, constructing instead foundational myths around unexamined assumptions of American innocence, progress, and innovation.[4]

As antipathies between settlers and Indigenous people deepened throughout the era of the early republic, and especially during and after the War of 1812, when Native warriors fought with the British against American soldiers, the myth of the vanishing Indian spread more widely. The idea that Indians were destined to fade away, their disappearance preordained by the Almighty rather than a consequence of federal policies or the actions of independent settlers, offered both an explanation and a kind of exculpation for what might otherwise have been an unnerving transition in a nation proud of its postcolonial origin story and its publicly anti-imperial posture. A commonly held perspective suggested that settlers in the United States, looking only to better themselves and improve the landscape around them, had neither sought a fight with Native peoples nor hoped to overrun their homelands. Regrettably, Indians had allied themselves with Great Britain, making themselves America's enemies, the argument went, and employed tactics that had no place in civilized warfare—never mind that Patriot soldiers had sometimes used similar methods in their fight with redcoats during the Revolutionary War. That Indigenous peoples might disappear in the wake of the War of 1812 seemed to many onlookers like just deserts.[5]

As the years passed, pressure on Indians living between the Atlantic coast and the Appalachians became unbearable. Around the time of the Louisiana Purchase, President Jefferson had mused about exchanging Native ground to the east of the Mississippi for federal lands to its west. By the 1820s, even though the so-called Five Civilized Tribes included among their ranks Christians, farmers, and slaveholders, settlers in the Southeast viewed those Native nations as an impediment to progress. In 1830, President Andrew Jackson decided to remove those tribes to a so-called permanent Indian frontier, territory beyond the Mississippi guaranteed to Native nations "in perpetuity." President Jackson and his supporters, working against the backdrop of the myth of the vanishing Indian, often recast the policy of removal as a kind of humanitarianism. They suggested that either Indians would willingly go into the West or they would disappear entirely. "All good citizens, and none more zealously than those who think the Indians oppressed by subjection to the laws of the States," Jackson suggested in justifying removal, "will unite in attempting to open the eyes of those children of the forest to their true condition, and by a speedy removal to relieve them from the evils, real or imaginary, present or prospective, with which they may be supposed to be threatened." The myth of the vanishing Indian became a self-fulfilling prophecy.[6]

With the United States hurtling toward civil war, racial scientists grew more authoritative by crafting planks for the South's pro-slavery platform and, in doing so, amplified the myth of the vanishing Indian. Adherents of the American school of ethnology, drawing on Samuel George Morton's *Crania Americana*, argued for the theory of polygenesis. Different races of human beings had been created during different episodes, they claimed, and therefore differences found among them, including apparent inequities of ability or variations in intellect, would remain immutable. Pointing to variegations in human skulls, Morton insisted that they came from entirely separate species of human beings. Josiah Nott, a physician and racial theorist in Mobile, Alabama, expanded on Morton's work, arguing that Native peoples, a distinct race created in a discrete moment, were incapable of change and that God and nature had sealed their fate: "To one who has lived among American Indians, it is vain to talk of civilizing them." He concluded, "It is as clear as the sun at noon-day . . . the last of these Red men will be numbered among the dead."[7]

During the Civil War, the Republican Party passed landmark pieces of legislation—the Homestead Act, the Pacific Railroad Act, and the Morrill Land-Grant Act—remaking the United States into an empire that stretched from coast to coast. Native peoples responded by fighting for their families, their homelands, and their sovereignty. Early in the war, southern diplomats guaranteed that a new Confederate nation would safeguard its allies' political and cultural prerogatives. Some Cherokees, weary of the federal government's broken promises, agreed to fight with the South. In 1862, Dakota peoples in Minnesota launched a territorial and cultural counterrevolution, burning towns and pushing settlers out of large swaths of the state. Federal troops then marched to restore order, smashing Native soldiers before staging the largest public execution in the nation's history: thirty-eight Dakotas hanged the day after Christmas, 1862. Two years after that, on November 29, 1864, volunteer soldiers in Colorado Territory descended upon a peaceful Arapaho and Cheyenne village and slaughtered more than 150 people, the vast majority of whom were women, children, and the elderly. In the wake of what became known as the Sand Creek Massacre, Native nations on the plains fought together during Red Cloud's War.[8]

Westward migrants and federal officials were shocked and infuriated as Indigenous people, supposedly hardwired by racial destiny to disappear when faced with adversity, kept adapting and fighting, sometimes securing stunning victories in struggles with the United States. Just days before the nation's centennial celebration, an army made up of Arapaho, Cheyenne, and Lakota warriors destroyed George Armstrong Custer's Seventh Cavalry. Onlookers around the United States grappled with the hard truth that Indians had bested one of the Civil War's heroes. When he took office in 1869, President Ulysses S. Grant had initially hoped to feed rather than fight Native people. He claimed that he did not want to destroy what remained of Indigenous America. But after the Battle of the Little Bighorn, he reversed course. The Indian Wars would not end until federal troops, responding to a perceived threat associated with a religious revival known as the Ghost Dance, killed hundreds of Native people at the Wounded Knee massacre.[9]

With the Civil War over and the Thirteenth Amendment ratified, many abolitionists searched for good works to occupy their idled hands. Some turned to the cause of Indian reform. In 1879, an author named Helen Hunt Jackson began writing an exposé of how Indians had been mistreated throughout the nation's history. Published in 1881, *A Century of Dishonor* revealed "the robbery, the cruelty which were done under the cloak of this hundred years of treaty-making and treaty-breaking." Rather than assuming that Native people would inevitably vanish, Jackson suggested that the people of the United States should understand their culpability in what today might be called a genocide. She warned that a day of reckoning drew near: "The history of the United States Government's repeated violations of faith with the Indians thus convicts us, as a nation, not only of having outraged the principles of justice, which are the basis of international law; and of having laid ourselves open to the accusation of both cruelty and perfidy; but of having made ourselves liable to all punishments which follow upon such sins." Only by repenting, she insisted, and also by shifting federal Indian policy, could the United States avoid the "natural punishment which, sooner or later, as surely comes from evil-doing as harvests come from sown seed."[10]

Around the turn of the twentieth century, the American West, despite the death and degradation associated with the Indian Wars, remained a place of hope and promise for the United States. But anxieties over the implications of imperialism troubled many observers of the region's landscape and history. Frederick Jackson Turner fretted over the closing of the frontier. He worried that a dearth of unoccupied land accessible to settlers would imperil American democracy. Indians disappeared in the West of Frederick Jackson Turner's "frontier thesis." In these same years, conservationists, including Teddy Roosevelt, unspooled their own declension narratives, predicting the impending destruction of the bison—a synecdoche for the West—and the Native peoples who depended on those beasts. An emerging field of professional anthropology, theorized by scholars such as Franz Boas, employed familiar rhetoric, warning colleagues that Native peoples would soon vanish: "Day by day the Indians and their cultures are disappearing more and more before the encroachment of modern civilization, and fifty years hence nothing will remain to be learned in regard to this interesting and important subject." Famed ethnographers, including George Bird Grinnell and James Mooney, went into the field to try to capture that culture before it was gone.[11]

Vanishing Indians featured prominently in popular culture and the arts early in the new century. Photographer Edward Curtis captured images of Native peoples who he believed would soon disappear. His haunting work rendered static figures who were, outside his frame, dynamic, embodying the misconception that Native Americans were trapped in the amber of a bygone era. He titled the most iconic of his compositions—a group of Navajos on horseback, riding away from the photographer toward an uncertain fate—*The Vanishing Race*. As Curtis tried to preserve evidence of a Native presence in the United States, he contributed to a deepening sense that Indians would soon be gone forever. Around the same time, readers consumed dime novels about cowboys and Indians. Zane Grey's *The Vanishing American*, released first as a book and then as a silent film in 1925, told the story of federal exploitation of the Navajo people. The book is relatively sympathetic to the plight of its subjects; the movie is less so. In both cases, beleaguered Indians ultimately realize that their traditional ways of life are doomed in a changing world.[12]

Ironically, as the myth of the vanishing Indian spread from the realms of pseudoscience and scholarship into the popular imagination, becoming more deeply ingrained in American culture than ever before, federal treatment of Indigenous people improved somewhat. At the same time, what had been a demographic decline seemingly began reversing itself—although census data are notoriously unreliable when it comes to Native Americans, who sometimes live in hard-to-reach places and frequently prefer not to be counted by investigators on the federal payroll. During the era of the New Deal, President Franklin Delano Roosevelt appointed John Collier, a sociologist and advocate of Native rights, to the post of Commissioner of Indian Affairs. Collier crafted the Indian Reorganization Act of 1934, reversing decades of policy devoted to assimilating Indigenous peoples—making Indians vanish, in other words, through a process of officially sanctioned amalgamation—and instead respecting their political and cultural sovereignty. As Collier explained in a rejoinder to critics, the goal of the legislation was "to recognize and respect the Indian as he is." In 1938 Collier reported that "Indians are no longer a dying race."[13]

In the three decades between Collier's statement and publication of *Bury My Heart at Wounded Knee*, Native nations, despite popular misunderstandings and the ongoing impact of settler colonialism—economic, environmental, and demographic devastation; public health catastrophes, including epidemics of substance abuse and malnutrition; and social, cultural, and political dislocation—survived and even thrived in some instances. These were years in which Indigenous peoples increasingly eschewed assimilationist pressures and fought for recognition on their own terms. Tribal peoples organized themselves to protect their ways of living: creating language-preservation programs, safeguarding sacred sites, and fighting for sovereignty. By 1970, the year of *Bury My Heart at Wounded Knee*'s publication, *Time* reported that American Indians were "no longer vanishing" and were instead "the nation's fastest growing minority." Nevertheless, Dee Brown, no matter how sympathetic he intended his portrayal of Native history and peoples, recapitulated antiquated rhetoric about the disappearance of Indians.[14]

Bury My Heart at Wounded Knee sprawls beyond any single region and sweeps across a vast temporal arc. From start to finish, Brown intends his book as a corrective for pervasive myths about the nation's character and history, which, in *Bury My Heart at Wounded Knee*, are inextricably intertwined. By incorporating Native voices into the national narrative, Brown helps readers understand that the United States achieved its status as a continental empire not merely by dint of Manifest Destiny but also because expansionist visionaries abetted the flow of settlers into the West. The cruel logic that accompanied demographic change at this scale, Brown suggests, hinged upon the assumption that treaties could be shredded, that communities could be dehumanized, and that Native people could be dispossessed and slaughtered. Brown relies on unsparing, even voyeuristic, storytelling. Readers bear witness as soldiers chop genitalia from the bodies of their victims and rip unborn children from their mothers' wombs; across the book's chapters, as Brown debunks notions of national innocence, corpses stack up like cordwood. In the end, there can be no conclusion other than that American exceptionalism is a deceit as self-serving as it is grotesque. But at the same time, a book written to debunk one pernicious myth unwittingly reifies another, hammering home the message that by the start of the twentieth century, Indians had vanished.

Intent on centering the experiences of Native peoples in his work, Brown featured their voices, but only as echoes of the distant past. His writing predated insights about mediated texts and linguistic sovereignty that now circulate widely in the field of Native American and Indigenous studies. Rather than exploring cultural positionality and multivocality, Brown could not believe that the polished rhetoric punctuating *Bury My Heart at Wounded Knee*'s pages had come from the mouths of Indians. An intrepid researcher, he "spent hours tracking down identities of the official interpreters" before reaching "the conclusion that in most cases it mattered little who the interpreters were. The words came through into English with the same eloquence." What Brown overlooked was the fact that those translators often worked in service of federal authority; they were agents of empire, and the documents they produced were later collected as part of a settler-colonial project and housed in the National Archives and the Library of Congress. Brown never bothered working with Native informants or tribal elders. He ignored Indigenous protocols for the collection and reproduction of conversations and stories. He had little interest in conducting oral histories or ethnographies. Indians were, he thought, relics of the past. They had, in his telling, effectively vanished wholesale in the aftermath of the massacre at Wounded Knee.[15]

Brown, the author of twenty-nine books throughout his career, never enjoyed better timing than with the release of *Bury My Heart at Wounded Knee*. Published against the backdrop of the modern civil rights movement, which generated popular interest in the nation's history of mistreating people of color; the so-called New Age, which featured seekers fascinated by Indigenous peoples and cultures; and declining support for the United States' war in Vietnam, which sparked anti-imperialist sentiment, Brown's book offered readers a scathing indictment of misbegotten federal authority, enduring bigotry and racial violence, and American empire. In 1968, tribal activists formed the American Indian Movement.

A year after that, some of the organization's members seized control of Alcatraz Federal Penitentiary—located on an island a bit more than a mile offshore of San Francisco—a triumphant debut of Red Power. Just a week before the siege at Alcatraz started, Seymour Hersh, then a young investigative reporter, broke news of American soldiers killing more than a hundred villagers in the Vietnamese hamlet of My Lai. The next year, *Bury My Heart at Wounded Knee* arrived in bookstores. As a critic noted, "Brown is clearly one of a few authors who manage to write the right book at the right time."[16]

After spending more than a year on the *New York Times* best-seller list, *Bury My Heart at Wounded Knee* sold well over five million copies before Dee Brown's death in 2002. It remains the most popular and likely the most influential work of western history ever written, its impact lingering into the present. In the half century since *Bury My Heart at Wounded Knee*'s publication, Native writers and activists have pushed back against the book's legacy and the myth of the vanishing Indian more broadly. In 1999, for example, Gerald Vizenor theorized the notion of "survivance" for Indigenous peoples, suggesting that "Native survivance stories are renunciations of dominance, tragedy and victimry." In other words, Vizenor rejected the notion that Indians should be understood as Dee Brown had cast them. Twenty years later, Tiffany Midge, a Lakota writer and humorist, poked fun at the ongoing impact of Brown's work, publishing an essay collection titled *Bury My Heart at Chuck E. Cheese's*, in which she acknowledges the impact of settler colonialism but focuses more of her attention on the reality of Native American lives as persistent and complex. Finally, in that same year, 2019, David Treuer, an Ojibwe scholar, author, and cultural critic, published *The Heartbeat of Wounded Knee: Native America from 1890 to the Present*.[17]

Treuer's book explicitly rejects Brown's framing of history, picking up the story of Native peoples after the violence at Wounded Knee—a time when, Brown had insisted, they should have disappeared. Treuer explains his inspiration: "the simple, fierce conviction that [our] cultures are not dead," that "[Native] civilizations have not been destroyed." Wounded Knee, he notes, often serves as a coda in discussions of Indigenous people. Many textbooks and scholarly monographs feature Native nations, if they are featured at all, only during the decades between Jacksonian removal and the end of the Indian Wars, after which they seemingly vanish. But Treuer insists that the tragedy at Wounded Knee should instead be understood as the "point from which much of modern Indian and American life has emerged." It is "not just that 150 people were cruelly and viciously killed," he mourns, but also "that their sense of life—and our sense of their lives—died with them." He suggests that "the victims of Wounded Knee died twice—once at the end of a gun, again at the end of a pen." In Treuer's view, it is only by rewriting the history of Native peoples—acknowledging their ongoing resilience and complexity—that the work of authors like Dee Brown can be effaced and Wounded Knee and the years since reclaimed and redeemed.[18]

Yet the myth of the vanishing Indian—despite the presence of so many actual Indians, including those increasingly working in the public eye, demanding that onlookers acknowledge their existence—persists. For someone like Rick Santorum, keen to signal support for American imperialism, excising the contributions and persistence of colonized peoples serves as a kind of shibboleth. Critics noted that Santorum chose not just to denigrate but also to erase the history and cultural contributions of Native peoples in the United States. Simon Moya-Smith, a Lakota journalist, suggested that "American history textbooks routinely—and, for men like Santorum, conveniently—leave out the deep and textured history of this continent's Indigenous peoples, as well as the details of the shocking brutality of the white men who invaded our land and claimed it for themselves." Moya-Smith concluded: "America desperately tried to get rid of us. Yet here we stand, Rick Santorum. Our stories and histories and bodies are going nowhere, white man. We are resilient." Nick Estes, a Lower Brule Sioux scholar who has written about the struggle over the Dakota Access Pipeline, observed that "the erasure of Native people and histories, which existed before and survived in spite of a white supremacist empire, is a foundational sin of a make-believe nation." Other onlookers, including Fawn Sharp, president of the National Congress of American Indians, labeled Santorum a racist and suggested that his remarks were predictable.[19]

On social media, in newspapers, and on TV, Native and non-Native people called on CNN, Santorum's employer, to fire the controversial commentator. Santorum engaged in what appeared to be a halfhearted effort at damage control, insisting that he had been misinterpreted. "The way we treated Native Americans was horrific," Santorum clarified, adding that "it goes against every bone and everything I've ever fought for, as a leader, in the Congress." Observers noted that he did not apologize for his remarks. Less than a month later, CNN's head of strategic communications, Matt Dornic, announced that the organization had "parted ways" with Santorum. An unnamed executive explained that "none of the anchors wanted to book him. So he was essentially benched anyway." Summing up management's decision, Dornic added: "I think after that appearance, it was pretty clear we couldn't use him again." Santorum would, at least for a time, vanish. It seemed likely, though, that the myth that had contributed to his disappearance would persist.[20]

4

IMMIGRATION

Erika Lee

THE GRAINY BLACK-AND-WHITE FOOTAGE CAPTURES A DOZEN DARK-skinned individuals swarming over a fence and running past a border checkpoint on Interstate 5 in San Diego County. They hop the freeway barrier and disappear into the US. "They keep coming," a deep-throated narrator ominously tells us. "Two million illegal immigrants in California. The federal government won't stop them at the border, yet requires *us* to pay billions to take care of them." Thus began California governor Pete Wilson's 1994 reelection ad. Playing to the xenophobic fears of a growing number of Californians, the ad was effective. Wilson was reelected, and voters approved Proposition 187, the "Save Our State" ballot initiative that proposed to deny nonemergency health care and public education to undocumented immigrants.[1]

Both the Wilson spot and the Proposition 187 campaign drew upon deep-rooted and well-known stereotypes about Mexican immigrants as criminals and undeserving lawbreakers. It explicitly demonized undocumented migrants, but it was a classic expression of what anthropologist Leo Chavez calls the "Latino threat narrative": all Mexicans in the United States—with papers and without—constitute a Hispanic "invasion" of the United States that will destroy America.[2]

The commercial's characterization of immigration also repeated one of the most enduring and powerful myths in the United States—the "They Keep Coming" myth. This is how it works: immigrants are "they," not "us." Typically nonwhite and non-Protestant, they are dangerous foreigners who come here uninvited to take jobs away from Americans and to harm its people and institutions. Once started, immigration continues without end: *"They keep coming."* Immigration unleashes an unwanted and unending inundation of foreigners who, along with their US-citizen children, will eventually outnumber "us," meaning white and "real" Americans, and take over. In short, immigration is nothing less than a hostile invasion of the nation.

Like all myths, this one distorts and obscures complex realities. For starters, it ignores the role of US foreign, economic, and immigration policies in promoting migration and obscures how global migration actually works. The United States has long been a particularly powerful actor shaping the movement of people by causing human displacement through war and foreign and economic policies. It also has a long history of coercing, recruiting, cajoling, and incentivizing foreigners to come to the country to serve its own economic needs. The US has rarely acknowledged its role in creating and directing migration and settlement. Rather, Americans typically view immigration through the "push-pull" framework, whereby the United States is responsible only for pulling foreigners to its borders and shores with the promise of jobs, freedom, and economic opportunity, but not for pushing them from their homelands in the first place.

Far from being a harmless misinterpretation, the immigration myth has had dire consequences. When Americans have believed that the disadvantages of immigration have outweighed its advantages—or when certain immigrant groups have outlasted their usefulness—the immigration myth has been dusted off to justify new restrictions and forms of control. We have deployed it and adapted it to demonize multiple and

successive groups of immigrants and refugees while celebrating an ex-
clusionary and nativist definition of *American*. It has been used to restrict
both immigration and the rights of immigrants already in the country. It
has been adopted to justify discriminatory immigration bans, the militarization of the US-Mexico border, and the expansion of America's deportation machine. It has allowed anti-immigrant xenophobia to become
part of systemic racism and discrimination in America.[3]

The "They Keep Coming" immigration myth has deep roots in our past.
We might even identify founding father Benjamin Franklin as inventor of
the myth (along with his other inventions like the lightning rod, bifocals,
and the Franklin stove). In 1755 he anxiously characterized Germans,
the largest non-English group of white settlers in colonial America, as
"swarthy" aliens who "herd[ed] together." Left alone, he predicted, they
would soon "be so numerous as to Germanize us instead of our Anglify-
ing them." Pennsylvania would become "a Colony of Aliens," he worried.
Franklin's anxiety over German immigration was expressed in ways that
would become familiar to Americans across the centuries: there were too
many foreigners; they did not assimilate; they were a danger that must be
stopped.[4]

These anti-German sentiments established an important pattern of xenophobia in colonial America. But it was not just about a fear of foreigners. It was also about where non-English settlers fit into a colonial society
defined and driven by white (English) settler colonialism, slavery, and
white supremacy. Germans represented an unpredictable and growing
danger to English settlers' power and dominance in the colonies at a time
when they were vulnerable to a whole host of threats: mounting anti-
Indian violence; an all-out war involving Pennsylvanians, the British, the
French, and North American Indians; and a growing population of and
dependence on enslaved Africans.

This early example of the immigration myth not only provides an opportunity to see how deeply embedded it has been in American history; it
also reveals how it neatly and deliberately obscures the realities of migration, including who has come and why. Franklin's message ignored how
white settlers, especially Protestants like the Germans, were essential in

furthering US settler colonialism. For example, the colony of Pennsylvania depended upon the migration of Europeans as part of British colonial expansion, the dispossession of Indigenous peoples and land, and the establishment of white-settler control over territory and resources. The need for settlers was so great that William Penn recruited them through pamphlets and promotional writings and through agents posted in London, Dublin, Edinburgh, and Rotterdam.[5]

In the mid-nineteenth century, xenophobes and nativists warned of the new threat of Catholic immigration. Protestant preachers such as Lyman Beecher argued that Catholic foreigners were an invading force sent by the pope. And because they had the power to become naturalized citizens and vote, they would also be able to "throw down our free institutions." These immigrants, Beecher concluded, should be viewed as a hostile "army of soldiers, enlisted and officered, and spreading over the land." When up to 1.5 million Irish fled their homeland and came to the United States from 1846 to 1855, anti-immigrant activists formed the American (Know-Nothing) Party and devoted themselves to curbing the rights and influence of immigrants. They promoted and elected anti-immigrant candidates, and in states like Massachusetts forcibly removed more than 15,000 immigrants from 1850 to 1863.[6]

As in the colonial era, the immigration myth identified foreigners as a threat to the country during a time of great economic, social, and political upheaval in the decades leading up to the Civil War. The myth also included the identification of white, Anglo-Saxon Protestants as "true" or "native" Americans who should remain the dominant force in the country. One of the Know-Nothings' favorite slogans was "Americans must rule America." The promotion of the immigration myth in the nineteenth century also neatly glossed over how immigrants were not simply "coming"; they were being driven out of their homelands. Famine-era Irish had suffered for centuries under harsh Protestant British rule that stripped Catholics of their ability to vote, hold office, and own land. When the potato blight struck, around 15 percent of the total Irish population died of starvation and disease. Irish migration to North America was a bid for survival.[7]

The immigration myth also obscured the fact that the United States continued to rely upon foreign immigration. Large-scale European migration continued to advance the US settler colonial project of seizing Indigenous land. For example, the 1862 Homestead Act fueled European immigration with its promise to grant any person 160 acres of land recently ceded by Indigenous peoples (who viewed the act as a treaty violation). Notably, the promise extended not just to established American citizens but to new immigrants as well. Prospective settlers from Norway, Sweden, and Denmark were recruited to the new territories. In the Upper Midwest, the foreign-born population ballooned while the Indigenous population dramatically declined. Serving the important needs of the expanding nation, these "Nordic" immigrants were never subjected to organized anti-immigrant campaigns.

But on the West Coast, it was a different story. In 1876 the California State Senate described Chinese immigration as "dangerous unarmed invasion" that imperiled the state and the country. With Chinese immigration, the "They Keep Coming" myth became more tightly connected to racism and immigration restriction. Lawmakers identified Chinese as a "separate" race "distinct from, and antagonistic to our people." They claimed that the Chinese would soon occupy the entire Pacific coast and that it would become but a "mere colony of China."[8]

The US Congress eventually heeded the call of West Coast activists to protect them from the so-called Chinese invasion with the passage of the 1882 Chinese Exclusion Act. The first federal law to single out an entire group for immigration exclusion based on their race and class, the Chinese Exclusion Act legalized xenophobia on an unprecedented scale. Chinese immigration plummeted. Chinese immigrants became victims of massive racial violence and were expelled from cities and towns across the US West. New immigrants were subjected to interrogations, medical examinations, lengthy detentions, surveillance, arrest, and deportation.[9]

The passage of the Chinese Exclusion Act again masked the falsehoods upon which the immigration myth was built: Chinese immigrants didn't simply "come." They were pushed, lured, and brought. Chinese men had been heavily recruited to work on the country's railroads and in its factories, canneries, fisheries, and fields. In the 1860s, labor recruiters sent twelve thousand Chinese workers to build the great transcontinental railroad. But when that work was done, calls that the "Chinese Must Go!" started gaining traction.

Although Chinese immigrants were excluded after 1882, others continued to come. From 1905 to 1914, almost 9.9 million immigrants entered the United States. Many were from southern, eastern, and central Europe, new groups that were labeled "racial inferiors" by eugenicists such as Madison Grant. Immigration was, once again, labeled a source of economic, social, and political problems facing the country and an invasion that threatened America. "Swarms of Alpine, Mediterranean, and Jewish hybrids threaten to extinguish the old stock," Grant warned in his best-selling 1916 book, *The Passing of the Great Race*. Grant expressed a special animosity toward Jewish immigrants, who he and other leading thinkers believed were a particularly "deficient" and dangerous "race." If the United States failed to act, Grant predicted the "passing of the great race" that had made America so great. Anglo-Saxons needed to "reassert" their "class and racial pride by shutting them out."[10]

Grant was just one of several voices clamoring for the gates to be closed to undesirable immigrants. Xenophobia and racism merged with "America first" nativism in James Murphy Ward's 1917 book, *The Immigration Problem, or America First*. It was also expressed in President Theodore Roosevelt's 1916 call for a "nationalized and unified America" as well as in the Ku Klux Klan's defense of an "America for Americans."[11]

By the 1920s, Congress acted again to close America's gates to dangerous foreigners. In 1924 the Johnson-Reed Act established national-origin quotas designed to cut immigration from southern and eastern Europe. It also banned "aliens ineligible for citizenship," which effectively barred all Asians. The restrictions put in place in the 1920s greatly reduced immigration. But continued US territorial expansion and rapid industrial growth required a massive number of workers, and between 1900 and 1930 at least half a million Mexicans, mostly male laborers, migrated north to the United States. An immigration backlash grew, with Mexicans embodying the latest version of the immigration myth. But unlike other groups, Mexicans had deep and historical ties in (and often

predated) the United States, especially in the Southwest. They were neither *foreign* nor *strangers*. They were also white. Thus, one of the first tasks
that xenophobes faced in mounting the campaign against Mexican immigrants was to make them *nonwhite, alien*, and *"illegal."* This strategy
continued to rely upon the already established immigration myth but also
tailored it to specifically apply to Mexicans.[12]

Xenophobes first characterized Mexicans as a racially inferior race.
Congressman John C. Box of Texas described Mexicans as a mixed
race comprising "low-grade Spaniard[s], peonized Indian[s], and Negro slave[s] mixe[d] with Negroes, mulattoes, and other mongrels, and
some sorry whites, already here." Others likened Mexican immigration
to a reconquest of the Southwest, a rhetorical strategy that conveniently
erased Mexicans' historical presence in and claims to the US Southwest
and instead remade them as foreign invaders of their former homeland.
Testifying before a congressional committee on immigration in 1930,
for example, economist Roy Garis described the "Mexicanization" of the
Southwest that jeopardized its future as the "home for millions of the
white race." "Mexicanization" included the birth of Mexican American
children in the United States. In 1930 California governor Clement C.
Young reported that Mexican immigrants were having far more children
than white Californians, a data point that he used to predict that Mexicans would soon eclipse the white population.[13]

The campaign to restrict Mexican immigration gained momentum.
The US Border Patrol was established in 1924 to regulate immigration
at the border and prohibit unauthorized immigration. In 1929 another
law made illegal entry a criminal offense. During the Great Depression,
Mexicans were targeted for restriction and deportation like no other
group. From 1929 to 1935, 82,400 Mexicans were deported by the federal
government. They constituted 46.3 percent of all deportees even though
they made up less than 1 percent of the total US population. Federal deportation drives were accompanied by local efforts to remove destitute
Mexican American families. Social workers and local relief officials pressured, coerced, and deceived Mexican and Mexican American families
to go to Mexico and never return. In the final count, nearly 20 percent
of the entire Mexican and Mexican American population in the United

States, up to one million people, were expelled to Mexico during the Depression. Sixty percent were American citizens by birth. For most, expulsion was final.[14]

Applying the "They Keep Coming" myth to Mexicans was extremely effective. That it led to such cruelty as the mass deportation efforts during the 1930s did not seem to matter to its proponents. Nor did the false claims upon which it was based. Like the Chinese before them, Mexicans had not just "come." In fact, American banks financed much of the construction of Mexican railroads that first made Mexican migration possible. During the 1880s, the Southern Pacific Railroad operated between Mexico City and Nogales; the Santa Fe–administered Mexican Central Railway ran from Mexico City to El Paso, the Huntington-owned International Railroad Company connected Durango, Mexico, with Eagle Pass, and the American-controlled National Railways linked Mexico City to Corpus Christi, Texas. By 1900, 14,573 kilometers of railroads directly linked Mexico City and the mineral-producing regions of northern Mexico with major trading cities in the American Southwest. These railroads brought agricultural goods, petroleum, and, increasingly, people northward. In addition, southwestern farmers, mine operators, railroad corporations, and large construction-firm owners aggressively recruited Mexican laborers to come north. During the 1920s, Mexicans became the largest ethnic group of farmworkers in California, and they made up nearly 60 percent of the workforce that was building and maintaining railroads in the West. Mexicans were also found in Minnesota's sugar-beet fields, Chicago's factories, and Pittsburgh's steel mills. Before 1924, the US government aided this mass movement with a deliberate policy of "benign neglect" at the US-Mexico border. Border Patrol agents literally looked the other way when Mexican workers were needed to harvest crops, build railroads, or work in the mines or factories.[15]

Both world wars ushered in a new era of recruited Mexican immigration. From 1917 to 1921, at least 72,000 guest workers were recruited to work in the United States. From 1942 to 1964, 400,000 Mexican men migrated to the US as part of the Bracero Program. After the war, the program continued, and what began as a binational agreement shifted into a program of imperial labor exploitation as the United States government and employers gradually gained control over the terms of the contracts. In addition, the direct recruitment and hiring of undocumented workers (and their families) grew alongside the program as employers increasingly sought to avoid the contract and transportation fees.[16]

Although this labor recruitment continued in Mexico, many in the United States promoted the immigration myth to close the border whenever it was deemed necessary to maintain control over an expanding pool of exploitable and deportable labor. In June 1954 the US Border Patrol announced that it would launch "Operation Wetback," an aggressive paramilitary law enforcement campaign against undocumented Mexican immigrants (i.e., "wetbacks," the derogatory term used to describe migrants who entered the country without authorization by wading or swimming across the Rio Grande). A total of 1,075,168 Mexican nationals were reportedly apprehended.[17]

The immigration myth also shaped congressional debates leading up to the passage of the 1965 Immigration and Nationality Act. Best known as a civil rights law that ended the discriminatory national origins system, the law also replicated immigration inequality, especially when it came to Mexican immigration. Lawmakers repeatedly pointed to the specter of a Latin American "population explosion" that would send millions to the United States unless some restrictions were put in place.[18]

These concerns were translated into policy. The 1965 Immigration Act opened the nation to new mass migration, but it also established the first global ceiling on immigration to the United States and the first-ever numerical cap on immigration from the Western Hemisphere. These restrictions, combined with the termination of the Bracero Program in 1964 and other measures specifically designed to scrutinize Mexican immigrants, set new limitations on Mexican immigration. What had been a massive amount of "legal immigration" (200,000 braceros and 35,000 regular admissions for permanent residency) was reduced to the annual 20,000 quota. However, the need and desire for immigrant laborers, especially from Mexico, kept demand for such immigrants high. What followed was an increase in undocumented immigration and a growing number of undocumented individuals remaining in the United States rather than risking multiple trips across an increasingly militarized border.[19]

Undocumented immigrants were not the only ones to come. From 1980 to 1989 a record 6,244,379 immigrants were admitted into the United States for legal permanent residence, followed by 9,775,398 from 1990 to 1999. In stark contrast to immigration patterns earlier in the century, 80 percent of all new immigrants came from either Asia or Latin America. In addition, 1.2 million Vietnamese, Cambodian, Lao, and Hmong refugees were resettled in the United States following the end of the wars in Southeast Asia.[20]

As in decades past, immigration became a flashpoint for culture wars and social, economic, and political anxieties that troubled Americans. In the last two decades of the twentieth century, these included a rapidly changing and deindustrializing economy that was displacing millions of blue-collar workers; new (and more radical) campaigns for social justice that challenged systemic racism, sexism, and homophobia; and the formal end of the Cold War, which raised new questions about the role of American leadership in the world. The immigration myth continued to be used to justify new restrictions on new immigration coming into the US and on immigrant communities already in the country.[21]

By the 1990s, some of the country's most prominent conservative intellectuals, writers, media commentators, and politicians helped to refine and mainstream a xenophobic message that relied upon the immigration myth to mobilize voters, gain political power, and attack the Left. Among the most prominent were writer (and British immigrant) Peter Brimelow, former presidential candidate Patrick Buchanan, and Harvard political scientist Samuel Huntington. All argued that immigration was just one of the many forces eroding the nation: a cult of multiculturalism and diversity that had gone too far; the rise of group identities based on race, ethnicity, and gender that threatened a unified national identity; and globalization that siphoned away jobs. They agreed that immigration was the largest and most dangerous threat.[22]

The so-called war on illegal immigration that they helped to launch became a bipartisan effort. President Bill Clinton implemented new border-enforcement initiatives that accepted, rather than dispelled, the idea that immigration was a dangerous invasion. For example, Operation Gatekeeper deployed increased numbers of Border Patrol agents and expanded the use of surveillance technologies to deter unauthorized immigration across the US-Mexico border near San Diego. From 1993 to 1997, Congress increased southern border enforcement funding from $400 million to $800 million. After the terrorist attacks on 9/11, President George W. Bush turned immigration into a national security issue by moving all immigration enforcement into the newly created Department of Homeland Security. He also increased investment in the Border Patrol and the deployment of six thousand National Guard troops to guard the border.[23]

By the time that President Barack Obama took the oath of office, the "They Keep Coming" myth had become institutionalized into federal immigration policy in the form of a legally robust, highly resourced immigration-enforcement regime. Obama tried to push comprehensive immigration reform through Congress and announced a series of executive actions that granted temporary reprieve from deportation to millions of "Dreamers," young undocumented immigrants who were brought to the United States as young children and who have lived and gone to school in the US. At the same time, his administration increased immigration-enforcement funding from $7.5 billion in 2002 to $18 billion in 2012. The federal government completed 651 miles of a 700-mile border fence, and immigrant detention expanded to 360,000 people by 2016. During the eight-year Obama administration, deportations also increased dramatically: 5,370,849 individuals were apprehended, 5,281,115 individuals were deported, and another 3,307,017 were apprehended at the US-Mexico border.[24]

In 2015 Donald J. Trump announced his candidacy for the presidency of the United States with a message that perfectly articulated the "They Keep Coming" immigration myth: "When Mexico sends its people, they're not sending their best. . . . They're sending people that have lots of problems, and they're bringing those problems with us. They're bringing drugs. They're bringing crime. They're rapists. And some, I assume are good people." Many Americans expressed outrage at these views, but in fact Trump was just repeating a message that had long been normalized on both sides of the political aisle.[25]

What was so curious about Trump's view of Mexican immigration was how outdated it was. Trump blamed Mexico for "sending its people," but in fact, Mexican migration was overwhelmingly shaped by US economic, political, and military policies. For example, the North American Free Trade Agreement allowed American agricultural companies to flood Mexican markets with corn and other grains. Unable to compete with US corporations, two million Mexican farmers and farmworkers were forced out of agriculture. They migrated first to large Mexican cities and then to the United States in search of economic survival.

Mexican immigration had indeed increased during the late twentieth century. But it was no invasion. In 2000, foreign-born Mexicans accounted for only 3 percent of the total US population. In fact, by the time Trump was running for president, net migration from Mexico was *below zero*, meaning that more immigrants were returning to Mexico than were heading to the United States. Despite its many inaccuracies, Trump's message resonated with voters, propelled him to the White House, and shaped his domestic policy agenda.[26]

In his first week in office, Trump signed executive orders to ban Muslims, deport millions, and build a wall along the US-Mexico border. Under his direction, the US government also separated more than three thousand children from their families and required asylum seekers trying to enter from Mexico to remain in that country for months while they awaited their US court hearings. During the global coronavirus pandemic, the president referred to COVID-19 as the "Chinese virus" and claimed that immigrants were dangerous carriers of infection. His language helped to fuel anti-Asian racism and historic levels of violence targeting Asian Americans across the country. President Trump eventually put in place more than one thousand immigration-related actions that made immigration harder and reduced the number of immigrants coming to the United States. Although President Joseph R. Biden Jr. reversed some of these policies, many remained in place during the first year of his administration. Immigration reform efforts stalled, and many Trump allies continued to keep the "They Keep Coming" immigration myth alive.[27]

From the colonial era to the Trump era, the "They Keep Coming" immigration myth has been used by xenophobes to demonize immigrants and lobby for immigration restriction. It has created a climate of fear and fueled discrimination and exploitation. At the same time, it has promoted a false and incomplete narrative of how immigration works. No part of the myth is actually true. Immigrants are not outsiders. "They" are "us." Immigrants have not "kept coming." They have been driven, recruited, lured, and incentivized to come to the United States, often with the direct help and encouragement of the US government and businesses. Only by fully understanding the origins, endurance, and contemporary relevance of the "They Keep Coming" myth can we begin to dismantle it and the xenophobia and racism that it fuels.

5

AMERICA FIRST

Sarah Churchwell

W HEN DONALD TRUMP REVIVED THE PHRASE "AMERICA FIRST"
as a campaign slogan in 2016, it was widely defended as a reasonable foreign policy doctrine espousing pragmatic nationalism and
economic protectionism. Insisting that the motto had shrugged off
its earlier history of interwar isolationism and associations with anti-
Semitic fascist sympathizing, Trump's supporters claimed that a re-
tooled twenty-first-century America First would prove a unifying
force to heal the nation's divisions. "'America First' is not a threat but
a promise," Michael Barone pronounced after Trump's inauguration in
the conservative *Washington Examiner.* "The phrase 'America first' in an
inaugural address in, say, 1949 or 1953 would have been disturbing for
many for understandable reasons. But it doesn't have any resonance for
today's voters. . . . A healthy nationalism based on 'America first' points
toward a less polarized, more inclusive country."[1] Another conservative,

Michael Anton (famed for a 2016 essay comparing Trump voters to the passengers on Flight 93 who saved America from terrorists), later agreed, declaring that "'America First' . . . is almost tautologically unobjectionable. After all, what else is the purpose of any country's foreign policy except to put its own interests, the interests of its citizens, first?"[2] America First was, they insisted, a forthright statement of pragmatic realpolitik, a direct expression of growing isolationism and protectionist sentiment among the American populace.

These defenses were prompted partly by the fact that Trump's critics had not actually forgotten the slogan's "disturbing" resonances, detecting in America First an enduring ethno-nationalist dog whistle. "Nativism is afoot in our politics once again," as one observer put it, explaining that nativism's "core message is simple: America first . . . America belongs to those who consider themselves here first."[3] The idea that some citizens have political or moral priority over others by virtue of historical priority is intrinsic to nativism, weighing the entitlements of those who were supposedly "here first" above those of more recent immigrants—while also ignoring the claims of other groups who demonstrably arrived before these supposedly "real Americans," including Indigenous people.

America First has never been—and was never intended to be—a simple statement of patriotic self-interest, and it has certainly never worked as a unifying national motto. On the contrary, it has consistently served as a divisive code camouflaged by its ostensible harmlessness, a frequently conspiratorial cover story for internal power struggles. The history of America First, unlike the myths about it, reveals a story less about isolationism abroad than bigotry at home. There are reasons why four years after Michael Barone promised that America First would make the nation less polarized, insurrectionists carrying "America First" flags stormed the nation's Capitol, threatening to kill lawmakers, reasons that the long history of the phrase makes clear.

Political myths are never far from conspiratorial thinking: the idea that Barack Obama was not born in the United States is both a conspiracy theory and a myth, one promulgated in the name of putting "America First," defining "real Americans" as a threatened minority forced to protect their interests against the menace of infiltration. Throughout its history America First has been deeply entangled with exactly this type of mythic conspiratorial thinking, from the anti-Catholic conspiracies of the 1850s and anti-British free trade conspiracies of the 1880s and 1890s, through anti-Semitic conspiracies that bridge the 1920s and 2020s, and up to the Islamophobic and QAnon conspiracies of today. America First works as a shield precisely because it imputes innocence to its adherents, maintaining a mythic image of the nation and their privileged place within it that is at odds with historical reality.

America First is a much older slogan than any of the debates over twenty-first-century uses of it have recognized. Most responses to Trump's resuscitation of the phrase located its origins in either the America First Committee (AFC) of 1940–1941 or the second Klan of the 1920s, while a bare handful noted that the phrase was popularized by Woodrow Wilson in 1915.[4] But the expression goes back much further, to the first nativist movement in the United States, when the American Party (nicknamed the "Know Nothings") emerged during the 1850s to defend what they considered the real American culture of Protestantism from the threat of immigrant Catholicism. It is from these original debates over nativism and immigration restriction that the motto appears to have emerged, and it has continued as it began, articulating hostility against those its users deem insufficiently American.

At an "American convention" in 1855, as nativists adopted a platform to restrict or repeal naturalization laws and prohibit anyone but native-born citizens from holding political or legal office, a New York politician gave a speech proclaiming himself for "America first, last and always"—thus establishing what is (to date) the earliest recorded use of America First as a political slogan:[5]

You have the true spirit of Americans in your hearts; I know it is unpleasant both for speakers and hearers to be standing here in this drenching rain, but, for one, American as I am, I decidedly prefer this rain to the reign of Roman Catholicism in this country. (Cheers) I, as an American citizen, prefer this rain or any other rain to the reign of foreignism. (Renewed cheers) I go for America first, last and always.[6]

America First's fundamental opposition to all forms of "foreignism" has never substantially altered—but what counts as "foreignism" has. As ideas of American identity continue to evolve, so America First must continually produce new enemies against which to define its own supposed pure vision of America.

In the second half of the nineteenth century, many Americans saw in Catholicism a plot to undermine American democracy, and used "America first, last and always" to rhetorically defend against the "foreignism" of popery. The depression of 1893 was widely supposed to have been plotted by an international Catholic cabal, while the myth of a Catholic crusade of heretic extermination and infanticide persisted well into the twentieth century. An enduring suspicion also held that the British Empire was trying to reclaim its lost colonies, and the two myths were by no means mutually exclusive. Thus, for example, after denouncing "the nefarious designs" of Catholics in the United States, an 1876 editorial titled "Romanism in America" urged every American "in this Centennial year, to renew the declaration of independence, to declare himself and the nation free, as it ought to be, from the thraldom of every foreign power—whether England or Rome—and to begin again where our forefathers began, with America first, last and always."[7] In practice, as this example shows, declarations of America First patriotism were consistently prompted by conspiratorial fears of foreign plots. This hostility against "every foreign power" abroad found expression at home as hostility against foreigners, making Catholics the target of mob violence in America through the second half of the nineteenth century.

"America First, and the World Afterwards" had become a Republican motto and a presidential campaign slogan by 1888, as candidates promised to protect America's "industrial patriotism" against domination by foreign interests.[8] When William Jennings Bryan's populist 1896 campaign attacked the gold standard as the mainstay of international finance, his supporters cheered that Bryan stood for "America first, the world afterwards," whereas William McKinley was maintaining "England's grip on this country [by] secret means."[9] International cabals would remain the target of America First agitation: the only thing that changed was which foreign group was accused of pulling the strings.

In the early decades of the twentieth century an enormously popular domestic tourism campaign called "See America First" helped transform the phrase from a Republican slogan rejecting free trade (itself suspected of being a British plot) to a more generally jingoistic expression.[10] When President Woodrow Wilson adopted the phrase in 1915 to intervene in debates about the loyalty of "hyphenate Americans"—immigrant Americans who had recently naturalized—it thus fell on the fertile ground created by a decade of advertising. "Hyphenates" were accused of a dual loyalty that made them less than "pure American." As hysteria against "hyphenates" mounted, Wilson joined in, declaring that it was necessary to demand of immigrant Americans: "Is it America First, or is it not?" In an editorial titled "Hazing the Hyphenates," the *New York Times* endorsed the president's "suggestion of humor" when he told the nation's citizens to harass those "who have failed in their loyalty," ending on a note of explicit menace: "There is no alternative if they are to continue to live among us, to do business in the United States, to retain their citizenship. Life is hardly worth living under continual 'hazing.'"[11] One senator criticized anyone who supported "aliens when they should be for America first, last and all the time."[12] Another announced that the "next big national issue will be America for pure Americans," an issue "defined by President Wilson in two words, 'America First.'"[13] The problem, then as now, is how to measure the "purity" of Americans.

After Wilson's speech, the slogan began to reverberate through American politics. "As if the cry 'America first' had rung through the halls of both houses," it gained bipartisan appeal ("'America First' Unites Factions") in response to a putatively "authentic" "German plot."[14] The phrase became not only Wilson's reelection slogan and the 1916 Democratic National Convention's keynote but also the slogan of his Republican opponent, Charles Evan Hughes ("America First and America Efficient"), who gave speeches promising "undiluted Americanism"[15] with "America First, Last and Always and No 'Hyphens.'"[16] When Theodore Roosevelt was asked to consider a third-party candidacy in 1916, his remarks were printed under front-page headlines announcing "Bars the Hyphen; America First": "Don't be for me unless you are prepared to say that every citizen of this country has to be pro–United States, first, last and all the time. . . . Every American citizen must be for America first and for no other country even second and he hasn't any right to be in the United States at all if he has any divided loyalty."[17]

American neutrality during World War I was in part a reaction to the mutual suspicion with which both the British and German empires were held by much of the American populace. "The President was right in his statement that it is America First," declared the *Washington Post* in 1915, endorsing neutrality. "The United States is not to be swerved from this absolutely correct position by either survile [*sic*] adulaters of British forms and customs or by enthusiastic admirers of German militarism and its practices. . . . It is America first with the true patriots of the United States."[18] At the same time, the internationalist Wilson was frequently accused of being "avowedly pro-British," prompting editorials urging Republicans to oppose him by going "America First" one better and promising "Pure Americanism against the universe."[19] Joining the spirit of escalation, a former Indiana senator caught the country's attention by declaring the nation's motto should be not "America First" but "America Only," as politicians jostled to establish who was the most American against the universe.[20]

While agitating to keep the United States out of the conflict, William Randolph Hearst declared "America First" the motto of his flagship *San Francisco Examiner*, invoking Washington's axiomatic (and semimythical) warning against "entangling alliances" to support it: "In two words, George Washington's farewell address consisted of the San Francisco 'Examiner's' motto, 'AMERICA FIRST.'"[21] The supposed threat of "entangling alliances" abroad rapidly became a shibboleth, another iteration of conspiratorial fears about international cabals. It bespoke the growing isolationism of Americans who were weary of foreign wars and resentful of cheap immigrant labor driving down domestic wages. They also feared that international elites were working to weaken American democracy—and thus their own grip on the levers of power.

When the United States finally entered World War I, America First effortlessly evolved into a patriotic wartime slogan. It continued to express a vicious anti-German animus, as well as violence against both foreign nationals and labor activists. Reports of Wobblies having been tarred and feathered ran alongside an illustration of the Statue of Liberty declaring

"AMERICA FIRST,"[22] as newspaper editorials defended citizens who were "expressing their feelings" against suspected spies and seditionists "in tar-and-feather parties and lynching bees" under banners proclaiming "The United States of America, First, Last and All the Time."[23] Newly naturalized Americans tried to protect themselves by waving "America First" banners and taking out ads in local papers to declare their loyalty. ("Peter Dorzuk, an Austrian shoemaker, is for America first, last and all the time. He was sent back from Camp Lee because of physical disability.")[24]

The Paris Peace Conference did nothing to allay suspicions of international conspiracies to undermine the United States. The proposal for the League of Nations included the power to arbitrate international free trade (still a trigger for America Firsters), while the Treaty of Versailles's Article X committed the United States to ongoing European intervention; the eventual proposal for a world court promised to add internationalist insult to isolationist injury. These "entangling alliances" earned not only Hearst's formidable opposition but also that of Republican leaders, including Henry Cabot Lodge. Together, Lodge and Hearst made "America First" the slogan for their implacable, and victorious, battle against Wilson's postwar settlement. As the fight against the League of Nations was culminating in early 1920, Hearst ran full-page editorials calling it a "conspiracy to surrender our country to the thieving diplomacy of Europe," urging readers "to stand up against this conspiracy of the International Plunderbund," a pro-German cabal representing "the International Banking Trust." To fight it, Americans were urged to pressure their representatives to "take up our good old watchword—'America First!'"[25]

As one international conspiracy subsided, another rose to take its place. Anti-Catholic and anti-British conspiracies were quickly superseded in the early decades of the twentieth century by fears of new waves of immigrants from Eastern Europe and the Far East. Suddenly, the cabals seeking to undermine American society looked like the Jews, Russians, and Asians who were arriving in American cities. The Red Scare charged "the international Jew," accused of financing and engineering the Bolshevik Revolution, with a secret plan to replicate it in the United States. Once again, America First was raised as a rallying cry as groups like the "American Defence Society" sprang up to combat the supposed Jewish-Communist plot and "stifle red flagism and uphold Americanism . . . for America first."[26] The Red Scare helped fertilize the anti-Semitic conspiracies that flowered in the United States in the early 1920s, in large part thanks to Henry Ford's circulation of the fraudulent *Protocols of the Elders of Zion* in his *The International Jew*. Reports of the Palmer Raids deporting supposed Bolshevik organizers ("300 More Reds Nabbed") arrived in American homes beneath Hearst's "America First!" masthead, as did hysterical warnings of an impending "Yellow Peril," the conspiracy theory that the Japanese and Chinese would unite the "yellow races" to invade and overpower "white civilizations" like the United States.[27]

When Warren G. Harding campaigned for the presidency in 1920 on an "America First" platform of isolationist protectionism, he used the slogan to answer every question, including the "Japanese Question": "Americans on the [West] coast are troubled in their minds about the Oriental question. . . . That question raises every interpretation of our watchword, 'America first.' . . . There is abundant evidence of the dangers which lurk in racial differences."[28] Meanwhile, Harding's supporters declared that his opponent supported the elite international bankers behind the League of Nations. Democrats, they charged, did "not favor American interests. Their motto is not 'America first'" because "international banking is not conducive to simon-pure American viewpoint [sic]."[29] The Republican Party promised to uphold "America First" against "international bankers" who were "money lenders first, and . . . not Americans at all,"[30] at a time when Henry Ford was making national headlines in declaring the existence of a plot by "the Jew money lender" to take over American business.[31]

At the same time, another nativist group was taking possession of the slogan as well. The Ku Klux Klan had declared itself reborn in 1915, and by 1919, a Klan leader in Texas was declaring "I am for America, first, last and all the time," he said, and "we don't want any of the foreign element telling us what to do."[32] The second Klan issued a pamphlet declaring its "ABCs," which began "America First, Benevolence, Clannishness," while the *Kloran* enshrined it: "[The Klan] stands for America first—first in thought, first in affections, and first in the galaxy of nations."[33] "We stand for 100 per cent. 'American' and for 'White Supremacy,'" declared a Kleagle in 1921. "We are not anti-Catholic, anti-Jewish, nor anti-Alien. We are non-Catholic, non-Jewish, and non-Alien. We are for America first, last and all the time,"[34] he insisted, even as the Klan was lynching Catholics, Jews, and foreign nationals, and tarring and feathering other Americans who aroused its ire.

In Illinois a Klan minister told his congregation that "the fiery cross which is the emblem of the Ku Klux Klan, is the symbol of the Christian religion and that this organization is for America first."[35] An Indiana newspaper, where the Klan had its highest membership during the 1920s, maintained the Klan was protecting America from being "overrun by a set of people from foreign countries" or having "their children intermarry with those of other races than the Anglo-Saxon race."[36] By the mid-1920s, as the Klan was spreading across the country, America First traveled with it. In 1923, a Klansman in Binghamton, New York, used the same formula: "I stand for America first, last and always. . . . I am opposed to any organization which tries to bring in foreign and alien ideals. This country was founded on Christianity."[37]

This nativism was inextricable from the eugenicist scientific racism that upheld Jim Crow racism and said that putting America First meant protecting the (mythical) Anglo-Saxon purity of the United States, ending "our policy of putting the alien and his interests first, and America last."[38] Americans were warned against "the enemy within our gates": "We must prevent the entry into this country of races which cannot be assimilated, whose children cannot intermarry with our own. . . . We want America first."[39]

The series of restrictionist immigration measures that culminated in the 1924 Johnson-Reed Act were widely understood in terms of "America First." Hearst trumpeted the legislation's earliest versions under his "America First!" masthead,[40] and everyone knew what the phrase meant in practice: a Republican congressman supporting Japanese exclusion cited "the doctrine of America first for Americans."[41] When a Polish-language newspaper in Milwaukee denounced this "most discriminatory piece of legislation," an Iowa editorial retorted that "real Americans" "should learn to think of America first."[42] It was clear to its critics at the time that the Johnson-Reed Act was politically proving "the theory of the Ku Klux Klan," which sought to change "the spirit of America" "from 'Humanity First' to 'America First' and 'America for Americans.'"[43]

By the late 1920s, the association of America First with mythic foreign conspiracies abroad and demonstrable white nationalism at home had become indelible. William "Big Bill" Thompson ran for Chicago mayor in 1927 on an America First platform, absurdly charging the English monarchy with planting pro-British propaganda in the Chicago schools. Exploiting any xenophobic conspiracies he could find, including charges that "'international bankers' are getting the upper hand,"[44] Thompson promised to "keep it on the issues, America first, no entangling alliances, no King George in the public schools."[45] His opponent accused Thompson of dog whistling—"'America first' was lifted from the Klan,"[46] he said, and "they understand him very well"[47]—but Thompson's conspiracy-mongering worked, and soon he had started a successful string of "America First" clubs.

As the second Klan declined and European fascism rose in the early 1930s, America developed a host of its own proto-fascist paramilitary groups. One of the most notorious was a rabidly anti-Semitic outfit established in 1934 called "America First, Inc." Aggravated by the seniority of prominent Jews in FDR's administration, paranoid fears of a Jewish-Communist plot long associated with "America First" finally found a powerful American target. Right-wing circles began calling Roosevelt "Rosenfeld" and his policy the "Jew Deal," while "America First, Inc." regularly circulated reports that the Roosevelt administration was "completely controlled by the international Jewish movement for world domination," urging America to "definitely settle the (Jewish) problem by the simple elimination process."[48]

By 1936, a "rising tide of nationalism" was again discernible, thinking only of "America first, last, and always," as local politicians continued to campaign on "America First, Against Foreign Entanglement" platforms.[49] Another anti-Semitic group soon declared itself incorporated and for America First: "American Nationalists, inc." were "for America first, last and always." The group promised to "shoot it out with the communists on the streets when they try to take America over. . . . The

American nationalists want to see the American people freed from the clutches of the gang of international bankers, shysters and pawnbrokers. We do not want the United States of America to become known as the western dominion of the international house of Rothschild."[50] By 1940, the Far Right in the United States was not unlike the constellation of groups orbiting there eighty years later, a miscellany of extremists clashing internally over fine doctrinal points, espousing various versions of nativist, racist, xenophobic, eugenicist, and Christian nationalist mythologies, but united in their resentment of a perceived racialized threat to economic opportunities and of a cultural pluralism that did not put their idea of America first.

By the time the America First Committee (AFC) formed in 1940, the phrase had been in use for almost a century, and in political life had never uncoupled from nativist conspiratorial nationalism. Americans had grown up with the slogan's connotations, knowing that it signaled not only political isolationism but also a herrenvolk, anti-Semitic white nationalism that strongly resembled the European fascists against whom the AFC did not, for some reason, want to take arms. They knew that it frequently incited violence and always spelled intolerance. One early spokesman of the AFC was Henry Cabot Lodge Jr., giving "Defend America First" speeches to make his father proud;[51] another was isolationist Senator Burton K. Wheeler, condemned as "Hitler's Megaphone" when he argued that the Lend-Lease Bill would aid "international bankers with their friends, the royal refugees, and with the Sassoons of the Orient and with the Rothschilds and the Warburgs of Europe."[52]

When war broke out in September 1939, Charles Lindbergh began delivering national radio broadcasts rehearsing familiar eugenicist arguments for isolationism, invoking persistent hysteria about the old idea of the "Yellow Peril" as he argued the United States need not intervene because there was "no Genghis Khan or Xerxes marching against our Western nations. This is not a question of banding together to defend the white race against foreign invasion."[53] Only if the United States were defending the white race would it be putting "America First." Lindbergh joined the America First Committee in April 1941 as its official spokesman, his speeches routinely raising old nativist ghosts. They were praised by the Nazi press, which applauded Lindbergh under the headline "America First" as "a real American of Swedish descent" who understood that "the danger of invasion of [the United States] is not from Germany 'but from the increasing British influence on the American continent.'"[54]

In September 1941, Lindbergh denounced the foreign elements he said were coercing America into joining an alien conflict: "The three most important groups who have been pressing this country toward war are the British, the Jewish and the Roosevelt Administration."[55] Suddenly, the dog whistle was audible, the outcry swift and peremptory. Even Hearst's papers condemned the "un-American" anti-Semitism of Lindbergh's address. Three months later, the Japanese bombed Pearl Harbor, deciding the question of intervention as "America First" subsided into rapid disrepute. The meaning of "America First" underwent an almost instant reversal from jingoism to sedition as it suddenly denoted "un-American" fascist sympathies against the all-out Allied war effort.

In 1944 Roosevelt's Justice Department prosecuted for sedition some of the more extreme right-wing groups that had been associated with America First, further discrediting the phrase, but its implications hadn't changed. The Rev. Gerald L. K. Smith, once Huey Long's deputy and "America's most notorious anti-Semite," built a political career out of loudly attacking the "international bankers," who were "our constant rulers." Smith founded the "America First Party" in 1943, promising to address the nation's "Jewish problem" in his 1944 presidential run.[56] Two years later Smith was still promoting his "America First Crusade" and distributing copies of Henry Ford's *International Jew*.[57] Then Smith tried rebranding: "The America First Party is trying to turn over a new leaf by changing its name to the Christian Nationalist Party."[58]

Before long, America First was being recuperated. During the Cold War's second Red Scare, conservatives were urged to stand "for 'America first' against the flaccid forces of political liberalism that would sacrifice our national sovereignty and free-world leadership for a system of international federalism potentially favorable to only the Communist conspiracy."[59] John F. Kennedy faced a primary opponent in 1960 who campaigned in an Uncle Sam suit on an "America First" platform.[60] Barry Goldwater was regularly characterized as a candidate who would

take the country "back to a policy of 'America First.'"[61] Voters wrote to
their local papers, declaring that "I'm for Goldwater! . . . let's again teach
an 'America First' doctrine,"[62] and "Senator Goldwater has long been an
'America first' statesman. . . . He will have our country and its interest
first. The United Nations will not dictate to us."[63] Goldwater "would find
no quarrel with Harding's 'America First' program" from 1920, noted a
journalist with a longer memory than most, quoting Harding's six campaign promises: "To stabilize America first; to safeguard America first;
to prosper America first; to think of America first; to exalt America first;
to live for and revere America first." The Republican conventions of 1920
and 1964, he observed, bore strong similarities: "The names and the dates
may change, but the plot remains the same."[64]

White supremacism remained intrinsic to that plot. George Wallace
was described by his supporters in 1968 as offering "strong leadership for
the United States of America, first, last, and all the time!," demonstrating
the endurance of the phrase's implications in right-wing circles.[65] David
Duke, America's most notorious Klansman in the second half of the twentieth century, has been associated with America First since at least 1976 ("a
new-image Ku Klux Klan is . . . still bent on riding its white-supremacy,
anti-Semitic, America-first stance to glory").[66] Fifteen years later, Pat Buchanan ran for president espousing "America First" "neo-isolationism" to
appeal to "insular, inward-looking" voters.[67] Buchanan surprised the conservative establishment in 1991 by announcing his presidential candidacy
on an "America First" platform, to defend against the economic dangers
"presented by the rise of a European super state." Buchanan's paleocon-
servative arguments were straight from the 1920s: he claimed that his political opponents "would put America's wealth and power at the service of
some vague New World Order," whereas "we will put America first."[68] His
isolationism was out of touch with an age of accelerating globalization, but
America First still stoked conspiratorial myths of international elites to
rouse populist sentiment at home.

After Buchanan announced a "Reform Party" for the 2000 election
with an America First platform, Donald Trump, a bankrupt playboy
billionaire, unexpectedly entered the lists. Because "the Republicans are
just too crazy right," Trump said he'd decided to challenge Buchanan, "a

Hitler lover" and "anti-Semite" who was going after the "really staunch right wacko vote," for the nomination of his own party.[69] The following year Trump withdrew from the Reform Party, announcing that "the Reform Party now includes a Klansman, Mr. Duke, a neo-Nazi, Mr. Buchanan, and a communist, Ms. [Lenora] Fulani. This is not company I wish to keep." A few days later Trump repeated the rejection: "Well, you've got David Duke just joined—a bigot, a racist, a problem. I mean, this is not exactly the people you want in your party."[70]

But then, in 2016, Trump announced his own presidential candidacy on a platform of America First, and he stopped repudiating the really staunch Right wacko vote. David Duke quickly endorsed Trump, saying he was "overjoyed to see Donald Trump and most Americans embrace most of the issues that I've championed for years. My slogan remains America first." That summer, Duke announced his own Senate run on "America First."[71] Challenged to disavow the support of America's most notorious Klansman, Trump prevaricated before claiming under pressure: "I don't know anything about David Duke. OK? I don't know anything about what you're even talking about with white supremacy or white supremacists."[72]

On November 9, 2016, Trump became the fourth president in a century to run successfully on a slogan of America First and the first to openly court fascism. On the day Trump was inaugurated, promising "it's going to be only America first, America first," Duke gave an inaugural talk on the neo-Nazi platform Stormfront.com titled "White Revolution and America First," declaring the first day of Trump's presidency "the official first day of the White Revolution!"[73] Trump had launched his presidential campaign by promising to build a wall to keep out Mexicans—whom he described as mostly rapists—and repeatedly attacked Muslim Americans. His first legislative act was a ban on travelers from seven Muslim-majority countries.

After Trump's (protracted) loss in 2020, Republican members of Congress Matt Gaetz of Florida and Marjorie Taylor Greene of Georgia attempted to maintain the momentum of his ethno-nationalist America First movement. "'America First' isn't going away. We're going on tour!," Gaetz declared in May 2021, as he and Greene announced the formation of the "America First Caucus"—to which they gave the familiar initialism AFC.[74] Their partner in this venture was Congressman Paul Gosar, who had joined forces in the summer of 2020 with Nicholas Fuentes, a Christian nationalist and Holocaust denier who has hosted an "America First" program on various online platforms since 2017, where he sells "AF" merchandise and promotes white supremacism.[75]

The platforms endorsed by the Trumpist AFC included a restrictionist, assimilationist, and nativist approach to immigration:

> America is a nation with a border, and a culture, strengthened by a common respect for uniquely Anglo-Saxon political traditions. History has shown that societal trust and political unity are threatened when foreign citizens are imported *en-masse* into a country, particularly without institutional support for assimilation . . . we cannot ignore the impact that mass immigration has on reducing job opportunities and depreciating wages for Americans.[76]

The implications of the "uniquely Anglo-Saxon political traditions" endorsed by the America First Caucus were not lost on observers who were quick to denounce its racism ("Immigrants out. Anglo-Saxons in") without always noting that its version of white nationalist history was not only dangerously racist but dangerously mythical as well.[77] Greene had already gained notoriety for her advocacy of any number of wild conspiracy theories, especially her support of QAnon, which claimed that Democrat leaders, Jewish financiers, wealthy philanthropists, and well-known liberal celebrities were members of a satanic cult of sex trafficking, blood-drinking pedophiles who control world governments. Only Donald Trump could overthrow them with his secret plan, sometimes called "The Great Awakening," sometimes "The Storm," as evangelical millenarianism fused with Nazi rhetoric.

Availing itself of an array of stock conspiratorial tropes, QAnon's cabal of satanic global elites was recognizably the heir of all the conspiracies that used "America First" to defend against anti-Catholic plots of heretic mutilation, or anti-Semitic vampiric blood libels, or red-baiting Jewish-Communist plots, or Jewish international bankers. Today, instead of the

Rothschilds controlling American finance, conspirators claim it is the Jewish financier and philanthropist George Soros, whom QAnon supporters like Greene accuse of having sent Jewish people to die in the Holocaust (when Soros was a teenager in Hungary).[78] Insurrectionists who stormed the US Capitol on January 6, 2021, included not only "Women for America First" but also standard-bearers waving the "AF" flags of Nicholas Fuentes, who is partly of Italian and Hispanic descent and identifies as Catholic. A century earlier, Fuentes might well have been the target of rage and violence perpetrated in the name of America First rather than its instigator. America First promulgates a myth of American homogeneity that the heritage and politics of people like Nicholas Fuentes disprove. The reality is that America has always been a fluid, heterogeneous collective that expands and evolves. Any effort to define America in static racial or ethnic terms was defeated before it began—that ship had sailed long before 1855. Today it is an exercise in futility—which is precisely what makes it so dangerous, as people like Fuentes and his supporters endorse violence to bring about a fantasy version of "pure Americanism" that has never existed and can never exist.

In a long essay that detailed the presence of America Firsters at the January 2021 insurrection, the *New Yorker* reported that Fuentes "distilled America Firstism into concise terms" for his followers when he gave a speech declaring, "It is the American people, and our leader, Donald Trump, against *everybody else* in this country and this world."[79] Pure Americanism hasn't defeated the universe yet, but because America First keeps trying, its list of enemies only grows. The names and dates may change, but the plot remains the same.

6

THE UNITED STATES IS AN EMPIRE

Daniel Immerwahr

Iɴ Nᴏᴠᴇᴍʙᴇʀ 1999, Gᴇᴏʀɢᴇ W. Bᴜsʜ ʟᴏᴏᴋᴇᴅ ᴏᴜᴛ ғʀᴏᴍ ᴛʜᴇ ᴘᴏ-dium of the Ronald Reagan Presidential Library. It was a crucial moment in his presidential campaign. He'd recently failed to name the leaders of four countries that had been in the news, and journalists wondered whether he knew enough about world affairs to be president. The Reagan Library speech, his first address on foreign policy, was his chance to prove that he did.

Bush debuted varied positions that day, from closer ties to Japan to a firmer hand with Russia. But there was a common thread linking them, he believed: they were "not imperial." "America has never been an empire," Bush explained. "We may be the only great power in history that had the chance, and refused."[1]

Bush was hardly the first president to search for the soul of US foreign policy and discover its long-standing antipathy to empire. The

United States, Richard Nixon wrote, is "the only great power without a history of imperialistic claims on neighboring countries." "Americans never fought for empires, for territory, for dominance," agreed Bill Clinton. In the past century, nearly every sitting president has insisted that the United States isn't an empire.[2]

This belief is part of its founding myth. The country was born of an anti-imperial rebellion, the story goes, and has since been a champion of republican values in a world of domineering empires. After fighting the British Empire twice, the United States took on the Spanish Empire, Germany's Thousand-Year Reich, the Japanese Empire, and the "evil empire" of the Soviet Union. It now holds the sort of global power that they once sought, but without any of their acquisitive intentions. Rather, the United States is "a beacon to oppressed people everywhere," as a recent secretary of defense put it. This belief, which wraps the United States' military interventions in an aura of benevolence, is crucial to the country's self-image. Of all the forms US exceptionalism takes, the notion of the country's inherently anti-imperial character is one of the first, most enduring, and most consequential.[3]

But is it correct? Is the United States fundamentally different from the violent, acquisitive empires of old? The question is charged, for the label *empire* is relished by the United States' critics and abhorred by its champions. It is also confusing because there is earnest disagreement about what the term means. Yet this doesn't mean that empire lies in the eye of the beholder. By the narrowest definition, one that nearly everyone accepts—an empire is a country with colonies—the United States has been an empire and remains one today. And it is arguably one by broader and more contested definitions, too.[4]

The founders called their country *the United States of America.* Compared to *France*, *Russia*, or *Japan*, it was an awkward mouthful—more of an ingredients list than a name. At the time, however, those ingredients meant something. *United* meant that this new polity wasn't an empire but a union, its members having joined voluntarily, as in a marriage. And *states* meant that those members weren't colonies but self-governing.

The trouble was, by the time the treaty securing independence from Britain was ratified, that name was no longer accurate. By then, the eastern states had begun to relinquish to the federal government their clashing territorial claims west of the Appalachians. The ceded land wasn't part of any state. It had a different classification, *territory*, and it wasn't self-governing. So from day one the United States was not a union of states but rather a conglomeration of states and territories. By 1791, territories constituted around 45 percent of its land.

A distinctive feature of the early republic was its willingness to upgrade territories to states. Following the pattern of the Northwest Ordinance of 1787, the federal government set guidelines for how those territories, once they filled with white settlers, would join the union on "an equal footing with the original States in all respects whatever." European countries didn't operate like that. It was a hint that the Americas would represent a new politics, republican rather than imperial.

Yet the Northwest Ordinance pattern came with caveats. Until territories became states, the federal government held absolute power over them. Moreover, statehood wasn't guaranteed: federal legislators decided if and when territories could be states, and history's annals are full of proposed states (Lincoln, Sequoyah, West Dakota, Deseret, Montezuma) that Congress swatted down. The Northwest Ordinance proposed population thresholds, but these weren't binding—Congress both promoted territories before they met thresholds and held them back after. On average, contiguous territories took forty-five years after annexation to become states. Oklahoma took more than a century, which is, for perspective, longer than the French held Indochina or the Belgians held the Congo.

Oklahoma lingered so long as a territory because of who lived there. The familiar image of territories as "empty" lands awaiting enough inhabitants to sustain a government is badly misleading. The reason Congress held territories back from statehood wasn't that no one lived in them but because the wrong people did. White squatters, free Blacks, French people, Spaniards, Mexicans, and, above all, Native peoples represented threats to federal control. And the more land the United States bought or conquered, the more such people it enclosed involuntarily within its borders. Oklahoma's long territorial stint is best explained by the fact that for decades it wasn't "Oklahoma" but "Indian Territory," an all-Native zone that Congress deemed ineligible for statehood.

Indians fell within the borders but often outside the political community of the United States. Many weren't citizens, and until 1871 Washington dealt with Indigenous nations via treaty, as foreign countries. Or, when not by treaty, by war. Overall, the federal government counted 1,642 military engagements with Indigenous adversaries; by the 1890s, these had cost it more than $800 million. Native peoples paid a far greater price in deaths from disease, dislocation, combat, and massacres. Over the nineteenth century, the Indigenous population of the present-day contiguous United States likely halved, dropping from around 600,000 to around 250,000.[5]

The final contiguous territories didn't become states until 1912. Yet even then the country wasn't a legally homogeneous zone, carpeted wall-to-wall with self-governing states. Washington, DC, remains a highly visible exception—a plurality-Black district whose nearly 700,000 residents may vote for president but lack congressional representation ("End Taxation without Representation," DC's license plates read) and have been repeatedly denied statehood. Less visible are the 574 federally recognized tribal nations within US borders today, quasi-states lacking full sovereignty. And within US states—existing as partial legal carve-outs—are more than 300 federal Indian reservations, covering a collective acreage the size of Idaho.

Western territories and Indian reservations can be hard to recognize as colonial spaces because they don't conform to the stereotypical image of empire: Asian and African societies ruled by mustachioed white men in pith helmets. That image was set by the British, French, Belgian, German, and Dutch empires in the late nineteenth century. The model involved a colonizing country seizing overseas land, establishing a government, and sending forth officials to rule over unwilling subjects who were culturally, linguistically, and religiously different. One reason that people see the United States as exceptionally nonimperial is that it didn't, say, colonize the Congo.

Yet that familiar model isn't the only form empire can take. What the United States did in North America—annexing adjacent land, violently driving Indigenous peoples off it, and flooding it with settlers—was different from installing a small unelected cadre to rule large colonized populations, but it was still a kind of empire. Scholars call it *settler colonialism* to distinguish it from the administrative colonialism typified by European powers in Asia and Africa.

Moreover, the United States *did* engage in administrative colonialism abroad, just like its European rivals. In the 1850s, right after the United States incorporated its last swath of contiguous land (the Gadsden Purchase, from Mexico), the country began expanding overseas. First, it took dozens of uninhabited islands in the Caribbean and the Pacific, valuable for the nitrate-rich guano they contained— by 1900, it had claimed nearly a hundred. In 1867 the United States purchased Alaska from Russia. In 1898 it entered a war that Spain was already fighting with its colonial subjects and won three Spanish colonies: Puerto Rico, Guam, and the Philippines. It also, in a fit of imperial enthusiasm, annexed two non-Spanish colonies at the same time, Hawaiʻi and American Samoa. In 1917 it purchased a Danish colony, now the US Virgin Islands. Major figures in US history, including William Howard Taft, Dwight Eisenhower, and Douglas MacArthur, had time in colonial government on their résumés.

But the road from annexation to rule wasn't always smooth. Colonial officials sometimes encountered violent resistance, particularly in the Philippines. There, US forces had entered the war against Spain on the side of Filipino nationalists. But once Spain surrendered, the United States turned on those nationalists. The ensuing war lasted officially from 1899 to 1902, although the fighting continued long after—including enormous massacres in the southern Philippines—and parts of the colony remained under martial law until 1913. The most careful study of the war's lethality concludes that, by 1903, it had killed 775,000 Filipinos, mostly from disease. By that count, it was bloodier than the US Civil War.[6]

It was, but it is rarely recognized as such. Although Indian removal and the promotion of territories into states are familiar aspects of US history, the overseas territories aren't. "Most people in this country, including educated people, know little or nothing about our overseas possessions," a governmental report from the 1940s noted. "As a matter of fact, a lot of people do not know that we have overseas possessions. They are convinced that only 'foreigners,' such as the British, have an 'empire.' Americans are sometimes amazed to hear that we, too, have an 'empire.'"[7]

But the United States did have an empire—a considerable one. In 1940 the overseas territories held nearly nineteen million people, mainly in the Philippines. Those people were all US nationals, yet most weren't citizens. And citizens or not, they were ruled by a distant government that they couldn't electorally unseat. The overseas territories in 1940 made up about one-eighth of the US population. At that time the United States contained more colonized people than Black people or immigrants (although the categories overlapped).

When the United States annexed its most popular territories at the nineteenth century's end, pressing questions about their legal status arose. Were they parts of the country, as the older territories had been? In a series of judgments known as the Insular Cases, the Supreme Court ruled that they weren't. The bulk of the new territories were possessed by the United States but not "incorporated" into it, so the Constitution didn't fully extend to them. The reasoning was transparently racist—the main majority decision warned about bringing "savages" and "alien races" into the constitutional fold. Only Hawai'i and Alaska, the territories most conducive to white settlement, counted as "incorporated."[8]

The distinction between incorporated and unincorporated territories was novel, but its underlying logic was old. The notion that some parts of the country were racially eligible for inclusion and others weren't—or weren't yet—had been there from the start. But the Insular Cases formalized it, depriving the most populous territories of constitutional protections and suggesting that they'd never become states. Quite clearly, they were colonies.

Unsurprisingly, colonial life differed from life in the contiguous United States. The mainland grew rich, but the colonies stagnated. They suffered serious violence, too. The worst police massacre (in Ponce, Puerto Rico, 1937), largest military massacre (at Bud Dajo, the Philippines, 1906), and bloodiest war (World War II in the Philippines, in which US armed forces leveled many towns and more than a million Filipinos died) on US soil all took place in the overseas empire.

That empire endures. The Philippines gained independence in 1946, and Hawai'i and Alaska became states in 1959. But Puerto Rico remains an unincorporated territory, as do Guam, the US Virgin Islands, and American Samoa. The Northern Mariana Islands voluntarily became one in 1986, following a long US occupation of Micronesia.

In all, the United States today has five inhabited territories that contain more than 3.6 million people. Those people cannot vote for president, have no voting representatives in Congress, lack full constitutional protection, and suffer the predictable effects. All five territories are poorer, per capita, than the poorest US state.

Whether to call the United States an empire can be a confusing question because the term has multiple meanings. Nearly all would agree that annexing overseas territories makes a country an empire. Most would categorize settler colonialism as empire, too. The harder questions arise regarding less formal types of power. When is a country a "leader" with "influence" over its neighbors versus an "empire" that has made quasi-colonies of them? In the US case, such questions arise particularly in reference to the twentieth and twenty-first centuries, an era of vast US power. When and whether to classify that power as imperial is a matter of earnest debate about which well-informed experts disagree.

A core concept in this debate is "informal empire." As applied to the British Empire by John Gallagher and Ronald Robinson, the idea was that the British Empire's extent couldn't be measured simply by the places colored red on the map: the formal colonies. The British had ways of securing overseas investments and foreign leaders' compliance without colonization—for example, in Latin America. Such arrangements were not only viable but preferable. British policy in the Victorian age "followed the principle of extending control informally if possible and formally if necessary," Gallagher and Robinson wrote in 1953.[9]

It didn't take long for US historians to grab on to the concept. In 1959 William Appleman Williams's extraordinarily influential book *The Tragedy of American Diplomacy* argued that, even more than Britain, the

United States specialized in informal empire. Setting Indian dispossession and overseas territories largely to the side, Williams maintained that the pursuit of foreign markets represented the country's most characteristic imperial mode. Economic rather than territorial expansion, he wrote, was the main avenue by which the United States "would enter and dominate all underdeveloped areas of the world."[10]

An important model was Cuba. During its 1898 war with Spain, Washington seized the Philippines, Puerto Rico, and Guam but didn't claim Cuba because anti-imperialist legislators had passed a law forbidding that. So rather than annexing the island, the McKinley administration occupied it. Controlling the government, it sought to "stabilize" Cuba to the point, as the occupation chief put it, where "money can be borrowed at a reasonable rate of interest." In other words, the occupation's aim wasn't democracy or Cuban welfare but a comfortable environment for US investors. Upon wrapping up the occupation, Washington insisted that Cubans constitutionally grant the United States the "right to intervene" if it deemed it necessary. That astonishing clause stayed in Cuba's constitution for more than thirty years.[11]

This arrangement, which gave Washington the benefits of colonization with few of the costs, became a pattern. In country after country around the Caribbean, the United States seized control of finance, trade, and foreign policy while leaving sovereignty formally intact. "Dollar diplomacy" was the polite name for this—a reference to Washington's habit of imposing the gold standard to ease the way for US corporations. But "gunboat diplomacy" was an equally accurate name. To secure political and financial "stability" in the region, US troops entered Cuba (four times), Nicaragua (three times), Honduras (seven times), Panama (six times), Costa Rica (once), and Mexico (three times) between 1903 and 1934.

The disconnect between the United States' professed ideals and its actions toward its southern neighbors could be jarring. "The United States will never again seek one additional foot of territory by conquest," promised President Woodrow Wilson in 1913. Yet two years later he ordered a US Marine invasion to ensure that Haiti repaid its debts to US banks—the start of a nineteen-year occupation. Technically, Wilson hadn't broken his promise. Although the United States controlled Haiti's finances and politics, it annexed no territory. On paper, Haiti remained independent.[12]

In the early twentieth century, the US empire was a North American, Caribbean, and Pacific affair. It was World War II that transformed the United States into a truly global superpower. By 1945, the United States sat atop the international system, easily outstripping its rivals in arms, industry, and technology.

The United States could have seized the opportunity to go on an imperial shopping spree, gobbling up weaker countries. Yet it didn't. Although it occupied many former war zones, it didn't annex any territory directly after the war, and it even set free its largest colony, the Philippines. Since then, it has fought wars from Korea to Kuwait, but never with the goal of colonizing. This lack of territorial acquisitiveness is Exhibit A in the "not an empire" case.

But the US reluctance to colonize widely after 1945 can't be attributed simply to benevolence. Although presidents haven't pursued colonies, they've aggressively defended the diplomatic, military, and economic supremacy of their country. No post-1945 president, possibly save the volatile Donald Trump, has accepted the possibility that the United States should sit anywhere but "at the head of the table," as Joe Biden puts it.[13]

So why hasn't this hegemonic mission involved annexations? Two factors are relevant. The first is a global anti-imperial revolt, which by the 1950s made holding colonies difficult for all colonizers and ultimately drove formal colonialism to near extinction. The second is the US mastery of many methods, stopping short of annexation, that allowed control without colonization; these ranged from giving aid to staging coups. Whether such actions nevertheless made the United States an empire depends on where you draw the definitional line.

On the spectrum's softer end was US intervention into postwar Western Europe. This was the first arena where Washington sought to contain Soviet influence by firming up its own. It did so mainly by injecting billions of dollars through loans and Marshall Plan aid. The cash came with strings, though. Washington pressed recipient countries to curtail unions, marginalize leftist movements, open up to US investment and trade, and sever ties with Eastern Europe. More strings came in 1949 with the North Atlantic Treaty Organization (NATO), a permanent military alliance through which the nuclear-armed United States extended protection to Western Europe (and spent yet more dollars there). Economically and militarily dependent on Washington, European leaders understood the costs of antagonizing their patron.

Was this an empire? If so, it wasn't one seized by force. Historians using the e-word in this context have called it an "empire by invitation" or an "irresistible empire" to highlight the fact that cash-strapped European governments often *sought* US aid, trade, and military involvement. Not everyone welcomed these things, of course; French leftists grumbled about "coca-colonization" as US products swamped their markets and English words crept into their language. But there was nevertheless a world of difference between what the United States did in Britain or France after 1945 and what it had done in the Philippines after 1898. European leaders had to navigate the United States' large gravitational field, but they mostly made their own choices.[14]

Outside Europe, the United States wielded considerably more power, most notably via military aid. By flooding its allies with arms, the United States could tilt the scales in conflict-ridden regions. Accepting military assistance from Washington was never just a matter of receiving crates of machine guns and sending a thank-you card, though. Recipients found themselves training their officers in the United States, opening their countries to its troops, relying on it for maintenance and resupplies, and fighting its proxy wars.

The adhesive of military aid bonded foreign militaries and police forces tightly to the United States. When Guatemala's elected president Jacobo Árbenz launched a land-reform campaign that threatened the US-based United Fruit Company in the 1950s, Washington could seek help from a friendly Guatemalan lieutenant colonel, Carlos Castillo Armas, who had trained at Fort Leavenworth in Kansas. Castillo Armas was a good man with good intentions, believed Vice President Richard Nixon. With US arms and other support, Castillo Armas staged a coup, seized the presidency, imprisoned his opponents, and returned the United Fruit Company's land. "Tell me what you want me to do and I will do it" is the message that, in Nixon's account, Castillo Armas conveyed to him.[15]

Behind Castillo Armas stood the Central Intelligence Agency, a secretive federal agency that meddled widely abroad. Reporters and scholars have documented sixty-four instances during the Cold War when the United States secretly interceded to oust a government or tilt a contested election—and twenty-five times when it succeeded. More than two-thirds of those interventions, including now-infamous coups in Iran (1953) and Chile (1973), were in support of authoritarians. CIA officers went so far as to plot the assassinations of Cuban dictator Fidel Castro and the elected Congolese prime minister Patrice Lumumba. Such machinations placed a string of unelected or unfairly elected leaders in Washington's debt—and impressed on other leaders the price of defiance.[16]

Theoretically, military aid and covert operations could let Washington confront its adversaries without fighting them, but it fought, too—nearly constantly. Although classifying military engagements is tricky, arguably there have been only two years in the past seventy-five when US forces were not invading or fighting in some foreign country: 1977 and 1979. Interestingly, despite its advanced and copious arsenal, the United States fared poorly on the battlefield. Of its four largest conflicts—in Korea, Vietnam, Afghanistan, and Iraq—none can be called a victory. Yet even when it lost, the United States insulated itself from war's worst consequences; the Vietnam War cost some 58,000 US lives compared with 1–3 million Vietnamese ones. Other conflicts did enormous damage abroad while leaving even fewer marks at home, such as the Korean War, which killed some 3 million and yet is known in the United States as the "Forgotten War," or a steady stream of air strikes on Iraq in the 1990s that barely registered on the US consciousness.[17]

Fighting wars doesn't necessarily make a country an empire. Nor does giving aid. Still, the United States' post-1945 ability to project power has been prodigious enough that we inhabit a hierarchically ordered planet where English is the global language, the dollar is the global currency, and the US armed forces are the global police. Call that imperial or not, but the United States has been unrivaled in its ability to impose its whims on the world.

"Living with you is in some ways like sleeping with an elephant," Canadian prime minister Pierre Trudeau once told a Washington audience. "No matter how friendly and even-tempered the beast, one is affected by every twitch and grunt."[18]

The United States is an elephant, but is it an empire? The answer depends partly on whether you count such nonterritorial tactics as aid and covert action as imperial, but it doesn't depend entirely on that. That's because territorial empire hasn't entirely vanished. Not only does the United States maintain overseas colonies and Indian reservations; since the 1940s it has also invested heavily in another type of territory: military bases. Today it controls some 750 bases in territories and abroad—far more than any other power does. The world's other militaries, combined, control fewer than a third of that number.[19]

The US bases comprise very little land. Mash together all the overseas sites that the Pentagon publicly lists, and you'd have an area not much larger than Houston. Nor do the sealed-off enclaves encompass large colonized populations. Still, the presence of US outposts in foreign countries is a large imposition, one that critics frequently decry as empire.

Consider Japan. The United States stationed hundreds of thousands of troops there after World War II, turning the center of Tokyo into "Little America." Those troops frequently clashed with locals: fights and sexual assaults were regular sources of friction. So were accidents, as when a US jet crashed into an elementary school in 1959, killing eighteen and wounding more than a hundred. Making such incidents more infuriating was US service members' persistent ability to escape trials in Japanese courts. Although arrangements vary, the United States has sought jurisdiction over its bases and personnel, usually successfully. In Japan it also claimed the right to deploy nuclear weapons to its bases, placing the country in peril of nuclear accident or Soviet attack. Such issues grated enough that two Japanese prime ministers were forced to resign over basing-related controversies.

It's telling that the most famous anti-US slogan—"Yankee, Go Home!"—isn't a protest of the United States' commerce or values. It's a protest of US military bases.

And it's a protest that has mattered. In 1962 the Cuban Missile Crisis brought the world to the brink of oblivion. As the story is often told, the crisis began when the Soviet premier, Nikita Khrushchev, aggressively stationed missiles on Soviet bases in Cuba. Yet in Khrushchev's eyes, this was merely tit-for-tat retaliation for missiles that the Kennedy administration had dispatched to US bases in Turkey. "The Americans had surrounded our country with military bases," remembered Khrushchev. He'd armed the Cuban bases to show them "just what it feels like to have enemy missiles pointed at you."[20]

Khrushchev wasn't the only malcontent. During the Gulf War, Washington sent troops to Saudi Arabia, opening bases from which to repel Iraq's invasion of Kuwait. Although Defense Secretary Dick Cheney had promised that those bases would be temporary, the troops stayed long after Iraq's defeat. "It is unconscionable to let the country become an American colony with American soldiers—their filthy feet roaming everywhere," fumed one Saudi, Osama bin Laden. Although he had many reasons for opposing the United States, military basing was one that Bin Laden brought up over and over. In 1998 he attacked two US embassies on the anniversary of the US troops' arrival in Saudi Arabia. In 2001 he attacked the Pentagon ("a military base," he explained) and the World Trade Center.[21]

The United States is still fighting a global war provoked by Bin Laden's 2001 attack. It still has five overseas territories, more than five hundred tribal nations within its borders, hundreds of foreign bases, and the world's largest military. Understanding all that, it becomes hard to agree with the presidents who have insisted that there is nothing imperial about their country. The United States isn't exceptional for its abhorrence of empire. It's been an empire, and it remains one today.

7

THE BORDER

Geraldo Cadava

Dᴜʀɪɴɢ ᴛʜᴇ ᴛᴡᴇɴᴛɪᴇᴛʜ ᴄᴇɴᴛᴜʀʏ, ᴛʜᴇ US-Mᴇxɪᴄᴏ ʙᴏʀᴅᴇʀ ᴀɴᴅ undocumented immigration became synonymous for many Americans. And how could it have been otherwise? Almost all of our national debates about immigration focus on the border. On the news we are shown images of migrants piling into government vehicles heading for detention centers, wrapping themselves in Mylar blankets, peering through the slats of the border wall, awaiting their opportunity to cross. Politicians, activists, and ordinary citizens on both ends of the ideological spectrum use these images at the border to bolster their immigration-related arguments.

Those on the left emphasize immigrant rights, migrant humanity, the role of the United States in furthering political instability in Latin America and the Caribbean, economic inequalities driven by capitalist exploitation, and the current and looming climate catastrophes compelling migration. Meanwhile, conservatives stress that the border is a point of vulnerability—our "soft underbelly," they have called it—exposing us to all sorts of threats posed by immigration, including would-be terrorist attacks, overpopulation, financial disaster, and the racial transformation of the United States.[1]

Both sides play into the idea that undocumented immigration and the border are inextricably linked. Both hide a deeper truth. It is a myth that the border is only a place of danger, dysfunction, and illegality. It is even more so a place of creativity, community, cooperation, and connection. This is as true today as it has been for almost two centuries.

The spaces between communities, empires, and nations, which by the mid-nineteenth century had become international borders, have always seemed full of peril and possibility, but during the early twentieth century they became yoked to national and international debates over immigration. This is not to say that concerns over immigration and the drawing of borders were in no way connected before the twentieth century. Spaniards and Mexicans a century earlier sought to define the boundary between them and the United States in order to defend against Indian raids. One of the ways they tried to prevent the destruction of communities on their northern frontier was to fortify them with immigrants from the United States. Free and enslaved Black migrants also sought refuge south of the border, where slavery had been abolished in 1837. For them, the border between the United States and Mexico was also the boundary between slavery and freedom. To be sure, immigration and the drawing of borders were connected in the minds of a diverse range of actors. But more than clear lines of demarcation, the shifting boundaries of the United States and Mexico—after the War of 1812, the Texas Revolution, and the US-Mexico War, for example—remained a fluid borderland of human, cultural, and economic exchange.[2]

Things began to change in the first decades of the early twentieth century, with the growth of African, Asian, and Mexican communities in border cities such as El Paso; the violence of the Mexican Revolution; and the establishment of the Border Patrol amid rising concerns over so-called illegal aliens. Henceforth, the border and undocumented immigration were joined, one perfectly symbolizing the other.

The two should be decoupled, almost entirely. Violence against immigrants and citizens has been committed in the name of policing the border, so it is important to continue thinking of the border and undocumented immigration together if it helps shine a spotlight on abuse in order to condemn it. Yet ending violence against immigrants also depends on breaking the bond between the border and undocumented immigration. The border has always been about more than undocumented immigration. This is a plain historical fact, but it is also a moral imperative.

Undocumented immigration into the United States happens in places that are far from the US-Mexico border. Likewise, many other things happen at the border besides undocumented immigration. Nevertheless, when the border and undocumented immigration are joined, the border gets reduced to a site of violent crimes committed by and against migrants, migrant caravans crashing the gates of the United States, pregnant women sneaking into the country to give birth so their children can become citizens, the point of entry for undocumented workers who steal American jobs, and a playground for drug traffickers poisoning Americans.

For a more accurate portrayal of the US-Mexico borderland both in the past and the present, it is important to understand its core character as a social, cultural, ecological, political, and economic region that bridges the United States, Mexico, and the Americas. Workers, students, families, food, and consumer goods have crossed between the United States and Mexico every day for more than a century.[3] Artists and architects have transformed border spaces in order to highlight connections between the United States and Mexico. Communities on both sides of the border share environments and natural resources. These exchanges have been about cooperation and cultural and commercial exchange, and have had little to do with undocumented immigration and border enforcement.

Seeing the border and immigration as synonymous has also propagated the dangerous idea that our national well-being depends on division rather than connection. Or "good fences make good neighbors," following the logic of many conservatives, who appropriated the idea from the poet Robert Frost. The vision of the US-Mexico border as a line that divides rather than unites is a dark one. It is fueled by a small measure of truth—because, of course, like most other regions, crime and criminals have found a haven in the borderlands—but a much larger degree of paranoia, racism, misunderstanding, and nationalist mythmaking. These are dilemmas that extend beyond the border but that the border represents, perhaps as a symptom or a cause in itself.

The gravest threats to the United States have little to do with immigration and the border. New perspectives on both can help us properly understand our connections with other parts of the world, the alliances that make us safe, and our reliance on migrants to keep our economy running.

Even before the US-Mexico borderland became closely associated with immigration, it could be thought of as a dangerous and threatening space. Such thinking has been part of American social, cultural, and political life for a long time. It took root well before the establishment of the border in the mid-nineteenth century and has defined the thinking of conservatives, nativists, xenophobes, warmongers, and isolationists ever since. Today, liberals also call the borderland a dangerous and threatening space when conservatives force them to preen their patriotic, America-first feathers and say as loud as they can that they, too, care about defending the United States. But despite the perceived dangers of the borderland, the people who live there conceive of it differently.

To begin with, the borderland has formed a single environment that only in modern times has been divided by a border. The Colorado River, approximately 1,450 miles long, flows from the Rocky Mountains in Colorado south through Utah and Arizona, continues between Arizona and Nevada and California, and then crosses into Mexico at San Luis Rio Colorado, where it empties into the Gulf of California. For centuries, Mexican ranchers and farmers have depended on the river's water in order for their cows to eat and crops to grow.

The borderland has also been home to flora and fauna found on both sides of the international divide. The Rio Grande—or Rio Bravo, as it is called in Mexico—accounts for more than half of the entire length of today's southern border. It has served both as a commercial waterway and source of sustenance for humans and animals. Lands in Texas and Chihuahua encompass the Sierra Madre Mountain Range and extensive desert grasslands. The Sonoran Desert, which covers large parts of Arizona and Sonora, and smaller slices of California, Baja California, and Baja California Sur, is home to dozens of species of reptiles and amphibians and fish, hundreds of species of birds, and thousands of species of plants, including the saguaro cactus, which does not grow anywhere else in the world. Communities formed in close proximity to and benefited from the area's natural resources.

For centuries before other groups arrived, Indigenous peoples lived in what is today the borderland. When Spaniards began pushing into the region in the sixteenth century, they were looking for the riches of the New World, including the mythical Seven Cities of Cíbola, thought to be located in New Mexico and filled with gold. Over the course of hundreds of years of exploration, conquest, and settlement, Spaniards brought African slaves into the region and held Native Americans as captives, lovers, and family members. They established a frontier society and institutions including military presidios and Catholic churches, which promised peace and threatened violence.[4]

Despite the growing presence of settler societies, for much of the Spanish period of the Southwest, which lasted from the sixteenth through the early nineteenth centuries, Indigenous nations such as the Comanche and Apache held the balance of power. Even into the Mexican period, after 1821, when Mexico won its independence from Spain, their raiding practices gave Mexican settlements a tenuous hold on the new nation's northern frontier. Indigenous power and autonomy in the borderland diminished significantly when the United States—often with help from Mexicans and Mexican Americans—waged brutal campaigns of extermination against them.[5]

In the first decades of the nineteenth century, immigration into the borderland by families from the United States such as the Austins and the Houstons, who set up colonies for slaveholders who brought their chattel with them into Texas, loosened Mexico's grip on its northern provinces. The result was something that historians have called a race war between Mexicans and Anglo settlers in Texas, which resulted first in the Texas Revolution, next the formation of the Republic of Texas, and finally the annexation of Texas by the United States. The war against Mexicans in Texas and elsewhere was bolstered by animosities toward them that had to do with old ideas about the backwardness of Spain and theories of racial degeneration caused by race mixture. The conflict in Texas foretold what happened in short order throughout the region.[6]

In 1846 the United States instigated a war that only two years later led to the signing of the Treaty of Guadalupe Hidalgo, on February 2, 1848, which annexed half of Mexican territory, including California, Arizona, New Mexico, and parts of Nevada, Colorado, and Utah. With the ink of a pen, an estimated tens of thousands of Mexicans became US citizens. Teams of surveyors from the United States and Mexico drew the border, placing sporadically throughout the desert piles of stones that became the only indicators of where one country began and the other ended.[7]

As the US government and corporations became more established presences in the borderland, the effects on Indigenous and Mexican peoples were profound. The establishment of the border by treaty meant that Indigenous communities that had lived in the borderland for centuries were divided in two. Apache, Yaqui, Kickapoo, and Tohono O'odham Indians, among others, lived on both sides of the new border. For the most part, the international line meant little to them, and they continued to cross it freely to move between different villages, gather for religious ceremonies, and visit family members. But over time, even if they identified as members of the same tribal nations, they became alienated from one another. Indians on one side confronted what it meant to be Indigenous in Mexico, and on the other they negotiated their relationship to the United States. Many lost their native languages, and some left their homelands to live in the new cities of the borderland.[8]

Americans attempted to police the movement of Native peoples by placing them on reservations, but they in no way tried to stop the migration of Mexicans across the newly drawn border. To the contrary, Mexicans—especially after the Chinese Exclusion Act of 1882, which excluded Chinese as a matter of law if not practice—became desirable and exploitable laborers who dug mines, extracted minerals, built railroads, and harvested crops. Nothing about this changed until well into the twentieth century.[9]

Borderland cities themselves were created by the border, which acted like a magnet for transportation linkages, trade networks, and new immigrant communities. Railroads in Mexico and the United States connected at the border in the 1880s. The railroads carried people and food and consumer goods from the Mexican and US interiors, where they were unloaded and reloaded onto trains on the other side and continued their journey into the neighboring country. Smaller offshoots of the major lines linked local mining areas to provision miners and the small communities that grew around the mines. Businesses opened on both sides of the border to service growing cities such as San Diego–Tijuana, Nogales Arizona and Nogales Sonora, and El Paso–Ciudad Juárez, which by the end of the nineteenth century had many thousands of residents.[10]

Mexicans, Native Americans, African Americans, Chinese, and many others settled together in the border region. They were not treated as the equals of white settlers, but neither was their migration to and settlement in the borderland prohibited. Immigration and the hardening of the US-Mexico border had not become part of the same conversation.

Even in the first years of the twentieth century, America's immigration problems were elsewhere. The US government was more preoccupied with the poor Europeans amassing at Ellis Island or the politically radical Europeans sneaking into the United States across the US-Canada border. It was also more concerned with the incorporation of Puerto Ricans, Cubans, and Filipinos after the Spanish-American War. Some attention turned toward the Mexican border when the violence of the Mexican Revolution threatened to spill across it. The US military put up barbed wire to prevent Mexican soldiers from stealing livestock, and it established some of the region's first military bases. But the aim was to secure the border against revolutionary violence, not to prevent Mexican immigration. Indeed, more than 10 percent of Mexico's population immigrated to the United States during the decade of revolution without much impediment.[11]

The new immigration laws of 1917 and 1924 were not meant for Mexicans either. They were exempted from the 1917 law's literacy and head-tax requirements because employers in the United States needed their labor. They and all other immigrants from the Western Hemisphere were also excluded from the 1924 Johnson-Reed Act, which established national-origin quotas that, instead of Mexicans, targeted southern and eastern Europeans who were seen as dangerous radicals. The Johnson-Reed Act also authorized the establishment of the US Border Patrol, but more agents were stationed along the Canadian border than along the Mexican border throughout the 1920s.[12]

No, the need to protect the border against the threat of Mexican immigration did not become a matter of national importance until the Great Depression, when more than a million Mexicans were deported to Mexico. With such rampant unemployment, employers in the United States encountered more resistance when they tried to justify their continued reliance on Mexican immigrant labor. So did the congressmen who did their bidding by making sure they had access to a steady stream of workers. From the Great Depression forward, the border and undocumented immigration were hitched.[13]

The so-called wetback problem gained widespread attention in the years leading up to Operation Wetback, another episode of mass expulsion in 1954 and 1955 that Joseph Swing, the head of the Immigration and Naturalization Service at the time, modeled after the Depression-era deportations. Even so, more than four million Mexicans migrated to the United States as part of the Bracero Program, creating what scholars have called a revolving door of Mexican immigration; many thousands of Mexicans were deported at the same time that many thousands more were allowed to enter, only to be sent back through the revolving door once their employers were done with them.[14]

The Bracero Program was canceled in 1964, the year before President Lyndon Johnson signed the sweeping Immigration and Nationality Act of 1965, which ended the discriminatory national-origin quotas but for the first time set a cap on immigration from Western Hemisphere countries, including Mexico. The number of Mexican immigrants allowed to enter the United States each year was smaller than the number of necessary workers. Because Mexicans also needed the work, many ignored the law and entered illegally. Almost continuously from 1965 until the end of the twentieth century, the number of undocumented Mexicans arriving and settling in the United States grew, which fed the anti-immigrant frenzy we are still living with today.[15]

The immigration debate began to focus almost exclusively on the border. More Border Patrol officers were sent to police the international line. Chain-link fences were replaced with helicopter landing pads used by the US military during the Vietnam War. Congress began debating several comprehensive immigration-reform bills that included fines levied against employers who knowingly hired undocumented immigrants, a pathway to citizenship for certain immigrants, and increased financial support for the Border Patrol. These provisions were codified in the 1986 Immigration Reform and Control Act, signed by President Ronald Reagan in November 1986.

At the same time, vigilante organizations claimed that the US government had failed to defend the border against undocumented immigration, so they took matters into their own hands. Klansmen including David Duke patrolled the border, and ranchers detained and tortured Mexican immigrants crossing their land.[16] Like the vigilantes, states also said they would step in to defend the border and punish undocumented immigrants because the US government had failed to do so. Californians passed Proposition 187 in 1994. If it had not been deemed unconstitutional, the bill would have denied public education, health care, and other social benefits to undocumented immigrants. Other states, as well as the national Republican Party, promised to follow California's lead.

The anti-immigrant mood deepened and calls for increased border defense only grew louder after 9/11, when conservatives argued that dangerous immigrants—terrorists, even—could enter the United States across the Mexican border. Such thinking has continued to shape immigration and border politics into the present, with Republicans from John McCain to Donald Trump calling for more border fencing to protect the United States.

Despite the fact that our national immigration debates have focused increasingly on the US-Mexico border, the region has maintained its borderland character as a home to diverse communities and a space of international exchange and cooperation.

As borderland economies grew in the early twentieth century because of the successes of the agricultural, mining, and defense industries, the already diverse region became even more so with the arrival of Japanese, Puerto Ricans, and US citizens from other regions, especially the Midwest, who found work and rooted their families there. The trend continued during and after World War II, largely as a result of the military-industrial complex that transformed the Sunbelt borderland. The populations of many borderland cities grew by at least 200 percent between 1940 and 1960 as new arrivals from Mexico and other parts of the United States flooded the region. They inaugurated regional and international celebrations—rodeos, Mexican Independence Day, July Fourth—that were rooted in romantic notions of the region's multiracial and multicultural past and present. Native Americans, the descendants of Spanish colonizers, and Mexican and American settlers participated as representatives of the groups that were original inhabitants and settlers. African Americans and Chinese Americans, and Vietnamese and Central American refugees, participated as relative newcomers.[17]

As they had always done, borderland residents crossed the border daily as a way of life, not as immigrants. They saw themselves as members of transnational border communities, such as El Paso–Ciudad Juárez or San Diego–Tijuana. In the late nineteenth century, when stone obelisks but nothing else marked the border, postcards showed people milling back and forth across an invisible line. Even after physical barriers defined the border in the early twentieth century, businesses crowded both sides, inviting tourists and residents who lived on the other side to cross. The residents of Nogales, Arizona, and Nogales, Sonora, have told stories about a time when saloons straddled the border. When the saloon on the US side stopped selling liquor, which was earlier than establishments in Mexico, patrons simply walked to the Mexican side of the saloon to keep drinking.[18]

Even as barbed-wire, chain-link, and steel fencing began to separate the United States and Mexico—first to stop cattle, then people—the borderland remained open to cross-border movements of all kinds. When the growth of borderland communities in the mid-twentieth century led to a boom in consumerism on both sides of the international line, the borderland locations of stores like Sears became, per square foot, some of the busiest and most profitable stores in the country. When department stores were replaced by big-box stores such as Target, Costco, and Sam's Club, border cities were home to the most profitable locations of these stores as well. When the Mexican peso was devalued in the 1970s, 1980s, and 1990s, border cities were devastated because Mexican shoppers who were important customers could no longer afford the prices north of the border. In a very real sense, US and Mexican border cities were mutually dependent.[19]

Mutual dependency also described the postwar labor and educational landscapes of the US–Mexico borderland. Hundreds of thousands of borderland commuters—workers who lived in Mexico but held jobs in the United States—entered California, Arizona, New Mexico, and Texas as domestics, blue-collar workers, and educated professionals.[20] Students from kindergarten through college crossed the border to go to school. Mexicans with means sent their kids to institutions of higher education such as the University of Arizona, where they studied agriculture, engineering, business, or law, then returned home to northern Mexico and became part of the regional elite. Sometimes parents bought second homes north of the border so they could visit their children and shop in the malls that began to pop up in the 1960s. The border was more about profit than immigration restriction. It was also about finding solutions to shared environmental and political challenges.[21]

The International Boundary and Water Commission, in consultation with communities on both sides of the border, built dams to manage the flow of water to the region's agricultural fields. US and Mexican government agencies worked together to control the outbreak of disease among cattle because pathogens crossed borders freely. Scientists at universities in US and Mexican border states collaborated to solve the region's aridity, including through unrealized proposals to desalinate water from the gulfs of California and Mexico in order to make it drinkable.[22]

In 1964 Lyndon Johnson and Mexican president Adolfo López Mateos settled a decades-long conflict that arose when a stretch of the river near El Paso actually switched course, moving several miles to the south. Mexico claimed about four hundred acres of the disputed land, and the United States claimed almost two hundred.[23] The United States established the Chamizal National Memorial ten years later, in 1974, which became a symbol of international diplomacy and conflict resolution. The shifting course of the river underscored how nature drove politics and diplomacy, not the other way around.

Even during the past half century, when anti-immigrant sentiments and laws have risen in tandem with the undocumented population, the US-Mexico borderland has been characterized by more than immigration. The US government itself has tried to move the focus on undocumented immigration away from the border by offshoring immigration control. In the early 1980s, a new security perimeter between the United States and Mexico was set up along the Guatemala-Mexico border. Mexico entered into an agreement with the United States that Ana Minian described as a "Faustian bargain," whereby the Mexican government would crack down on Central American migration through Mexico in exchange for the US government's continued acceptance of Mexican immigrants. The crossing has become increasingly dangerous for Central Americans, but when they can be apprehended before reaching the US-Mexico border, US citizens do not have to experience the discomfort of their presence.[24]

In addition to the nonimmigrant students, shoppers, truck drivers, and tourists who cross the border habitually, no group of borderlanders has more creatively challenged the idea that the border is primarily about undocumented immigration than artists and architects. For them, the border has been both a canvas and a laboratory for experimenting with new forms of urban art, housing, and design. They have insisted on cultural hybridity and transnational connection as the borderland's core identity. For example, the performance artist Guillermo Gómez-Peña, who founded the Border Arts Workshop/Taller de Arte Fronterizo (BAW/TAF) in 1984, combines English and Spanish and mixes symbols, metaphors, and religious imagery from the United States and Mexico. He wears eyeliner, a leather vest, and elaborate headdresses that evoke Mesoamerica, embodying the borderland and making it plain through his performances that the border was neither Mexico nor the United States but both at the same time. In his 1996 book *The New World Border*—a play on George H. W. Bush's 1990 speech about the New World Order, in which the United States and its allies would unite to fight against evil in the world—Gómez-Peña universalized the borderland experience when he wrote that "all major metropolises have been fully borderized . . . they all look like downtown Tijuana on a Saturday night."[25]

Borderland architects have worked in the same vein, insisting on fluidity and connection rather than division. In 2006 the *New York Times* invited more than a dozen architects to participate in a competition to come up with new designs for a border wall. In response to rising calls for hundreds of miles of new border wall construction after 9/11, which George W. Bush included in the 2006 Secure Fence Act, the architects who submitted proposals instead reimagined the border wall as solar panels that could power the whole region or a series of highways connecting the United States and Mexico.[26]

In the twenty-first century, Donald Trump became the leading spokesperson for—the very embodiment of—the myth that the border and undocumented immigration were one and the same. He and his followers repeated the time-worn, distorted argument that the US-Mexico border is a site of lawlessness where criminals run rampant, a point of vulnerability that exposes the United States to national security threats, and the international crossing where racialized others pour into the country, contributing to the fraying of our social fabric and making the United States a brown nation instead of one defined by the patriots who fought in the American Revolution—many of whom, by the way, were also brown and not necessarily from Europe.

Trump argued that the construction of border walls, the prevention of undocumented immigration, and the maintenance of national identity were mutually reinforcing projects. During his 2016 campaign, he tweeted, "If we have no border, we have no country." And when he adopted the slogan "Make America Great Again," many Americans heard him to be saying that he wanted to Make America White Again. To him and his followers, the border was the physical symbol of national sovereignty and identity, which depended on stopping undocumented immigration. The connections they made among border enforcement, the rule of law, and the preservation of national identity relied on racist ideas about Mexicans and Central Americans, who were rapists, murderers, thieves, and invariably members of gangs like the Mara Salvatruchas, also known as MS-13.[27]

The conflation of undocumented immigration with the need for a border wall is representative of how many Americans think today, and their thinking is wrong. Much immigration and border enforcement does not even happen at the US-Mexico border. Instead, it takes place deep within Mexico or at interior checkpoints on the US side of the border, where Border Patrol officers search vehicles to ensure that all inside are in the country legally and that they are not carrying contraband with them. It also takes place in American cities, as Immigration and Customs Enforcement (ICE) officers raid homes and workplaces, evincing Gómez-Peña's point that all major metropolises have been "borderized." As many as half of all undocumented migrants in the United States entered legally and overstayed their visas, entering by boat or by plane in addition to crossing by land.[28]

All of these things together expose the fact that the border as Trump saw it is little more than a symbol—of national insecurity, of the xenophobia of many Americans living far from the border, of our government's habit of blaming others for problems of our own making, or of problems that do not have easy fixes.[29]

As the symbol of all US efforts to curb undocumented immigration, Trump's border wall was an expensive one. When it was first proposed, estimates of the wall's cost ranged from $8–12 billion, the figure cited by Trump, to $66.9 billion, the figure from the Democratic staff of the Senate Homeland Security and Governmental Affairs Committee. These estimates were outliers. Most ranged between $15 and $25 billion, and many fell right in the middle, at around $20 billion. As of October 2020, right before Trump was voted out of office, as much as $15 billion had already been spent on less of the wall than he hoped to build.[30]

Even if $20 billion were the final price tag for Trump's wall, that amount, as one Democratic representative noted, could pay for 1.5 aircraft carriers. But what else, beyond more war machines, could $20 billion cover? That amount is about twice the budget of the Environmental Protection Agency, twice the budget of the US Department of Commerce, and a little less than the budget of NASA. It is about a third of the US Department of Education's budget and a third of the entire budget of the US Department of Housing and Urban Development, which supports rent, homeless aid, support for poverty-stricken communities, and the housing and community needs of Native Americans.[31]

It is at least worth asking whether a $20 billion outlay for the construction of a border wall that, as a performative gesture, might make some Americans feel that their concerns about undocumented immigration are being addressed is justifiable when so many other needs go unmet. And it is an especially important question to ask when many of the arguments in support of the border wall have rested on the myth that the US-Mexico border and undocumented immigration are one and the same.

The vast majority of borderland residents do not want to live with a border wall that divides their communities. In surveys, two-thirds of borderland residents reported that they "absolutely" did not want Trump's wall to get built. Another 10 percent thought it probably should not get built. They believed it would separate them from family and friends, and was unnecessary because border communities were safer than many other communities in the United States.[32] It seems important to listen to the people whose lives have been most affected by the border wall's imposition instead of listening to those who live far from the border but believe that it is the only way to stop undocumented immigration.

We should resist uniformly negative associations of the border and undocumented immigration. They should be a relic of past politics, representative of debates that divided us at one point but that no longer will. All borders can be read as artifacts, and the miles of fencing that Trump built could become one as well. It will then be our duty to teach about how Trump sowed divisions instead of bridging divides. We have done this with all other walls, such as the Berlin Wall, which fell at the end of the Cold War.[33]

We should also pay more attention to all of the things that happen in the borderland besides undocumented immigration. More than

15 million people live within 100 kilometers, or 62.5 miles, of the US-Mexico border. Before the middle of the twenty-first century, the population of the border region is expected to double again. Also, millions of US and Mexican citizens still cross the border every year to eat, shop, attend school, visit family, and work, then return home at the end of their visits. Borderland businesses stay afloat because of customers from the other side.

The economic interdependence of border cities is a microcosm of the interdependence of the United States and Mexico more broadly. Mexico is second only to China as our leading trading partner in terms of the dollar value of goods flowing between countries. In July 2020 the total amount of trade between Mexico and the United States was $47.5 billion, which accounted for 15.2 percent of the total value of trade between the United States and all countries. Trade with China in the same month totaled $49.7 billion.[34]

The United States exports electronics, auto parts, medical equipment, computer accessories, petroleum products, and meat and poultry and corn. We import fruits and vegetables, crude oil, plastics, computers, automobiles, appliances, electronics, and many other parts and products. These exports and imports flow across the border in semitrucks whose operators pass through checkpoints with more lanes than the largest highways in either country, heading for points in the Mexican or the US interior, or neighboring countries such as Guatemala or Canada.[35]

No matter how much attention we focus on undocumented immigration, we will not interrupt other connections either, such as educational exchanges and shared cityscapes. At one private school in El Paso, more than 70 percent of the students live in Mexico and cross the border every day. Meanwhile, the greatest number of international students at universities in US border states come from Mexico. Thousands of Mexican college students cross the border to attend classes at San Diego State University, Arizona Western College in Yuma, or the University of Texas at El Paso. They wake up early and wait for hours in long lines. As they approach the border, the cities they leave and the cities they enter appear be joined. Buildings clump together and thin out the farther they are from the border.[36]

These exchanges are entirely unremarkable because they take place every day. The fact that they are so mundane means that it is possible to take them for granted. Their scale is massive, but we hardly learn about them because politicians have used crisis-driven news cycles to focus our attention on undocumented immigration instead.

Doing away with the myth that immigration and the border are synonymous, and instead shifting our perspective to see the border more fundamentally as a space of connection, innovation, and cultural strength, will not solve all of the problems that Americans face. It may not help us find solutions to partisan divisions that have eroded our connections to one another, and it may not help with solutions to immigration debates that seem intractable. But it could help us recognize that our obsession with building and policing the border has scapegoated immigrants and displaced anxieties about imperial and national decline, economic fragility, and demographic change, for which immigrants are blamed but do not bear the responsibility.

8

AMERICAN SOCIALISM

Michael Kazin

"AMERICA WILL NEVER BE A SOCIALIST COUNTRY," DECLARED DONald Trump in his 2019 State of the Union Address, given to a joint session of Congress. The president clearly believed that fear of such a radical transformation would help him win reelection against a Democratic Party in which socialists like Bernie Sanders were growing in numbers and influence.[1]

The former president and most of his political allies are probably unaware that nearly two centuries earlier, a wealthy socialist from abroad spoke before the same body. The friendly reception he received suggests that the philosophy of economic equality and cooperation instead of competition may not be "un-American" at all.

During the winter of 1825, Robert Owen, a rich manufacturer from Wales, gave two addresses, each about three hours long, to joint sessions of Congress. There was, he told the lawmakers, an urgent need

117

to establish "a New System of Society," one that would be based "upon principles of strict justice and impartial kindness." Owen condemned the reigning economic order, which he called "the trading system," as selfish and inhumane at its core. It trained people "to obtain advantages over others," he argued, and gave "a very injurious surplus of wealth and power to the few" while exacting "poverty and subjection on the many."

Owen predicted the coming of a new order that would liberate Americans from their plight. An economy organized for "mutual benefit" would enable men and women to leave the irrationality of relentless, often violent, competition behind them. "In the new system," he promised, "union and cooperation will supersede individual interest."[2]

The legislators treated Owen and his ideas with great respect. Several Supreme Court justices came to hear him; so did the outgoing president, James Monroe, and the incoming president, John Quincy Adams. Because neither Thomas Jefferson nor James Madison, who were then quite elderly, could leave their Virginia estates, Owen brought his message to them. He paid a visit to John Adams up in Massachusetts as well.[3]

Every living president at the time was thus willing to hear the visionary radical's sharp critique of the capitalist society emerging both in the United States and across the Atlantic. Their curiosity was a sign that the market system, for all its promise of plenty, was not yet a settled reality defended by all men of wealth and standing.

Robert Owen soon gave a name to the new system he advocated. He called it "socialism," and the term quickly caught on across the globe. Although future socialists would never enjoy such an elite audience in the United States, their ideas and the movements they built remained part of the mainstream of American history. Most have been committed to democracy, both as an electoral system and as the vision of a future in which ordinary people, in all their diversity, would make the key decisions in their workplaces and communities, as well as at the polling booth, that affected their lives and the fate of their society. Like it or not, socialism has been as impossible to separate from the narrative of the nation's history as the capitalist economy itself—and often posed the most prominent alternative to it. Socialists were also energetic advocates of federal and state policies such as Social Security, on which most Americans have come to rely.

Conservative politicians and commentators take quite a different view. For them, socialism has meant only a hankering for state tyranny and brazen assaults on property rights that, together, threaten the beliefs every patriotic citizen holds dear. For the Right, socialists are the sworn enemies of freedom and democracy; according to Representative Tom Cole, a Republican from Oklahoma, they defy the national creed that "the ultimate sovereign power [in the US] lies with the people."[4]

The congressman might be surprised to learn that, a little more than a century ago, his own state had been home to one of the strongest contingents of socialists in America. In 1912 one-sixth of Oklahoma voters cast their ballots for Eugene Debs, a former railroad union leader, who ran for president on the Socialist Party (SP) ticket. Debs drew a little less than half as many votes in Oklahoma that year as did William Howard Taft—the White House incumbent. Soon there were then six Socialists in the state legislature; more than three thousand Sooners belonged to the party—one of every three hundred adults in the state.

Part of their attraction to socialism was practical: the Oklahoma party appealed to small farmers, then the majority of residents, with a program that featured a plan for the state government to purchase arable land for the use of those willing to cultivate it and vowed to remove all property taxes on farms worth less than $1,000. State banks and warehouses would help growers stay in business. And nearly all socialists, like most other Oklahomans, were devout Christians. They flocked to yearly encampments that blended a faith in Jesus with a belief in socialism. At one gathering, a preacher proclaimed, "Christ's church was a working class church" and cited the verse from Ecclesiastes that decrees "the Profit of the Earth is for all."[5]

The passion for reform that moved many Oklahomans to vote for socialists or look favorably on their ideas was not unique to that prairie state. Socialists, then and later, played a major role in initiating and rallying support for changes that most Americans have no desire to reverse. These include women's right to vote, Medicare, the minimum wage, workplace safety laws, universal health insurance, and civil rights for all races and genders. All were once considered radical ideas. But vast majorities now consider them the cornerstones of a decent society.

Americans also overwhelmingly favor curbs on the power of big business that conservatives since the nineteenth century have condemned as socialist. Most citizens believe that the superrich should pay much higher taxes than the middle class. They believe that businesses should be subject to rules that require them to act responsibly and that banks shouldn't engage in predatory lending. They also agree that energy corporations shouldn't endanger the planet and public health by emitting carbon-based pollution. Companies, they believe, should be required to guarantee that consumer products like cars, food, and toys are safe and that companies pay decent wages and provide safe workplaces.

Another way to gauge the influence of socialism in US history is to list some of the prominent American writers, artists, intellectuals, activists, and scientists who either publicly embraced the label or favored a socialist blueprint for the nation. It's quite a distinguished roster. At various times it has included Ralph Waldo Emerson, Walter Lippmann, John Dewey, Charles and Mary Beard, W. E. B. Du Bois, Jack London, Carl Sandburg, Upton Sinclair, Theodore Dreiser, Helen Keller, John Reed, Eugene O'Neill, Randolph Bourne, Florence Kelley, Isadora Duncan, Thorstein Veblen, Walter Rauschenbusch, Clarence Darrow, Max Eastman, George Bellows, John Sloan, Charlie Chaplin, Ernest Hemingway, John Steinbeck, Orson Welles, Norman Mailer, Woody Guthrie, and Jacob Lawrence. Two of the most influential labor leaders in US history— Walter Reuther and A. Philip Randolph—were also open about their sympathy for socialism. So, at some points in their lives, were Margaret Sanger, Betty Friedan, and Gloria Steinem—a trio who did much to create the modern feminist movement. Several of these people remain controversial today. But it would be impossible to write a history of American culture that did not devote attention to nearly every one of them. And conservatives who view socialism as unpatriotic might also ponder why Francis Bellamy, author of the Pledge of Allegiance to the Flag in 1892, was an avowed Christian socialist.

The world-famous physicist Albert Einstein and Charles Steinmetz, who developed the alternating current vital to machines that run on electricity, also expressed a fondness for the socialist vision. "I am convinced," wrote Einstein in 1949, that "there is only *one* way to eliminate these grave evils" of capitalism, "namely through the establishment of a socialist economy, accompanied by an educational system which would be oriented toward social goals. In such an economy, the means of production are owned by society itself and are utilized in a planned fashion."[6]

What's more, the only nonpresident to have a federal holiday named after him favored both "a massive program by the government" to create a job for every citizen who could not find one in the private sector and the abolition of poverty in the entire nation—as well as complete equality of the races. In a 1961 speech to the Negro American Labor Council, he proclaimed, "Call it democracy, or call it democratic socialism, but there must be a better distribution of wealth within this country for all God's children."[7] Such views help explain why conservatives opposed a holiday dedicated to Martin Luther King Jr. as long as they did.

So if individual socialists and their proposals gained a good deal of popularity throughout American history, why didn't socialist parties fare better in the electoral arena?

During the first two decades of the twentieth century, several thousand members of the Socialist Party of America did win a share of local power—from the mayor of Milwaukee to the mayor of the little town of Antlers, Oklahoma. Yet only two Socialists became members of the House of Representatives, and none came close to winning a seat in the US Senate or a high executive office in any state. The charismatic Debs ran fives times for president on a socialist ticket, but he never won more than 6 percent of the vote, with about a million ballots in 1912. At that point the socialist movement had managed, wrote the critic and historian Irving Howe, to escape "the isolation of the left-wing sect" without becoming a mass movement of enduring size and power. In the end, the "working class party" was unable to woo more than a small minority of workers away from voting for politicians beholden to the "capitalist class."[8]

For over a century, scholars and activists have been arguing about why it failed to make that leap. Serious debate began in 1906 with a short book, *Why Is There No Socialism in the United States?* by the German academic Werner Sombart. At the time, anyone who visited the hungry coal towns of Appalachia or the fire-prone sweatshops of the Lower East Side

could have refuted Sombart's contention that incomparable prosperity—
what he called "reefs of roast beef and apple pie"—prevented American
workers from emulating their European counterparts. So the question remained alive among historians and political scientists through the twentieth century, even as the program of most Socialist and Labor parties on
the continent came to resemble that of liberal Democrats in the United
States and vice versa.

Some prominent critics blamed American socialists for their own mar-
ginality or viewed their cause as doomed by conditions particular to the
nation's history. Thus, Daniel Bell contended that socialists "could not
relate to the specific problems" of the "give-and-take, political world."
Aileen Kraditor claimed they spoke to working people as if they were the
ignorant dupes of capitalism, with no ideas or cultures of their own. Louis
Hartz maintained that the hegemony of liberal thought, with its vaunting
of the classless individual, made Marxists politically superfluous. Many
commentators have focused on the absence of a feudal past, with its deep
class feelings; on ethnic and racial and religious divisions in the United
States; or on the ideological flexibility of the two-party system.[9]

In recent years, scholars on the left have altered the terms of discussion. They defend the achievements of socialists as the deeds of prophets
without honor in an unjust society. Nick Salvatore portrayed Debs as
a union leader who gradually came to believe that monopoly capitalism was betraying the American Dream. Mari Jo Buhle paid tribute to
"the tens of thousands of rank-and-file women who formed the Socialist
women's movement . . . the defeated and now forgotten warriors against
triumphant capitalism." Such views echo a remark by Mr. Dooley, the
fictional Irish American bartender created by Finley Peter Dunne, who
delighted newspaper readers at the turn of the twentieth century. Dooley
disdained the kind of historians who, like physicians, "are always lookin'
f'r symptoms" and making "a post-mortem examination." "It tells ye
what a countrhy died iv," he complained. "But I'd like to know what it
lived iv."[10]

Even the minority of American radicals who admired dictatorial regimes abroad spent most of their time fighting for the same causes as did
the nation's scrupulously democratic socialists. The Communist Party,

formed in 1919, yoked its reputation to the Soviet Union run by Vladimir Lenin and then Joseph Stalin, one of the most repressive regimes in modern history. But their party went into swift decline during the Cold War that began in the late 1940s and barely exists today.

But in their brief heyday in the 1930s and early 1940s, most rank-and-file American communists were busy advocating badly needed changes at home. During the Great Depression, they mobilized jobless men and women to demand immediate aid from the government. They organized low-paid industrial workers into such unions as the Electrical Workers and Auto Workers. They battled discrimination by race and religion and national origin. And they advocated for a good education, health care, and access to cultural resources for every American. Communists were also the most vigorous foes of fascism—except for twenty-two notorious months beginning in late August 1939, when the USSR signed a nonaggression pact with Nazi Germany. Knowing that the tyrants in the Kremlin approved all these activities does not negate their positive impact on American society. Ordinary members of the Communist Party helped make the US a more tolerant, more democratic society—and put pressure on liberals to dismantle barriers between people deemed worthy of government help and those who were not.

As part of mass movements, socialists have followed the same pattern throughout American history: they do all they can to compel elites to make reforms in the existing order. The paradox of their success is that it often limits the growth of socialism itself. Perceptive politicians understand that a rising opposition force that aims to replace the entire system has to be co-opted, not simply repressed.

Take the example of Progressivism in the early twentieth century. This drive for reform was a tree with multiple roots—the social gospel, pragmatic philosophy, a desire for efficiency and honesty in government, and more. But the socialist challenge (with sizable parties in Europe as well as the United States) posed the promise (or threat) of an upheaval that would, to paraphrase the Russian revolutionary Leon Trotsky, hurl every old order into the dustbin of history. So leading figures in both major American parties shifted to the left in rhetoric and program to ensure that the essential structures of the capitalist republic would remain intact.

On trips to Europe in between his three campaigns for the presidency, the Democrat William Jennings Bryan praised the public ownership of utilities and railroads and marveled that the German Socialists "have educated the working classes to a very high standard of political intelligence and a strong sense of their independence and of their social mission." The progressive Republican Theodore Roosevelt, who despised class-conscious radicals, nevertheless worked hard to steal their thunder. He declared that "property shall be the servant and not the master of the commonwealth" and promoted corporate regulation and craft unions. As governor of New Jersey, Woodrow Wilson told his fellow Democrats that "the service rendered the people by the national government must be of a more extended sort and of a kind not only to protect it against monopoly, but also to facilitate its life." Later in the White House, he struck up an alliance with organized labor that frustrated some socialists who had believed such a cross-class partnership was immoral.[11]

Socialists of various stripes also played a critical role in building movements during the Great Depression that helped persuade President Franklin D. Roosevelt and his fellow liberals in Congress to initiate the New Deal. General strikes in 1934 led by radicals in Minneapolis and San Francisco nudged Congress to pass the National Labor Relations Act, which, for the first time, gave the federal government the power to punish employers for firing workers attempting to organize a union. Socialist-minded artists employed by the Works Progress Administration (WPA) created the historical murals that still exist in public buildings all over the land. And the 1935 Social Security Act, one of the most enduring and popular of all New Deal programs, built on pensions for the aged and relief for the unemployed that were already common in many European nations, where socialist parties were stronger. Even so, two decades earlier, it was Victor Berger, the Socialist Party congressman from Milwaukee, who introduced the first bill in Congress to provide an annual income for the elderly.

Conservatives routinely condemned such programs as steps down the road to a terrifying, dystopian order. In 1961 Ronald Reagan, then an actor and corporate spokesman, recorded a warning about the consequences of enacting the proposal that would become Medicare. "Behind it," he predicted, "will come other federal programs that will invade every area of freedom as we have known it in this country. Until, one day . . . we will awake to find that we have socialism." A year earlier, Reagan wrote in the same vein to Richard Nixon about John F. Kennedy, his rival in the 1960 presidential campaign: "Shouldn't someone tag Mr. Kennedy's bold new imaginative program with its proper age? Under the tousled boyish haircut is still old Karl Marx—first launched a century ago." But when Reagan became president in 1981, he kept Medicare intact. He knew that it had become one of the most popular—as well as expensive—federal initiatives in history.[12]

Democratic socialists have never been content with a program like Medicare that only covers a minority of Americans. They favor paying for the health costs of *all* citizens through progressive taxation, as well as guaranteeing them affordable housing and decent employment (backed by strong unions). Yet throughout US history, most have practiced what Michael Harrington, the last leader of the Socialist Party, liked to call "the left wing of the possible." They were eager and sometimes able to use their talents as intellectuals and activists to spur changes that improve lives for millions of people, even if doing so did not build a radical movement.

A prime example comes from Harrington's own work and career. In 1962 he published *The Other America*, a book that became a best-seller and brought him a measure of fame. It challenged the conventional wisdom that the nation's post–World War II prosperity left hardly any Americans in poverty. In the book Harrington revealed that almost one-third of all Americans lived "below those standards which we have been taught to regard as the decent minimums for food, housing, clothing and health." He told stories that humanized the poor as people trapped in difficult conditions not of their own making. He described them living in slum housing, suffering with chronic pain because they could not afford to see a doctor, and often going without enough food for themselves or their children.

"The fate of the poor," Harrington concluded, "hangs upon the decision of the better-off. If this anger and shame are not forthcoming, someone can write a book about the other America a generation from now and it will be the same or worse." He added, "Until these facts shame us, until they stir us to action, the other America will continue to exist, a monstrous example of needless suffering in the most advanced society in the world." Harrington was soon in great demand as a speaker on college campuses, at union halls, and before religious congregations. He appeared often on television.[13]

But the word *socialism* did not appear in *The Other America*. Harrington aimed to tug at people's consciences and urge them to take action. He argued that poverty was caused and perpetuated by institutions and public policies, not by individuals' own faults. But he did not maintain that it was caused by capitalism or that socialism would abolish it. The solution, he wrote, was full employment, more funding for housing and health care, and better schools and job training.

The popularity of the book gave Harrington a national platform to talk about democratic socialism as well as poverty. He mesmerized audiences, especially on college campuses, with eloquent, funny, and morally uplifting lectures. He also functioned as a talent scout, recruiting young activists and plugging them into different movement activities. When he talked about democratic socialism, he made it sound like common sense—rational, practical, and moral at the same time.

In 1964 Sargent Shriver, one of President Lyndon Johnson's closest advisers, invited Harrington to help design a new initiative called the War on Poverty. Harrington coauthored a background paper in which he argued that "if there is any single dominant problem of poverty in the U.S., it is that of unemployment." The remedy was a massive public-works initiative similar to the New Deal's WPA and Civilian Conservation Corps (CCC). Harrington disagreed with Johnson, who did not want to spend the money that such a program would cost, especially while he was escalating the war in Vietnam. Harrington's stint as a government adviser lasted only about a month. But with programs like Head Start and SNAP (which provides food stamps) and Medicaid, the poverty rate did decline, and even Americans who stayed poor had access to food, health care, and aid in preparing their children for formal schooling.[14]

Since the Great Recession of 2008–2009, socialism has staged something of a revival in the United States. The leading organization with that name, Democratic Socialists of America (DSA), which Michael Harrington helped found back in 1982, has increased its membership tenfold to close to 100,000. Bernie Sanders, the Vermont senator who has long described himself as a socialist, ran two competitive campaigns for the Democratic presidential nomination. In 2021 he became chair of the powerful Budget Committee. In public opinion polls, over two-fifths of Americans say they have a positive opinion of socialism; a majority of younger Americans feel that way. After the election of 2020, some 101 DSA members held office around the country, all in progressive districts and cities. Four were members of Congress, double the number the old Socialist Party was able to elect a century before.[15]

That nearly all these officials ran as Democrats shows they are not bent, as their adversaries on the Right allege, on a revolutionary overthrow of the capitalist system. Like most of their predecessors, they dream of a far more egalitarian society but fight for realistic goals such as Medicare for All and an economy that would run on renewable sources of energy. As Harrington liked to tell audiences, "You must recognize that the social vision to which you are committing yourself will never be fulfilled in your lifetime." So his ideological progeny work zealously to improve the country for the living. Would that it were the actual goal of every American politician.[16]

9

THE MAGIC OF THE MARKETPLACE

Naomi Oreskes and Erik M. Conway

CLIMATE CHANGE IS A MARKET FAILURE—PERHAPS THE "BIGGEST market failure the world has seen."[1] But as great a market failure as it is, it is by no means the only one. Many of America's most serious problems—the opioid crisis, the lack of affordable housing in major American cities, the epidemic of obesity, gun violence, the disease burden of toxic chemicals, and, arguably, COVID-19—are market failures of one kind or another. So is the persistence of tobacco use, which annually kills eight million people around the globe, and air pollution, which annually kills seven million.

Many of these problems could be addressed by appropriate government regulation and reshaping of markets. For example, the greenhouse-gas emissions that drive anthropogenic climate change could be reduced through a "Pigouvian tax"—in lay terms, putting a price on carbon. Other problems could be addressed through better regulation—of guns, chemicals, fast food, cigarettes—or public investment in alternatives, such as housing, renewable energy, and public health. History demonstrates that solutions of these kinds can work. Tobacco use in the United States was greatly reduced by a combination of bans on smoking in public places, taxes on tobacco products, and health education; the stratospheric ozone layer was protected by banning the chemicals that were causing its demise.[2]

Yet conservative politicians, business executives, libertarian think tanks, and millions of ordinary Americans resist these solutions, clinging to the notion that the best way to solve our problems is through the workings of the marketplace. They suggest that the private sector can handle these matters and that any government action is likely to fail, perhaps making things worse than they already are. They adhere to the notion, as Ronald Reagan famously put it, that "government is not the solution to our problems, government is the problem." Some even go so far as to state that it is reasonable to *worship* markets, a perspective famously encapsulated by Reagan when he declared that what united the world's prosperous nations was "their belief in the magic of the marketplace."[3]

Where did the belief in the magic of the marketplace come from? Certainly not Adam Smith, the eighteenth-century economist whom those same conservatives consider to be the founding father of capitalism. Smith recognized the need for taxation, for government provision of public goods, and for regulation in cases where self-interest failed to serve the greater good. Why then have so many educated people accepted the assertion of market omnipotence, even in the face of overwhelming evidence of market failure and the obvious limits of self-interest? How were millions of Americans persuaded to accept the myth that markets are magic?[4]

Market fundamentalism is not restricted to the United States, but that is where it finds its fullest expression and most wide-ranging support. This is not historical contingency. Rather, it is the result of a decades-long propaganda campaign to persuade the American people of the efficacy and benevolence of markets, the inefficacy and malevolence of "big government," and the centrality of economic freedom in American life.

In this essay we focus on the American businessmen in the mid-twentieth century who worked to lay the foundations for that myth by insisting that economic freedom has been as central to the fabric of the American nation as political and civic freedom, that markets underwrite that freedom, and that any economic constraint on business is a threat to freedom overall. The truth is that American governments have always been involved in managing and at times even directing the economic life of the nation, and economic freedom does not guarantee political freedom. The myth of the magic of the marketplace was invented to defend the prerogatives of business leaders while denying many prerogatives of workers and consumers. It centered on a false claim about the historic significance of "free enterprise."

Founded in 1895, by the early 1930s the National Association of Manufacturers (NAM) had a history of fighting business regulation by state or federal governments, and fighting unionization.[5] It had had some success, but the Great Depression threatened to undermine its efforts, for it seemed to prove once and for all that unsupervised markets not only did not protect us from evils like child labor, workplace injury, and starvation wages; they didn't even protect prosperity.

In response, NAM envisaged a bigger, broader, and more aggressive role for itself: not just defending business interests in matters of direct concern but also providing a broad-ranging voice in public debate. In the words of Wendy Wall, NAM "tried to convince the American public that their interests and those of the nation's largest corporations were virtually indistinguishable."[6] But it went further. NAM sought to change the way the American people viewed business, government, and, above all, American history, by promoting a historical narrative about the centrality of "free enterprise."

At its 1939 annual convention, NAM issued a declaration of principles premised on the concept of "inseparability," sometimes also called "indivisibility." In a letter to libertarian journalist Rose Wilder Lane in December 1948, NAM board member and president of Sun Oil Company J. Howard Pew explained:

I . . . am an ardent supporter of freedom, and all that it comprehends—religious freedom, political freedom, industrial freedom, freedom of speech, of the press and of assembly, and I might add freedom of choice,

which is probably the most important of them all. I believe, too, that freedom is indivisible; when a part is taken away, that which remains is no
longer freedom. . . . Suppose we should lose our industrial freedom; then
it would require a compulsory form of government in order to enforce the
decrees having to do with the conduct of industry, and a compulsory state
can brook no freedoms.[7]

Pew's indivisibility thesis was a restatement of Herbert Hoover's claim
that there could be no freedom of any kind where there was not also economic freedom; Pew's example of industrial freedom was not incidental.
From the early twentieth-century defense of child labor to the mid-century attacks on the New Deal, American business leaders had argued that
any compromise to business freedom threatened the fabric of American
social and political freedom and therefore the American way of life. Constitutional representative democracy, free enterprise, and civil and religious liberty were "inseparable fundamentals of freedom to be cherished
and preserved."[8]

The 1939 declaration of principles was embedded into NAM's "Tripod of Freedom" campaign, launched in 1940 by NAM president
H. W. Prentis. American democracy, he asserted, was founded on three
legs: (1) free speech, free press, and free religion; (2) representative government; and (3) Free Enterprise (the latter made into a proper noun). If
any leg were compromised, the argument went, the entire tripod would
collapse.[9] The implication was that any prominent government role in
the marketplace was a departure from American history and that the
founding fathers had valorized economic freedom as equal to the other
legs of the tripod. Neither of these claims was true.

Corporations were originally products of the state. Throughout the
first half of the nineteenth century, state governments had used the right
to charter corporations as means to influence, direct, and even control
the private sector. Gary Gerstle quotes fellow historian Louis Hartz explaining that in the early history of the republic, "state governments had
'assumed the job of shaping decisively the contours of economic life.'"[10]
In particular, city and state governments and the federal government had
authorized and helped finance internal transportation improvements such

as canals, roads, and railroads as a means to foster growth. By the early 1840s, New York State had constructed more than six hundred miles of canals at a cost of more than $50 million.[11]

Slavery of course refuted the NAM claim that America had been built on free enterprise and respect for the rights of individuals. It wasn't merely that individual plantation owners had insisted that it was their right to buy and sell other human beings—who had no say in the matter and therefore, obviously, no freedom—but also that government had insisted that it was its prerogative to sanction (or prohibit) this form of business, no less than the building of the Erie Canal. One can easily multiply examples: the development of the "American System of Manufactures," the creation of the intercontinental railroads, and of course the expropriation of Native American lands were examples of major, consequential government action in the marketplace, as was the widespread use of trade tariffs to protect American industry against foreign competition.[12] The idea that twentieth-century government involvement in the marketplace was a departure from American history was false.

Equally false was the elevation of free enterprise to parity with the First Amendment guarantees of free speech, a free press, and freedom of religion. "At the core of [our] strategy," Pew professed, "has been the idea of establishing free enterprise where it rightfully belongs, as one of the three great elements (along with the civil liberties of free speech, free press, and religious freedom, and the representative form of democratic governments) which go up to make the American way of life."[13] This was at best misleading: *free enterprise* appears nowhere in the Bill of Rights. Larry Glickman has shown that the phrase *system of free enterprise* was not even coined until 1919.[14] Free speech, freedom of religion, and representative government were guaranteed to the American people in the Constitution; free enterprise was not. NAM was transmogrifying a self-serving argument for protecting business privilege into a seemingly virtuous defense of American freedom.

Although NAM characterized its activities as "education," it was in fact building a myth. And the myth began to take hold. A survey early in 1941 found that 71 percent of respondents believed that "the disappearance of the free-enterprise system would be harmful to their personal liberty." By late 1941, NAM's polling showed that the majority of Americans believed that industry was the entity that could best protect Americans against the threats posed by the conflicts overseas.[15]

Still, most Americans in the early 1940s supported New Deal reforms intended to supervise the marketplace, protect workers from unfair labor practices, safeguard investors from dubious financial practices, bring electricity to rural America, and get America back to work—all reforms that NAM opposed. As Wall has noted, in the face of the Great Depression the "narrative of capitalist-driven growth" seemed "questionable at best, a monstrous delusion at worst."[16] It was a bit rich for the captains of industry to insist that businessmen knew what was best for the country when that argument had in living memory so conspicuously failed. Moreover, as Eric Rauchway shows in this volume, the New Deal had largely *worked*.

For Pew and his allies, this was a serious problem. How could they persuade the American people to accept a view that available evidence refuted? In the mid-1940s they found their answer in the work of two Austrian economists: Ludwig von Mises and Friedrich von Hayek.

NAM often insisted that socialism and communism were foreign theories—alien to the American way of life—but in the 1940s it imported foreign theorists to promote the primacy of economic freedom in the United States. Those theorists were the neoliberal economists Mises and Hayek, famous for their defense of free markets and the belief that any compromise to economic freedom would necessarily lead to compromises to political freedom and from there to totalitarian tyranny.

Hayek is best known today as a conservative hero. His most famous book, *The Road to Serfdom* (first published in 1944), has been touted by right-wing Americans from Glenn Beck and Rush Limbaugh to Paul Ryan and Ted Cruz. President George H. W. Bush—who granted Hayek the Presidential Medal of Freedom in 1991—once called *The Road to Serfdom* a book that "still thrills readers everywhere."[17] Few Americans know that his position and influence—along with that of his mentor, the Austrian economist Mises—was secured by powerful businessmen linked to NAM.

Ludwig von Mises was a strident free-market absolutist who sympathized with Austrian fascism, opposed laws restricting child labor, and doubted the virtues of public education.[18] By the 1940s, his views were taken by most economists to be (at best) out of step, and when he fled Europe he had trouble finding work in the United States. But his career and influence were salvaged by acolytes in the American business world. They included Henry Hazlitt, an editorial writer for the *New York Times* and a fierce opponent of the New Deal, and Leonard Read, the president of the Foundation for Economic Education. (FEE had been founded in 1946 to promote the idea that a free society hinges on free enterprise.)[19]

Hazlitt introduced Mises to NAM, where he worked closely with Noel Sargent, the principal architect of the 1930s NAM propaganda campaign. Hazlitt and Read also joined forces with Lawrence Fertig—an advertising executive, journalist, and later a trustee of New York University—to arrange for Mises to lecture at the NYU Graduate School of Business Administration at their expense. And in 1949, Kansas City businessman Harold Luhnow, director of the libertarian William Volker Fund, provided the salary for Mises to continue to teach at NYU as a "visiting professor," where he would profess his neoliberal views for the next three decades.[20]

Hayek was Mises's most influential student. Hayek (like Mises) was trained as an economist, but the central argument of *The Road to Serfdom* is not an economic one. It is a political one: that capitalism and freedom are linked, and if we wish to preserve political freedom, we must preserve economic freedom as well. Conversely, if we abandon our economic freedom to centralized planning, whether in the name of fairness, efficiency, equality, or equity, it is only a matter of time before we will lose our political freedom, too. Despite the best of intentions of even its most benevolent exponents, Hayek argued, socialism must inevitably lead to totalitarianism. Socialism is therefore not just irrational; it is dangerous. "The unforeseen but inevitable consequences of socialist planning create a state of affairs in which, if the policy is to be pursued," Hayek wrote in an oft-quoted passage, "totalitarian forces will get the upper hand."[21] Hayek's argument *is* the indivisibility thesis: political freedom and economic freedom cannot be decoupled.

The appeal of Hayek's central argument to men like J. Howard Pew is obvious: it offered a principled defense of the position they already held. Not surprisingly, Pew and his colleagues were thrilled. What in the hands of NAM had looked like a raw defense of ruthless self-interest, in the hands of Hayek became a principled case for the benefits of government restraint.[22]

Pew and his allies took steps to promote both the book and its author in the United States. The key figures in this work were Harold Luhnow and his colleague Jasper Crane. The latter was a former DuPont executive who had been closely associated with NAM in its fight against the New Deal, but by 1945 had become disenchanted, finding NAM insufficiently ambitious. Crane was also a FEE trustee and, like Leonard Read, believed that NAM businessmen focused too much on the details of commerce and not enough on a larger vision of the society they wanted to build and sustain. They were also too willing to compromise. The battle for a free society, Crane argued, needed to be carried forward by "a cadre of intellectuals and businessmen that would be absolutely committed to the market."[23]

Luhnow had already paid for Hayek to come to the United States on a five-week book tour; now he and Crane decided to bring Hayek to America permanently and to find a way to get his message to the masses.[24]

They faced two problems, however. The first was that no prominent American university wanted to hire Hayek. Therefore, as they did for Mises, they found one that would, in part by their promising to pay Hayek's salary. Luhnow met personally with University of Chicago president Robert Maynard Hutchins and offered $150,000—$15,000 per year for ten years—to cover Hayek's cost. Hutchins agreed, and Hayek was appointed in 1950 (although as a professor on the Committee on Social Thought, not in the Department of Economics, which still did not want him).[25]

The second problem was that *The Road to Serfdom* was a nuanced and qualified book. For example, Hayek explicitly rejected *laissez-faire* and recognized the warrant for social insurance and government regulation of hazards such as pollution and deforestation. He was *not* suggesting that governments should do nothing and let the world unfold without regard to consequence. Indeed, the critique of government "interference" in the marketplace did not make sense, he insisted, because governments would always be involved to some extent: "The question whether the state should or should not 'act' or 'interfere' poses an altogether false alternative, and the term 'laissez faire' is a . . . misleading description of the principles on which a liberal policy is based. Of course, every state must act and every action of the state interferes with something or the other."[26]

This formulation yielded considerable ground to the critics of unregulated capitalism, so Crane, Luhnow, and their allies worked to create an unmistakable statement of the book's thesis. In 1945 *Reader's Digest* published a twenty-page version, and *LOOK* published an actual cartoon version the same year. General Motors distributed it to its employees.[27] These transmogrified Hayek's qualified argument about the risks of governmental control into an unqualified antigovernment polemic.

This was a start, but what was really needed, Crane and Luhnow believed, was a single book, accessible to American audiences, encapsulating the key ideas connecting capitalism and freedom. Communists had *Das Kapital*, Nazis had *Mein Kampf*, but market fundamentalists lacked their epitome. Luhnow now took steps to establish the "Free Market Project" at the University of Chicago. The successful outcome of the project would be not just a book, but *the* book that would become "The New Testament of capitalism."[28] It would be the bible of market fundamentalism. This, in turn, would enable conservatives to change the American social contract and build a society that valorized and protected economic freedom above other considerations. Although Luhnow and Crane hated Marx, they believed—as he did—that the point of philosophy was not to study the world but to change it. Under their guidance and financing, the Free Market Project would produce a manifesto to move society in the spirit of Marx but in the opposite direction.

Despite their alleged belief that competition was required to yield optimal results, there would be no competition in staffing the Free Market Project. To ensure that the message would not be mixed—as academic messages often were—they would hire men who would not step out of "character as a libertarian." One of these men was Milton Friedman. In 1962 Luhnow and Crane finally got their bible of market fundamentalism.[29] It was Friedman's *Capitalism and Freedom*.

In the original preface to *Capitalism and Freedom*, Friedman implies that his connection to Luhnow and the Volker Fund was more or less incidental, saying that the book was based on a set of lectures he gave in 1956 at a Volker-funded conference in Indiana and some miscellaneous lectures he gave at Volker conferences at Claremont College, the University of North Carolina, and Oklahoma State.[30] In the book's first chapter, however, Friedman not only acknowledges but celebrates the role of rich men's money in advancing his own work.

In a socialist society (Friedman alleges), dissenting views are crushed, but in a capitalist society anyone with money can freely promote his views. Wealthy individuals can support whatever ideas suit them—including outlier ones—and influence society. But rather than see this as a problem requiring redress, Friedman sees this as a virtue. In a capitalist society, "it is only necessary to convince a few wealthy people to get funds to launch any idea, however strange." In this manner, "a free market capitalist society fosters freedom."[31]

It's an old socialist joke that capitalist societies run on the golden rule: he who has the gold makes the rules. What Friedman not only added but defended was that the man with the gold could pay clever people—like himself—to offer the best defense of those rules that they could muster, a resource not available to the poor and middle class.

Hayek had recognized this problem in 1956, when he explained why he did not consider himself a conservative: "A conservative movement, by its very nature, is bound to be a defender of established privilege and to lean on the power of government for the protection of privilege."[32] In Friedman's vision, anyone could be a benefactor to men of ideas, but in practice only the wealthy were positioned to do so. In this and many other ways that Friedman would rarely acknowledge, the rich are a good deal freer than the poor: philanthropy is not a level playing field, and free speech is not free.

Of course, Luhnow didn't *pay* Friedman to hold the views he did. Mises, Hayek, and Friedman were not bought; patronage doesn't generally work that way.[33] It's rather that patrons find people whose views they like and then succor and sustain them. It's a form of unnatural selection, an environment in which the rich can select the ideas they want and ensure their survival and propagation. And that is exactly what, for thirty years, these American businessmen did.

Capitalism and Freedom was hugely successful. First published in 1962, the book would sell more than half a million copies, see numerous editions, and be translated into eighteen languages. Above all, it would be accessible to just the audience that Luhnow and Crane had envisaged. The Foundation for Economic Education has described it as "much more accessible to intelligent undergraduates than Hayek's, which was intentionally addressed to intellectuals." Friedman, they suggest, was "the best communicator of the political-economic ideas of the classical liberal tradition of the last century." The book was just what the patrons of the Free Market Project had imagined: a capitalist manifesto that insisted that "the great threat to freedom is the concentration of power" in government, that government must stay out of economic affairs, and that unrestrained capitalism was the only system that could protect freedom.[34]

Not surprisingly, given its heritage, the central argument of *Capitalism and Freedom* is the indivisibility thesis: the inextricable link between capitalism and freedom, and, conversely, between socialism and freedom's negation. But Friedman's version is much more doctrinaire than Hayek's was. It has all of Hayek's confidence with few of his caveats.

In 1977 Friedman began working on a televised version of *Capitalism and Freedom*, *Free to Choose*, which aired on PBS starting in 1980. The project was a giant success. Its first episode, *"Power of the Market,"* recorded at the University of Chicago, garnered fifteen million viewers. It boosted the revised edition of *Capitalism and Freedom* to number-one nonfiction book of the year.[35] That same year, Ronald Reagan would reduce the myth to a sound bite. At the annual Mises lecture at Hillsdale College, in Michigan, he demanded: "Will we, before it is too late, use the vitality and the magic of the marketplace to save this way of life, or will we one day face our children, and our children's children, when they ask us where we were and what we were doing on the day that freedom was lost?"[36] Markets were no longer just an efficient means to deliver goods and services; they were the underwriter of American freedom. The construction of the myth of the magic of the marketplace was now complete.

And, as we have shown, it *was* a myth. NAM's portrayal of American history had always been a half truth at best, and even in the 1940s there was good reason to conclude that Mises's, Hayek's, and Friedman's claims were overblown. By the 1960s, the reforms of the New Deal and the experiences of European social democracy had proved that governments could both act assertively in marketplaces and strengthen social safety nets without undermining democratic governance. By the end of the century, it was clear that the central premise of the myth was just plain wrong.

From 1973 to 1990, Chilean dictator Augusto Pinochet implemented pro-market reforms advised by Friedman and a group of his acolytes known as the "Chicago boys," while overseeing a totalitarian political system in which opponents were systematically kidnapped, tortured, and murdered. In China, after the death of Mao Tse-tung in 1976, a new system emerged—sometimes called "market authoritarianism"—in which economic liberalization went hand in hand with continued political oppression; something similar happened in Russia after the collapse of Soviet communism.[37] In America, decades of neoliberal policies have made many people *less* free as they struggle to stay afloat financially or remain healthy in the face of the opioid crisis and the COVID-19 pandemic.

Anatole France once famously said that "the law in its majestic equality forbids rich and poor alike from sleeping under bridges, begging in the streets, and stealing loaves of bread."[38] Economic freedom makes some people rich and enhances their freedom, to be sure. But it leaves others sleeping under bridges. Political and economic freedom are not indivisible, and markets are not magic.

10

THE NEW DEAL

Eric Rauchway

On March 5, 2019, Senator Charles Grassley, Republican of Iowa, offered a history lesson to his fellow legislators: "The New Deal in the 1930's didn't work," he said. "It didn't get us out of the Great Depression. The Depression didn't end until we entered World War II." Grassley's concern was not scholarly; he was arguing against his Democratic colleagues' proposal for a Green New Deal. But, Grassley warned, any kind of new New Deal could only, "like the original . . . dampen economic growth and will hurt jobs."[1]

Not long afterward, a journalist asked a group of historians to evaluate the senator's scholarship. On a scale running from "All bunk" to "True as it gets," Grassley's history earned marks near the bottom; the most generous academic rated the senator's analysis "more or less false."[2]

Yet Grassley is not the only one who says this sort of thing; you may commonly hear similar claims. About ten years before Grassley's speech, the senator's fellow Iowa Republican, Representative Steve King, argued that the New Deal "broadened and, perhaps, deepened the trough the Great Depression was in."[3] Like Grassley, King was using the myth of the New Deal's failure for political purposes. Grassley wanted to forestall a Green New Deal; King wanted to forestall a New Deal–style response to the 2008 recession—particularly, large-scale public-works programs and other federal measures to relieve unemployment.

Myths have consequences, and insofar as people like Grassley and King have used the myth of the New Deal's failure to prevent or diminish effective policy responses to economic and climate crises of the twenty-first century, this myth may turn out to be the most consequentially pernicious and indeed catastrophic in all of human history.

You may wonder if claiming that the New Deal failed really qualifies as a myth. Unlike some of the myths in this collection—the vanishing Native American, for example, or the absent US empire—the New Deal's failure is not a tale tightly woven into the national story. It is not enshrined in public monuments or an integral part of American patriotism. Rather, politicians revive it to justify opposing specific policies, and it otherwise falls dormant. So perhaps *myth* seems an inappropriate term for the tale that the New Deal failed. Maybe another would suit it better. There are many analytical categories of falsehood; in this essay we will see how a few of them contribute to the creation of myth.

Possibly the historians surveyed about Grassley's remarks were asked the wrong question—that is, whether his account of the New Deal was true. Maybe, as the philosopher Harry Frankfurt says of statements like the senator's, Grassley's disquisition was "produced without concern for the truth." An honest person tries to tell the truth; a dishonest person tries to conceal it. The senator was attempting neither. He was misrepresenting *something*, but that thing was not primarily the history of the New Deal. Rather, Grassley was misrepresenting his own attitude toward history; it was useful to him to appear to care about history, even though he did not. To borrow further from Frankfurt's description, "He does not care whether the things he says describe reality correctly. He just picks them out, or makes them up, to suit his purpose." Frankfurt supplies a technical term for statements uttered to misrepresent oneself, without regard for their apparent substance: they are properly known as "bullshit."[4] And bullshit like Grassley's serves a vital function. It allows people to oppose evidently well-intentioned legislation out of an apparent—although nonexistent—concern for the lessons of history.

This use elevates the story of the New Deal's failure from ordinary bullshit to the standing of myth. As the anthropologist Claude Lévi-Strauss explains, to the historian the past is past, even if its "remote consequences . . . may still be felt at present." But to a "politician, as well as to his followers," the history of an event like the New Deal "is both a sequence belonging to the past . . . and an everlasting pattern which can be detected in the present."[5] This abuse of history, Lévi-Strauss observes, serves the function of myth. The New Deal has occupied this mythical category since before its enactment. In December 1932 Herbert Hoover told an aide that his own opposition to the New Deal was part of just such an everlasting pattern as Lévi-Strauss describes: "In all history there had been contest [sic] between the nationalists and what we now call 'bolsheviks.' . . . It existed thousands of years ago in Egypt."[6] Hoover's conviction that the New Deal could not work preceded the myth that it did not work, and the latter was necessary to support the allegedly timeless truth of the former.

Setting myths momentarily aside, suppose that you actually wanted to know whether the New Deal worked according to Grassley's two criteria: Did it "dampen economic growth" and "hurt jobs"? You could start your investigation by going to the library or even doing a responsible internet search. The dates of US business cycles, as determined by the Business Cycle Dating Committee of the National Bureau of Economic Research (NBER), appear on the NBER website and also in the current edition of a standard reference work, *Historical Statistics of the United States*. A chart plotting these dates atop a monthly series showing economic activity, the index of industrial production, appears in Figure 1.

As you can see, the decade after the Great War featured four periods of expansion (the unshaded portions of the graph), each lasting around two years, with three intervening periods of contraction (the shaded portions of the graph), each lasting somewhat more than a year. Together, each expansion and contraction makes up a business cycle. But then we see an

Figure 1: US Index of Industrial Production and Business Cycles
1919–1945

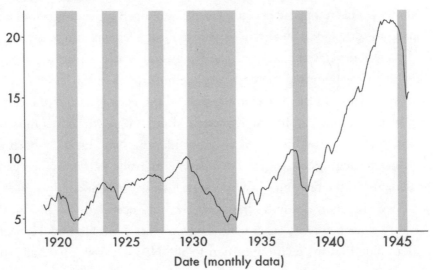

Data from Susan B. Carter, et al., eds., *Historical Statistics of the United States,*
Millennial Edition (hereafter HSUS), Table Cb5-8 and series Cb31

anomaly: almost four straight years of contraction—nearly all of Hoover's presidency. This great slump ended in March 1933, with Roosevelt's first inauguration. Afterward came a period of recovery lasting slightly more than four years, followed by a downturn of similar length to previous ones—thirteen months—then a resumption of expansion lasting nearly seven years, almost to the end of Roosevelt's presidency. This second, longer period of expansion included mobilization for war and war itself. But the first fifty months of expansion coincided with the introduction and operation of the New Deal's recovery measures.[7]

Not only did the US economy begin to grow during the New Deal; it grew rapidly. As the economist Gauti B. Eggertsson writes,

Indicators rebounded strongly once Roosevelt took office. The stock market . . . increased by 66 percent in Roosevelt's first 100 days and commodity prices skyrocketed. Similarly, investment nearly doubled in 1933 with the turnaround. . . . Roosevelt's inauguration also marked a turning point in monthly industrial production, which bottomed out in March 1933 after falling for three consecutive years. . . . Hoover's . . . term resulted in 26 percent deflation, while Roosevelt's first [term] registered 13 percent in-flation. Similarly, output declined 30 percent from 1929 to 1933. This was the worst depression in US history. In contrast, 1933–1937 registered the strongest output growth (39 percent) of any four-year period in US history outside of wartime.[8]

The economist Christina D. Romer likewise writes that "these rates of growth are spectacular, even for an economy pulling out of a severe depression."[9]

A plot of US real GDP appears in Figure 2. You can easily see the col-lapse and recovery. The data plainly show that if we wanted truthfully to describe what happened to the US economy during these years, we would say that a downturn began in 1929 and continued until Roosevelt's inau-guration, whereupon a speedy recovery began and continued—interrupted by a recession in 1937–1938—until war mobilization began. Afterward, economic growth continued powerfully until the end of the war.

We cannot necessarily say, based on this information, that the New Deal promoted this recovery. But we *can* say that even if—to use Grass-ley's phrase—the New Deal dampened economic growth, it did not

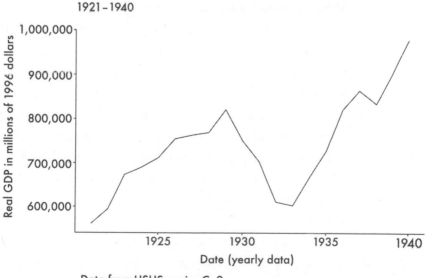

Figure 2: US Real Gross Domestic Product
1921–1940

Data from HSUS, series Ca9

dampen it sufficiently to prevent an extraordinarily rapid rate of recovery from the Great Depression. This observation means that if you consider the benefits of the New Deal—among them, saving Americans from starvation and idleness; rescuing banks and the currency; bringing electricity to people who never had it; building a national road network; controlling flooding; eradicating diseases in much of the nation; and establishing the right to join a union, secure an old-age pension, obtain unemployment insurance, and earn a minimum wage; and in doing so, renewing Americans' faith in democracy because they could see that their government would work for them and attend to their needs—then you can say Americans were able to enjoy all those gains without forgoing a robust economic recovery. Even if one wished, by contrast, to condemn those innovations as an un-American, socialistic drag on the economy; even if, like Hoover, one saw these changes not as gains but as a program to "break down the enterprise and initiative of the American people" and to embrace "the negation of the ideals upon which our civilization has been based"—even then, an honest person would have to acknowledge that the wholesale wrecking of enterprise and equality of opportunity and the rejection of American ideals did not prevent a rapid economic recovery during the New Deal.[10] That is the least one can truthfully say about the New Deal: even if it was terrible, it did not stop a speedy economic recovery.

Moreover, there are reasons to believe that New Deal policies *did* encourage recovery. Stabilizing the banks and inducing inflationary expectations stopped hoarding and encouraged spending. Wages from public-works jobs allowed people to buy more goods, increasing demand.[11]

Furthermore, Americans in the 1930s realized the New Deal improved their economic situation. Roosevelt won reelection in a record landslide in 1936, with 60.8 percent of the popular vote and an Electoral College tally of 523–8. His 1932 victory represented hope for what the New Deal might do; the 1936 victory represented endorsement of what the New Deal had done. Many voters—notably, African Americans—switched to the Democratic Party based on the New Deal's success.[12] Christopher H. Achen and Larry M. Bartels find that voters' endorsement of the New Deal owed to economic growth; the more that personal income rose for a given state in 1936, the larger the increase in Roosevelt's vote share.[13]

Many Americans who lived through those years remembered them that way. Robert Wood, the president of Sears, told the oral historian Studs Terkel that "things began to pick up around '34 and '35. It was '36 before they began to pick up strong. . . . The Depression ended in '33. But it didn't begin to recover on a big scale until '36."[14]

Yet others, including Terkel himself, seemed to ignore the testimony of Wood and instead concluded that World War II, not the New Deal, healed the economic wounds of the Great Depression. "True," Terkel writes, "the New Deal had created jobs and restored self-esteem for millions of Americans. Still, there were ten, eleven million walking the streets, riding the rods, up against it, despairing. All this changed under the lowering sky of World War Two."[15] Terkel's assessment is not Grassley's—the senator had nothing to say about the New Deal's creating millions of jobs or restoring self-esteem. And Terkel's remarks contain some truth: unemployment had not fully recovered by the time World War II began. But that does not mean the New Deal "hurt jobs," as Grassley claimed.

If you want to know about employment during the New Deal, you could turn again to the current edition of *Historical Statistics of the United States*. Although modern unemployment accounting did not begin until later, economic historians have made retrospective estimates for the 1930s. Some of them appear in Figure 3.

The top measure represents unemployment as a percentage of the civilian labor force. It is similar to a common modern measure of unemployment. As you can see, this rate shoots up beginning in 1929, peaks in 1932, and falls during the New Deal, with the exception—in a mirror image of Figure 2—of the 1937–1938 recession.

The middle chart, also from the current edition of *Historical Statistics of the United States*, takes agriculture and government out of the data and shows the civilian, private, nonfarm unemployment rate, which demonstrates a similar pattern.

The bottom graph shows numbers you will not find in the current edition of *Historical Statistics of the United States*, only in the older edition. It too shows a sharp rise in unemployment after the 1929 crash, and a fall during the New Deal, but the fall is more gradual. The reason

Figure 3: US Jobless Measures
1921–1940

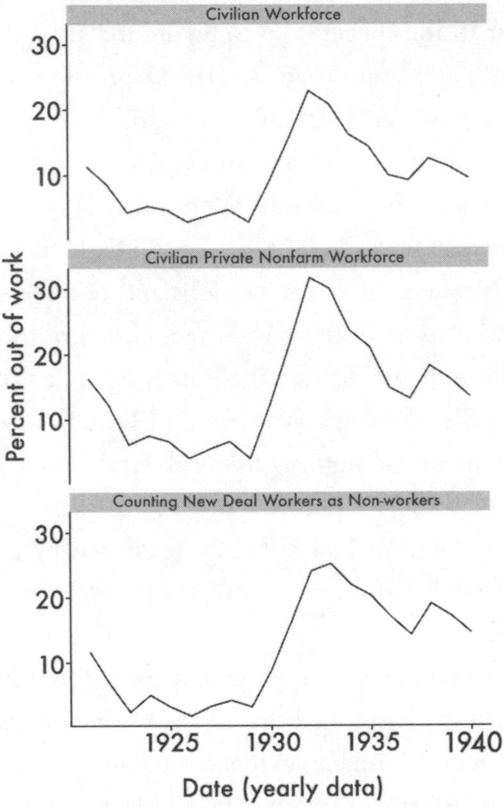

Date (yearly data)

Data from HSUS series Ba475 and Ba476;
Historical Statistics of the United States,
Bicentennial Edition, series D9

for unemployment falling less sharply on this graph is both simple and frankly political: this older data series counts New Deal workers as unemployed. The economist Stanley Lebergott, who composed this series, explained his reasoning as follows: "In the United States we are concerned with measuring lack of regular work and do not minimize the total by excluding persons with made work or emergency jobs. This contrasts sharply, for example, with the German practice during the 1930s when persons in the labor-force camps were classed as employed."[16]

It's not clear if Lebergott was comparing New Deal workers to the inmates of forced-labor camps like Mauthausen, whose imprisoned workers toiled in quarries in exchange for such privileges as access to an on-site brothel, or if he was referring to the Reichsarbeitsdienst (RAD), a compulsory labor service designed to cultivate loyalty to the Nazi Party among ethnic Germans. In either case he is using apparently neutral numbers to hide a profoundly political point by likening Nazi labor programs to New Deal public-works jobs.[17] The two were nothing alike. Most Americans employed by the New Deal worked for the Works Progress Administration (WPA). Unlike Nazi programs, the WPA was purely voluntary. The WPA paid a security wage; some of its workers unionized and even went on strike. It was prohibited by law from discriminating on the basis of race.[18] It did useful work, especially on roads; as one economic historian concludes, WPA work "literally helped pave the way for the postwar suburbanization boom."[19] WPA workers understood they were employed.[20] "We WPA workers want to work and be treated as workers," as one said.[21] To count them as unemployed and the equivalent of Nazi laborers, as Lebergott did, is indefensible, which is why the *Historical Statistics of the United States* stopped doing so in its 2006 edition, following three decades of careful scholarship on the subject.[22]

If someone now uses the older series without a strong explanation why, they either have not done due diligence or they want to score political points. It's unfortunately easy to be careless: the old version of *Historical Statistics* is freely available online because it was a government publication, while the current edition was outsourced to Cambridge University Press and can therefore be accessed only for a fee, usually through a research library. Worse, scholars often pull figures from old books without checking the underlying data. As the scholar Ole Bjørn Rekdal writes, relying on secondary sources in this manner propagates "academic urban legends."[23] But occasionally a writer will knowingly use the deceptive data for no substantive reason, as when Amity Shlaes justifies use of Lebergott's numbers because they are "traditional."[24]

Still, an honest person consulting even the old data must acknowledge that employment improved significantly under the New Deal. As David M. Kennedy says, looking at Lebergott's numbers, "The FDR administration managed to knock the unemployment rate down from 25% in 1932 to about 14% in 1936—a pretty impressive counter-punch to the greatest economic shock in modern history."[25] Writers who want to avoid

Kennedy's observation can, of course, go beyond myth or bullshit and resort to other forms of falsehood.

Consider this assertion from a *Wall Street Journal* column of 2008: "As late as 1938, after almost a decade of governmental 'pump priming,' almost one out of five workers remained unemployed," calling the 1930s "a lost decade of economic growth" (a statement we already know to be untrue) and blaming New Deal policies for this unfortunate outcome.[26] The writer is, like Kennedy, referring to Lebergott's numbers, which put unemployment at about 19 percent in 1938, rather than the revised series, which puts it at about 12.5 percent. But he reaches the opposite conclusion to Kennedy. How? Look at the bottom of Figure 3: for a start, the writer is cherry-picking, choosing the recession year to report the effects of New Deal policies. But he is doing more: by saying "as late as 1938" the unemployment rate "remained" nearly 20 percent, he is engaged in another kind of deception, which Harry Frankfurt also analyzed.

As Frankfurt writes, "An act with a sharp focus . . . designed to insert a particular falsehood at a specific point in a set or system of beliefs, in order to avoid the consequences of having that point occupied by the truth," is called "telling a lie."[27] In this case the writer could truthfully state, like Kennedy, that the New Deal at least coincided with, if it did not cause, substantial jobs growth. Instead, the writer substitutes the concept that "as late as 1938" the unemployment rate "remained" nearly as high as it was at the start of Roosevelt's presidency. If we use Frankfurt's definition, this is a lie.

To help understand why, consider the similar (made up for this purpose) assertion that Grover Cleveland first became president in 1885 and that *as late as* 1896, he *remained* president, thus creating a "lost decade" of the Cleveland presidency. This is plainly a lie: it is framed deliberately to conceal some historically important not-presidenting that occurred to Grover Cleveland from 1889 to 1893, between his two nonconsecutive terms in office. Likewise, the *Wall Street Journal* column contains what Frankfurt defines as a lie: an assertion framed to assert the continuity of economic catastrophe through the 1930s and to conceal the powerful recovery that occurred during Roosevelt's presidency prior to the 1937–1938 recession and resumed afterward.[28]

But such lies are rarer than bullshit, like Senator Grassley's statement, which creates deception based on elements of both fiction and fact, as when he says "the Depression didn't end until we entered World War II." Now, as Terkel's remarks indicate, there was a grain of truth in that assertion: only in 1942 did unemployment at last fall below 5 percent. But the conclusion you should draw from the data we now have in hand is not that the New Deal "didn't work"—it is that the New Deal worked, just not quickly enough. Saying that the war ended the Depression is simply noting the greater effect of larger government spending and hiring. During the New Deal, the federal budget sometimes reached the neighborhood of 10 percent of GDP; during the war, federal spending soared to more than 40 percent of GDP. The argument that the war ended the Depression is an argument that the New Deal should have been bigger, sooner, to provide adequate economic stimulus. As the economic historian Gabriel Mathy finds, the Depression created not just high unemployment but also long-term unemployment; people lacking work for longer found it correspondingly more difficult to get hired. The massive demand for labor created by war mobilization wiped out this backlog of the long-term unemployed. Therefore, one may reasonably conclude that the New Deal should have provided such a massive demand for labor sooner. If federally created jobs building tanks and airplanes could wipe out the Depression, so could federally created jobs building schools and roads.

That the New Deal should have been bigger, sooner, is a conclusion of long standing: John Maynard Keynes told Roosevelt he needed to approximately double the rate of "direct stimulus to production deliberately applied by the administration" in 1934, at a time when Roosevelt had reduced such expenditures in response to political pressure just like the kind that later came from Grassley or King.[29] Roosevelt soon moved in the direction that Keynes suggested, getting the so-called big bill—amounting to nearly $5 billion—from Congress and allowing him to create the WPA to employ Americans nationwide under the direction of Harry Hopkins. But a few years afterward, once recovery seemed well under way, Roosevelt again cut relief spending—again in response to political pressure. For many economists—including Keynes—that premature reduction in fiscal stimulus was the cause of the 1937–1938 recession.[30] Only after making that fiscally cautious error did the Roosevelt administration adopt a deliberately Keynesian budget. Soon afterward, mobilization for war began.[31] In 1941 Hopkins took a new job, directing Lend-Lease operations; Congress approved nearly $50 billion for the program—an order of magnitude more than the "big bill" that created the WPA.[32] So when Grassley says the war ended the Depression, he is not stating an argument against the New Deal: he is stating an argument for a bigger New Deal, an argument that New Dealer Harry Hopkins at WPA should have had a budget more like World War II–era Harry Hopkins at Lend-Lease.[33]

But, maybe most important, we should remember that judging the New Deal mainly by its success at making conventional indicators of economic welfare move in the right direction is poor historical analysis. For New Dealers, the point of the New Deal was not to return the US economy quickly to the precrash status quo but to promote a recovery in which all Americans could share, to demonstrate that the US government could still work for the American people. When Roosevelt first took office, democracy was under threat throughout the world; he became president the same year that Adolf Hitler became chancellor of Germany. For New Dealers, the emergency government employment of citizens was no mere matter of replacing deficient private demand with public funding; it constituted what Roosevelt called an effort "to preserve our democratic form of government."[34]

Roosevelt campaigned on, and governed by, a phrase we would recognize today: "social justice." The Depression showed, to use Roosevelt's preferred word, the "interdependence" of all Americans and indeed all people. No one group could enjoy the benefits of prosperity if all did not. Therefore, the New Deal aimed to introduce a "broadening conception of social justice" to American life, and after the war, with the terms of the peace Roosevelt hoped to achieve, to the world. The nation could not "restore"; it must "remodel." Roosevelt rejected the idea that "recovery means a return to old methods" and proposed instead "a permanent readjustment of . . . our social and economic arrangements."[35] We are not taking the New Deal seriously if we look only at its effect on unemployment or GDP; we need to consider its effect on democracy.

On January 11, 1944—seventy-five years before Grassley's speech in the Senate condemning the New Deal—Roosevelt delivered an address to Congress declaring that Americans had rights not spelled out in the Constitution, including the right to a decent job that would support a decent standard of living, to housing and proper medical care and education, to protection when injured or aged. He campaigned on these rights when he first promised a New Deal, and during his presidency he did much to see them enshrined in law. And upon making a renewed pledge to the New Deal in 1944, and by running on the federal obligation to provide full employment, he won reelection to an unprecedented fourth term.[36] Senator Grassley was ten years old then; he probably remembered it, even as he condemned it.

11

CONFEDERATE MONUMENTS

Karen L. Cox

FEW MYTHS HAVE THE STAYING POWER AND SUCH A STRANGLEHOLD on the American imagination than that of the Lost Cause. Born out of Confederate defeat, nursed by generations of white southerners, cradled by sympathetic white northerners, raised by popular culture, and defended by politicians, this myth of Civil War history might be a senior citizen, but it is still a long way from the grave. In many ways, it is no longer a southern myth but an American myth instead, and in its latest iteration it is modified by debates over Confederate monuments. These monuments, memorials to the Lost Cause, have served as tangible symbols of this mythology since the end of the Civil War. They tell the tale of its evolution as a narrative, which has been less about history and more about cultural shifts tied to racial progress.

Confederate monuments have, throughout their history, represented white supremacy. These statues are not, and have never been, static symbols. They are not simply physical memorials made of bronze or granite; they represent a system of beliefs. The groups that erected them, whether postwar Ladies Memorial Associations (LMAs), the United Daughters of the Confederacy (UDC), or men's organizations that have erected the most recent ones, did not just build them and walk away. They were, and still are, reanimated on an annual basis through rituals held on Confederate Memorial Day, the birthdays of Confederate generals, and during Civil War–era reenactments. For more than a century, white southerners have gathered at these memorial sites to recall the Confederate past and reassert their commitment to the values of their ancestors, the very same values that resulted in a war to defend slavery, as well as the right to expand the institution.

How the Confederate past is remembered is tied to the narrative of the Lost Cause, a term adopted by southern whites after the Civil War to describe defeat. The evolution of that narrative is complex. Not only did it offer a means for white southerners to come to terms with defeat; they also used it to justify their failure to create a separate nation and to reject the idea that slavery was a primary cause of the Civil War. It made Teflon heroes out of its generals, especially Robert E. Lee and Thomas "Stonewall" Jackson, and it also romanticized the Old South and recast Reconstruction as the "Tragic Era" that had allowed uncivilized and ignorant freedmen to govern their former masters.

White southerners were first aided in their efforts to explain what went wrong, but also why their cause was just, by Edward A. Pollard, the wartime journalist for the *Richmond Examiner*. In 1866 Pollard, a native Virginian, wrote a tome he titled *The Lost Cause: A New Southern History of the War of the Confederates*. A "new" southern history immediately suggested that this was intended as a partisan assessment of the war even before the first volumes of history about the war were ever produced. Over the course of 752 pages, Pollard laid out a Confederate history of the war, as well as a narrative that proved useful to white southerners reeling from defeat and the devastation of their world. Not only did he coin the term *Lost Cause*, but he also provided former Confederates with a rhetorical balm to soothe their psychological wounds. In doing so, he helped to lay the foundation of a mythology that reassured them that their cause was just and their values were worth fighting for even in the face of a thoroughly crushing defeat.[1]

The Lost Cause was Pollard's paean to southern nationalism and a rally cry to not give up on it. The war might be over, but the fight to maintain the region's values still existed. Southern nationalism, under Pollard's pen and those who followed in his footsteps, was reinvented in order to align with their current postwar reality. As a Lost Cause evangelist, Pollard gave future generations the language and arguments to defend white supremacy and dismiss slavery as a cause of war. That the Confederate generation were the true inheritors of the Revolutionary generation was just one argument that played out repeatedly for decades, particularly the South's defense of the Tenth Amendment to the Constitution, which preserves states' rights. A second argument, a complete reinterpretation of southern nationalism, was that slavery had been necessary to preserve white supremacy and prevent race war. Pollard and others still justified slavery as a paternal system that benefited the enslaved, but in the shadow of defeat, it now needed to be understood as necessary. This narrative allowed Confederate soldiers to be understood not as defenders of slavery but of the region and of their race. In sum, these false memories of the Confederacy and southern nationalism still had value, even in defeat. Therefore, the Lost Cause was nothing to lament. It was a "just cause," and in the postwar South, white supremacy was front and center.[2]

Pollard also argued that despite the war's outcome, the South did not have to admit to defeat but rather only what was "properly decided." For him, only two issues were determined in 1865—the restoration of the Union and a legal end to slavery: "It did not decide negro equality; it did not decide negro suffrage; it did not decide State Rights . . . and these things which the war did not decide, the Southern people will still cling to." In this, Pollard was prophetic. White southerners remained committed to the supremacy of their race, even in the face of federal Reconstruction.

One cannot overstate how quickly the Lost Cause, sometimes referred to as the Confederate tradition, evolved after Reconstruction. There was more widespread participation from the white community, and new rituals emerged. LMAs continued to lead the charge to raise funds and build monuments, as well as orchestrate unveilings, such that even placing the cornerstone for a monument came with its own ceremony, as the case of Augusta, Georgia, demonstrates. Just ten years after the end of the Civil War, in April 1875, locals witnessed more than a simple procession to Magnolia Cemetery to decorate the graves of Confederate dead with flowers. That year the white community reclaimed the town for the Lost Cause, something that towns across the region would do with increasing frequency after Reconstruction.

The myth of the Lost Cause was on full display during monument unveilings as a male speaker, usually a Confederate veteran or a politician, perpetuated its narrative tropes. In Augusta, Confederate hero General Clement Evans, a Methodist minister and Lost Cause stalwart who later headed the Georgia Division of the United Confederate Veterans (UCV), spoke to a crowd of ten thousand that gathered for the unveiling. His address contained many of the elements of speeches given during such ceremonies. He articulated the South's anger with Reconstruction, lauded the work of southern women, linked the American Revolution to the Confederate cause, and remained defiant that secession was just.

Even as he told the assembled crowd that he advised against "[keeping] alive the passions of war" and claimed that the "voice of the monument will not be for war, but peace," he asserted that "it was right to repel aggression . . . it was right to set up a separate government. . . . It was right to hold out to the bitter end. Right! Right!" He also made clear, for those who wished to understand their meaning, what these statues represented: "I have no doubt of the public utility of these monuments [to] keep the popular heart drawn to the original principles and policies of this [Confederate] Government," concluding that "in common with others of like character which shall adorn every city of the South, this monument will mould and preserve Southern opinion." In other words, Confederate statues were not simply commemorative; they also represented the values as well as the "principles and policies" of states' rights and the preservation of white supremacy in the absence of slavery. Evans finally conceded that the Confederacy was dead: "We buried it. We do not intend to examine its remains. We were utterly defeated, and we dismiss our resentments." Yet his pronounced resentment very much underlay his message.[3]

In 1878, when the Augusta monument was unveiled, the LMA chose Charles Colcock Jones Jr. as its speaker. Jones, a lieutenant colonel in the Confederate army and former mayor of Savannah, began by addressing the work of women to erect a monument in memory of the soldiers from Richmond County who died during the war. He was unrepentant in his defense of the Lost Cause. Speaking to the enormous crowd, which included Georgia's governor, he reassured his fellow white southerners that Confederate veterans "have no apologies to offer, no excuses to render, no regrets to utter, save that we failed in our high endeavor." Yet he followed that statement with the well-worn excuse for defeat: "We were overborne by superior numbers and weightier munitions." Jones also echoed Edward Pollard's pronouncement of twelve years earlier when he said that "nothing has been absolutely determined except the question of comparative strength."[4]

Jones also commented on the irony of the day since the white citizens of Augusta were dedicating an elaborate monument to those who were "overcome in the contest, to a cause which seemingly lost." Significantly, he used the word *overcome*, rather than *defeated*, but even more noteworthy was his use of the adjective *seemingly* because the monument itself appeared to suggest that all had *not* been lost. He also believed that the day was coming when anyone "with the candor to confess," even northerners, would acknowledge the Confederacy was right in its fight for an "independent national existence." Last, he hinted at what became a key component of the Lost Cause, indoctrinating southern children, noting that they should "be taught to emulate the example of their Confederate ancestors."[5]

As the case of Augusta shows, post-Reconstruction monument building became a public enterprise that moved the Confederate tradition from mourning into the realm of celebration. No longer limited to decorating the graves of soldiers on Confederate Memorial Day, that annual ritual now included a stop at the monument to pay homage to a mythologized past. It also demonstrates how quickly entrenched the Lost Cause narrative had become, with its emphasis on a just cause and a sacred duty to Confederate principles, such that going forward it also included a commitment to perpetuate a false history among future generations of white children in the South.

For three decades after the Civil War, white southerners continued their efforts to commemorate the Lost Cause, but between 1890 and World War I the narrative assumed a different tone and new intensity. Monument building expanded to every town and hamlet throughout the South, and statues now appeared on local courthouse lawns, in town squares, and on the grounds of state governments. Commemoration took many forms. Highways were named for Lee, Jackson, and Confederate president Jefferson Davis, and images of these same men were cast into the stained-glass windows of churches. Confederate Memorial Day became an official state holiday in southern states, too, but monuments continued to be the most tangible reminders of the Lost Cause myth and the white South's continued loyalty to the principles of states' rights, which in the late nineteenth and early twentieth centuries meant the right to maintain a system of segregation based on white supremacy.

The 1890s was also a decade marked by the disenfranchisement of Black men across the region. Southern states had long rejected Black citizenship, but during this decade they amped up their efforts to eliminate it altogether. Southern legislatures passed laws that reversed voting rights, and white men across the region used racial violence, especially lynching, not only to intimidate Black voters but also to subdue entire Black communities. The result was that by the turn of the twentieth century, Black men, even those who once served in Congress, were eliminated from voting and holding office. This left an opening in the southern polity for southern white women to assume an even more public role as leaders of the Confederate tradition. When they did, it was primarily through the United Daughters of the Confederacy (the UDC or "Daughters"), which became the most influential southern women's organization for the next several decades.

The UDC grew rapidly after its founding in 1894. What began as a small gathering of thirty women in Nashville, Tennessee, became thirty thousand women within ten years. By the time of World War I, they were an army of one hundred thousand. The growth in monument building paralleled the growth of the UDC's membership, for the Daughters were primarily responsible for the vast majority of monuments and memorials built throughout the South, and even beyond its borders, during those years. In fact, the period between the mid-1890s and World War I represents the peak period of monument dedications, and it demonstrates how seriously southern women took their role as leaders of the Lost Cause. The mark they made on the social, political, and physical landscape of the region in the early twentieth century is undeniable, such that the term *New South* is practically a misnomer.

The Daughters' heightened visibility and their broader agenda to cement a loyalty to Confederate principles among future generations of white southerners was yet another stage in the evolution of the Lost Cause. In fact, their efforts in the early twentieth century provided the cultural underpinning for the Jim Crow legislation created by their male counterparts throughout the South. This was not a coincidence. Not only did southern white women share similar views on racial supremacy; they were also related by blood or marriage to men of influence within the region: local attorneys and judges, governors, state legislators, and even US senators.

The UDC's monument campaigns were always supported by a narrative that Confederate veterans fought nobly and that defeat did not erase the justness of their cause. These monuments also reflected the beliefs held by the Jim Crow generation—whites who regarded African Americans as second-class citizens and whose leaders sought to preserve the racial status quo through both legal and extralegal means. And if there were any doubts about the larger meaning and purpose of Confederate monuments within the context of the Lost Cause, the Daughters made it clear in the minutes of their meetings, in the essays they wrote, in the speeches they gave, and in the actions they took. Moreover, the men they selected to give speeches at monument unveilings or on Confederate Memorial Day, as they reiterated the message of honor and sacrifice, also furthered the Lost Cause narrative about slavery, the war, and Confederate soldiers as valiant heroes who not only fought to defend the South against an invading North but who withstood Reconstruction and became stalwart defenders of white supremacy, sometimes as members of the Ku Klux Klan.

North Carolina Supreme Court justice Heriot Clarkson was one such man. In his Confederate Memorial Day speech to the local chapter of the

UDC in Raleigh, he addressed many of these themes. Standing along-side the monument, Clarkson asserted that the Civil War was not fought over slavery but that the institution was a burden on white people because it fell upon them "to civilize and Christianize a barbarous race." Like-wise, he described the years-long effort it took for white leaders to regain control of government in the decades following Reconstruction. By dis-franchising Black male voters, he asserted, white lawmakers succeeded in restoring "white supremacy through white men."[6]

By the time of World War I, the reputation of Confederate soldiers was nearly restored in the eyes of the white South. The North's capitulation to the Lost Cause narrative, which began with veterans' reunions in the 1880s, had hastened reconciliation. In American popular culture, there was evidence of a cultural reconciliation between white northerners and southerners that allowed for the glorification of the Confederacy, whether through films like *Birth of a Nation* (1915), where former Confederates become heroes in the guise of the Ku Klux Klan, or in popular songs like "The Dixie Volunteers," published in 1917, whose lyrics compared south-ern soldiers to their Confederate forebears. "See those great big southern lad-dies, just like their dear old dad-dies," the chorus went, "and they're going to be, fighting men like Stonewall Jackson and Robert E. Lee." It was the vindication that the white South had wanted since the surrender at Appomattox.[7]

Monument building renewed after World War I, but the pace had slackened considerably. World War II once again interrupted those ef-forts, but by then memories of a war that had ended seventy-five years earlier meant less than it had a generation earlier. After the war, but par-ticularly in the 1950s and early 1960s, there was a renewed interest in the Lost Cause and monument building in the years leading up to and during the Civil War Centennial. Those decades also marked enormous changes to the "southern way of life" as the civil rights movement challenged the political system that had kept Black southerners from enjoying the full rights of citizenship. Somewhere in the center, the monuments of Jim Crow remained, not as static symbols of a long-dead culture but as daily reminders of racial inequality. Significantly, the Lost Cause evolved once

more as Confederate Memorial Day speeches contained references to racial segregation as a states' rights issue.

It is important to understand that the myths used to justify the Lost
Cause and the building of monuments did not go unchecked. Criticism
of this damaging myth and Confederate symbols stretched back to as
early as 1870, when Frederick Douglass called out the "*nauseating* flat-
teries of the late Robert E. Lee" that poured in after the Confederate
general's death, asking, "Is it not about time that this bombastic laudation
of the rebel chief should cease?"[8] Until his death in 1895, Douglass engaged in an uphill battle trying to dislodge the Lost Cause narrative that
had gripped the national consciousness, while still seeking to preserve
the memory of Emancipation. But the pull of this southern mythology
was so strong that even white northerners made a devil's bargain with
the South's Confederate tradition for the sake of sectional reconciliation.
And the race to build "monuments of folly," as Douglass called them, had
yet to peak by the time of his death.[9]

Still, while Frederick Douglass waged a battle against the Lost Cause,
the real war against it was in the South, where Black southerners were on
the front lines. They were keenly aware that Confederate symbols in their
communities were imbued with racism and white supremacy, and they
protested them publicly and privately, especially in the pages of African
American newspapers both in and out of the South.

Black citizens in Richmond, Virginia, did not hesitate to challenge the
Lost Cause narratives associated with the massive equestrian statue to
Robert E. Lee in their hometown, which they expressed through the local
Black newspaper, the *Richmond Planet*, edited by John Mitchell Jr. When
the Lee monument was unveiled in May 1890, the paper reported that
"Confederates from New York to Texas," who were in town for the unveiling, demonstrated their continued commitment to Confederate values,
behaving as if the South had not lost the Civil War. The display of "rebel
flags," including one "mammoth Confederate flag" that covered the entire length of City Hall, alongside the gathering of Confederate veterans
giving a full-throated "rebel yell," Mitchell editorialized, "told in no uncertain tones that they still clung to theories which were presumably to be

buried for all eternity." Doing so was not only a deterrent to progress, the paper lamented; the Confederate tradition also "forge[d] heavier chains with which to be bound." He also worried that the movement to glorify the Lost Cause was inextricably tied to nascent efforts to disenfranchise Black men.[10] He was right. Throughout the 1890s, as Confederate monuments increased in number, states across the region took steps to undermine Black male suffrage.

Despite the loss of political power, African Americans continued to express their contempt for Confederate symbols, especially in the pages of leading Black newspapers. The *Chicago Defender*, founded in 1905, swiftly became the nation's most respected Black newspaper, its pages a lively space for both journalists and readers to voice their opinion on Confederate flags and monuments. Many of its columnists were migrants from the South, and the paper was read and shared where Confederate monuments claimed public spaces in their hometowns.

From the outset, the *Defender* published pieces that linked monuments to both slavery and treason, and writers were very clear about what should be done with them. In 1921, for example, a staff correspondent writing from Thomasville, Georgia, published an article under the headline "Tear the Spirit of the Confederacy from the South—Destroy All Flags, Records and Other Symbols of Ante-Bellum Days." Given the tenor of the piece, it is clear why the author remained anonymous; his life would have clearly been in danger. The article began as a response to protests against a statue of John Wilkes Booth in Alabama, placed there in 1906, but that had recently received national attention, including in the northern press. This monument to the "murderer of the Emancipator" led the author to rail against Confederate iconography in southern communities as well as present a searing critique of the Lost Cause: "In every Southern city, town or hamlet one sees relics of the Confederacy kept intact. Confederate flags fly triumphantly, monuments are erected to Lee, the victories of rebels are celebrated, museums gather obsolete weapons, libraries store the infamous records, white school children are studiously taught to believe in the righteousness of the lost cause." And all of it was done "to reproduce the spirit of ante-bellum days."[11]

The author's detailed description of Confederate culture in the South, much of it a result of the UDC's efforts, is a vivid reminder of how widespread the Lost Cause was and how embedded it had become in communities with a significant African American population. He recognized a direct link between the symbols of white supremacy and the disenfranchisement of his race. "Every Confederate flag in the South should be sought out and burned," he wrote, adding that "it should be made a misdemeanor to display one" and that parades that honored rebels "should be made a crime." Sectionalism was the problem, he argued, because it "propped up" Confederate traditions. And he pointed the finger at public schools, churches, and newspapers for the "incalculable wrong" they were doing to Black southerners, especially in public schools. He rightfully noted how the continued instruction of Lost Cause ideals—a key component of the UDC's agenda—perpetuated racism among the next generation of white southerners: "The Southern white child goes to school to find an emblem of Jefferson Davis' South hung beside Old Glory. He is taught that the old ideals are still right," and, he warned, "The Southern white child is taught and led to believe that he is a superior being; that the law which granted freedom and opportunity to our Race may be easily glossed over; that he does not have to obey it."[12]

The *Defender* regularly engaged its readers, asking them their thoughts about any number of topics that were of interest to the race in a column called "What Do You Say About It?" On September 10, 1932, the paper printed the answers to the question it posed the prior week. The question—"Would you favor a federal law to abolish all patriotic monuments erected in the South to the memory of Confederate soldiers?"—elicited several favorable responses. Spencer Hilt of Columbus, Georgia, wrote that "I am highly in favor of such a law," pointing to the federal government for "[tolerating] the unpatriotic spirit of the South to the Stars and Stripes." Hilt added, "Rebels should not be honored, and any section of the country producing traitors should be ashamed of them." John Upcher, a reader from Omaha, Nebraska, was troubled by what monuments taught young white southerners. "Every time children of the men [Confederate veterans] look at the monuments it gives them a greater desire to . . . carry out the wishes of their forefathers," he worried, adding that "if those monuments weren't standing the white South wouldn't be so encouraged to practice hate and discrimination against our people." In short, he said, "They stand as emblems of hate and envy" and "shouldn't have been permitted" to be erected. A letter from Scott Boydston of Birmingham, Alabama, began by calling out the Confederate cause, saying, "The dirtiest blot on the pages of American History was written by rebel statesmen of the South. Why honor them?" Boydston suggested that Confederate monuments were the equivalent of erecting a monument "to the memory of Benedict Arnold." He believed that the South held the nation back and concluded that "only fools would want to glorify men who fought in defense of human slavery."[13]

Asking readers what they thought about a federal law to remove monuments provides us with insight into how African Americans from various places around the South saw the monuments in their communities on a daily basis. The letters also demonstrated a keen understanding of American history and what patriotism meant to them. Further, they recognized the hold that the Lost Cause had on the region, so much that "the South has never admitted defeat," M. K. Quigley of Marietta, Georgia, wrote. Quigley expressed his belief that the North went too easy on the South at war's end. "Jeff Davis should have been shot at sunrise and his whole staff imprisoned for life," he said, and "to honor these skunks with monuments for the future generation to gaze upon is the rawest insult to the memory of noble men like Lincoln and Grant." His fellow Georgian, Marshfield Gregg of Waynesboro, agreed: "It is a blot on civilization that at this time and day we are faced with granites that depict men who attempted to perpetuate human slavery."[14]

The responses of African Americans to the *Defender*'s question offer stark evidence that Confederate monuments meant something far different to them than what white southerners claimed they symbolized. Confederate organizations, especially the UDC, were still busy building monuments when the paper queried its readers about a federal law banning such iconography. By the early 1930s, there were already several hundred monuments erected throughout the region. Black southerners may not have publicly expressed their contempt for such symbols in their hometowns for fear of being physically attacked for such views, but they did so in the pages of the nation's leading African American newspaper. And the contents of their letters reveal not simply the opinion of an individual writer; they also suggest that entire communities of Black southerners had concluded that Confederate monuments represented white supremacy and treason, as well as honored white men who would have kept them enslaved.

The evolution of the Lost Cause myth offers proof that it was never tied to a factual history but was always about an alternate reality. This has been proven repeatedly, especially since the passage of the Voting Rights Act of 1965, as monument defenders have co-opted the language of racial progress to redefine what Confederate heritage and southern monuments represent. During the 1970s, for example, following the changes wrought by the civil rights movement and nascent protests against Confederate symbols by African American politicians, defenders claimed that to build and maintain a Confederate monument was about preserving "equal rights." During the late 1980s and early 1990s, when the myth of the Lost Cause expanded in reaction to multiculturalism, defenders of battle flags and monuments referred to themselves as "Confederate Americans." Following the 9/11 tragedy, and as talk of monument removal increased in the early 2000s, the myth once again shifted, with monument removal equated with the Taliban's destruction of religious sculptures. Since the emergence of the Black Lives Matter (BLM) movement in 2014, Lost Cause stalwarts amended the myth again by adopting the phrase "Confederate Lives Matter" to undermine BLM messages about systemic racism and return the focus to white power structures and patriarchy.

Following the 2017 Unite the Right rally in Charlottesville, Virginia, during which time white nationalists claimed that they were there to protest the removal of the monument of Confederate general Robert E. Lee, what had long been a regional myth was adopted by American whites at the rally who had no legitimate claim to southern heritage. Following the murder of George Floyd by a Minneapolis police officer in May 2020, a diverse group of southerners defaced monuments and challenged the myths associated with them. Yet as monuments were being removed throughout the region, defenders of the statues found an unlikely supporter in President Donald Trump, who expanded the Lost Cause myth again by suggesting that monuments, even Confederate ones, represented a "common inheritance."[15]

The legacy of monuments within the Confederate tradition is a legacy of historical distortion. As a revisionist narrative, the Lost Cause has not only damaged Americans' ability to determine fact from fiction; it has also served as a bulwark against racial progress and is its most insidious legacy.

12

THE SOUTHERN STRATEGY

Kevin M. Kruse

IN 2017 THE CONSERVATIVE MEDIA OUTLET PRAGERU POSTED A five-minute video that has since been viewed over twenty-two million times. In it, political scientist Carol Swain addressed the party realignment of the twentieth century, a process in which Republicans, originally based in the Northeast and committed to liberalism, and Democrats, once solidly southern and dedicated to conservatism, gradually swapped political ideologies, demographies, and geographies. Despite a half century of scholarly work on the topic by her fellow political scientists and historians, Swain asserted that "this story of the two parties switching identities is a myth." In particular, she called into question the "Southern Strategy," in which Republicans used race-based appeals to win over conservative whites in the 1950s and 1960s. Asserting there was no evidence of any such effort, Swain insisted it had been simply "fabricated by left-leaning academic elites and journalists."[1]

Despite such claims, the record is clear. There was, indeed, a long-term transformation in the two parties—first at the national level and then subsequently at the state and local levels—a process that stands at the core of twentieth-century political history. Over several decades, Democrats abandoned their role as the party of slavery, segregation, and white supremacy to champion civil rights; in response, Republicans retreated from their original racial liberalism and courted white resentment. The southern strategy—well documented in manuscript archives, public speeches, party platforms, contemporary reporting, polling data, oral interviews, memoirs, and elsewhere—has long been accepted as a wholly uncontroversial fact. (Indeed, Swain herself had acknowledged this reality in an earlier work.)[2] Only recently have conservative partisans challenged this well-established history, presumably seeking to blunt accusations that Republicans have embraced racism today by pretending that Republicans never embraced racism before. Clinging to the claim that the Grand Old Party is still "the party of Lincoln," today's conservatives have, ironically, tried to erase the considerable work that earlier generations of conservatives did to remake the Republican Party in their own image.

A quick glance at the political landscape of the mid-nineteenth century shows how drastically the two parties changed. Geographically, the political map of the 1860s largely inverted our own: Republicans ruled New England and the West Coast; Democrats dominated the South. Ideologically, the parties inverted as well. Republicans embraced economic liberalism and federal power; Democrats championed "states' rights." The line between the parties was clearest when it came to race. Republicans opposed slavery as a founding principle of the party, championed emancipation in the Civil War, and advanced an aggressive agenda to secure Black freedom in Reconstruction. Democrats, in contrast, committed to the successive causes of white supremacy: slavery, secession, and segregation. Given this stark split, racial conflicts mirrored partisan ones. When the Ku Klux Klan formed in the late 1860s, southern Democrats predictably embraced it while Republicans recoiled.[3]

This bright line soon blurred. Republicans, who sent nearly two dozen African Americans to Congress in the late nineteenth century, relaxed their commitment to racial equality as the twentieth century began.

Southern Democrats still led the way in entrenching disfranchisement and discrimination, but northern Republicans now offered tacit acceptance or explicit approval. Southern states constructed racial segregation under Democratic rule, for instance, but every Republican on the Supreme Court save one sanctioned that system in *Plessy v. Ferguson* (1896).[4] Likewise, when Democratic legislatures purged African American voters, Republicans responded by abandoning their interracial "black-and-tan" coalitions for a new "lily-white movement."[5] By the early decades of the twentieth century, Republicans and Democrats each had made peace with white supremacy. Notably, when the Klan revived in the 1920s, the second version found supporters in *both* parties: Democrats in the South, Republicans in the Midwest.[6]

As the parties converged on race, they diverged elsewhere. By the 1920s, the GOP had abandoned the economic radicalism of its founding generation and the trust-busting of Theodore Roosevelt's progressive Republicans and embraced corporations and economic conservatism. The Great Depression pushed Democrats in a new direction, too, as Franklin D. Roosevelt reoriented his party to the big-government liberalism that Republicans had abandoned. Importantly, however, FDR's brand of liberalism was narrowly economic. Although some New Dealers were racially liberal, Democrats as a whole were decidedly not. Southern Democrats controlled powerful committees in Congress and used that influence to protect their own interests, especially on matters of race. Despite segregationists' strength in Democratic circles, a majority of African Americans switched parties in the 1930s. Black voters had remained loyal to "the party of Lincoln," even through Hoover's reelection campaign, but once they benefited from FDR's New Deal, many voted accordingly.[7] The switch here was abrupt. In 1932 Roosevelt received only 23 percent of the Black vote; in 1936 he received 71 percent. Regardless of their votes for a Democratic president, many still formally remained Republicans. In 1936, 44 percent of Black voters registered as Democrats and 37 percent as Republicans. In 1940 and 1944, Black registrations were evenly split.[8]

When African Americans entered the party, white southerners saw it slipping away. "The catering by our National Party to the Negro vote,"

Senator Josiah Bailey of North Carolina noted, "is . . . very alarming to me."[9] As they panicked, segregationists found themselves stripped of tools to stop the change. At their 1936 convention, Democrats abandoned a long-standing rule requiring presidential and vice-presidential nominees to receive at least two-thirds of the delegates' votes, which had given the South a regional veto.[10] In the 1938 primaries, the shift in power came into focus, as Roosevelt backed liberal challengers to three conservative southern senators. All three incumbents survived, but FDR's "purge" attempt sparked concerns about the region's future.[11] "The South," Virginia's senator Carter Glass wrote, "would better begin thinking whether it will continue to cast its 152 electoral votes according to the memories of the Reconstruction era of 1865 and thereafter, or will have spirit and courage enough to face the new Reconstruction era that northern so-called Democrats are menacing us with."[12] Alarmed by this "new" Democratic Party, white southerners looked across the aisle. In 1937 Bailey joined Michigan Republican Arthur Vandenberg in drafting the "Conservative Manifesto," a clear articulation of limited-government principles shared across party lines. In the next session, a bipartisan coalition of thirty senators prevented FDR from pressing ahead with a new wave of economic and social reforms, stopping the New Deal in its tracks. This successful partnership convinced Republicans that their southern colleagues would come their way eventually. "I have no doubt," Vandenberg said, "that the realignment must occur."[13]

For another decade, the Democratic coalition awkwardly balanced segregationists with African Americans and white liberals. The tipping point came in 1948, when President Harry Truman endorsed recommendations of his commission on civil rights, and liberals seized the moment to push an aggressive civil rights program at their convention. "The time has arrived," Minneapolis mayor Hubert H. Humphrey declared there, "for the Democratic Party to get out of the shadow of states' rights and walk forthrightly into the bright sunshine of human rights."[14] A plank endorsing Truman's civil rights program passed narrowly, prompting delegates from Mississippi and Alabama to storm out. Political observers were stunned. As *Time* put it, "The South had been kicked in the pants, turned around and kicked in the stomach."[15]

Days later, thousands of southern Democrats gathered for another convention in Birmingham to launch the States' Rights Democratic Party, commonly called "the Dixiecrats." Governor Strom Thurmond of South Carolina was nominated for president and Governor Fielding Wright of Mississippi for vice president. In his acceptance speech, Thurmond complained that white southerners had been "stabbed in the back by a president who has betrayed every principle of the Democratic Party in his desire to win at any cost."[16] Despite a call for regionwide rebellion, the Dixiecrats couldn't capture the South. Indeed, Thurmond would win only four states: Louisiana, Mississippi, Alabama, and South Carolina. (Notably, these were the only states where his allies managed to block Truman from the ballot and replace him with Thurmond as the "Democratic" nominee. Elsewhere, loyalists kept the president in the top spot, delivering party-line ballots to *him*.)[17] As he held on to most of the South, Truman also won 77 percent of the Black vote nationwide, more than Roosevelt ever had. African Americans delivered the margin of victory for Truman in swing states and thus the election. Civil rights now stood as a decisive campaign issue.[18]

The year 1948 brought a different reckoning for Republicans. The party had now lost five straight presidential elections and had controlled Congress for only two years out of sixteen. Despite having a more aggressive stance on civil rights, Republicans had actually lost ground with Black voters. This realization prompted some Republicans to look to the South, which the national party had neglected for generations. (In his classic 1949 study of southern politics, V. O. Key observed that the GOP was so threadbare in the region that it "scarcely deserves the name of party.")[19] Nevertheless, some believed a Republican revival could be forged through concerted appeals to the disaffected Dixiecrats. J. Harvie Williams, a North Carolinian, spent 1949 fund-raising for a "Citizens' Political Committee" that would spark "political realignment" by strengthening the coalition of conservatives. A more "formal alliance between Republicans and Southern Democrats," he noted, would inspire "white, English-speaking stocks" to elect a "conservative president."[20] Others went further. Ohio senator John W. Bricker, the 1944 vice-presidential nominee, urged Republican and Dixiecrat leaders to coordinate "realignment" so "voters may have a chance to decide whether they believe in all this big government, high taxes and profligate spending, or believe in conservation of resources, of human energy and opportunity for the individual."[21] Liberal Democrats welcomed these proposals. Minnesota senator Hubert Humphrey encouraged the thinning ranks of progressive Republicans to become Democrats so that the remainder of the "Republican Party could join in holy wedlock with the Dixiecrats, thereby making legal the illicit marriage which now exists."[22]

The strongest case for a Republican-Dixiecrat coalition came from Senator Karl Mundt of South Dakota. Seeking "permanent realignment of party forces in this country," Mundt crisscrossed America on a years-long campaign of public lectures, radio interviews, and television appearances.[23] "Mundt's proposal for a merger of the Republicans and Southern Democrats is the most intriguing, and perhaps the most promising, party reorganization development," enthused the *St. Louis Globe-Democrat*.[24] The South proved especially excited. "Not mere applause," the *Jackson (Mississippi) Daily News* reported after an April 1951 visit, "but ear-splitting Rebel yells, the kind heard in political gatherings in this State three score years ago."[25] In July Mundt debated Representative Clifford Case, a liberal Republican from New Jersey, in the pages of *Collier's*. The question: "Should the G.O.P. merge with the Dixiecrats?" Mundt argued that Republicans' string of defeats demanded a new strategy: "We have tried . . . to echo Democratic appeals to minority and pressure groups, but this hasn't worked. We have tried just about everything except an alliance with the South." Whites there had closer "political kinship" with Republicans than with Democrats: "There is no chance for Southern Democrats to recapture their party. It is irrevocably committed to a viewpoint that is not Southern, and to non-Southern interest groups." In any case, he added, realignment had already begun: "The Republican and Democratic parties have exchanged positions about the functions of states. Once, State rights was the battle cry of Democrats; now it is a Republican tenet of faith. I am convinced it is still close to the hearts of Southern Democrats." Case insisted that Mundt's merger plan would never work because southern Democrats in Congress would have to forfeit their prized committee chairmanships and, as a result, their power.

But more fundamentally, Case warned that abandoning civil rights would be "a betrayal of our heritage."[26]

Despite objections from liberals and moderates, Republican leaders courted Dixiecrats in 1952. "Our friends call themselves States' Righters and we call ourselves Republicans," RNC Chairman Guy Gabrielson noted in an appeal in Alabama, but such labels were meaningless. "The Dixiecrat Party believes in states' rights. That's what the Republican Party believes in."[27] The shift in emphasis was evident at the convention, which adopted a milder civil rights plank than previous conventions. "We believe that it is the primary responsibility of each state to order and control its own domestic institutions," it read, allowing that the federal government might take "supplemental action." (Headlines that summer in the Black-owned *Atlanta Daily World* highlighted the contrast: "States' Rights Position on Civil Rights in GOP Platform" and "Democratic Party Nails Down Strong Civil Rights Plank.")[28] This GOP message enticed Dixiecrats, and so did the presidential nominee, Dwight D. Eisenhower. Leaders of the Dixiecrat revolt in Alabama and Louisiana—former state party chairman Gessner McCorvey and political boss Leander Perez, respectively—had been early backers of Eisenhower, but other prominent Dixiecrats soon lined up.[29] Walter Sillers, speaker of the Mississippi House and chairman of the Dixiecrat convention, supported Eisenhower.[30] In South Carolina, three prominent Dixiecrats also backed Ike: Congressman Mendel Rivers, Governor Jimmy Byrnes, and Senator Strom Thurmond, the 1948 Dixiecrat presidential nominee.[31] The Republican campaign welcomed their support. In Birmingham the Dixiecrats' national treasurer introduced Eisenhower at a rally; in Miami, a leading Florida Dixiecrat did the same.[32]

The 1952 drive for the Deep South came up short, but Republicans still made inroads. "Throughout the Deep South, but especially in Georgia, South Carolina, and Mississippi," Kari Frederickson concluded, "there was a strong correlation between counties that supported the Dixiecrats and those that endorsed Eisenhower," showing that "the Dixiecrat movement had effectively loosened the moorings of southern political allegiance at the national level."[33] Meanwhile, Eisenhower succeeded in the peripheral South, taking Virginia, Tennessee, Florida, Oklahoma, and

Texas, largely by winning over moderate, middle-class whites in metropolitan regions. Beyond the presidency, however, Republicans' southern
gains were limited because of a narrow focus on the top. "Do not try
to sell the Republican party to Southern voters," a GOP memo advised.
"Sell Eisenhower." The nominee never stumped for congressional candidates; accordingly, only six southern Republicans won House races: five
in mountain districts along the Tennessee-Virginia border and a sixth
in central Virginia. In 1954 the party lost a mountain seat but gained
two seats in Dallas and Tampa.[34] As these moderate Republicans gained
ground, ex-Dixiecrats floundered. In 1954 two former activists in the revolt, Alabama's Tom Abernethy and Florida's Tom Watson, won Republican gubernatorial nominations by promising to preserve segregation.
Both improved considerably on past GOP performances—Abernethy
won 27 percent, Watson 20 percent—but not enough to win.[35] Modera-
tion, it seemed, might be the clearest path to success in the South.

The civil rights revolution quickly upended that logic. The Supreme
Court's *Brown* decision, authored by Republican chief justice Earl Warren, gave segregationists second thoughts about Republicans' newfound
talk of "states' rights." Personally, Eisenhower loathed the decision,
grumbling that Warren's appointment was "the biggest damfool mistake I ever made" and dismissing suggestions that he announce support
for *Brown* or tour the South to urge compliance.[36] Three years later, he
finally intervened in Little Rock, but only after his presidential authority had been challenged. "President Eisenhower was a fine general and
a good, decent man," remembered the NAACP's Roy Wilkins, "but if
he had fought World War II the way he fought for civil rights, we would
all be speaking German today."[37] That said, Democrats were no better.
Illinois governor Adlai Stevenson, Eisenhower's opponent in 1952 and
1956, likewise tried to sidestep the subject, for he also sought votes from
segregationists and African Americans alike.[38]

But southern Republicans couldn't avoid the issue. After *Brown*, no
new Republican candidates won southern congressional seats for the rest
of the decade, and those already in office increasingly joined their Democratic colleagues in "massive resistance" to desegregation. In 1956, for instance, two of the region's seven House Republicans signed the "Southern

Manifesto," urging states to fight federal integration orders.[39] In 1957, five of the seven petitioned Eisenhower to withdraw troops from Little Rock, fearing that the intervention would cause "the destruction of the Republican Party in the South."[40] In Dallas, once-moderate representative Bruce Alger embraced segregation in his 1956 reelection campaign. When his opponent blamed Republicans for *Brown*, Alger noted that seven of the nine justices in that case had been appointed by Democrats, while *Plessy* had been written by a Republican and backed by almost every Republican then on the court. The segregationist doctrine of separate but equal, Alger argued with pride, came from a "Republican" ruling. He won the race.[41]

Importantly, this rightward turn for southern Republicans happened just as the national party finally devoted resources to the region. In 1957 RNC Chairman Meade Alcorn complained that most southern states had "no Republican organization. . . . No office, no staff, no telephone, no program of party action, no effort to develop candidates, no effort to do anything." Accordingly, he launched "Operation Dixie," creating a Southern Division at the RNC and dedicating more funding to recruit leaders and build up infrastructure. Eisenhower hoped that this would enable the party to repeat the moderates' successes of the early 1950s, but its timing, right during the Little Rock crisis, only helped reactionary forces take hold. In Mississippi, for instance, the RNC replaced its long-standing moderate leader, African American Perry Howard, with Wirt Yerger, the head of a lily-white organization who promised to "build the Mississippi GOP into a vehicle for conservatives who felt estranged from the national Democratic Party."[42]

As southern Republicans veered right, the national party wavered. Vice President Richard Nixon secured the 1960 presidential nomination only after making concessions to New York governor Nelson Rockefeller, leader of the GOP's liberal wing. More progressive than Eisenhower on civil rights, Nixon welcomed a return to the party's tradition of racial equality. Accordingly, a lengthy civil rights plank in the 1960 platform called for federal intervention on several fronts, a bold stance that Nixon believed would give him an edge in the election.[43] But when Nixon lost on that platform, conservatives urged Republicans to turn right and look south. "Their theory," Rockefeller's aide related, "is that by becoming more reactionary than even the Southern Democratic Party, the Republican Party can attract Southern conservatives who have been Democrats, and by consolidating them with conservative strength in the Middle West and Far West, the Republicans can offset the liberalism of the Northeast and finally prevail." The strategy was gaining adherents, the aide added: "Barry has been falling increasingly for it."[44]

Indeed, Arizona senator Barry Goldwater had been a trailblazer. As early as 1953, he noted privately that "the dictates of the stronger minority groups are felt in almost every decision [Democrats] make, in almost every debate they enter." Conservative white southerners were losing their ancestral home: "I sense here a realignment."[45] In 1959 he toured the South, impressing segregationists with his insistence that court-ordered desegregation represented an abuse of federal power. Headlining the Republican Convention in South Carolina, Goldwater declared that *Brown* should "not be enforced by arms" because it was "not based on law."[46] In a radio interview with the segregationist White Citizens Council, the Arizonan belittled "so-called liberals who are so vitally interested in civil rights" and insisted that "states' rights is the cornerstone, the keystone, of our whole constitutional republic."[47] Nixon's defeat the following year moved Goldwater's argument mainstream. In a postmortem meeting with Nixon and Kentucky senator Thruston Morton, chairman of the RNC, Eisenhower complained that "we have made civil rights a main part of our effort these past eight years but we have lost Negro support instead of increasing it." Nixon agreed, calling African Americans "a bought vote" beyond their reach. RNC Chairman Morton summed up the mood: "The hell with them."[48]

In 1961 the Republican National Committee intensified its southern outreach. Its new chairman, conservative Representative William Miller of New York, made the Southern Division a priority, devoting $500,000— roughly a third of his annual budget—to Operation Dixie. Party chairs and vice chairs were established in 87 percent of southern counties by 1964, but only because of a readiness to recruit segregationists. Former RNC chairman Alcorn later remembered that the program's "whole purpose was perverted" as new leaders "took over the Operation Dixie machinery and attempted to convert it into a lily-white organization.

They did succeed in some states, I'm sorry to say."[49] But conservatives welcomed this change. In June 1961, William Loeb, influential publisher of the *Manchester Union-Leader*, urged Republicans to ignore "the Negro vote in the North" and focus on whites. "By being the white man's party, they can definitely become the majority party of the white man in the South," he noted. "In this way, we will have finally brought the conservative and the States' Righters in the North and South together in the Republican Party."[50] At the RNC's first gathering of southern leaders that fall, Goldwater insisted that white conservatives represented Republicans' best hope. "We're not going to get the Negro vote as a bloc in 1964 and 1968," he famously announced, "so we ought to go hunting where the ducks are."[51]

An emerging generation of southern Republicans revealed what this meant. In Texas a 1961 special election for the Senate seat vacated by Lyndon Johnson resulted in the surprising victory of John Tower. An outspoken critic of desegregation mandates, Tower had bemoaned federal intervention in Little Rock and led the fight against civil rights at the 1960 convention.[52] In the Senate, Tower would make common cause with segregationist Democrats, voting against both the Civil Rights Act of 1964 and the Voting Rights Act of 1965. But even before those votes, his election—as the first southern Republican in the Senate since Reconstruction—showed that the segregationist vote was up for grabs. In South Carolina, Republicans recruited segregationist William D. Workman Jr. for the 1962 Senate race. A newspaper columnist and television commentator, Workman had recently published *A Case for the South*, which urged massive resistance to desegregation. Campaigning beneath Confederate flags, he argued that incumbent Senator Olin Johnston was simply incapable of defending "the southern way of life" as a Democrat. Workman, who abandoned that party as it turned to civil rights, likened himself to the Dixiecrats, who had also been "driven from the house of their fathers." Meanwhile, in Alabama, Democrat James D. Martin switched parties to run against Senator Lister Hill, who he likewise claimed was "soft on integration." When he accepted the Republican nomination, Martin called for "a return to the spirit of '61—1861, when our fathers formed a new nation. . . . God willing, we will not again be forced to take up the rifle and the bayonet to preserve these principles." Both made strong showings: Workman won 43 percent, while Martin took 49 percent, nearly unseating an entrenched incumbent.[53] Republicans were encouraged by the results. "I like to fish when the tide's coming in—that's when the fish bite," explained Operation Dixie's head. "And the tide is coming in now in the South."[54] Accordingly, the GOP kept recruiting segregationist Democrats. The next year in Mississippi, for instance, the Republican candidates for governor and lieutenant governor were Rubel Phillips, former Democratic chairman of the Mississippi Public Service Commission, and Stanford Morse, a Democratic state senator. They embodied the state GOP, which was, a reporter noted, "composed largely of former Democrats." Campaign material promoted Phillips as "a staunch segregationist [who] condemns the use of federal power or threats of reprisals to force integration on Mississippians to curry favor with minority voters in the big Northern and Eastern cities." He took nearly 40 percent of the vote, showing again that segregationist Republicans could compete in the Deep South.[55]

As Republicans welcomed segregationists, political observers took note. Liberal columnist Joseph Alsop scolded the GOP for embracing what he called "the Southern Strategy." "Closed doors are desirable for a discussion of the Southern Strategy," he noted in 1962, "because it is basically a segregationist strategy. The ugly word will not be used, of course. Powerful admiration for states' rights will be professed instead. But this amounts to the same thing."[56] What journalists discovered behind those closed doors alarmed them. In 1963 syndicated columnist Robert Novak attended the RNC's summer meeting in Denver. Over breakfast, one operative reminded colleagues, "This isn't South Africa. The white man outnumbers the Negro 9 to 1 in this country." At lunch, two southern chairmen casually used racial slurs. "The amazing part of it," an easterner marveled, "was that nobody criticized them for doing it." Wirt Yerger, head of the GOP's Association of Southern State Chairmen, even accused the Kennedy administration of fomenting racial trouble to win elections. "All this pointed to an unmistakable conclusion," Novak noted. "A good many, perhaps a majority of the party's leaders envisioned substantial political gold to be mined in the racial crisis by becoming in fact, though not in name, the White Man's Party."[57]

The 1964 election provided, at long last, a stark contrast on civil rights. President Lyndon B. Johnson had long been a typical southern Democrat, consistently voting against civil rights measures during his first twenty years in Congress. But as his national ambitions grew, he embraced the cause, helping pass the Civil Rights Acts of 1957 and 1960 as Senate majority leader. As president, Johnson devoted himself to strengthening Kennedy's civil rights bill and overcoming southern resistance. Underscoring his commitment to the issue, LBJ tapped Hubert Humphrey, Democrats' longtime trailblazer on civil rights, as his running mate. Meanwhile, the Republican ticket was the Southern Strategy personified. Goldwater won the nomination and picked RNC Chairman William Miller as his vice-presidential nominee. (Alabama governor George Wallace, a segregationist Democrat, offered to switch parties if Goldwater would make *him* his running mate, but the Arizonan thought that was a step too far.)[58]

The 1964 Republican National Convention displayed the party's reinvention. Liberals and moderates who had dominated for decades now found themselves on the outside. The moderate Ripon Society insisted that the party had to choose "whether or not to adopt a strategy that must inevitably exploit the 'white backlash' to the Civil Rights Movement."[59] The convention's verdict was clear. The 1964 party platform, columnists Rowland Evans and Robert Novak reported, had "the weakest Republican civil rights plank in memory."[60] The 1960 platform had devoted 1,250 words to a detailed civil rights plank; the 1964 plank was one-tenth as long and, as one newspaper put it, "weak and weasel-worded."[61] Nelson Rockefeller, who had pushed the prior convention to embrace civil rights, tried to add an amendment denouncing extremists in the John Birch Society and the KKK but was shouted down.[62] Notably, the convention floor was mostly white. For the first time in fifty years, there were no Black delegates in any southern delegation; even "polyglot California" somehow sent "no Negroes and no Jews," Evans and Novak marveled.[63] The few Black Republicans who attended were verbally abused and physically assaulted. One had his suit set on fire. His attacker screamed, "Keep in your own place!"[64] Longtime Republican Jackie Robinson left the convention deeply shaken: "I now believe I know how it felt to be a Jew in Hitler's Germany."[65]

As Blacks recoiled from the GOP, white southerners warmed to it. Goldwater led the way, making pointed appeals for party switching. "There is nothing left . . . of the principles that your fathers, grandfathers and great-grandfathers stood for in the Democratic Party," he assured a massive audience in South Carolina. "I wonder how many votes Hubert Horatio Humphrey would have gotten in the Deep South of your fathers and grandfathers?"[66] The campaign for party switchers climaxed with the announcement in September 1964 that Senator Strom Thurmond— the archetypical Dixiecrat—was leaving the Democratic Party and officially joining the GOP. This was "no surprise," newspapers yawned, as he had long sided with Republicans.[67] ("There is not enough difference between a conservative South Carolina Democrat like Sen. Thurmond and a conservative Republican to put a piece of paper between," Goldwater had told southern audiences.)[68] But working across the aisle was one thing, and moving there quite another. Southern Democrats had considered switching since the 1930s but always found reasons to stay put. Republicans' reputation for racial liberalism, long a sticking point, had faded. But career congressmen still balked because their power derived from two simple facts: Democrats had solid majorities in Congress, and within the party southern congressmen had seniority, which gave them prestigious committee chairs. Switching parties would have meant starting over at the very bottom, as junior members of the minority party. "None seemed willing to surrender one iota of seniority or other senatorial perquisites in the Congress," Thurmond's chief of staff later explained. "This is why so few party switches take place."[69] Conservative columnist William F. Buckley Jr. accordingly urged Republicans to be "generous with Strom Thurmond." If the perks of his seniority were protected, it would establish an enticing precedent and "six, or possibly eight, conceivably ten Democratic senators could be persuaded to move in a bloc to the Republican side of the aisle."[70] Republicans were indeed "generous" with Thurmond, but the sweetheart deal they struck was understood to be a one-off. As a result, other segregationist senators closed out their careers as Democrats. Outside Congress, party switching was more common. In Houston two thousand registered Democrats (including forty precinct workers) gathered for a mass "resignation rally" to announce their switch. In Illinois a Republican precinct worker announced his switch the other way, rationalizing that "the two major parties have changed sides in 100 years."[71]

Goldwater suffered a landslide loss that year. Aside from Arizona, he carried only five states, all of them in the Deep South: South Carolina, Georgia, Alabama, Mississippi, and Louisiana. But his impact there was remarkable. "Goldwater won a smashing victory in Mississippi," the *Jackson Clarion-Ledger* reported, becoming "the first Republican to win the state since Grant won it with the aid of reconstruction bayonets." He took 87 percent of Mississippi's vote, winning every county. His coattails helped a little-known candidate oust a twenty-two-year Democratic congressman and surely would have done more if Republicans had only bothered to run candidates everywhere. (Their oversight was "naïve and stupid," one activist regretted.)[72] In Alabama, Goldwater did nearly as well, winning 70 percent. Here, though, state officials had anticipated his strength and prepared to profit down-ballot. "The Barry Goldwater tidal wave," the *Birmingham News* reported, "swept Republicans into office at every level from constable to Congress."[73]

To be sure, Goldwater's impact was clearest in this new class of southern Republican congressmen. Prentiss Walker, the first Mississippi Republican representative in eighty years, was a former Democratic official and ardent segregationist. Unsubtly, his first public address after winning came before a Klan front called Americans for the Preservation of the White Race.[74] In Alabama segregationist Bill Dickinson likewise left the Democrats and won a House seat as a Republican. "I have joined the white man's party," he announced upon switching. "It behooves us to support those who support us and our way of life."[75] The other four Republican congressmen from Alabama—including Jim Martin, bouncing back from his narrow loss in 1962—were similarly outspoken opponents of civil rights. One said that the Civil Rights Act "paved the way for the destruction of our liberties"; another called the day that it passed "Black

Friday."[76] Howard "Bo" Callaway, who likewise abandoned Democrats over integration and promised to repeal the Civil Rights Act, became Georgia's first Republican representative since Reconstruction.[77] In South Carolina, Democratic congressman Albert Watson had campaigned for Goldwater, prompting House Democrats to strip his seniority. Watson resigned from Congress, switched parties, and reclaimed his seat with 70 percent of the vote. Regardless of party, Watson remained a solid segregationist, voting against the Civil Rights Act as a Democrat and against the Voting Rights Act as a Republican.[78] Most of his southern colleagues did, too. "So goes the GOP in the South," an Atlanta columnist noted in 1965, "with its crop of freshmen in Congress sounding just as Democrats and Dixiecrats have sounded for lo, these many years."[79]

Importantly, the nation now saw the two parties starkly divided on racial matters. In 1962 a survey asking whether Democrats or Republicans were "more likely to see to it that Negroes get fair treatment in jobs and housing" showed Americans evenly split: 23 percent said Democrats, and 21 percent said Republicans, but a solid majority of 56 percent saw the two parties as basically the same. Just two years later, public opinion had shifted dramatically. In 1964, 60 percent said Democrats were likelier to back civil rights measures in employment, 33 percent said the parties were little different, and only 7 percent said Republicans had the edge. Likewise, on the question of which party was likelier to support school desegregation, 56 percent picked Democrats, 37 percent said neither had an edge, and, once again, only 7 percent said Republicans.[80] The clearest sign of realignment on racial issues, of course, came from African Americans themselves. Well after the New Deal made most Black voters Democrats, roughly a third remained Republicans: in 1956, Eisenhower won 39 percent of the Black vote; in 1960, Nixon took 32 percent. Yet in 1964, Goldwater received only 6 percent.[81]

Although the election was transformative, the permanence of those transformations wasn't yet clear. The Voting Rights Act of 1965 promised to remake the electorate and, quite possibly, the electoral map. In its first year of operation alone, the number of African Americans registered in the Deep South doubled.[82] Given the 1964 patterns, observers expected new Black voters to vote Democratic, too. But how their rise would reshape politics in the South and elsewhere remained an open question. Would there be a "white backlash" in 1966?[83] If so, polls suggested that it would benefit Republicans. When the Harris Survey asked, "Which party in the next few years would do a better job slowing down the pace of civil rights?," 69 percent said Republicans, 31 percent Democrats.[84]

The 1966 election gave a mixed verdict on the power of white backlash. In the South, reactionary politics drove both parties right, as three Republican House freshmen took on prominent Democratic segregationists: Prentiss Walker challenged Senator Jim Eastland in the Mississippi Senate race; Jim Martin faced Lurleen Wallace, defending Alabama's gubernatorial seat as a surrogate for her husband, George; and Bo Callaway ran for Georgia governor against Lester Maddox, an Atlanta businessman who shut down his restaurant rather than desegregate it. All three Republicans lost. (Callaway actually won the popular vote, but the close election was thrown to the Georgia House, where the Democratic majority backed the Democrat.) Even with those departures from the House, southern Republicans doubled their numbers, from fourteen to twenty-eight.[85] Outside the region, though, the potential of backlash politics remained uncertain. Gubernatorial races in California and Florida, won by Democrats-turned-Republicans Ronald Reagan and Claude Kirk, "were both influenced by the backlash," the *Los Angeles Times* observed. But in Arkansas and Maryland, Democrats running reactionary campaigns lost to moderate Republicans; in Massachusetts, African American Edward Brooke won election to the Senate as a Republican.[86] The future of the GOP was unclear.

What the 1966 elections *did* make clear was the return of Richard Nixon. Hoping to build support for his next presidential run, Nixon spent the year campaigning for Republican congressional candidates, paying special attention to the South. Because of its strong showing for Goldwater, the region had been rewarded with additional seats for the next Republican National Convention, enough to control nearly half the votes needed for the nomination. Stumping for southern Republicans in 1966, Nixon repeated Goldwater's call for conservatives to switch sides. "The Democratic Party at the national level hasn't been conservative for thirty years and never will be," he insisted in Birmingham, "so get out of it and join the Republican Party."[87] Nixon tried to dodge discussion of segregation, although state parties often made that impossible. In 1964, for instance, the Mississippi GOP formally endorsed "segregation of the races as absolutely essential to harmonious race relations." Asked about it during a 1966 visit, Nixon insisted that he was "opposed to any so-called segregationist plank" in a Republican platform.[88] Meanwhile, in South Carolina the moderate leadership had been replaced in 1965 by Thurmond's aide Harry Dent, who switched parties with his boss.[89] ("Any major Republican you meet in the state is likely as not to be a former Democrat," a newspaper explained in what was now a routine observation.)[90] The 1966 South Carolina Republican convention, held beneath a huge Confederate banner, had no Black delegates; its gubernatorial candidate, a former Democratic state representative, called the incumbent soft on segregation.[91] When Nixon came to raise funds for this new South Carolina GOP, a reporter asked if it was awkward to be associated with "ole States' Rights Strom." Undeterred, Nixon vouched for Thurmond's character: "Strom is no racist. Strom is a man of courage and integrity."[92]

Nixon and Thurmond's alliance proved pivotal. "In the next two years," Harry Dent remembered, "the seed of the Republican Southern Strategy began to sprout and grow."[93] Looking ahead to 1968, Thurmond and Dent locked down southern Republicans for Nixon, setting up an Atlanta meeting with southern party chairmen. Nixon avoided supporting segregation openly, but his promises—conservative judicial appointments, relaxed enforcement of school desegregation, and opposition to busing—won them over.[94] At the Miami convention, Nixon provided more assurances to southern conservatives, especially his selection of Maryland governor Spiro Agnew as running mate. Elected as a moderate, Agnew gained fame lambasting civil rights leaders after a riot. Meanwhile, the Republican platform never even mentioned the phrase "civil rights." There were instead extensive calls for "law and order," which Nixon protested in his acceptance speech was *not* a "code word for racism."[95] "Taken together," Alsop observed, "the words and acts quite clearly mean that Nixon will follow the 'southern strategy' this year."[96]

But there was not a single "southern strategy," and Nixon's plan was not a simple rehash of Goldwater's. "The idea that Goldwater started the

Southern Strategy is bullshit," Nixon later fumed to a biographer. The GOP had already made inroads under Eisenhower, but Goldwater over-reached by chasing "foam-at-the-mouth segregationists." The Arizonan "ran as a racist candidate," Nixon argued, and therefore "won the wrong [southern] states," sweeping the Deep South but alienating the rest.[97] Nixon believed Goldwater's approach was generally flawed, but especially ill-suited to 1968. Segregationist Democrat George Wallace, running as an independent, seemed sure to sweep the Deep South. Accordingly, Nixon ceded that ground, focusing on winning the rest of the region.[98] A memo from Mississippian Fred LaRue spelled out this southern strat-egy: "The anti-Wallace message will be indirect—'between the lines' and 'in regional code words.'" Dent handled the details, although Nixon held off on officially hiring Thurmond's aide until after the election.[99] As he stressed similarities with Wallace to white southerners, Nixon em-phasized differences elsewhere, using the segregationist to seem states-manlike by comparison. Still, when it came to Wallace's and Nixon's challenges to the civil rights movement, these were differences of degree, not kind. (Sociologist Jonathan Rieder has aptly invoked the strategies that anticommunists proposed for the Cold War: "If Wallace offered roll-back, Nixon suggested containment.")[100] Nixon's plan worked. Wallace took only five Deep South states, while LBJ's Texas stayed Democratic. Nixon captured the rest of the South, which, along with the Midwest and West, won him the election.[101]

Having narrowly won a three-way race, Nixon sought to solidify the South for 1972. "The southern strategy was just pure election politics," remembered Clarke Reed, chairman of the Mississippi GOP. "The South was going for Wallace and Nixon could get it next time."[102] Publicly, Nix-on's aides repeatedly denied they had any "southern strategy," hoping to maintain the middle-of-the-road image they had drawn between the seg-regationist Wallace and the liberal Humphrey. To maintain that illusion, Nixon aide John Ehrlichman noted, the administration strategically took a range of stances on civil rights issues, adding liberal "zigs" to balance conservative "zags."[103] But the "zags" were there nonetheless—the attor-ney general's testimony against renewal of the Voting Rights Act, an ap-peal for desegregation delays in Mississippi, and, most important, the nomination of two southern conservatives to the Supreme Court.[104] Political rhetoric backed up policies, with Dent orchestrating the plan and Agnew serving, one journalist noted, as "chief agent of the President's Southern Strategy."[105]

Despite their denials, Nixon's administration soon confirmed the Southern Strategy. In the fall of 1969, Kevin Phillips, a campaign strategist and special assistant to Attorney General John Mitchell, published *The Emerging Republican Majority*. In it he observed that the old liberal Democratic coalition was being surpassed by a new conservative Republican one, rooted in suburbia and the South and the Southwest, which he christened "the Sunbelt." The "principal cause of the breakup of the New Deal coalition," Phillips stated bluntly, was "the Negro problem."[106] Counterintuitively, he argued that Republicans should back the Voting Rights Act because it would only accelerate the process of party realignment. "The more Negroes who register as Democrats in the South, the sooner the Negrophobe whites will quit the Democrats and become Republicans," he informed the *New York Times*. "That's where the votes are."[107] Wallace's independent run had merely represented a "way station" for "Democratic traditionalists following party realignment into the Republican Party."[108] Phillips confidently predicted that "we'll get two-thirds to three-fourths of the Wallace vote in 1972."[109]

The Emerging Republican Majority panicked the administration. Speechwriter William Safire warned it was the "most dangerous new book to come out," not because it was wrong about Republicans looking south but because it suggested they would "write off" the Northeast in doing so. To blunt the book's impact, Safire urged Dent to "pooh pooh" it and urged Nixon to deny having read it. Both did exactly that.[110] In a December 1969 memo, "Re: 'Southern strategy' and the Northeast," Dent exhorted Nixon to reframe southern outreach "so we effectively get across the point that nobody is being written out, the South is only being written in."[111] Publicly, the GOP followed that exact line. "The 'Southern Strategy' is a bum rap," RNC Chairman Rogers Morton told reporters. Republicans *were* pursuing the South, but the suggestion that Nixon might ignore other regions was "a deeply cynical view of the office of the presidency."[112]

Although the administration insisted that the Southern Strategy had been exaggerated, privately it worried that the strategy had not gone far enough. In January 1970, Dent warned that "George [Wallace] has a 'counter Southern strategy' to deny Southern electoral votes to the President in 1972."[113] Journalists likewise saw Nixon and Wallace competing for the same southern white votes. At the 1970 Gridiron Dinner, for instance, the president was treated to a song titled "Rock-a-Bye Your Baby with a Dixie Melody," whose lyrics included the lines:

> *Rock-a-bye the voters with a Southern strategy;*
> *Don't you fuss; we won't bus children in ol' Dixie!*
> *We'll put George Wallace in decline*
> *Below the Mason-Dixon line . . .*
> *A zillion Southern votes we will deliver;*
> *Move Washington down on the Swanee River!*
> *Rockabye with Ol' Massa Nixon and his Dixie strategy!*[114]

Nixon and Agnew played along with the joke during their own performance, engaging in banter behind pianos on stage. "What about this 'southern strategy' we hear so often?" Nixon asked his vice president. "Yes suh, Mr. President," Agnew answered in exaggerated dialect. "Ah agree with you completely on yoah southern strategy."[115]

Worried about being outflanked by Wallace, the administration backed archconservative Republicans in the 1970 midterms. In South Carolina, Representative Albert Watson ran for the governor's office in a starkly racist campaign. One of his first television ads depicted Black rioters in Los Angeles asking "Are we going to be ruled by the bloc?" ("Only thing folks are talking about is if the colored are gonna run our schools or we are," a white truck driver told a reporter. "For my money, only one man is standing up for white folks, and that's Albert Watson.")[116] Meanwhile, Florida governor Claude Kirk tried to hold his seat with delays on public school integration and "complete resistance to forced busing." Kirk pressed racial resentment so hard that the editor of the *Gainesville Sun* had to ask: "Does he want re-election so badly that he will pull a George Wallace and split Florida's people asunder?"[117] When Watson and Kirk both lost their races to more racially moderate Democrats, many concluded that they—and the Nixon administration—had overplayed their hand. *New York Times* reporter R. W. Apple scoffed that 1970 was "the year of the non-emerging Republican majority."[118]

Having gone too far in the midterms, Nixon's team recalibrated for 1972, returning to its 1968 plan of backing conservative policies while disavowing extremist politics. "It is not a Southern strategy," Nixon insisted. "It is an American strategy. That is what it is, and that is what the South believes in and what America believes in."[119] In noting that "southern" appeals worked well across the nation, the president was wholly right. Nixon won a landslide reelection, taking in 60.7 percent of the popular vote. He won every state of the Confederacy—the first time a Republican *ever* did that—and by commanding margins. Indeed, the South was Nixon's strongest region. Across America, Nixon won over 70 percent of the vote in eight states; six of them were in the South. He did best in Mississippi, winning 79 percent. He won roughly 80 percent of the white vote across the South, an estimated 92 percent from rural whites in the Deep South. Voters who had opted for Wallace in 1968 swung to Nixon by a three-to-one margin, just as Phillips had predicted.[120] "In many ways, the Republican and Democratic parties are exchanging their historic roles and constituencies," the strategist crowed. "The Republicans are becoming the presidential party of the Old Confederacy, while the Democrats are beginning to pivot on the Northeast, Upper Midwest, and Pacific Northwest, virtually reversing the old post–Civil War pattern."[121] Dent believed this realignment was permanent: "The South will never go back."[122]

Though significant, this shift in voters' presidential preference was simply the first stage in regional realignment. Typically, changes in local, state, and congressional preferences follow presidential shifts, but at a slower pace. Republicans hoped to speed the process, Dent noted to Nixon, by encouraging "more switchovers throughout the South."[123] They had some successes. In 1968 five top Democratic officeholders in Georgia became Republicans at once; state legislators switched parties there and elsewhere, too.[124] Negotiations to get Georgia's governor, Lester Maddox, to turn Republican fell apart, but another former segregationist, Virginia's governor, Mills Godwin, changed parties as a prelude to his successful return to that office in 1973.[125] Former Texas governor John Connally, who joined Nixon's cabinet in 1971 as a rumored replacement for Agnew, switched parties in 1973 as well. "The GOP 'Southern Strategy,'" Phillips gloated again, "seems to be rolling along—and rolling up local victories."[126]

In Congress, however, a mass defection of conservative southern Democrats remained a pipe dream. In its first term the Nixon administration championed "Project Okinawa," an attempt to lure Senator Harry Byrd Jr., head of Virginia's Democratic machine, into the Republican ranks. Byrd did leave the Democrats after the 1970 election but stopped short of joining the GOP, declaring himself an Independent. In early 1972, House Minority Leader Gerald Ford hoped to boost Republican ranks through "Operation Switchover," but that plan fizzled, too.[127] After Nixon's 1972 landslide, however, mass switching seemed plausible. The president's coattails produced "a narrow but durable conservative majority" in Congress, reflected *National Review* publisher William Rusher, prompting "serious consideration" for major realignment.[128] Even as the national party had moved left, southern Democrats remained reliably on the right. In its 1972 congressional ratings, for instance, the American Conservative Union gave eight senators a "100" for their perfectly conservative records: five Republicans and three southern Democrats.[129] Newspapers speculated in late 1972 that a small number might switch parties; later reports suggested more.[130] According to journalist Godfrey Hodgson, "Some forty Democrats entered into negotiations about becoming Republicans." In early 1973, Democratic congressman Joe Waggonner of Louisiana, a former leader of the White Citizens' Councils, discussed with GOP officials under "what terms Democrats would be welcomed into Republican ranks." The main obstacles, as always, were Democrats' concerns over seniority. "It went committee by committee; the ranking [Republican] member in each case was asked whether he would be willing to stand aside and let a Democratic convert take over the chairmanship," Hodgson noted. "In the end, half of those who were asked said they were willing to do just that." Before Waggonner's work could be completed, however, the Senate Watergate inquiry began, quickly making the Republican Party much less attractive for disaffected Democrats.[131]

Instead of a sudden shift, congressional realignment happened piece-meal, with older conservative Democrats being slowly replaced by younger conservative Republicans. Consider Mississippi representative William Colmer. First elected in 1932, he had witnessed firsthand Democrats' shift from segregation to civil rights. Part of the Mississippi delegation that stormed out of the 1948 convention, he helped launch the Dixiecrat movement. Like most Dixiecrats, though, he returned to the Democrats, waging a losing battle against civil rights inside the party. By 1966, Colmer was grumbling that conservatives should leave the Democrats for good. But his seniority made him the powerful head of the House Rules Committee, so he stayed put. When he finally retired in 1972, Colmer tapped his administrative assistant—thirty-year-old Trent Lott—as his replacement. Crucially, Lott ran as a Republican, with newspaper ads presenting him as "a conservative in the Colmer tradition." Lott won and over the next decades rose through Republican ranks to become Senate majority leader (a position he later resigned, ironically, for praising Strom Thurmond's Dixiecrat candidacy).[132]

Most new southern Republicans had a less direct connection to Democrats they replaced, but the general pattern held. In 1972 Mississippi Republican Thad Cochran replaced another retiring House Democrat; six years later, he succeeded Senator Jim Eastland.[133] Dave Treen, a Louisiana Dixiecrat who joined the GOP in 1962, replaced another retiring Democrat that year. (The state's first Republican representative since the nineteenth century, in 1979 Treen became its first Republican governor since Reconstruction.)[134] In North Carolina, Jesse Helms—who worked as an aide to segregationist Democratic senator Willis Smith and served as a Democratic city councilman in Raleigh before switching parties in 1970—won election in 1972 to become the state's first Republican senator in seventy years.[135] As with negotiations for switches by senior congress-men, this replacement process stalled with Watergate and the reckoning it brought Republicans in the 1974 and 1976 elections. But that was merely a short-term setback. As RNC chairman George H. W. Bush predicted in 1973, "The current realignment of the GOP will continue long after Watergate is forgotten."[136]

Indeed, the shift of southern white conservatives only accelerated. Republicans' regional domination of the Nixon era was interrupted in 1976, when Democrat Jimmy Carter, a born-again Christian from Georgia, swept all of the South except Virginia. That proved a temporary reversal as Reagan retook it all (except Carter's Georgia) in 1980. Revered in the region, Reagan persuaded southern whites to register as Republicans. Ads across the South framed switching as the only option for conservatives: "I didn't leave the Democratic Party; it left me."[137] "I know what it's like to pull that Republican lever for the first time, because I used to be a Democrat myself," Reagan joked. "But I can tell you—it only hurts for a minute."[138] The plea worked. Election returns showed that southern white men, who had identified as Democratic by a four-to-one margin two decades earlier, now split evenly between the parties. "It was," political scientist Warren Miller concluded, "a realignment of massive proportions."[139]

The reasons for Reagan's success with southern whites, however, remain contested. A former Goldwater surrogate, Reagan seemed intent on reviving that brand of "southern strategy." For his first major event after the 1980 convention, Reagan accepted Lott's invitation to come to Philadelphia, Mississippi—the infamous site where three civil rights activists were murdered in 1964 with the local police's complicity. "I believe in states' rights," Reagan told the lily-white crowd, promising to "restore to states and local governments the power that properly belongs to them."[140] Civil rights leader Andrew Young warned that "these code words have been the electoral language of Wallace, Goldwater and the Nixon southern strategy."[141] Campaign surrogates such as South Carolina congressman Carroll Campbell insisted that Reagan's invocation of "states' rights" had no connection to segregation.[142] But such claims of innocence were often undermined by those surrogates' own past links to segregation. (Campbell, for instance, gained fame in 1970 as spokesman for a South Carolina group working to slow school integration. He won his first election that same year.)[143]

Like Nixon's administration, Reagan's denied it had any race-based Southern Strategy. In 1981 strategist Lee Atwater readily admitted that racism *had* been the foundation for "the Harry Dent–type Southern

Strategy. The whole strategy was . . . based on coded racism. The whole thing." But Reagan's regional appeal was different, the South Carolinian protested, because it focused on economics and national defense, and "the whole campaign was devoid of any kind of racism, any kind of reference."[144] Despite Atwater's spin, Reagan made campaign references to a "Chicago welfare queen" in addition to the "states' rights" talk across the South.[145] But Atwater was right, in another sense, for Reagan's regional appeal wasn't simply the "old Southern Strategy" of coded racism. As political scientists Angie Maxwell and Todd Shields have noted, "too often the Southern Strategy is remembered as a fixed, short course, relegated to a few election cycles and singularly focused on exploiting racial animus." Instead, they argue convincingly, there was a "long Southern Strategy" that evolved and expanded from the coded racism of the Goldwater-Nixon appeals to a broader social conservatism attuned to religious fundamentalism and "family values" as well.[146]

In the Reagan era, Republican campaigns blended these three themes in equal measure, delighting southern conservatives. (Trent Lott told the Sons of Confederate Veterans that "the spirit of Jefferson Davis lives in the 1984 Republican platform.")[147] The GOP presidential nominee took every single southern state in 1984, 1988, 2000, and 2004, losing only parts of the region in 1992 and 1996, when Democrats ran *two* white southerners on the same ticket. The surge of southern Republicans in Congress was equally remarkable. In 1950 there were no southern Republican senators and only two congressmen in the South's 105-member House delegation; by 2000, the South's delegations to the House and Senate were both majority Republican. State legislatures were the last to change because of the GOP's initial focus on statewide races and an according lack of grassroots investments.[148] But the process that political scientists Christopher Cooper and Gibbs Knotts termed "trickle-down realignment" reached state legislatures in the 1990s and 2000s. Reviewing the "firsts" for Republicans in twentieth-century South Carolina shows how slowly that realignment spread. Strom Thurmond and Albert Watson became (in the modern era) the state's first Republicans in the Senate and House in 1964 and 1965; James Edwards didn't become the state's first Republican governor until 1974;

the state's House and Senate became majority Republican only in 1994 and 2000, respectively.[149] "It is not surprising that the big change did not come all at once," political scientist James Glaser noted. "Old-time, hard-line southern Democrats in the mass public had to die out and be replaced."[150]

Ultimately, party realignment over civil rights stands as one of the central arcs of twentieth-century political history. The Democratic Party's evolution from being a defender of slavery, segregation, and white supremacy to a champion of civil rights represented a massive revolution in the political scheme, one that prompted an equally significant reaction, as the Republican Party retreated from its roots in racial liberalism to embrace and exploit the politics of white grievance. Realignment was a glacial change, in both senses of the term: moving slowly but thoroughly transforming the landscape that it left behind. Amply chronicled by journalists at the time and thoroughly detailed by historians and political scientists in the decades since, this long-conventional narrative has been grounded in the private words and public deeds of Republican presidents and presidential candidates, administration figures and campaign strategists, and even national, regional, and state leaders of the Republican National Committee. These individuals' embrace of the Southern Strategy was cemented in changes at the party level, such as official platforms and convention delegations, and readily recognized by outside observers, ranging from political journalists to public opinion surveys and polling data.

These realities of the Republican Party's past, of course, do not dictate its future. Just as one generation of political figures chose to enflame white resentment for their own gain, later generations could reject that path. At the start of the twenty-first century, Republicans seemed intent on turning the page. Under President George W. Bush, the GOP strengthened its outreach to African Americans and other racial minorities. The Bush administration featured a racially diverse cabinet, with African Americans and Latinos in prominent posts, and promoted policies such as immigration reform.[151] Notably, in 2005 RNC chairman Ken Mehlman directly apologized for the Southern Strategy in an address to the NAACP: "Some Republicans gave up on winning the African

American vote, looking the other way or trying to benefit politically from racial polarization. I am here today as the Republican chairman to tell you we were wrong."[152] Michael Steele, another RNC chairman and the first African American in that role, echoed Mehlman in 2010, acknowledging that "for the last forty-plus years, we had a 'Southern Strategy' that alienated many minority voters by focusing on the white male vote in the South."[153]

This frank reckoning with Republicans' past racism proved short-lived. Pundits on the Right denounced it as weakness, or worse. Radio star Rush Limbaugh compared Mehlman's decision to "go down there and basically apologize for what has come to be known as the 'Southern strategy,' popularized by the Nixon administration," to sexual assault: "Once again, Republicans are going to go bend over and grab the ankles."[154] When Democrats rallied around Barack Obama, the first African American candidate from a major party and the first to serve as president, Republicans retreated from the racial outreach of the Bush years and returned to the politics of resentment. During the reign of President Donald Trump, who pandered to white nationalists and promised to protect monuments to the Confederacy, the GOP reverted to its earlier form with a vengeance. Due to the success of the Southern Strategy, Republicans are now unrecognizable as the party of Lincoln.

13

THE GOOD PROTEST

Glenda Gilmore

THE RIGHT TO PROTEST IS ENSHRINED IN THE BILL OF RIGHTS' First Amendment, and most Americans cherish it. Our textbooks and national lore celebrate moments in our history when individual and collective acts of civil disobedience—for example, the Boston Tea Party—seemed to change the course of history. We see protest as a part of civic life—indeed, as an international human right.

The current national myth of the "good" protest is based on the civil rights movement (CRM) that began with the Montgomery bus boycott in December 1955 and continued until Martin Luther King Jr.'s death in April 1968. Historians call this period the "classical phase" of a longer struggle. They recall orderly people who marched in the streets flying flags and holding signs, or took part in sit-ins practicing nonviolent passive resistance. Moreover, the CRM, as Americans like to remember it, simply sought to end legal segregation of the public sphere, which most people now agree was undemocratic. If a protest does not resemble the movement's classical-phase demonstrations, critics often call it a usurpation of the nation's noble past.

Many contrast protests of the 2010s and 2020s with those of the classical phase of the CRM to suggest that if they were more like those in the past, most Americans would readily support them now as they had then. For example, on September 4, 2020, *New York Times* columnist David Brooks argued that if Donald Trump tried to hold on to the presidency after losing the then-upcoming election, citizens' protests should follow those of the classical phase. Pointing to their nonviolence and tight organization, he wrote, "That's how the movement captured the moral high ground and won the mind of the nation." He explained that "through epic acts of self-discipline, the nonviolent civil rights marchers in the 1960s forced their foes to reveal that if there were to be any violence and anarchy, it would come from the foes."[1] That restraint, he implied, would win large-scale support today.

That simplified myth of the "good" protest and others like it do the country a disservice. They shorten more than a century of diverse antiracism protests to roughly a decade, implying that it was relatively easy to win total victory over racism and also producing a national amnesia of the much longer struggle. They suggest that protesters should take action against only the most egregious, state-sponsored laws, excluding a broader definition of racial justice and equity. Problematically, the myth holds subsequent demonstrations to a model of behavior that arose from a peculiar context at one moment in time. If protests do not conform to the orderly marches staged by people practicing passive resistance in the face of violence, then they aren't "good" protests. The narrative rests on four misconceptions: that the demonstrations from 1955 to 1968 were the first of their kind, that most Americans gave their support to the protests and their leaders, that they quickly exposed and vanquished hatred, and that they ended happily by bringing racial equality to America.

This essay challenges that mythology. First, it chronicles a long civil rights moment from the 1890s to the 1950s that ultimately led to the classical phase of the movement. This longer look demonstrates that winning civil rights was much more difficult than most Americans believe and that African Americans had always fought for equality. Second, it dispels the notion that most Americans supported the protests. Leaders such as Martin Luther King Jr., who have been "canonized" in the past thirty-five years, were vilified then.[2] Third, it proves that classical-phase protests were, and had always been, about issues other than simply abolishing segregation. Police brutality, economic equity, voting rights, and cultural symbols have always been on the civil rights agenda. Fourth, it sees the classical phase as incomplete, with issues that remain on the national agenda. Reshaping the national myth of the "good" protest uncovers a more useful past in the face of growing antiprotest sentiment.

The longer history of protest demonstrates that the years that it took for Black people to be able to sit where they liked on Montgomery buses or to order a grilled-cheese sandwich at Greensboro's Woolworth lunch counter represented only a culmination of countless other protests that had preceded them. Those protests most often failed and were disorderly. People condemned them as lawless, and police brutally suppressed them.

Homer Plessy and Rosa Parks both became famous for a day when they refused to participate in segregated transportation, but those refusals were separated by 63 years and 177 days (June 7, 1892, to December 1, 1955). As they began their commutes, both protesters anticipated what would happen. They expected that the driver would tell them to move, they knew they would refuse, and they braced themselves for what would follow. With organizational backing, they would fight the inevitable ejection, publicize it, and rally community protesters to support them. By the time that Parks refused to move to the back of the bus in 1955, countless others had followed Plessy's 1892 refusal to move to the Jim Crow trolley car, been arrested, and challenged the Jim Crow laws under which they were charged. Nonetheless, most Americans know Parks as the "first" person who challenged segregated transportation when she refused to move to the back of the bus and ignited more than a decade of novel civil rights actions in the 1950s and 1960s.[3]

As Blair L. M. Kelley documents, after the *Plessy* decision in 1896, cities and states across the South quickly passed public-transportation segregation laws. In 1900 in Parks's home of Montgomery, Black residents responded to their city's passage of a segregation law with petitions, mass meetings, and a two-year-long boycott and picketing. In 1903 the Montgomery city council responded by passing a law prohibiting "boycotting, . . . picketing or other interference with . . . lawful business."[4] That is the same law under which police arrested Parks. In 1955 a few Montgomery elders must have remembered the turn-of-the-century protests, even if Parks and Martin Luther King Jr. apparently remained unaware of them.[5] Most historians also failed to connect them as part of a long history of protest.[6]

The streetcar demonstrations were not the only precedents on which the 1955 Montgomery marchers drew.[7] In the fifteen years before Parks's action, Black southerners had launched almost daily protests against segregation on crowded buses and trains as the country mobilized on the home front for World War II. In Virginia, Pauli Murray, a young Black woman, had been studying nonviolent techniques when she refused to stay seated in the back of a bus in 1940 in Petersburg, Virginia. After her arrest and conviction for disorderly conduct, she chose to go to jail rather than pay a fine. Moreover, Montgomery's bus boycotters would have known that during World War II in Birmingham, only ninety-three miles away, fights and arrests over seating on crowded buses had been commonplace.[8] And in 1944 in Virginia, Irene Morgan refused to give up her bus seat, a refusal that the US Supreme Court ratified when it found that forcing interstate passengers to abide by Virginia segregation laws put an "unconstitutional burden on interstate commerce."[9]

Nearly every iconic protest in the classical phase of the civil rights movement shared goals, venues, and methods with those that came before them. The "first" sit-in at the Woolworth lunch counter in Greensboro, in 1960, followed a formula that began over a quarter of a century earlier in Washington, DC. There, a Black assistant to Representative Oscar DePriest, the nation's only Black congressman, was shocked on January 23, 1934, to find himself suddenly denied service at the Capitol's public restaurant, where he had customarily eaten over a five-year period. Indeed, some fifteen years earlier, Woodrow Wilson's administration had segregated the dining rooms on the Hill, but managers had enforced the rule "only sporadically." Then managers manhandled and ultimately evicted a Black Chicago woman who was attending a congressional hearing. NAACP officials, students, and Professors Ralph Bunche of Howard University and Howard Beale of the University of North Carolina, who was white, mounted sit-in demonstrations.

Kenneth Clark, a twenty-year-old Howard undergraduate, led thirty male Howard students in a sit-in at the House restaurant. A fracas, disorderly conduct charges, and threats of expulsion from Howard ensued. Representative DePriest worked to get a compromise behind the scenes, but he failed. Sporadic sit-ins on Capitol Hill continued for years.[10] During World War II, Pauli Murray, by then a Howard University law student, led another sit-in movement in 1943 and 1944. Murray perfected the "stool sitting technique," the method of nonviolent confrontation inside privately owned restaurants, with robust picketing outside, all trademarks of the protesters from Greensboro's universities who took their own seats on Woolworth's lunch-counter stools seventeen years later.[11]

The national amnesia concerning early protests leaves most Americans with the impression that African Americans complied for decades with Jim Crow's outrages and theft of rights, even as it hides the continual remaking of the racist regime that whites built and rebuilt to enforce them during the decades that Jim Crow lasted. Moreover, the omission of protest history also makes it seem that when the evil of segregation became apparent to white people in 1955, the federal government quickly solved it with the Civil Rights Act of 1964.

That narrative allows space for redemption by implying that white people had been unaware of the extent of their own oppressive acts before the movement began. But the CRM's classical phase did not reveal previously hidden wrongs to an unaware white public. Instead, it initially cast those long-visible wrongs in a new light for a small group of people who became allies. Finally, the horror and duration of those struggles unseated the national narrative of a progressive twentieth century and placed responsibility for Black inequality not on faceless ancestral slaveholders but on living white people's grandpas and grandmas.

In the 1950s and 1960s, a vast majority of Americans condemned the civil rights protests. The notion that the movement won "the mind of the nation" at the time is fallacious. In 1966—even before urban riots, before the rise of Black Power—only 36 percent of white people said that Martin Luther King Jr. "was helping the cause," and 72 percent of white people "had an unfavorable opinion" of him. Moreover, most white people at the time were outraged at the protesters, not at the police, Birmingham commissioner of public safety Eugene "Bull" Connor, or the violent white supremacist groups who beset demonstrators. In 1964, the year after Connor turned fire hoses and dogs on the crowds, he won election as president of the Alabama Public Service Commission. Two years later, despite a decade of "good" protests and the Civil Rights Act, some 85 percent of white Americans and 30 percent of Black Americans thought that "demonstrations by Negroes on civil rights hurt the advancement of that cause."[12]

Conservative and mainstream politicians smeared King as a "communist" throughout his career. Federal Bureau of Investigation Director J. Edgar Hoover testified to Congress that there was "communistic influence infiltration in the civil rights movement." Mainstream columnist Joseph Alsop wrote in the *Washington Post* that King ignored FBI warnings about communists in the movement. As late as 1966, the FBI continued to pursue what it saw as communist activities within the Southern Christian Leadership Conference (SCLC).[13] Both King and Parks came under fire when they visited the Highlander Folk School, which white southerners called a "Communist training school."[14] It wasn't.

Vilified at the time, King and Parks have become role models whom most Americans claim. In 2008, eleventh and twelfth graders, given complete latitude to include anyone, responded to the question "Who are the most famous Americans?" by naming King and Parks in first and second place.[15] Yet this celebration has come at the cost of obscuring what made them so controversial. With increasing intensity, conservatives have remade King into a caricature of his former self in an effort to hijack his legacy. It began in 1985, when Ronald Reagan argued that King would have opposed affirmative action: "The truth is, quotas deny jobs to many who would have gotten them otherwise but who weren't born a specified race or sex. That's discrimination pure and simple." Reagan then quoted King's "I Have a Dream" speech: "I have a dream that my four little children will one day live in a nation where they will not be judged by the color of their skin but by the content of their character."[16]

Nothing could be further from King's position than fabricating his opposition to affirmative action. In 1965, as President Lyndon Baines Johnson considered implementing affirmative action by executive order, writer Alex Haley asked King, "Do you feel it's fair to request a multi-billion-dollar program of preferential treatment for the Negro, or for any other minority group?" King replied, "I do indeed. Can any fair minded citizen deny that the Negro has been deprived?"[17]

Donald Trump's press secretary Kayleigh McEnany used King's words to praise law enforcement's aggressive conduct against Black Lives Matter demonstrators: "And I just want to leave you with a quote from Martin Luther King Jr. that, 'We must learn to live together as brothers or we will perish together as fools.'"[18] She didn't quote another line from King: "We can never be satisfied, as long as the Negro is the victim of the unspeakable horrors of police brutality."[19] Collectively, the nation has rewritten support for the CRM and recast King's passive resistance as passivity.

If the classical movement was roundly vilified at the time, it was in part because of its challenges to structural and systemic racism, the questioning of patriotic norms, and its calls to alleviate poverty. Protests from the mid-1950s until King's death were always about issues other than simply abolishing segregation. For example, fair economic policies always had a place in civil rights work.

On the eve of World War II, Americans nervously awaited what promised to be the largest protest movement in the country's history, the original March on Washington Movement (MOWM). Demanding jobs in defense industries and the federal government, and desegregation of the armed forces, the MOWM became the quickest and most immediately successful protest movement that never happened. In the spring of 1941, officials in the Office of War Production tried to open jobs to African Americans with Eleanor Roosevelt's endorsement, but failed. Asa Philip Randolph, a powerful Black labor leader, realized that "Negroes are not getting anywhere with National Defense." In three months he organized a movement that promised to bring 100,000 African Americans to

Washington. He organized thirty-six MOWM chapters, including ten in the South; held mass meetings; and worked through churches to get people to sign up for the march.[20] In May, Randolph sent a manifesto to President Franklin Delano Roosevelt with the marchers' demands.[21] The Black press ratcheted up the pressure with headlines such as "Roosevelt Gives Only 'Lip Service' to Aid Negroes."[22] In the weeks leading up to the scheduled march on July 1, 1941, demonstrators across the country carried signs such as "Hitler Must Run This Plant: They Won't Employ Negroes."[23]

Roosevelt responded that he could simply use his influence to promote hiring African Americans, but Randolph stuck to his demand of an executive order. Ultimately, Randolph won an incomplete victory: jobs, but not desegregation of the military. Executive Order 8802, which FDR issued just six days before the scheduled march, banned discrimination in "defense industries or government" and created a temporary committee on fair employment practices. Randolph called off the march.[24] He kept the structure of the MOWM, and its followers continued during the war to protest discrimination when it occurred. Despite Randolph's success in ending discrimination in federal employment, the vast majority of the country remained segregated for another twenty years.

When SCLC member and civil rights leader Ella Baker spoke to the founding conference of the Student Nonviolent Coordinating Committee in 1960, she said that students had already made it clear that "the current sit-ins and other demonstrations are concerned with something much bigger than a hamburger." Instead, they "are seeking to rid America of the scourge of racial segregation and discrimination—not only at lunch counters, but in every aspect of life . . . we will no longer accept the inferior position of second-class citizenship." Students, she continued, have a "feeling that they have a destined date with freedom, . . . not limited to a drive for personal freedom, or even freedom for the Negro in the South."[25] More than sixty years ago, in the middle of the classical phase of the civil rights movement, Baker declared war on structural racism, just as the Black Lives Matter movement has done.

As protesters won victories for integration of public space in the 1960s, the movement and its leaders began to emphasize economic issues. In

1968 King organized the Poor People's Campaign, which, after his assassination, brought fifty thousand multiracial protesters to camp in Resurrection City on the National Mall.[26] His assassin acted, as Keeanga-Yamahtta Taylor reminds us, just after King called for a general strike during the 1968 Memphis sanitation workers' campaign.[27]

In the classical phase of the civil rights movement, leaders and participants also grappled with police brutality. In "Letter from a Birmingham Jail," King addressed those who praised Bull Connor's forces for "preventing violence": "I don't believe you would have so warmly commended the Birmingham police force for keeping 'order' . . . if you had seen its angry violent dogs literally biting six unarmed, nonviolent Negroes" or observed "their ugly and inhumane treatment of Negroes here in the city jail; if you were to watch them push and curse old Negro women and young Negro girls; if you would see them slap and kick old Negro men and young boys."[28] After King turned to the urban North in the final years of his life, he called on police to "cease being occupation troops in the ghetto and start protecting residents."[29] Despite honoring King, most Americans remain unaware that King protested issues that today might be considered outside of the model of the "good" protest. As Brandon M. Terry writes, "Canonization has prevented a reckoning with the substance of King's intellectual, ethical, and political commitments."[30]

The myth of the "good" protest excludes those who protest to question the inclusivity of national symbols in an effort to reform the country. But this also has a long history. In his 1935 "Let America Be America Again," poet Langston Hughes wrote on the exclusion of African Americans from the polity: "America never was America to me."[31] Baseball hero Jackie Robinson wrote in his 1972 autobiography that "I cannot stand and sing the anthem. I cannot salute the flag; I know that I am a Black man in a white world."[32] The irony was not lost on Colin Kaepernick, who tweeted those words on April 15, 2018.

The narrative that the civil rights movement ended and ended well works to delegitimize the protests that followed it. Certainly, the classical phase protests did a great deal, but they failed to resolve the problem of racial inequality. Their successes did not herald the end of the struggle, but the beginning of a new struggle to enforce new laws and to apply those gains to everyday life.[33]

Alondra Nelson recently argued that there is a "*longue durée* of Black Lives Matter."[34] In fact, that movement follows on from the long history of protests outlined here. Yet as protests took new forms, occurred in unfamiliar venues, and targeted systemic problems through complicated symbolism, many Americans discounted or even condemned them. In a Pew Research Center poll conducted in the last week of July and the first week of August 2020, alarming trends emerged. Some 40 percent of respondents "doubted that people could count on their right to peacefully protest," up 13 percent from 2018. Even more troubling, six of every ten people interviewed believed that "the statement, 'the rights and freedoms of all people are protected,' did not accurately describe the situation in the country today." There were stark partisan divides in the responses: some 80 percent of Republicans thought that the right to protest "was safe," but only 43 percent of Democrats did. Astonishingly, just a bare majority of Republicans—53 percent—said that it was "highly important that protestors be able to peacefully assemble."[35]

Subsequently, the right to protest came under fire in twenty-nine states. By July 2021, eight states had passed laws "cracking down on protest activity," and similar legislation was pending in twenty-one others.[36] In Arkansas you can be arrested for blocking a sidewalk and face a mandatory sentence of thirty days in jail. If you do it near "critical infrastructure," you face six years in prison. In Florida, if your protest blocks traffic "even temporarily," the sentence could be fifteen years in prison. In Oklahoma, if you stand on the street, making it "unreasonably inconvenient" for cars to pass, you could serve a year in prison. But if a driver "unintentionally" and "exercising due care" hits and kills you, he or she "cannot be held civilly or criminally liable."[37]

The myth of the good protest has fostered a national belief that the purpose of the civil rights movement was to gain access to fora previously reserved for whites; when such access became legal, many Americans assumed that minorities had achieved equality even as governmental and private institutions continued to privilege whites over minorities. The "good" civil rights movement had come and gone. Now African Americans were on their own. The classical phase of the civil rights movement was an extraordinary political era that toppled a legal regime that mandated racial oppression, but it fell short of achieving equality. But most white Americans believe that it settled things. A Gallup poll in 2008 "revealed that nearly ninety percent of Americans believed that protestors in the Civil Rights Movement had 'achieved some or all of their goals.'"[38]

The idea that the protests of the classical phase of the civil rights movement remade the United States into a color-blind country is one reason that by 2021, a majority of white Americans experienced no cognitive dissonance in believing that Rosa Parks's action to desegregate bus seating was right and just but could not countenance the slogan "Black Lives Matter" as a tool against structurally racist police violence. Or, instead of remembering African Americans' Depression-era boycotts in the "Don't Buy Where You Can't Work" campaign, led by Black women practicing gendered consumer politics, they deplored boycotts as "cancel culture."[39] They condemned, rather than embraced, Colin Kaepernick's humble and harmless kneeling for the national anthem, a timeless religious gesture against oppression in the tradition of King's own kneeling in 1965 in Selma, Alabama.[40] Jeanne Theoharis argues that the "civil rights movement became a weapon some used against these new movements for justice, as comparison after comparison was made to the Civil Rights Movement to find the BLM wanting."[41]

Many white Americans came to believe that it is acceptable to ask for admission to a system but not to challenge its structure if it continues to disadvantage minorities. But by the late 2010s, protesters sought structural change. A deeply divided country began to speak two different languages. People of all ethnicities routinely used the terms *systemic racism*, *racial capitalism*, *police violence*, and *carceral reform*, but others spoke of *snowflakes*, *socialism*, *cancel culture*, *Blue Lives Matter*, and *law and order*. Nonetheless, some historians have found ways to honor the demonstrations of the classical phase of the civil rights movement without drawing vast divides among them, their antecedents, and those that followed them. They recognize that the myth of the mid-twentieth-century model works to foreclose possibilities for recognizing current demonstrations as a civil rights movement.[42]

The tendency to condemn all demonstrations as lawless gained speed in the 2020 presidential election. That summer, Trump and Republican allies mounted a law-and-order campaign that painted national protests against police brutality as un-American, violent, anarchist, and the Democrats' fault. Heather Cox Richardson documented eighty-nine tweets by Trump in a single evening, most of them condemning protesters, including his retweet of One America News claiming that "it appears this coup attempt is led by a well-funded network of anarchists trying to take down the President."[43] As journalist Charles P. Pierce asked of Trump's fantasy of "thugs" on planes headed to demonstrations, "Isn't this pretty much the same thing as the 'busloads of armed blacks' that we heard about during every urban disturbance in the 1960s?"[44]

Change is possible, but painfully hard. Democratic progress arises from group actions that may be messy and flawed. Civic problems run deeper than any single protest can possibly solve. Protests rarely succeed in isolation; instead, they succeed when they open up new ways to express citizenship rights and slowly erode structural inequities. More than most Americans believe or are willing to accept, radical ideas and actors often accompany more mainstream protests and help extend the limits of possibility closer to equality for all. Even the most successful protest is only a partial victory, a prelude to the hard work that follows to change hearts, minds, and laws, and to root out systems of oppression.

Nonetheless, there is some evidence that recent protests worked. In the midst of the Republican attacks on protests in September 2020, a *Washington Post* poll offered a glimpse of Americans coming to terms with the protests of the recent past. Some 63 percent of Americans—73 percent of Democrats and 36 percent of Republicans—"support athletes speaking out [and] say anthem protests are appropriate."[45] Minds change, and society and institutions change with them.

Kenneth Clark, the Howard student who organized the 1934 Capitol Hill sit-ins, found himself a victim of tactics similar to those Trump used on Black Lives Matter. His future at risk, Clark held his ground: "I have no apologies to make for participating in the protest of such an ungodly crime, and if my participation places me in the category of a hoodlum, I am proud to be one. If seeking our rights as American citizens makes us communists, then I am also proud to be among the ranks of communists."[46] Clark wasn't a communist any more than the vast majority of today's protesters are anarchists. Twenty years later, psychologist Kenneth Clark's joint research with his wife, Mamie Clark, demonstrated the pernicious effects of racism and proved instrumental in changing the minds of the Supreme Court justices who determined *Brown v. Board of Education*.[47]

14

WHITE BACKLASH

Lawrence B. Glickman

O N SEPTEMBER 27, 1966, *CBS REPORTS* AIRED A DOCUMENTARY called *Black Power–White Backlash*. The documentary began with chants of "Black Power" followed by Mike Wallace's somber narration: "Summer 1966 was a season of revelation for the white man in the North. For the first time, he began fully to comprehend the intensity of his feelings and his fears about the black man." Throughout the documentary, Wallace didn't simply foreground white fears and anxieties; he claimed that "Black power was the catalyst" of those fears, comparing white backlash to a chemical reaction. White people had become "fed up with racial turmoil," he claimed, and, as a result, were now "countermarching, counterdemonstrating" in opposition to Black Power.[1]

Contrary to Wallace's narrative, summer 1966 was far from "the first time" that white people acted on their "fears and anxieties" about the Black struggle for freedom and equality. Indeed, just a few days after the documentary was broadcast, Martin Nolan of the *Boston Globe* observed that the "'white backlash' is now 3½ years old." And less than a month later, the syndicated columnists Rowland Evans and Robert Novak claimed that "the backlash is becoming a permanent feature of the political scene," noting a lingering "bitter anti-Negro resentment." Yet the *Black Power–White Backlash* documentary reversed that history. Even the ordering of the words in its title—like much journalistic and scholarly writing about opposition to the civil rights movement—implied that the "white backlash" was a response to "Black Power." But the title got the history wrong. Whereas *white backlash* had been coined in 1963 to describe extant white resistance to emerging policy initiatives toward racial equality, *Black Power* was a brand-new phrase when the documentary aired in September 1966. The activist Stokely Carmichael, who appeared in the documentary, had brought the phrase to the public square in a speech only two months earlier.[2]

By the time the documentary aired, more than three years of polling data showed a trend of accelerating white backlash. Starting in May 1963, even before President John F. Kennedy promoted civil rights (his legislation having been stalled in Congress for several months), a Gallup poll asked a question every month about whether the Kennedy (and later the Lyndon B. Johnson) administration "is pushing racial integration too fast, or not fast enough." For the next fifteen months, George Gallup reported that those who thought things were moving "too fast" grew, with the ratio of person who said "too fast" to "not fast enough" increasing every month from two-to-one to four-to-one. By October 1963, 50 percent of Americans said JFK was going "too fast." Headlines like "Gallup: Too Fast," and "Integration Push Too Fast in Feeling of Those Surveyed" appeared regularly.[3]

The reversal of agency on display in the documentary—in which civil rights extremism caused white counterreaction—was not an aberration but was actually typical of how white backlashes have long been explained and continue to be understood today. Commentators often misassign responsibility for backlashes, as Wallace did, by implying that African American activists are the responsible party, assigning agency and causality not to the backlashers but to the movements for social equality to

which the backlashers are allegedly responding. In one common formulation, for example, the journalist and historian John Judis wrote in 2019
that "the rise of the civil-rights movement sparked a powerful backlash
among some white voters." If the movements had acted more cautiously
and not been as bold, then, according to the conventional wisdom, the
backlash might have been averted.[4]

This essay examines how the mythology about backlashes developed,
showing how, since the era of Reconstruction (1865–1877), both commentators and backlashers have minimized and often denied their agency,
instead explaining the movements they joined, supported, and celebrated
as an inevitable and even natural reaction to what they characterized
as excessively rapid campaigns for social change or overly aggressive
government policy promoting civil rights. Many other backlashes—
against feminism, LGBTQ rights, and the New Deal, to give only a
few examples—followed a similar dynamic. This essay is devoted to the
"white backlash," focusing on its three most intense phases: the eras of
Reconstruction, the civil rights movement, and the Obama/Trump presidencies. Understanding how the mythology about backlash emerged and
became clichéd tracks a largely continuous thread across the US history
of white resisters to racial justice claiming exemption from three fundamental principles of politics: agency, responsibility, and causation. If
most social-movement actors see themselves as seeking to initiate, produce, and consolidate change, backlashers, by contrast, consistently self-
describe as acted upon rather than acting, and as the victims of changes
that are being foisted upon them and that they fear.

The idea that backlashers are acted upon rather than actors coincides
with an equally common myth about backlashes that Wallace also put
forth, which is that they are a defensive response to Black militance. As
the Gallup polls of 1963–1964 reveal, however, backlashes are typically
preemptive rather than reactive. Although the Pulitzer Prize–winning
reporter Relman Morin, like Wallace, defined the backlash in 1966 as
"the term for white reaction to recent Negro riots and . . . to the Negro militant's cry, 'Black power,'" this does not capture how backlashes
actually occur. More accurately understood as persistent, not episodic,
backlashes are the continuous—long-term and ongoing—attempt by

white conservative reactionaries to stand in the way of Black people's demands for equality. Indeed, it was this pattern of white opposition that made African American campaigns for equality necessary in the first place.[5]

Although the phrase *political backlash* had been used occasionally in the past, it was only in the early 1960s that it came to stand as shorthand for specifically conservative reaction to civil rights agitation. For example, an article in February 1960 noted that presidential candidate Lyndon B. Johnson "is feeling a backlash from the South for his efforts to get Senate action on a civil rights bill." In June 1963, the month when President John F. Kennedy began his push for serious civil rights legislation, Evans and Novak spoke of the "first backlash of civil rights turmoil," and the term quickly became what one columnist the following year called "the word of the year in American politics," a key analytical category in the presidential election between Johnson and Barry Goldwater. It came to stand for a topsy-turvy rebellion in which white people with relative social and political power perceived themselves as victimized by what they described as the overly aggressive actions of African Americans demanding equal rights and their white supporters in the political world. Backlash, as the *New York Times* columnist Tom Wicker wrote, "is nothing more nor less than white resentment of Negroes."[6]

White backlash was a novel phrase, but the phenomenon it described was "nothing new," as Martin Luther King Jr. pointed out in "Racism and the White Backlash," an essay he wrote shortly before his assassination in 1968. (The sports journalist Howard Cosell said something similar during the 1968 Olympic Games in response to those who condemned the protests of African American athletes: "He's aware of backlash, but says he's had it for 400 years.") Indeed, as King noted, it captured one of the deepest patterns in American history, which we can date back to the Reconstruction era at least, when the country's first experiment in interracial democracy was met with fierce opposition. "As soon as the first Republican governments were inaugurated," wrote Lerone Bennett Jr. of Reconstruction, "counter-revolutionaries sprang into action." Bennett called this "the first white backlash."[7]

You cannot have a backlash without backlashers. This may seem like a truism so obvious that it is barely worth noting. But backlashes are almost unique among political movements in how they are—or, more accurately, fail to be—explained. When we seek to understand, say, the agrarian rebellion of the nineteenth century or the women's and civil rights movements of the twentieth century, we usually start by exploring not only the conditions that led to their actions but the motivations of those who led and joined these campaigns, how these movements were built, and how their actions succeeded and failed. Yet in the world of political commentary, backlashers are rarely treated as agents of history, the people who participate in them seen as bit players rather than catalysts of the story, reactors rather than actors, ciphers playing a prescribed and predetermined role rather than protagonists making choices and taking action. Backlashers are often described not as choosing to participate in backlashes but as, in a variety of ways, being forced, almost against their will, into them, "wearied and angered by all the placard waving and demonstrating," as the journalist Dick Nolan wrote in October 1963, or, as Judis put it, "sparked" into action.[8]

Social movements, however, do not magically happen. As the great historian of populism Lawrence Goodwyn has written, "History does not support the notion that mass protest movements develop because of hard times. . . . The masses do not rebel in instinctive response to hard times and exploitation because they have been culturally organized by their societies not to rebel." His point was that propitious conditions alone do not, indeed cannot, make popular movements. To become movements, they require not just an impetus, which is a necessary but not a sufficient cause, but the actions of large numbers of people acting in concert. The claim of a Virginia newspaper in 1968 that a white candidate's "appeal to Negro voters set off a backlash" was typical of how the media often assigned agency for the cause of backlashes, assuming the "instinctive response" that Goodwyn warned against. That a candidate's appeal for Black votes would automatically spark a white backlash—not a self-evident proposition—was assumed rather than explained.[9]

Goodwyn was describing subaltern protest, but we can apply his lessons to top-down social movements of the relatively powerful, such as

white backlashes, as well; his argument that social movements are a matter of agency as well as conditions applies to reactionary as well as radical
ones. Movements of the Right are no more inevitable than those of the
Left. In her study of grassroots conservatism, Lisa McGirr argues that
the "Age of Reagan" did not spontaneously arise in response to the liberal
policies of California Democrats. She shows that the growth of conservative political power in Orange County was a gradual process requiring
the activism of many engaged men and women who held coffee klatches,
ran for local school boards, leafleted their neighbors, and organized campaigns for elected officials at all levels of government.[10]

This is to say that backlashes are long-term political projects, not one-
off natural events. Yet backlashes are often described, as Mike Wallace
did in the *Black Power–White Backlash* documentary, as automatic and
mechanical, a reflexive response to the speed and depth of social change
or political or legal frameworks.

This mode of explanation began in the opposition to Reconstruction,
arguably the first significant backlash movement in American history and
the one that set the template for backlashes in the twentieth century and
beyond. "Your reconstruction acts were calculated to make [the] Ku Klux
Klan," said Senator Allen G. Thurman of Ohio in 1870. Although the
term wouldn't be employed for nearly a century, Thurman's comment encapsulated the essence of backlash discourse: laying the blame for reactionary anti-Black violence not on those who participated in it but on
those seeking to promote racial equality. Although he insisted that he
was not "justifying [the] Ku Klux," the senator argued that the terrorist organization was the inevitable result of radical policies. Inevitabil-
ity was key: in describing the Klan as "made" by Radical Republicans,
Thurman obfuscated the agency of actual KKK members and supporters.
After listing the indignities that whites faced—putting white southerners
"under the heel of the military men" and "putting a set of ignorant negroes above all the intelligence of the white race," some of whom served
in Congress—Thurman reiterated: "I do not wonder it [Reconstruction]
made the Ku Klux."[11]

Andrew Johnson, the accidental president, who presided over the nation at the onset of Reconstruction—an effort he vigorously opposed—put

forward the blame-the-victim causal template that future backlashers employed. Not only did Johnson maintain that the push for legal and political freedom for African Americans was "too rapid a movement"; he also claimed that the efforts of African Americans and their Radical Republican allies amounted to a form of "military tyranny" that would "precipitate" a violent response "more damaging than the last civil war." Choosing another word from the lexicon of chemistry—*precipitate*—to describe a white reaction, Johnson's language—like Mike Wallace's "catalyst"—had the effect of describing the campaign against Reconstruction as inevitable and somehow "scientific" or natural: outside the agency of Reconstruction's opponents. The responsibility for what Johnson predicted would be unavoidable violence lay with those advocating Reconstruction, not with those who opposed it.[12]

In what became a characteristic way of framing backlashes, opponents of Reconstruction also used passive language to elide their responsibility for participating in an extralegal campaign of violence. William P. Wells, a law professor and a Democratic member of the Michigan legislature, for example, said in 1868, alluding to the policies of the Radical Republicans, "Nothing can be surer than that there will be a reaction if this is persisted in, which will result, not in the subjection of the white race at the South, but in the utter destruction of the black race." This phrasing ("there will be a reaction") was characteristic backlash language: it threatened violence as an inevitable outcome without acknowledging that such genocidal violence, if it was to occur, would be as a result of the choice of white opponents to Reconstruction.[13]

Ninety years later, opponents of the civil rights movement described a similar mechanism: being compelled by the actions of activists and politicians. In an open letter to President Lyndon Johnson, a couple in Louisiana said in 1964 that those members of Congress who voted for the Civil Rights Act were "absolutely forcing the good American citizen . . . into a revolution" and that if he signed the bill into law, Johnson would be "equally responsible." Those in favor of the law were doing nothing less than "instigat[ing] a revolution." The letter writers suggested that they had little choice but to participate in that "revolution" for which their political enemies were culpable.[14]

As in the Reconstruction era, the two most frequent modes of backlash rhetoric were to blame the victim and to claim that the movements for racial justice were moving too quickly, both of which mandated reaction. As the *Atlanta Constitution* said in a 1961 editorial praising President John F. Kennedy's go-slow approach to civil rights, "Time after time, we have witnessed these futile and divisive battles in Congress over civil rights legislation which Southern politicians in particular are forced to oppose." Why they were "forced to oppose" the paper did not say. In 1964 a Wisconsin newspaper predicted that "the civil rights bill, like the prohibition amendment, will foment trouble for many years to come." It predicted that "Congressional decrees, too unpopular to stomach for many, just won't be accepted." And congressmen claimed that they were "forced to oppose" the civil rights bill for a variety of reasons, including that it was too extreme ("so drastic"), that it was too "fast," or that their (white) constituents opposed it. In 1966 a columnist for the *Jackson (MS) Clarion-Ledger* said that if the members of Johnson's administration "insist upon ignoring and trampling majority rights in efforts to favor minority groups, they may in time provoke a White Revolution." The language of *fomenting, provoking*, and *forcing* not only placed the onus for the backlash on pro–civil rights activists and politicians; it also denied the persistence of white supremacy.[15]

Although scholars have produced some exceptionally nuanced examinations of white-grievance politics, many commentators have echoed these mythologies, underemphasizing the actions of participants and locating the emergence of backlashes in the social movement or government policy that they opposed. In the process, the motivations and actions of backlashers have sometimes gone unexplored, and their reactionary movements understudied, though deemed to be important. They are treated as inevitable rather than a conscious political effort aimed to stifle change. For example, in his excellent book *The Unraveling of America*, Allen J. Matusow wrote that "ghetto rioters, antiwar protesters, and pot-smoking hippies created a backlash against liberalism." This frequently repeated formulation mistakenly locates the agency of backlashes in the "rioters," "protesters," and "hippies" rather than in the participants in the backlashes themselves. In a review of Matusow's book, Gordon

Turtle made an even stronger claim: "The emergence of blacks and the search for a just society did not create a more tolerant America . . . as the liberals predicted; it unraveled America and caused a backlash that elected Richard Nixon before the liberals had a chance to knit together a more new, improved America." The claim that it was "the search for a just society," rather than people mobilizing in opposition to it, that "caused a backlash" denies agency to the backlashers because it assigns the "cause" to the quest for justice and thus minimizes the importance of recognizing the motivations, organization, and political leadership of the backlashers. In this manner, backlashes have often been naturalized rather than explained.[16]

Such analysis continued after the civil rights era into the twenty-first-century presidencies of Barack Obama, Donald Trump, and Joe Biden. Dan Balz of the *Washington Post* wrote in 2020 that "Obama's election produced a backlash, that gave rise to a tea-party movement fueled by anti-government resentment but also by racial resentment," which implies that his election was the causal agent. Jim Tankersley and Jason DeParle, writing in the *New York Times* in 2021, explained that Biden's popular COVID-relief package, which the Republicans unanimously opposed, might backfire: "The law could provoke a Tea-Party style backlash of the sort generated by the Obama administration's efforts to jolt the economy back to health in 2009." The words *produced* and *provoke* suggest that Obama and, later, Biden caused the backlashes and bear the main responsibility for their appearance. If we agree that backlashes are not inevitable and sometimes do not happen in the wake of campaigns for social equality, then we must be careful about explanatory devices that treat them as "stimulated," to use political scientist Ronald Inglehart's term, by social movements, legislation, or cultural change. These framings evade important questions of agency and offer an unconvincing account of causality.[17]

Here we should pause to think about causation in history. In his classic 1961 study *What Is History?*, E. H. Carr wrote that "the study of history is a study of causes." Historians, who have become equally interested in "how" as well as "why" change (or continuity) happens, might not fully concur with Carr, but they continue to agree with him that almost any historical event has "a multiplicity of causes" and that part of the job of the historian is to sort through them to determine which are most important. As Carr wrote, "The hierarchy of causes, the relative significance of one cause or set of causes, is the essence of" historical interpretation.[18]

Carr offers a thought experiment to show why it is important to think hard about causation: Jones is driving home from a party at which he drank too much alcohol, in a vehicle with defective brakes. At a "blind corner whose visibility is notoriously poor," he hits and kills Robinson, who "was crossing the road to buy cigarettes at the shop on the corner." Although all these facts are technically conditions of Robinson's death, Carr's point is that not all of them count equally as causes. It is true that "of course, Robinson was killed because he was a cigarette-smoker," but that Robinson went to buy cigarettes is not on par with the facts that Jones was drunk and driving a car that did not work properly on a dangerous stretch of highway. History is a "process of selection in terms of historical significance," says Carr, meaning that historians have to sort among causal factors to pick the most decisive ones. It is in this process of selecting, of distinguishing between conditions and causes, where commentators on backlashes have tended to be lax.[19]

In some sense, the backlashers can be analogized to "Jones" because they bear primary responsibility for the backlash. But there is a significant difference: Carr is describing an accident; nobody in his scenario intended the deadly outcome. Robinson's death had multiple causes, which we can hierarchize, starting with Jones's drunkenness. But Jones, although criminally negligent, did not wish to kill Robinson. By contrast, those who participated in backlashes did seek to slow down or reverse social changes or government policies with which they disagreed. The outcome they sought was not an accident but a long-term goal.

Backlashes have occurred for many reasons, but, surely, chief among them was the decision of large numbers of people to participate in protests, threats, and statements of support or other reactionary efforts to roll back the threat of civil rights advances. Writing of civil rights demonstrations, a reporter speculated in 1963 that they would "strengthen the counter revolution against the Negroes."[20]

But this counterrevolution was not fated to occur. We know this because, just as oppression doesn't always lead to social movements, not all progressive reforms or social movements are met with organized opposition. In this context, it is instructive to return to the 1963–1964 period, when the term *white backlash* was popularized. Notwithstanding all the talk about the power of this new social force and the polls showing that many white Americans thought civil rights were proceeding too quickly, Lyndon Johnson, who championed the Civil Rights Act, overwhelmingly won the 1964 presidential election. Johnson's pollster, Oliver Quayle, even coined the term *frontlash* to highlight the push that LBJ gained because of his support for civil rights.[21]

Recognizing that backlashes are political and contingent is not to deny that they have been a powerful force in shaping American politics. However, it does highlight the role of agency. As the Black newspaper editor Norman Lockman wrote in 1995, "White backlash is more mood than movement. It comes and goes." Even though Lyndon Johnson bragged about the "frontlash" that led to his overwhelming victory, he was well aware that a powerful backlash sentiment could well be mobilized in the future. (And even in that very election: in 1964 Goldwater won Mississippi, previously a Democratic stronghold, with more than 87 percent of the vote.) "We may have lost the South for a generation," LBJ reportedly told some of his aides, shortly after he signed the Civil Rights Act. Over time, Johnson's prediction proved correct, and in 1968 the two backlash candidates, Richard Nixon, the eventual winner, and the segregationist, George Wallace, running on a third-party ticket, won almost 57 percent of the popular vote. This history suggests that backlash is not an automatic reflex but a long-term political process, with many twists and turns.[22]

African American labor leader and civil rights activist A. Philip Randolph made this distinction in 1958 by labeling what came to be called backlashes as "counterrevolutions," purposeful efforts to undo and reverse social change. In doing so, he reversed the backlash framing that posited civil rights activism as their cause. Instead, he described backlashers as the active, not passive, agents of reaction: "Just as the counter revolution against the Civil War revolution nullified the 13th Amendment to the Constitution of 1865, the 14th Amendment of 1868, and the 15th Amendment of 1870, the second counter has begun in massive and ominous dimensions." For Randolph, backlashers acted to "nullify" civil rights advances; they were not forced to do so.[23]

Indeed, we need not rely only on Carr's abstract discussion of causation to show why a claim that civil rights efforts cause backlashes is incomplete. A long tradition of African American thinkers and activists, including Randolph, Bennett, and Lockman, have challenged the view that they are responsible for backlashes or that backlashes are inevitable. Martin Luther King Jr. provided perhaps the most robust response in his posthumously published book *Where Do We Go From Here?*: "Our white liberal friends cried out in horror and dismay: 'You are creating hatred and hostility in the white communities in which you are marching.'" But he rejected the view that African American marchers "created" or "developed" the white backlash; instead, he said, "white America must assume the guilt."[24]

King made two arguments to support his point. First, he drew upon a medical metaphor to question the notion of causality that he attributed to skeptical white people: "How strange it would be to condemn a physician who, through persistent work and the ingenuity of his medical skills, discovered cancer in a patient. Would anyone be so ignorant as to say he caused the cancer?" King also made a point about chronology; the backlash could not have been caused by a movement that had not yet begun: "This is not a new backlash caused by the Black Power movement; there had been no ominous riots in Watts when white Californians defeated a fair housing bill in 1964." Backlashes, as King noted, were often preemptive rather than reactive, or, as he put it, the white backlash should be thought of as the "resurfacing of old prejudices, hostilities and ambivalences that have always been there." It is a tragic but fitting postscript to King's essay that, after he was assassinated, Alan Stang, writing in the publication of the John Birch Society, claimed that "the ironic truth is that King contributed to his own murder" by "provok[ing] violence." Stang's statement revealed precisely the "blame-the-victim" backlash dynamic that King had exposed.[25]

In *Black Power–White Backlash* Mike Wallace interviewed Stokely Carmichael, the popularizer of the *Black Power* phrase, and asked him to clarify his position on the "white liberal," who, Wallace claimed, might be backing away from support for the civil rights movement. Carmichael responded by questioning the backlash framework that Wallace offered: "There is no reason why they should stop supporting the movement now." Carmichael's point was that backlashes do not have to happen. They are not preordained. Backlashes are part of our history, but as an examination of that very past reveals, they do not have to be our fate.

15

THE GREAT SOCIETY

Joshua Zeitz

In a blistering address delivered before the John M. Ashbrook Memorial Dinner in Ashland, Ohio, in May 1983, President Ronald Reagan, then halfway through his first term in office, condemned the Great Society as a bundle of expensive and failed initiatives that increased, rather than lightened, the burden of poverty for tens of millions of American citizens. The vast expansion of the federal state that marked the five-year tenure of his predecessor, Lyndon B. Johnson, had only reinforced the "central political error of our time," Reagan warned—the flawed notion that "government and bureaucracy" were the "primary vehicle of social change." For Reagan, the historical syllogism was simple: "The Great Society coincided with an end to economic progress for America's poor people"; thus, the Great Society was responsible for the wage stagnation and rising income inequality of the 1970s that effectively marked the end of the postwar economic boom.[1]

Reagan gave voice to an emerging consensus among movement conservatives that the Great Society had immiserated the very people it intended to help. In the decades following his speech, leaders on the Right drew this theme out, arguing not only that the Great Society hobbled the American economy but also that it "perpetuated a debilitating culture of dependency" among its beneficiaries, thereby "wrecking families and communities," as Wisconsin congressman and vice-presidential candidate Paul Ryan claimed in 2012.[2]

So did the Great Society fail? The short answer is "no."

Conservative faultfinders tend to cherry-pick those pieces of Johnson's legacy that seem not to have worked—notably, the War on Poverty's "community action" programs and experiments in public housing—and ignore programs now inextricably woven into the fabric of American civic and economic life.[3] These critics ignore the many lasting successes of the Great Society because, a half century after the fact, it is all but impossible to conceive of a United States without Medicare and Medicaid, public television, integrated hotels and restaurants and polling places, federal aid to primary and secondary schools, or federally guaranteed college loans—programs that continue to command wide backing. Some of this selectivity owes to confusion over what exactly the Great Society actually *was*. Like Franklin Roosevelt's New Deal, it was an elastic term that accommodated a broad range of sometimes divergent ideas and programs. Should it include the 1964 Civil Rights Act and the 1965 Voting Rights Act? The War on Poverty (and if so, which specific programs under *that* broad umbrella)? Federal aid to schools and universities? Hospital insurance for the elderly? Because of this definitional challenge, it is all too easy for both defenders and critics to fasten on to what they love or abhor about the Great Society and leave the rest unaccounted for.

But the conservative argument with the Great Society is about far more than the value of particular domestic policies and programs. It's a debate over the very role of government. In short, is big government the solution to systemic economic and social problems or the cause?

If we are to use the Great Society as a litmus test for the argument against "big government," it's critical to assess whether the Great Society succeeded on its *own* terms—to consider the context in which LBJ's

administration labored: the ideas that guided it, the political circumstances that constrained it, the problems that it set out to solve, and the
shifting economic reality that in later years forced the Great Society to
compensate for challenges its architects never anticipated. Judged by those
standards, the Great Society proved a successful and lasting experiment.

In the bleakest days of the Great Depression, consensus emerged among
liberal policy makers that capitalism was irrevocably broken. Economist
Alvin Hansen warned in 1938 of a future marked by "sick recoveries
which die in their infancy and depressions which feed on themselves and
lead a hard and seemingly immovable core of unemployment." But the
experience of World War II and the early Cold War era altered this bleak
thinking as the United States experienced a period of record economic
expansion, driving a transition for millions of Americans from renter
to homeowner, blue-collar worker to white-collar worker, and a world
of Depression-era scarcity and wartime rationing to postwar consumer
plenty. The success of the federal state in mobilizing for World War II
convinced many postwar liberals that through a deliberate application of
Keynesian measures, policy experts could calibrate government spending to ensure sustained growth, full employment, and low inflation—
in perpetuity. This point, in turn, led many Democrats to rethink their
long-standing ideas about the nature of inequality. A "generation ago, it
would have been taken for granted that a war on poverty meant taxing
money away from the haves and . . . turning it over to the have nots,"
observed the journalist Walter Lippmann. "But in this generation . . . a
revolutionary idea has taken hold. The size of the pie can be increased by
invention, organization, capital investment and fiscal policy and then a
whole society, not just one part of it, will grow richer."[4]

Some voices in the administration argued that what poor people
needed most was income, which the government could furnish through
public-sector relief jobs reminiscent of the New Deal. Prominent figures on the Left—including the Swedish economist Gunnar Myrdal;
the socialist writer Michael Harrington; Todd Gitlin and Tom Hayden,
founders of Students for a Democratic Society; Irving Howe, the editor of *Dissent* magazine; and Stewart Meacham of the American Friends

Service Committee—concurred, calling for an "incomes policy" that would furnish "every family with an adequate income as a matter of right." It was the only way, they believed, by which "the quarter of the nation now dispossessed and soon-to-be dispossessed by lack of employment can be brought within the abundant society." But most liberal policy makers disagreed. The economy, after all, was humming. Those who had been left behind, whether because of cultural deprivation or geography, only needed to be equipped with the means to claim their fair share of an ever-growing pie. The president also agreed. Early in his administration, when Labor Secretary Willard Wirtz proposed a New Deal–style public works program, LBJ responded with an "absolute blank stare," a participant in the meeting recalled.[5]

Instead, LBJ and his administration advanced a series of qualitative measures aimed at empowering poor and vulnerable people to lift *themselves* out of poverty, while helping those who could not work—the elderly, disabled, and (so the thinking went) single mothers—enjoy a more comfortable and dignified life. Some of these programs, like federal aid to primary and secondary education and government health insurance for senior citizens, had been bedrock liberal aspirations dating back at least twenty years. Others, like job training and nutrition assistance, began as pilot initiatives during JFK's presidency. Still others were products of their time: community-action programs intended to help poor and politically marginalized citizens organize and advocate for better services in their own neighborhoods; Head Start, to furnish poor children with pre-K classes and medical and nutritional assistance; a job corps for young men in rural and urban areas; and free legal aid for the poor. What joined these diverse programs into a coherent idea was the belief that disadvantaged people needed qualitative help in tapping their share of opportunity—not income assistance.

To be sure, not everyone bought into the logic behind "growth liberalism" or "opportunity theory." By 1965, Sargent Shriver, LBJ's poverty czar and a onetime proponent of qualitative measures to fight inequality, believed that to "end poverty in the United States, as we know it today, within a generation," the administration ought to adopt a "negative income tax." Qualitative measures would not suffice. (The concept had bipartisan draw. As president, Richard Nixon proposed substituting cash assistance for social services.)[6] But layering a minimum income on top of existing antipoverty programs would cost at least $7.5 billion in incremental spending. It was a political nonstarter, particularly as the Vietnam War bloated the federal budget and threatened to inflate the economy at dangerous levels.[7] And for most Great Society architects, income redistribution—even if politically feasible—was a solution better suited to a stagnant economy, not a growing one.

The same worldview influenced the administration's decision to walk back long-standing aspirations to build a government-run health care system for all Americans—a liberal hope since as early as 1934. Throughout the 1940s, dogged opposition from the American Medical Association (AMA) and congressional Republicans stymied progressive efforts to make this dream a reality.[8] But the problem wasn't just conservative opposition to "socialist" medicine. By the 1960s, many Democrats no longer believed that universal government health care was necessary. After World War II, major employers began extending new benefits to workers, including paid vacations, annual cost-of-living adjustments to wages, and defined-benefits pensions. By 1960, 100 million Americans enjoyed access to private health plans.[9] What many liberals once assumed that government would need to do for working-class citizens, private industry now offered on a contingent basis.

Many people—including many African Americans, Latinos, and unmarried women; most nonunionized workers; the unemployed; and children of uninsured adults—did not enjoy access to such benefits. But Democrats turned their focus to a narrower subset of the population that, by definition, could not access employer-based health programs: senior citizens, most of whom were no longer in the workforce, and indigent people of all ages, many of whom were expected to be either widows or disabled people no longer able to work.[10]

It made enough sense in its own time. What LBJ and his supporters did not anticipate was that by the early 1970s, the era of boundless growth—of low inflation, broadly distributed incomes, and a growing unionized workforce enjoying strong wages and stable benefits—would grind to a screeching halt.

If Great Society liberals failed to anticipate an end to postwar economic expansion, their eyes were wider open to systemic racism, which made a mockery of opportunity theory. All the education and training in the world would not help a citizen who was artificially barred from participating fully in housing or labor markets. Dismantling Jim Crow became fundamental to the liberal project and a central current that ran throughout most of the Great Society's key initiatives.

The Civil Rights Act of 1964 famously mandated the desegregation of places of public accommodation. Equally important, Title VI of the bill also empowered the government to withhold federal funds from state and local authorities that failed to comply with the law. In the early months of Medicare's existence, in 1966, the Department of Health, Education and Welfare (HEW) sent more than a thousand inspectors to ensure that southern nursing homes and hospitals had desegregated their facilities. More than twelve thousand facilities swiftly acquiesced.[11] The federal guidelines were sweeping. To be eligible for Medicare and Medicaid reimbursements, nursing homes and hospitals were compelled to admit people regardless of color, race, or national origin. Where there was a "significant variation between the racial composition of patients and the population served," the facility had an affirmative obligation to justify that discrepancy to HEW. Each facility's "rooms, wards, floors, sections, and buildings" were to be integrated; officials were not permitted to ask if patients preferred to share quarters with someone of a particular race. "Employees, medical staff and volunteers of the hospital are to be assigned to patient service" on a color-blind basis, the rules continued. Hospital and nursing home employees would be required to use "courtesy titles" such as "Dr.," "Mrs.," and "Mr." without regard to race, and formerly segregated institutions were required to conduct proactive outreach to nonwhite physicians, nurses, and civil rights organizations—and take out advertisements in local media outlets announcing the change in their policy.[12]

The administration also used Title VI to cajole local schools into desegregating. Districts were required to submit desegregation plans and demonstrate progress in meeting them. Much of the onus for compelling compliance fell on Francis Keppel, the administration's "chief SOB with the Southerners," who regularly reviewed district-level desegregation plans with LBJ's domestic policy aide, Joe Califano. During these meetings in the West Wing, the president would routinely "wander in and out saying, 'Get 'em: Get 'em: Get the last ones!'"[13]

Debates over what constituted desegregation, and whether the standard should be desegregation or integration, persisted into the 1970s and beyond. Court-imposed busing plans would overtake Title VI compliance as a political lightning rod after Johnson left office. But the combination of administrative and judicial firepower ultimately worked. From 1965 to 1968, the number of Black students in the South who attended majority-white schools rose from roughly 2.3 percent to almost 23.4 percent. That ratio would continue to climb over the following two decades until it peaked at 43.5 percent in 1988. Further, from 1968 to 1980 the portion of southern Black children attending deeply segregated schools— schools where they made up over 90 percent of the student population— fell from 77.5 percent to 26.5 percent. In those same years, the portion of white southern students attending deeply segregated public schools dropped from 68.8 percent to 26 percent.[14]

The administration also moved quickly to force compliance with the Voting Rights Act of 1965. Four days after the bill-signing ceremony, federal examiners arrived in twelve counties in Alabama, Louisiana, Mississippi, and Georgia to assume control of enrollment. By the following January, they added over ninety thousand voters to the rolls in those jurisdictions alone. Violence and intimidation persisted, but for the most part southern authorities acquiesced in the face of strong executive enforcement. As late as 1965, only 6.7 percent of African Americans in Mississippi and 19 percent in Alabama had surmounted the complex of legal and extralegal measures in place to prevent them from exercising the franchise. By 1970, roughly two-thirds of African Americans in these Deep South states were registered to vote, and most were able to exercise this right without interference.[15]

The Great Society did not eliminate systemic racism. Far from it. But the gulf between the world as it existed in 1960 and as it exists today is wide, in no small part because Lyndon Johnson committed to spending down much of his political capital on civil rights.

The Great Society was predicated on the belief that America would long enjoy sustained economic growth, low inflation, and strong wages and benefits for a growing portion of its population. But the subsequent history speaks for itself. Owing in part to the runaway spending on the Vietnam War, as well as a series of supply shocks in the food and energy sectors, Americans absorbed over a decade of runaway inflation.[16] Inflation was accompanied by rising unemployment, particularly in the manufacturing sector, which for many years had formed the backbone of America's prosperous postwar middle class. Stagflation—the combination of high unemployment and inflation—undermined the concept of opportunity theory. Experts had lost control of the economic levers, and increasingly it became clear that all the education and training in the world would not help poor people in urban ghettos, declining coal towns in Appalachia, or midsized cities in western Pennsylvania and eastern Ohio, where in the coming decade empty steel mills stood as skeletal reminders of the country's bygone industrial might. Poor people needed income, not qualitative assistance, to capture their share of a shrinking pie.

During the Kennedy and Johnson years, the American economy expanded at an average annual rate of 4.6 percent each year.[17] The country has not seen growth like that since. To be sure, America has experienced periods of sustained economic expansion since the 1960s. But in recent decades the blessings of limited economic growth have accrued principally to the wealthiest Americans. When Lyndon Johnson left office in 1969, the poorest quintile of American households earned 4.1 percent of the nation's aggregate income, and the richest quintile took home 43 percent. By 2010, the bottom quintile saw its share of income drop to just 3.1 percent, while the top quintile saw its share rise to 51.9 percent.[18]

Stagnant incomes are central to this story. Between World War II and 1973, real wages grew steadily at a rate of between 2 percent and 3 percent each year, enabling millions of American workers to enjoy upward mobility. Then wage growth slowed dramatically for many Americans. Over the next three decades, household wages remained essentially flat, principally because more women entered the workforce, even as men's wages fell in real dollar terms.[19] In the main, families with two wage earners were able to keep their heads above water and maintain what they had; families headed by single parents fell behind as wage growth stalled. These economic trends also strained the New Deal/Great Society safety net. Programs like Medicaid and SNAP (originally known as food stamps) were initially designed to help a small subset of poor people—particularly, single mothers and their children, or disabled workers—escape the grind of hunger and sickness. But by 2021, some 51 percent of Black children, 29 percent of Latino children, and 22 percent of white children resided in single-parent households. Given the stagnation of wages since 1973, single-parent families are more likely to be poor.[20] At the same time, record-setting numbers of working-age adults have slipped out of the workforce; they are neither employed nor seeking employment, and many have filed for permanent disability benefits—a trend that has alarmed conservatives and liberals alike.[21]

In the fifty years since LBJ's presidency, the social contract between employers and employees has broken down considerably, driven in large part by the sharp decline of private-sector unions. Great Society programs had to work harder for more people than they were originally intended to help.[22] As more families fell below the poverty line, Medicaid, SNAP, and general antipoverty programming have had to cover a larger body of constituents. The result has been a steady expansion of programs that were initially intended to plug holes in the dam—not constitute the dam itself.

Great Society programs such as SNAP, which covered 500,000 recipients in 1965 but roughly 40 million in 2020, and free or subsidized school meals (a product of the 1966 Child Nutrition Act), whose enrollment grew from 22.5 million in 1970 to 29.4 million in 2019, have evolved into a hidden form of income support. The same is true of Medicaid, CHIP, and Medicare, which cover 147 million Americans—roughly 45 percent of all the country's population.[23]

Because these benefits qualify in budgetary terms as a "near-cash" benefit—meaning that they are not technically income—the federal government does not include their value when measuring poverty. Using the alternative Supplementary Poverty Measure (SPM), which counts the value of such benefits as part of household income, census figures in 2010 revealed that food stamps cut the child poverty rate by three percentage points.[24] Taken in sum, noncash benefits associated with LBJ's domestic initiatives cut the poverty rate by 26 percent between 1960 and 2010, with two-thirds of the decline occurring before 1980.[25]

Ronald Reagan famously quipped that "Lyndon Johnson declared war on poverty, and poverty won."[26] Yet even without accounting for near-cash assistance, the national poverty rate declined from 20 percent to 12 percent under LBJ's watch. By contrast, it stood at 13 percent when Reagan was elected president, and it remained at 13 percent when he left office.

The poverty rate among African Americans was roughly 55 percent in 1959. It dropped to 32 percent by 1969, when LBJ left office, and stood at 23 percent in 2020.

Among people of all races living in households led by single mothers, the poverty rate dropped from 49 percent in 1959 to 38 percent in 1969. It stood at 26 percent in 2020.

None of this is to say Johnson bears sole credit for sharp reductions in poverty over the past fifty years, although the Great Society's civil rights legislation surely helped erode racial and gender disparities in employment and housing. Even so, the trend line refutes the claim that poverty "won" the war.[27]

In other fundamental ways, the Great Society has proven a lasting success. Although entire libraries could be shelved with debates over the correlation (or lack thereof) between education expenditures and educational achievement, federal funding for K–12 education undeniably closed yawning gaps between wealthier and poorer regions and addressed a clear deficiency in resources that states would otherwise have been ill-equipped to remedy. Between 1958 and 1968, federal spending on primary and secondary education rose from less than 3 percent to more than 10 percent of total education funding. As LBJ himself predicted, once formalized as policy, it grew. By 1985, the federal government's share of all K–12 school spending rose to 16 percent, the percentage provided by state governments rose from 41 percent to 55 percent, and the portion shouldered by local governments fell from 51 percent to 31 percent. Because many local and state governments rely heavily on regressive property and sales taxes, in many cases these swings shifted some of the burden for funding schools from working-class and poor families to middle-class and wealthy taxpayers. In the early 1970s, Congress plugged some of the loopholes in the program by imposing "maintenance of effort" (MOE) requirements on states and localities; to continue receiving funds, they had to set their own education budgets at a high fraction of the prior year's appropriation, thus ensuring that federal dollars truly were supplementary.[28] As the federal government gradually imposed additional restrictions governing the allocation of federal education funds, state authorities centralized and professionalized their education departments and school systems to ensure ease of compliance and the continued flow of federal dollars. In this way, too, the Great Society proved not just a funding source but also an engine of reform and modernization.[29]

Fifty years after the fact, liberals are looking for ways to supplement and surpass the Great Society. Some are revisiting ideas that Johnson's White House considered but ultimately rejected, like a guaranteed basic family income. In her campaign memoir, Hillary Clinton revealed that in 2016 she came very close to proposing such a policy.[30] Even as this book goes to print, Joe Biden's administration has quietly rolled out means-tested child tax credits. They came in the form of monthly cash transfers deposited directly into people's bank accounts and entitled families to $3,000 in annual payments per child ($3,600 for children under six years old). Estimates suggest that this program, which Congress allowed to sunset after Biden's first year in office, temporarily cut the child poverty rate in half overnight.[31] It remains to be seen whether the program will be renewed in some form. The Biden administration also summarily recalibrated the government's SNAP payment tables to increase household food assistance by an average of 25 percent each month—the largest expansion of Johnson's food stamp program since its inception.[32]

The Great Society was a creature of its time. It succeeded in many of the things it set out to do. It also formed a critical safety net as American society changed in ways that few people could have anticipated in LBJ's time. Alone, the safety net may no longer be enough to ensure that all

Americans enjoy basic economic security—and with it, food and health security. But when critics home in on its alleged failures, they more generally hope to establish a case against government intervention in the economy. That case falls apart on reconsideration of the Great Society's many achievements.

Hours after ascending to the presidency, Johnson marveled that "every issue that is on my desk tonight was on my desk when I came to Congress in 1937."[33] Civil rights. Health insurance for the elderly and poor. Federal aid to primary and secondary education. Support for higher education. Antipoverty and nutritional programs. It has now been a half century since LBJ addressed those challenges. He did so while operating in a specific time and context. Today, the same challenges are as urgent as ever before, even as the context is starkly different.

16

POLICE VIOLENCE

Elizabeth Hinton

D URING THE SUMMER OF 2020, POLICE, FEDERAL TROOPS, AND THE
National Guard flooded the streets of American cities with a frequency and intensity the nation had not witnessed since the "Long, Hot Summers" of the 1960s. After hundreds of people took to the streets to protest the murder of a forty-six-year-old Black man named George Floyd by white police officer Derek Chauvin on May 25, 2020, police dressed in riot gear responded to a peaceful protest on May 26 by firing tear gas and rubber bullets into hundreds of demonstrators. Some of the protesters responded with violence of their own, breaking the windows of a police precinct and eventually burning it down. As the situation escalated, and as the video of Floyd's horrific killing became widely distributed across social media platforms and major news outlets, the National Guard assisted local police in teargassing crowds. From there the protests and the state-sanctioned violence spread to St. Louis, Memphis,

Louisville, and other urban centers across the United States. On May 29, President Donald Trump took to Twitter, as he so often did to blow off steam during his tenure in the White House. "When the looting starts, the shooting starts," the president wrote. Knowingly or not, Trump had quoted word for word Miami police chief Walter Headley's response to the city's unrest in 1967.

From Headley to Trump and in between, officials and much of the American public have widely assumed that police violence primarily occurs as a reaction to community provocation. The myth holds that the fires and the looting of the immediate post–civil rights period, and in our own time, began with disaffected groups themselves; the police were merely "doing their jobs" in reacting to a dangerous situation with force. As Arkansas senator Tom Cotton put it in a *New York Times* op-ed that ran at the peak of the nationwide protests on June 3, 2020, it was the "rioters" in Minneapolis and other cities who "plunged many American cities into anarchy." Police officers "bore the brunt of the violence" and, in Cotton's telling, were the victims of "bands of miscreants." Ignoring the reality that the vast majority of the protests remained nonviolent, Cotton urged law enforcement to crack down. "One thing above all else will restore order to our streets," he argued: "an overwhelming show of force to disperse, detain and ultimately deter lawbreakers."[1]

Contrary to the fearmongering rhetoric of politicians, history reveals that police violence very often inflamed community violence, not the other way around. Although protesters are often blamed for creating violent situations where the police are forced to respond in kind, from Miami in 1967 to the George Floyd uprisings in 2020, law enforcement officials were the instigators. Indeed, protests have grown more peaceful since the fiery post–civil rights era, but the police response to them has escalated in its violence. Dominant narratives have confused where the responsibility lies, in part because of the police's increased reliance on tear gas and other chemical weapons that tend to be regarded as relatively benign riot-control tactics.

What happened during Labor Day weekend in St. Paul, Minnesota, in 1968 is one striking example. After hundreds of young Black people in their teens and early twenties gathered downtown at a community dance, the preemptive application of force—in this case, tear gas—on the part of the police brought what should have been a fun event to a violent end.

The young partygoers had ventured two miles from the segregated Rondo neighborhood to Stem Hall, where local funk bands The Exciters and The Blazers were playing that Friday night. In anticipation, the attendees had selected cute, freshly pressed outfits to wear and had fixed their hair. Some of them hoped to dance with their crush, or even get past first base. The youths weren't there to protest anything, by violent or nonviolent means, but to enjoy themselves. By 10 p.m., a crowd of five hundred had arrived to hear the bands and move their bodies, and one group of friends, all young men, left the dance floor and headed to the restroom in Stem Hall's basement, where they could hang out away from everyone else. Two cops followed the group downstairs. The officers were white, and they stood out. Although the policemen were off duty and not in uniform, they came to Stem Hall with their guns and their radios, just in case anything suspicious happened.

The officers walked into the restroom, ready for trouble, just as one of the teens they followed pulled a pistol from his jeans to show his friends. In no time, the officers moved in to make an arrest, but they were easily outnumbered, and the young men began to yell in protest, hoping to keep their friend from being carted off to jail. Surrounded among the urinals, the officers called for backup, drawing their guns to hold the teens off. A scuffle ensued, ending with a shot to the shoulder of one of the officers. Reinforcements arrived at the scene around 10:30 p.m.

The partygoers dancing upstairs were unaware of the standoff taking place below or that anything out of the ordinary was happening until tear gas suddenly came pouring into the hall. It was difficult to see: people's eyes started to tear, their nostrils burned, their throats became clogged as if they were being choked, they coughed as their chests tightened. But it was impossible to find relief: police had trapped them in Stem Hall with the gas, using their nightsticks to lock the doors. Only after all the on-duty police in St. Paul arrived, 150 officers total, plus five reinforcement squads from the Ramsey County Sheriff's office, did the police open Stem Hall. The youths—anxious and traumatized—poured into the streets to breathe in fresh air. The first thing they saw was the fleet of law enforcement, ready and waiting to make arrests. Or worse.

Tensions between St. Paul's Black residents and the mostly white police department, with only four Black officers among its rank and file, were already high. The city had been on alert since the uprising in nearby Minneapolis during the previous summer of 1967, when an officer threw two Black teenage girls to the ground during an altercation at the city's Aquatennial Torchlight parade and hundreds of Black residents mobilized to hold the officers accountable. After the police arrived at the protest and a cop hit a pregnant woman's belly, residents fought back. They hurled rocks at police and Molotov cocktails at buildings. The National Guard and state troopers assisted local police in bringing the violence to an end after four nights.[2]

Similar incidents of police brutality or aggressive enforcement had ignited some 2,239 rebellions across the United States from 1964 to 1972. This era of political violence began with Harlem in July 1964, after a New York City police officer shot and killed a fifteen-year-old Black high school student named James Powell. The community burned for six consecutive nights, with the fire spreading to Brooklyn's Bedford-Stuyvesant neighborhood. Two days after calm was restored in New York City, Black residents in upstate Rochester threw rocks, bricks, and Molotov cocktails at police following the arrest of a twenty-year-old Black man for disorderly conduct at a block party. Lasting for several days, the violence came to an end only after Governor Nelson Rockefeller summoned between eight hundred and a thousand National Guardsmen. Black residents in Chicago's Dixmoor suburb and Philadelphia rebelled the following month, although these incidents were subdued by comparison. In total, more than two thousand people were arrested, seven died, and thousands were injured that July and August.[3]

The fires through the summer of 1964 had prompted President Lyndon Johnson to declare the "War on Crime" in March 1965, an effort that began an unprecedented federal investment in law enforcement. The federal allocation for local police forces went from nothing in 1964 to $10 million in 1965, $20.6 million in 1966, $63 million in 1968, $100 million in 1969, and $300 million in 1970—a 2,900 percent increase in five years.

These funds enabled the twinned expansion and militarization of police in targeted low-income communities of color. The size of the police force in America more than doubled during this early stage of the crime war, as federal policy makers delivered surplus army weapons and technologies— including riot and crowd-control training, military-grade weapons such as AR15s and M4 carbines, steel helmets, armored vehicles, two-way radios, three-foot batons, bulletproof vests, and tear gas—to local departments.[4] Despite these measures, the collective violence only escalated for the remainder of the decade and into the 1970s.

Black residents in thousands of communities across the United States were fighting back against more than just the police officers who interrupted them or brutalized them as they went about their everyday lives. Although the tactics may have differed, the people who attacked police, smashed windows, set fires, and plundered local stores shared the same demands as the mainstream civil rights movement. They were fighting against the process of their own criminalization, as well as making unanswered calls for socioeconomic inclusion and against racism more broadly. As a group of teenagers who participated in a 1970 rebellion in Akron, Ohio, clearly explained to Mayor John Ballard, the causes of the collective violence were routine police harassment, the dearth of resources available to Black residents, "200 years of repression and frustration from the white man," and unemployment. "Everybody's been turned down this summer for employment," one of the teens said.[5]

Instead of addressing lack of access to decent jobs, housing, educational opportunities, and other drivers of inequality with a structural transformation that surpassed the self-help and training programs of the War on Poverty, the Johnson administration and Congress believed that increasing police patrols and granting weapons arsenals to police departments under the banner of the War on Crime would function as the most powerful deterrent to disorder in the short term. As such, police were deployed in neighborhoods with high rates of reported crime that seemed vulnerable to rebellion in anticipation of *future* violence. Rather than responding to incidents that had already occurred (as is the general police function in middle-class and white areas), in low-income communities of color police were tasked with identifying a group that the Johnson administration and Congress called "potential delinquents" or "potential criminals" and arresting them before they went on to cause trouble or harm.[6] This preemptive strategy explains why the plainclothes officers were surveilling the dance at Stem Hall in the first place, with their guns and their radios.

When the young people came pouring out of Stem Hall that Friday night, the police instructed all attendees to disperse and go home. Most followed orders, but about 150 remained, a match for the police force. The night had ended much earlier than expected, and the teenagers were just getting going. Their rides home had yet to arrive. Many of the concert-goers wondered where to go next, what to do. And many of them were angry, having just been violently teargassed out of nowhere and for no apparent reason. "The gas affected the crowd indiscriminately," the local chapter of the Urban Coalition later observed in a report. "It is clear that from the time the gas was thrown into the hall, a wider disturbance was beyond prevention."[7]

This cycle of over-policing and community rebellion was not unique to St. Paul. It played out frequently through the early years of the War on Crime. Just three weeks before the incident at Stem Hall, a fight between two attendees at a dance held at Washington Park High School in Racine, Wisconsin, led to police teargassing a crowd of 250 Black teenagers. The youths proceeded to move through the streets of the Black neighborhood in the south side of the city, smashing store windows, stoning cars, and setting fires, much as their counterparts did in St. Paul. In Harrisburg, the capital of Pennsylvania, a peaceful protest against police brutality in June 1969 quickly turned into a rebellion lasting for several days after police teargassed an angry crowd. The violence ended only after a Black high school student was shot and killed by a local policeman who claimed the teenager was preparing to ignite a Molotov cocktail.[8]

As in Racine and Harrisburg, the decision on the part of St. Paul police to throw gas grenades at a grouping of residents created violence even if the purpose was to prevent it before it began. Some of the teens began hurling bricks, bottles, rocks, and even chairs at the police outside Stem Hall. They taunted them. After a rock hit an officer in the head, causing him to fall to the ground, the police felt they had to move in and break up the crowd by force. The youths quickly split up, running in two opposite directions. The police followed their lead, separating to pursue both groups as the teens made their way back to their small, often deteriorating homes, smashing the windows of white-owned businesses, breaking into cars and stores, assaulting white civilians, and pulling fire alarms along the way.

At the time, the conditions in the city's Rondo community, home to 85 percent of St. Paul's Black residents, clearly resembled those of Harlem, Watts, Detroit, and other low-income Black communities across the United States that had also erupted. With just over 300,000 residents, the Black population in St. Paul had surged 35 percent as southern migrants fled the terror of Jim Crow in the two decades leading up to the uprising. As the flood of newcomers settled in the Rondo neighborhood through the 1950s and early 1960s, and in part to make way for the construction of Interstate 94, a total of more than a thousand units in the area had been demolished, causing a severe shortage of low-income housing that provided tenants with standard or even decent conditions. As St. Paul became a Blacker city, middle-class white residents moved to modern, more comfortable housing at affordable prices in the suburbs. Black residents were essentially limited to segregated projects where the Housing Authority was unresponsive or often insensitive, or to the oldest housing stock in the city, where slum landlords who were very rarely subject to housing inspections allowed the dwellings to deteriorate further while charging exorbitant rents. Urban renewal policies and neglect left the already vulnerable Rondo district vastly overcrowded.[9]

Adding to these desperate conditions, Black residents paid more for decrepit homes in St. Paul and many other cities at the same time as they suffered from a rate of unemployment that was more than three times that of their white counterparts, and those with jobs were most often in the lowest-paying, unskilled sector. As a result, 26 percent of Black residents in St. Paul lived below the poverty line, more than double the rate of white households in the city. Although craft trades and apprenticeship programs had recently opened up to Black residents, affirmative-action measures had made very minor changes in the overall situation. And the public schools, which that state had flagged as "racially imbalanced" for the segregation within them, were becoming increasingly punitive for Black students, who were frequently suspended and who dropped out at disparate rates.[10]

In effect, by holding a group of young people at gunpoint and then unnecessarily teargassing several hundred more, the St. Paul police force set the violent cycle in motion that escalated as the night went on. A total of twenty-two policemen were injured during the unrest, all of whom recovered quickly, including officers who suffered gunshot wounds, and thirty residents suffered physical harm at the hands of police.[11]

Twenty-year-old Teretha Glass-Kelly was one such victim. Glass-Kelly came to Stem Hall with her sister, and they sprinted off together when it seemed an attack by police was imminent. Glass-Kelly was six months into her pregnancy at the time and struggled to keep up. Her stomach started cramping, and the tear gas still lingering in her lungs didn't help. An officer discovered Glass-Kelly as she stopped to catch her breath near the local library, her belly protruding from the dress she had carefully selected for the evening. He struck the young girl with his riot stick, causing her to fall to the ground. He continued to kick her in the stomach and pull her hair before eventually moving on to hunt others in the dead of night.[12]

Glass-Kelly made her way to the hospital with the assistance of a policeman who treated her far more kindly than the first officer (her baby was fine, and she suffered only bruises), and by 4 a.m. the uprising had seemed to subside. But residents prepared for retaliation the following night, making Molotov cocktails and throwing them at three white-owned businesses in the Rondo neighborhood just before 9 p.m. When firefighters arrived to extinguish the blaze, they were reportedly hit by sniper fire. Officers, too, were shot at as they patrolled the neighborhood, seeking to prevent additional destruction. For the most part, however, property damage was "light," as reporters described it: "confined mostly to broken windows." A total of twenty-six young Black people were sitting in jail by that point, the vast majority on charges of unlawful assembly, others for aggravated assault and gun possession.[13]

Once peace had been restored in St. Paul on Sunday, September 1, the local Urban Coalition and Human Rights Department commissioned studies to determine the causes of the rebellion. Together they interviewed hundreds of witnesses and residents throughout the fall and released their reports in February 1969. "The tensions and frustrations of the St. Paul Negro Community have been created by so many factors and been bottled up so long that disorder seemed inevitable," Human Rights Department director Louis H. Ervin wrote. "Something had to give." The investigators identified the crises in housing, employment, and education as the fundamental causes of the violence, but their recommendations to remedy these inequalities—regulating slum landlords, constructing new affordable housing units, desegregating public schools, and creating jobs—never came to fruition. And although the Human Rights Department criticized "some ineptitude, even misconduct," among local police, "it ought not to, and will not, detract from the exemplary conduct" on the part of the officers who consistently "maintained discipline" during the rebellion.[14] Ultimately, the Human Rights Department defended the use of force against hundreds of innocent teenagers in Stem Hall that evening.

Even if authorities consistently upheld the fundamental logic of policing in targeted neighborhoods, the fact that law enforcement very often inflamed community violence did not entirely escape policy makers and law enforcement officials. The widely distributed 1967 FBI manual called *Prevention and Control of Mobs and Riots* recognized that the application of force was a delicate matter, for its premature use would only "contribute to the danger, aggravate the mob, and instill in the individual a deep-rooted hatred of police." Likewise, in its 1969 report the National Commission on the Causes and Prevention of Violence concluded that "excessive force is an unwise tactic for handling disorder" that "often has the effect of magnifying turmoil not diminishing it."[15]

When riot-control methods came in for criticism as rebellions flared through the summers of Johnson's presidency, tear gas offered a solution. Officials regarded the chemical as a "measured" response to domestic political violence, a way to control crowds without resorting to outright brutality. A combined total of some eighty Black residents had been killed by police, National Guardsmen, or paratroopers during the 1965 Watts uprising and in the 1967 Newark and Detroit uprisings. "Equipping civil police with automatic rifles, machine guns, and other weapons of massive and indiscriminate lethality is not warranted by evidence," the National Advisory Commission on Civil Disorders (known popularly as the Kerner Commission) wrote in its 1968 report. "Weapons which are designed to destroy, not to control, have no place in densely populated urban communities." However, the commission and federal policy makers across the political spectrum determined that tear gas provided "police forces with an effective and appropriate weapon" that could quickly disperse a mob without resorting to beating people with billy clubs or shooting them with bullets, and was essentially harmless beyond its immediate effects. It is now understood that tear gas, in any form, can cause significant damage to the lungs, liver, and heart. The chemicals that tear gas contains are so powerful that pregnant women who have been exposed to chlorobenzylidene malononitrile (CS) fumes are vulnerable to miscarriage.[16]

The tear gas that the St. Paul Police Department unleashed on the dancing teenagers, and that thousands of other departments frequently used on the streets of American cities in the late 1960s and early 1970s, had been initially formulated toward the end of World War I. Then, military officials used the nonlethal chloracetophenone (CN) gas to move people from trenches and force enemies into retreat. Tear gas had been banned under international law in 1925, but the United States and many other nations consistently relied on it as a weapon of domestic law enforcement and a riot-control measure for the remainder of the twentieth century and beyond. The British developed the more potent o—CS or "super" tear gas in the 1950s to put down uprisings in its colonies. The weapon proved to be useful in inflicting both physical and psychological torture on those who might challenge the empire. The United States quickly adapted its own version for use, viewing tear gas as an effective way to leave riotous crowds demoralized, stomping the collective spirit of the protest or gathering and preventing participants from engaging in further action (at least temporarily).[17] Yet it was not until the 1960s, in the context of the Vietnam War and the launch of the War on Crime at home, that tear gas became popular among US military and law enforcement officials. The more pronounced impact of CS gas, in particular, proved effective in pursuing the Vietcong through underground bunkers and tunnels, and in putting down so-called riots in Black American neighborhoods from St. Paul to Los Angeles.

Tear gas had been intended for the battlefield, to harm enemy forces for a brief period of time without leaving a trail of blood. The chemical weapon produced immediate effects, attacking the senses of its intended targets, leaving them incapacitated anywhere from ten seconds to ten minutes and causing, as the army manual *Military Chemistry and Chemical Agents* described it and as the young people in Stem Hall experienced it, "extreme burning of the eyes accompanied by copious flow of tears, coughing, difficulty in breathing, and chest tightness, involuntary closing of the eyes, stinging sensations of moist skin, running nose, and dizziness or swimming of the head."[18]

Following the Kerner Commission's best-selling 1968 report, tear gas became the weapon of choice to suppress both nonviolent and violent protests for racial justice (or, as the story of St. Paul shows us, simply controlling crowds) in Black communities that seemed prone to both rioting and crime. Of course, tear gas had been used during civil rights protests, such as the planned fifty-four-mile march from Selma to Montgomery, Alabama, in March 1965 after police killed twenty-six-year-old Jimmie Lee Jackson during a peaceful voting-rights demonstration. As six hundred marchers proceeded on Selma's Edmund Pettus Bridge, state troopers sporting gas masks shot forty canisters of tear gas into the crowds, twelve canisters of smoke, and eight canisters of nausea gas, and then they proceeded to beat the marchers with clubs and whips under the smokescreen of the chemicals in an incident remembered as "Bloody Sunday." This was only the beginning of what would come in the era of Black Power and Black rebellion. Police, state troopers, and National Guardsmen used the chemical to punish protesters for challenging the racial status quo as much as for its stated purpose of quelling disturbances. By 1969, tear gas had become so ubiquitous that the Department of Justice had enabled the low-cost sale of more than seventy thousand gas masks to local law enforcement.[19]

Tear gas remained an essential riot-control device through the collective violence that rocked Miami in 1980, Los Angeles in 1992, Cincinnati in 2001, and Ferguson, Missouri, and Baltimore in the mid-2010s.

The 1993 Chemical Weapons Convention upheld the international prohibition on tear gas and other chemical weapons in warfare, but they are still regarded as humane alternatives to violently arresting or shooting into crowds of people, and law enforcement officials around the world are still permitted to apply the devices at their discretion. For the most part, the composition of CS gas hasn't changed from the formula developed in the 1950s, but the canisters that contain the weapon have become more advanced and powerful (and therefore more destructive on impact). A host of other projectiles that have been developed in recent decades, such as rubber bullets, beanbag rounds, and stun grenades, are likewise often misused against protesters and can cause debilitating injuries and permanent disabilities.[20]

During the largest social movement in American history, sustained by tens of millions of protesters through the summer of 2020, law enforcement in at least a hundred cities discharged tear gas and other "nonlethal" weapons. The demonstrations in Minneapolis in the days after George Floyd's murder were the opening act, when the National Guard hurled tear gas canisters to disrupt the protest "like a knife cutting butter," in the words of President Trump, an action that produced "a beautiful scene." One of the most egregious incidents of that summer involved US Park Police and Secret Service agents who used tear gas, riot batons, and other weapons against nonviolent protesters in Lafayette Square near the White House to make way for a photo opportunity for Trump in front of the nearby St. John's Church.[21]

From Sacramento to Providence, the fog of tear gas dominated the police response to unanswered calls for social justice and racial equality once again. Yet unlike the earlier rebellions, which typically began with demonstrators throwing rocks, bottles, and other objects when police arrived to patrol their communities (or when police used tear gas and other forms of blatant violence preemptively, as in St. Paul), the demonstrations from Ferguson onward started as peaceful marches and vigils in response to flagrant acts of brutality. When police responded aggressively to these nonviolent protesters, some of them quickly turned violent, and so the cycle began.[22]

The tear gas used in St. Paul in 1968, and in Minneapolis and Washington more recently, is part of the recurring pattern of police violence and community violence that took hold roughly a half century ago and has remained unbroken. The history of protest—past and present—demonstrates that aggressive policing tends to incite violence, especially when residents are protesting the very thing to which they are then subjected. Because police force is almost always viewed as legitimate, tear gas and other forms of state-sanctioned violence will remain the go-to, short-term solution that policy makers and officials embrace whenever people challenge racial hierarchies and the systems that uphold them. The long-term solution that will finally break the cycle involves dismantling the underlying socioeconomic drivers of inequality that extend far beyond a single law enforcement agency. Until then, nonviolent and violent protesters alike will continue to be harmed when toxic substances are used against them, and all of us will continue to live with the violent legacies of American racism and the myths that sustain it.

17

INSURRECTION

Kathleen Belew

O N January 6, 2021, throngs of protesters stormed the US Capitol Building intent on disrupting the certification of the presidential election. The crowd included seasoned militiamen and organized white power activists, Trump supporters with varying degrees of intensity of feeling, and adherents to QAnon, a conspiracy that accuses global elites of trafficking and murdering children. They breached the building, threatened lawmakers, carried zip ties, roamed the hallways, defaced offices, and scrawled "Murder the Media" on the edifice. Five people died, including a police officer beaten by the crowd. As the action unfolded, journalists began to insist upon the word *insurrection*—not *protest*—to describe the day's violence. But many commentators, as well as policy makers and ordinary people, also voiced and repeated one reaction that quickly became its own myth: "This is not who we are."[1]

Although in this case it is an understandable, emotional reaction meant to decry antidemocratic violence, the notion that January 6 is "not who we are" is one manifestation of what has become a regularly deployed Republican Party and right-wing media strategy: to deny the workings of overt and violent racist activism even when those actions threaten American citizens and democracy itself. In the months that followed January 6, this intentional denial became even more pronounced. One lawmaker—even as the *New York Times* assembled a long-form video piece that clipped footage together to depict multiple close brushes with violence on 1/6—called the insurrection "a normal tourist visit." Another—while the House Select Committee tasked with investigating the attack began to subpoena witnesses—attempted to distort the very category of "insurrection" by calling the border policies of the Democratic Party a "permanent election insurrection" meant to replace white American voters. Trump administration officials and confidants, at the time of this writing, were preparing to refuse subpoenas, and the January 6 committee was filing contempt-of-Congress charges just to get testimony. In other words, the GOP, the right-wing media, and most Republican lawmakers did *not* condemn the events of January 6, particularly in the long term.[2]

Furthermore, the very element that shocked so many that day, the presence of militant Right and white power activists in propelling the violence, has been with us for decades, if not generations. January 6 is exactly who we are.

As historians pointed out immediately, January 6 was American in the truest sense, its action harkening all the way back to the founding of the United States: a moment that both built upon and produced deep and enduring legacies of violence, racism, and settler colonialism. Indeed, one can trace vigilante violence and lynching as foundational to American life and culture from the beginnings of the nation to the present. Such violence occurred not only in its most well-known incarnation, the spectacle lynching of Black men in the American South between 1890 and 1930, but in other places too. Mexicans and Mexican Americans faced vigilantes on the border in the early twentieth century in stunning numbers. Women who refused to marry faced the possibility of lynching in the American West, as did union organizers in the forests of the Pacific Northwest. Violence meant to seize and shore up power—a claim to sovereignty through the violence of the mob—is fundamentally American.[3]

The recent white power movement, however, is distinct in many ways from earlier mobilizations of racist and vigilante violence in American history. Here I'm talking about the broad and diverse social movement that brought together Klansmen, skinheads, neo-Nazis, militiamen, and more beginning in the late 1970s. White power was bigger than simply another version of the Ku Klux Klan, which had already experienced three different "eras" after the Civil War, World War I, and World War II and the war in Korea. By contrast, proponents of the white power movement were not really interested in seizing local power through mob violence. Instead, they advocated wholesale revolution through race war.[4] By 2020, this organized groundswell represented the greatest domestic terrorism threat to the American homeland, according to both the FBI and the Department of Homeland Security.[5] This was bigger, more dangerous, better armed, better organized, revolutionary, and endemic in every region of the country. How did we reach not only the crisis of January 6 but also the repeated assertion that *this is not who we are*?

The white power movement convened a broad array of groups and people engaged in overt racism and violence. Indeed, it remains an incredibly diverse social movement in every way but race, uniting men, women, and children; people in every region of the country; felons and religious leaders; people in suburbs, rural areas, and cities; high-school dropouts and people with advanced degrees; people across social classes; and veterans, active-duty military personnel, and civilians. When it formed in the late 1970s, it brought together several groups that had previously been at odds with one another, including Klan, neo-Nazi, radical tax resister, Christian identity, white separatist, and, later, skinheads and militia activists. These groups united with the explicit goal of waging war on the United States and its democratic institutions.

Another historical myth provided the terms of the movement's unification: a shared narrative of the Vietnam War. By telling the story of betrayal by the government and failure of the state, white power activists mobilized both veterans and those who had not served. The loss of the war, in this powerful narrative, operationalized their violence and focused their anger and sense of betrayal on the federal government. Many of them traded white robes and hoods for camouflage fatigues and adopted the weapons and tactics of the Vietnam War. Here they followed a long pattern: the aftermath of warfare has been the most consistent predictor of such violence (more so than poverty, immigration, populism, or racial diversity) throughout the recent past. Klan membership surges have aligned neatly with the aftermath of every major war in recent history. In the case of the Vietnam War, loss provided a particularly potent example, one that drew together a small number of veterans with many other disaffected people who felt betrayed by the government and sought radical change.[6]

These activists were motivated by a sense of urgency: they believed that immigration, feminism, abortion, interracial marriage, and other social changes would lower the white birthrate and lead to the end of the white race. In other words, they saw not a soft demographic transformation— the much anticipated moment of transformation when a town, city, state, or nation would no longer be majority white—but an apocalyptic threat.[7] Today the same constellation of ideas goes by the label "replacement theory" or the "Great Replacement," and it has found purchase in mainstream politics and cable news commentary.

The unifying event of the white power movement was the shooting of leftist protesters in Greensboro, North Carolina, in 1979. There, neo-Nazis and Klansmen calling themselves the United Racist Front opened fire on a "Death to the Klan" rally, killing five people and injuring more. The eighty-eight-second shooting was captured by multiple news cameras on scene, clearly revealing what had happened: heavily armed gunmen had fired into a crowd.[8] A state trial of the Klan and Nazi gunmen featured an all-white jury, achieved through peremptory challenges—the dismissal of Black jurors without cause, a vestige of white supremacist legal systems in the South that was eradicated in North Carolina shortly thereafter. The court acquitted every one of the Greensboro defendants. A federal trial similarly attempted to prove that the gunmen had deprived the victims of their civil rights (by killing them) but specified that it was concerned with conspiracy to do so *for reasons of race*. But the victims in Greensboro had been one Black woman and four men who appeared white, and the United Racist Front said it was there to kill communists, not Black people. And because the long and complex regional relationship between anticommunism and racism—one documented at length by scores of historians—was ignored, the gunmen walked free yet again.[9]

Perhaps the most stunning is the finding of the later civil case, in which the only death at Greensboro deemed "wrongful" was that of the one victim who was not a card-carrying communist at the time of his death. In any case, the white power movement opened fire on leftist protesters and killed five of them, and it did so with no real legal penalty because the city of Greensboro paid the damages in the civil case. The white power movement celebrated this victory and took it as a green light for further violence.[10]

The most pervasive misunderstandings of the white power movement come from the early 1980s, when its activists declared open war on the federal government and adopted an organizational strategy called "Leaderless Resistance" to achieve that goal. Simply put, this meant cell-style domestic terrorism in which white power activists could carry out individual or small-group acts of violence on an agreed-upon set of targets with no demonstrable ties to other cells or group leadership.[11] This strategy was designed to foil the government informants who had infiltrated the civil rights–era Ku Klux Klan and to make it more difficult to prosecute white power groups in both criminal and civil cases. Even trials like the one in Greensboro, a victory for the movement, had high personal and financial costs. At the time of the implementation of Leaderless Resistance, the Southern Poverty Law Center had succeeded in using civil cases to disband Klan paramilitary training camps, gag particular white power leaders and prevent them from associating with one another, and even to seize the assets, membership lists, and headquarters of one Klan group. Although criminal cases broadly failed to return similarly decisive verdicts, they did cost the movement time and money. Leaderless Resistance offered a solution to this problem.[12]

Leaderless Resistance had a much more catastrophic outcome, how-ever, one largely unanticipated even by white power adherents when it was implemented. It erased public understanding of white power activ-ism as part of a movement, producing the most damaging myth about this history: that of the "lone wolf."[13] Let me be perfectly clear: there *are* crimes carried out by individuals. There are some mass shootings that are not motivated by politics. But there is no such thing as a "lone wolf" white power terrorist. The actions carried out by white power activists are part of a coordinated social movement, one that has united people in common purpose and around a coherent white supremacist ideology. They are legible events that require more than an individual response.

Leaderless Resistance did several things to change how the white power movement worked, ultimately letting it disappear from broad public under-standing as a social movement. First, it disconnected rising membership numbers from rising levels of violent activism. In other words, the move-ment became less focused on mass demonstrations and emphasized tar-geted acts of violence. After it declared war on the United States in 1983, the white power movement wasn't looking for six thousand people to march down Main Street; it was looking for six people willing to detonate a bomb. To be sure, the movement still used public actions to recruit and to disperse its ideology, but the violent center of its activity was not interested in large numbers as much as it was interested in total dedication. Therefore, from 1983 forward, falling membership in white power groups sometimes corre-sponded with *rising* levels of violent activism.[14]

One way that the white power movement implemented Leaderless Resistance was to go online. This is another misunderstanding reaching the level of cultural myth: people erroneously believe that the movement began to use the internet in the social-media bonanza of the present mo-ment, or even with the founding of the major white power website Storm-front in the mid-1990s. Instead, the white power movement pioneered proto-internet, web-based social network activism in 1983–1984, with the founding and implementation of Liberty Net. Using early computer networks, the white power movement set up a series of password-pro-tected message boards where activists could access content. Their posts included not only hit lists and ideological screeds but also personal ads and other social content. Liberty Net, in this sense, was an example of how social media could motivate network activism and spread misinformation and conspiracy theory decades before the invention of Facebook.[15]

The importance of Liberty Net was also evident in the resources and manpower devoted to its setup and implementation. As the historical archive shows, white power activists stole millions of dollars from department stores and armored cars in the Pacific Northwest and Northern California in the mid-1980s. They took this money around the country, distributing those funds to a network of white power groups with instructions to purchase Apple "minicomputers." Then a key movement leader traveled the same circuit, teaching people how to use the computers and the network. In a dispersed social movement that attempted to avoid keeping and revealing membership networks, the activity around Liberty Net illustrates the breadth and coordination of previously separate white power groups. Liberty Net also helped to operationalize the strategy of Leaderless Resistance by laying out a series of targets held in common between cells. Activists then pursued these targets with real-life acts of violence, including attempted assassinations, infrastructure attacks, the murder of federal judges and state troopers, bombings, and a cyanide attack on a public water supply.[16]

Leaderless Resistance also allowed the movement to organize around differential levels of involvement. We might consider these in concentric circles. Scholars who have attempted to estimate the size of the movement in the 1980s broadly agree that the innermost circle would include only 25,000 people but that this inner ring would be quite dedicated. Here we would find the people who live their full lives in the movement, marry other white power activists, raise their children in the movement, visit churches in the movement, and also attend to daily life—rides to and from the airport, homeschool curricula, recipe exchanges—within the movement. These activists would also provide the pool from which to recruit Leaderless Resistance cell operatives. Outside this dedicated center, we would find another 150,000–175,000 activists: those who attend public actions, subscribe to movement literature, and similar actions. Then there is a larger circle of some 450,000 people who would not themselves subscribe to movement literature but who regularly read that literature all the same.[17]

On January 6, it was not just the inner circle who stormed the Capitol but people from each of these rings, and a new one. Scholars little understand the circle of people just outside of that outer ring, which is much larger and somewhat more amorphous. That group includes the people who would never read a newspaper titled, for instance, *White Aryan Resistance*, but who might agree with some of the ideas and even the broader ideologies of white supremacy presented therein. This outer circle becomes critically important in an action like the January 6 insurrection.

The concentric circle model of organization did two important things: it allowed activists who could be radicalized to be pulled to the center, and it pushed extremist ideas from the center into the mainstream, even beyond the outermost circle. The most notable example of the second impact from the pre-Trump years is the presidential campaign of former Klan leader and lifelong white power activist David Duke. Sociologist Sara Diamond documents how some elements of Duke's presidential platform were deliberately adopted by populist primary challenger Patrick Buchanan, and his by the Republican nominee George W. Bush, who was elected president. In other words, white power ideas percolated into mainstream politics far before the 2016 election of Donald J. Trump.[18]

The work of pulling people from casual membership to what both scholars and white power activists called "hard-core" activism happened in myriad ways: there were, perhaps, as many routes to radicalization as there were radical activists in the movement. So, too, did white power leadership in this period prioritize the recruitment of targeted populations, such as incarcerated people, veterans, and active-duty troops, all of whom were thought to have operational and weapons expertise valuable to the movement. But it is difficult to overstate the importance of women in doing crucial radicalization work. Indeed, this reveals another durable myth: the idea that white power activism is a men's movement. To be sure, the movement used a paramilitary command structure and espoused antifeminism, but the role of women was critical to its success, and the women who participated in it subscribed to this ideology and organization as well.[19]

Sociologist Kathleen Blee documents that across the twentieth century, from the Ku Klux Klan to the white power movement, women have done critical work in normalizing and mainstreaming such fringe groups, and in the social interactions used to recruit, radicalize, and bind white power activists.[20] The historical archive of the white power movement also bears this out. One might think of the Aryan Nations World Congress, the major summer summit that convened different groups in northern Idaho regularly in the 1980s. There, women were in charge of matchmaking schemes, social events, volleyball, and a big spaghetti dinner.[21]

Women's activism also provides a window into a period of white power activism that has largely been misunderstood, that of the bridge between the paramilitary movement of the 1980s and the militia movement of the early 1990s. Women's publications, auxiliary groups, home-school curricula, fund-raising, and coupon-sharing campaigns did not just persist but actually boomed in the period from the crest of paramilitary activism in the 1980s to the militia movement peak in the early 1990s.[22]

Because the militia movement represented a change in rhetoric, uniforms, and, to some extent, membership, some journalists and scholars have treated it as distinct from the earlier white power movement. This is a mistake. The militias, while antigovernment, were not always overtly racist. But the white power movement's weapons, funds, and activists nevertheless flowed into militia groups. On a Venn diagram, we could think of a large circle representing the militia movement and a smaller circle of white power activism. Some militia groups and actions were not within the white power circle. However, the white power movement circle was almost entirely enclosed within the broader circle of the militia movement in this period. The money, people, weapons, and energy of the 1980s white power war on the federal government flowed directly into militias. Furthermore, many militias unaffiliated with overt racism and white power violence marched shoulder to shoulder with groups that *were* affiliated.[23]

Both Leaderless Resistance and the opportunistic adoption of militia movement trappings were moves calculated to disguise the white power movement for what it was: a coordinated and socially networked movement of men and women that connected activists across multiple regions and different kinds of places in a violent war on the federal government, and in an attempt to attack democracy and provoke race war.

It would be impossible to understand how a small number of activists thought they could wage revolution without *The Turner Diaries*, a novel that imagined the success of Leaderless Resistance. A central text and cultural lodestar for the movement, *The Turner Diaries* appeared at critical points and in the hands of important activists throughout its history. The White Patriot Party in North Carolina distributed it to new recruits in the mid-1980s. The Order, a white terrorist group in the Pacific Northwest, kept a stack of copies in the bunkhouse. Oklahoma City bomber Timothy McVeigh sold it on the gun-show circuit in the early 1990s.[24]

The Turner Diaries, first printed in serial form in the late 1970s and then published as a paperback, was important not because of its quality but because it answered a critical question: how could a fringe movement possibly hope to overthrow the most militarized superstate in the history of the world? The novel answers this question by laying out a series of strategies, beginning with cell-style terror, infrastructure attacks, and targeted assassinations, and rising to the theft and deployment of nuclear weapons and other mass-casualty attacks. *The Turner Diaries* lays out the assassination of all "race traitors" on the "Day of the Rope" and then, after the white power activists win, explains in a postscript the annihilation of all people of color throughout the United States and the world. The novel is unflinching in its violence, prescribing the use of nuclear, biological, and chemical weapons and describing the massive human cost of white nationalist warfare as collateral damage. It also illustrates an important problem with the phrase *white nationalism* in describing the movement. People may hear "white nationalism" and assume it to be adjacent with patriotism, or at the very least consider it as pro-American. But after 1983 the nation at the heart of white nationalism was not the United States but rather the Aryan nation, imagined as a transnational polity of white people who would need to be saved from extermination through race war and violence. This is a fundamentally more violent and radical position than that implied by "nationalism."

The desire of the white power movement to disappear; the use of Leaderless Resistance, or cell-style terrorism, which prescribed denial of connection between groups and activists; and the rising tide of militia movement–era disaffection for the federal government set the scene for the explosion in Oklahoma City in 1995. So, too, did a disastrous attempt to prosecute thirteen white power activists and leaders on federal charges including seditious conspiracy in 1987–1988. That trial depended on plea bargains and investigative materials from several other prosecutions, all in an attempt to prove that the defendants had conspired together to violently overthrow the federal government. The archive here is quite clear: they said that's what they were doing, and they set out to do so on the model of *The Turner Diaries*. They were outfitted not only with the usual automatic and semiautomatic rifles but also with antitank LAW rockets, homemade napalm and Claymore mines, and machine guns. The Department of Justice (DOJ) had wiretaps showing the conspiracy—hundreds of calls between movement leaders and activists. But the trial was a disaster, with chain-of-custody problems obscuring the evidence, romantic relationships between two jurors and defendants, and a jury pool heavily sympathetic to the defendants.

The DOJ had poured resources into the trial, but the headline it got at the conclusion was "Jubilant Racists Win Trial." One of the main defendants, not contrite in the least, immediately started a quarterly titled the *Seditionist*. This embarrassing outcome was soon followed by standoffs at Ruby Ridge and Waco, where extremists died during government interventions—on live television in the case of Waco.[25] Even as these events galvanized white power and militia activism, they tamped down government response. After the failure of the sedition trial, the FBI institutionalized a policy to pursue only individual actors in white power violence, with "no attempts to tie individual crimes to a broader movement."[26]

This was the policy in place when Gulf War veteran Timothy McVeigh detonated a fertilizer bomb that destroyed the Alfred P. Murrah Federal Building in Oklahoma City. The act belongs on a short list of atrocities. It was the largest deliberate mass casualty on American soil between the Japanese attack on Pearl Harbor that marked the US entry into World War II and the terror attacks of September 11, 2001. We know the stories of Pearl Harbor and 9/11. Those events have entered the realm of common knowledge: they are taught in schools and represented in pop culture, and many, if not most, Americans have at least a passing understanding of what happened on those days.[27] Oklahoma City is different. Even as the nation marked the twenty-fifth anniversary of the attack that struck at America's heartland, slaughtering 168 people—including 19 young children in the building's day-care center—the nation lacked a coherent narrative of how the bombing happened, who perpetrated it, and what it stood for.

From the beginning, and even more intensely, perhaps, after the guilty verdict and his execution, our narratives of the Oklahoma City bombing have focused on McVeigh as a lone wolf. The evidence to the contrary is overwhelming. A simple social geography of McVeigh's life places him clearly within the white power movement. Indeed, the evidence of McVeigh's involvement in the white power movement is too extensive to document in full here, but a few highlights include his choice of a building that had been a movement target since the early 1980s; the use and distribution of movement novel *The Turner Diaries* in formulating his plan for the bombing; his presence as high-level security for movement leadership in the Michigan Militia; his contacts and attempted contacts with the white power groups Arizona Patriots, National Alliance, and a white separatist compound at Elohim City; and the date of the bombing on the anniversary not only of the Waco siege but of the execution date of a prominent white power activist who had once targeted, yes, the same federal building in Oklahoma City. Additional evidence abounds, and not at the level of conspiracy theory: he clearly subscribed to "leaderless resistance."[28]

The Oklahoma City bombing did not reduce the violent ambitions of white power activists. Militia group membership and activity *increased* in its aftermath, and white power activists flocked to Stormfront, the newest platform for web-based activism following the model of Liberty Net.

When the white power movement charged back into the limelight in recent years, it was not roundly condemned. In the aftermath of the violent Unite the Right rally and clashes in Charlottesville, Virginia, in August

2017, President Donald Trump gave an infamous sound bite about there being "very fine people on both sides."[29] In his full comment, he makes clear that he is not referring to white nationalists and neo-Nazis as "very fine people," and he says they should be "condemned totally." The "very fine people" he refers to are an imagined group of innocent and peaceful protesters who wanted to protest the removal of a statue and name of Confederate general Robert E. Lee from a public park. Trump's comment attempts to draw a bright line between neo-Nazis and white nationalists and the "very fine people," even as it blames "troublemakers" on the left for starting the confrontation.

The problem here is that the Unite the Right rally was not designed as a peaceful protest but as a deliberate and paramilitarized white power action. It featured torchlit acts of intimidation and the killing of a counterprotester. It also featured militia groups that were purportedly present as neutral peacekeepers but that in fact kept police from protecting counterprotesters because they were more heavily armed than the police.[30] Trump's lack of condemnation would only become more and more pronounced.

Even more concerning were deliberate attempts to distract from white power activism in the aftermath of mass attacks on American civilians, often with incontestable evidence about the motivation of the attackers. Several recent mass shootings carried out by white power attackers have been described in other ways. For this reason, we still read stories of "lone wolf" gunmen attacking Muslims in Christchurch, New Zealand; Jewish people at the Tree of Life synagogue in Pittsburgh; Black Bible-study worshippers in Charleston; Latinx people in El Paso. And these *were* acts of Islamophobic, anti-Semitic, racist, and anti-immigrant violence. But they were *also* carried out by white power activists, all of whom shared the same core motivating texts (including *The Turner Diaries*), ideology, concerns about white reproduction, and list of targets. They are all part of the same movement.

But a GOP talking-points memo after the 2019 El Paso shooting suggested steering "the conversation away from white nationalism to an argument that implies both sides are to blame."[31] This stance not only ignored the threat of the most violent domestic-terrorist movement attempting to attack American civilians but deliberately tried to aid it in its work of disappearance.

Here we see the evolution of the myth of "this is not who we are": the rising tide of white power activity and its overt, violent racism, on the one hand, and the deepening disavowal and complicity of Republican elected officials and their media allies on the other. If the historical archive of the earlier white power movement offers us one lesson for today, it's this: the movement has used, and will continue to use, the myth of the "lone wolf" to attempt to evade open confrontation with public opinion. It will continue to claim that it is simply one person, a few people, a few feuding groups. But even as we see the newest iteration of this tactic, we are surely in the midst of a rising tide of white power violence. According to FBI Director Christopher Wray, 2019 was "the deadliest year for domestic violent extremism since 1995, the year of the Oklahoma City bombing." Wray issued a similar statement when rates in 2020 and 2021 were even higher.[32] This is a problem deeply intertwined in American politics and culture, and one that will require sustained attention to resolve.

On January 6, 2021, the white power and militant Right actors were, among the larger crowd, the most organized and well armed, and they posed the greatest threat to the workings of democracy. So did January 6 follow *The Turner Diaries*, which features an attack on the Capitol meant as a show of force. And again, while much ink has been spilled trying to differentiate among groups such as the Proud Boys, Oath Keepers, Three Percenters, The Base, Boogaloo Boys, and Atomwaffen Division, all should be understood as part of the same broad white power and militant Right groundswell, one with decades of organizing and resources and, today, with increasing momentum.

On January 6, when the insurrectionists constructed a gallows and noose outside of the Capitol, they referred directly to a scene in *The Turner Diaries*; the entire action referenced a strike on the Capitol in that novel. This indicates that January 6 was not meant as a mass-casualty event but a recruitment and radicalization exercise to draw others into the fold. Certainly this happened immediately after the rally, as white power activists and others on the militant Right reached into the Trump base and QAnon groups in intensified recruitment campaigns.

Experts are quite clear on the danger we face. Political scientist Robert Pape has found that the outer circle of white power and militant Right membership—where it connects to and overlaps with our mainstream politics—is growing at an alarming rate. Some 47 million American adults polled after the January 6 insurrection said that they believed the 2020 election was stolen and Joe Biden was an illegitimate president. Of those, 21 million said they agreed with the statement that the "use of force is justified to restore Donald J. Trump to the presidency."[33] Pape, who has studied political violence and civil unrest in other countries, recognizes a storm brewing in our own.

All of this is, and remains, who we are. Knowing and understanding our history is the only path to a more democratic future.

18

FAMILY VALUES FEMINISM

Natalia Mehlman Petrzela

O N JUNE 30, 1982, CONSERVATIVE ACTIVIST PHYLLIS SCHLAFLY threw a party for more than a thousand guests in a Washington, DC, hotel ballroom festooned with red, white, and blue balloons and streamers. Resplendent in a long string of pearls and a white dress with butterfly sleeves, Schlafly was positively triumphant: the night before, the ten-year timetable for the ratification of the Equal Rights Amendment had expired, and the measure had failed to pass.[1] As Schlafly and Republican leading lights from President Ronald Reagan to Jerry Falwell saw it, she and the legions of homemakers she had mobilized at coffee klatches and PTA meetings over the past decade and a half were responsible for scoring a major victory for the ascendant conservative movement.

Specifically, killing the ERA protected the nuclear family from the depredations of evil feminists intent on undermining this bedrock American institution. Feminism, conservatives announced, was an antifamily movement. But such declarations denied nearly two hundred years of American history. Feminists have *never* been dead set on destroying the family before, during, or after Schlafly's heyday. On the contrary, American feminists have consistently championed policies that shore up the family—often in the face of intense conservative opposition. Schlafly exploited a moment when feminism had indeed expanded to support the rights of women as more than mothers, making the movement vulnerable to accusations of undermining the family. However, feminist activists have only continued to this day their two-century-long fight to *strengthen* families and to define this fundamental institution more inclusively.

This history was deliberately denied on that night in 1982. From the podium, Falwell lauded Schlafly's STOP ERA movement as "just the beginning" of the wholesale conservative renaissance he envisioned.[2] Ironically benefiting from the feminism she abhorred, Schlafly happily accepted such praise from the men who had until recently spurned her opinions on any policy outside of the "women's issues" they considered her turf. But as the band played "Ding Dong, the Witch Is Dead," Schlafly must have been especially buoyed by her own apparently prescient observation, reported three years earlier by the *Washington Post*, that "the women's lib movement is going to self-destruct because they are not going to have any babies—and if they do have them, they won't take care of them, so our children will be the ones who are well-cared-for and well-adjusted."[3]

History, it seemed on that summer night, was on Schlafly's side in a war that she and her conservative allies painted as a long-standing conflict between traditional, God-fearing Americans who valued the institution of the family and the radical feminists who sought to destroy it. The ERA victory was important, but it didn't mean that the fight was over. Schlafly announced she would next turn to eradicating "feminist influences" that undermined the family in the schoolhouse. "You can't show a picture of a woman washing dishes," she wrote of contemporary children's literature, not to mention the "family life education classes" in which liberals promoted sexual experimentation, inappropriate challenges to gendered family roles, and general immorality. Stocking school libraries with "pro-family" titles and eradicating such curricula was the next front, Schlafly and her followers believed, in vanquishing the feminists who would just as soon see teenagers get pregnant, wives go off to the office, and children be left in the care of government institutions or, just as bad, in the arms of an emasculated husband.

By the night of the pro-family ball, this dichotomy between feminism and family was an entrenched plank of conservative messaging, and it has endured. But the historical record on which this supposed opposition relies is dubious. Feminism has been an effort to strengthen the family and offer policies that allow parents and their children to flourish, rather than struggle, from the challenges presented by the marketplace, austerity policy, and restrictive ideas about gender and race.

Few activist American women in the antebellum era—many who were pious Protestants—used the term *feminism*, coined by French socialist Charles Fourier in the 1830s. But these women who worked to reform society were unquestionably the foremothers of those who soon adopted the label self-consciously; protecting the integrity of the family was at the heart of their activism.

For example, fighting against the social evil of alcohol in order to safeguard the home and marital sanctity animated many women who joined organizations such as the Woman's Christian Temperance Union. Drunken men were more likely to beat and cheat on their wives—cracking down on prostitution was another antebellum cause—and squandering one's wages on alcohol could ultimately leave a family destitute. Speaking out about social policy or curbing men's purchasing power did not conform with dominant ideas about female propriety, but to the extent that women were defending realms within their purview—the home and family—they enjoyed greater latitude.

Temperance activists made this argument explicitly when some men questioned the appropriateness of their activism: women were "not leaving [their] own proper sphere, or usurping the prerogative of the other sex; but acting strictly in accordance . . . with the word of God." Their gender "exerted a softening, enobling [*sic*], and purifying influence."[4] Indeed, nineteenth-century women reformers invoked their identities as caregivers to fight for children's welfare by supporting hospitals, common schools, and even an "Orphan Train" movement that relocated immigrant children to live with families in the rural West. These efforts were largely

advanced by native-born white women who celebrated a familial structure most familiar to them, but their invocation of family resonated with
abolitionists such as Harriet Beecher Stowe, who appealed for emancipation by arguing that the cruelest aspect of enslavement was the destruction of families.

The fight for women's suffrage came under fire as an attack on the family. Opponents decried that the political independence of women would
somehow prevent them from their traditional role of raising children. After all, the women who fought for suffrage made their pleas in the idiom
of Enlightenment individualism and independence. The 1848 Declaration of Sentiments was modeled directly on the Declaration of Independence, a document that severed what many considered a metaphorically
familial relationship between imperial parent and dependent, colonized
child. It took more than seventy years for women's suffrage to be codified
with the Nineteenth Amendment. Suffragists were successful at reframing the debate, arguing that the right to vote and what historians call
"maternalism" went hand in hand: (white) women should be granted the
franchise because they, especially as mothers, were moral beacons, and
the vote would enable them to instill this essential virtue in their families
and to transmit it broadly to a world that sorely needed salvation.

To be sure, the fight for women's suffrage involved a limited vision of the
family, one narrowly defined as white and straight. One of the most pernicious social ills facing families, argued suffragists such as Emma Willard,
who built her career through the Woman's Christian Temperance Union,
was the growing power of recently enfranchised Black men, whom she saw
as undisciplined drunks who, like "locusts," threatened the "safety of the
[white woman], of childhood, of the home."[5] Black women resisted this
racism, consistently fighting for a more expansive definition of equality.[6]

The women who were thought to deserve the protection of the state
were defined similarly narrowly by early twentieth-century feminists—
and only in relation to their familial status—as mothers. State support
for mothers, like children, was imperative because of their assumed, in-
herent dependence on a male breadwinner. Absent his presence, the state
must step in as a kind of surrogate father that upheld an idealized domestic economy. The Children's Bureau, as Linda Gordon has shown,

discouraged the single women to whom they dispensed aid from working outside the home, and the bureau would not collaborate with labor unions on its welfare efforts.[7] Single working women could have used such support, for their wages were often unfairly depressed by the assumption that they should be working only for "pin money" as opposed to supporting themselves or a household. Rather than establish a living wage, the successful legislation that recognized women's labor only reaffirmed their essential dependence and domestic responsibilities, establishing limits on working hours and physical and moral hazards, from lifting heavy loads to tending bar.[8] Establishing social welfare institutions and labor laws that recognized women as citizens and laborers was undoubtedly a feminist watershed, but the fights that activists of this era picked just as unquestionably upheld a family supported by a breadwinning father and a caregiving mother, rather than challenging it.

No feminist initiative shored up this traditional familial model as much as early twentieth-century activism around young women's sexual and reproductive autonomy, ironically the realms that social conservatives usually caricature as their progressive enemies' gravest assaults on this bedrock institution. Extending the "protective" ethos of labor legislation to the bodies of young women and girls, by 1920 women's rights activists advanced laws that raised the age of sexual consent to sixteen or eighteen in every continental state (except Georgia, where it remained at fourteen until 1995).[9] In the case of adolescent girls, the intention was to protect the vulnerable from abuse and seduction by older men, but raising the age of consent could also serve to criminalize young, sexually active—usually working-class—women who were punished as delinquents. Such legislation gave parents—who could invoke the law to separate their daughter from a slightly older suitor they disliked—greater power over their daughters, reinscribing the idea that the only appropriate place to express sexuality was within the marital bond.[10]

Planned Parenthood is probably the institution that has provided the most enduring grist for the myth that feminists hate families. The problem, according to conservatives, is the organization's role in promoting and disseminating contraception (and later providing abortion), which undermines women's fundamental social role as mothers. But Margaret Sanger, who founded the American Birth Control League in 1921, which became Planned Parenthood two decades later, envisioned her activism as a way to build healthier families through more deliberate planning. Her experience was personal, as she had watched her mother endure seven miscarriages that permanently debilitated her, to say nothing of the exhaustion of raising her eleven surviving children before dying of tuberculosis at age fifty. At a time when childbirth still proved fatal to many women, providing maternal health services was hardly a rejection of the institution of the family. Rather, it was a way to rescue women from the kind of suffering that Sanger witnessed firsthand. Still, Sanger's proposition that women exert some autonomy over their fertility was perceived as pornographic, and she was arrested for circulating "obscene, lewd or lascivious material"—articles about birth control—and later served thirty days in jail for "creating a public nuisance" by offering contraception to women who traveled across state lines to avail themselves of these services.

Planned Parenthood spawned another myth worth debunking here because it has proved durable: that Sanger embraced eugenics and sought to control the Black population through the "Negro Project" she developed in the 1930s with prominent Black leaders such as W. E. B. Du Bois and Adam Clayton Powell Jr. Building on her work with poor, white-ethnic immigrants, who were most vulnerable to quack doctors whose family-planning interventions ranged from ineffective to lethal, Sanger first worked with Black community leaders to open a clinic in Harlem, staffed by Black health professionals. Buoyed by this success and the suggestion of Black leaders such as Mary McLeod Bethune and Ida B. Wells, Sanger expanded the program to serve African American women in the rural South, where services were even more lacking and the clinic was well received. Sanger did identify the "over-fertility of the mentally and physically defective" as a social problem in an idiom that is alarming today and should have been then, but she never advocated for culling racial or ethnic groups through contraception. In fact, the Nazi Party banned and burned Sanger's publications because it believed that family planning would undermine the propagation of the Aryan race.[11]

Crucially, the sort of family planning that Planned Parenthood provided was so uncontroversial that for much of the twentieth century, prominent conservatives voiced their support for the organization. In 1964 former Republican president Dwight Eisenhower joined former Democratic president Harry Truman as honorary chairmen of the organization.[12] During his tenure, President Nixon actively backed the Family Planning Services and Population Research Act, Title X of which built on liberal Great Society programs to become the only federal program that provided family-planning services, focusing on low-income citizens. Celebrity evangelist Billy Graham, who would become one of the most vocal proponents of a narrowly defined conservative "family values" movement, a linchpin of which was condemning Planned Parenthood, had openly told the press in 1959 that "nothing in the Bible prevents birth control." Nine years later, he convened the Protestant Symposium on the Control of Human Production, and its influential attendees overwhelmingly supported the use of contraception among married couples.[13] Not only did feminists perceive Planned Parenthood as an institution that would empower families; conservatives enthusiastically signed on to this vision. The notion that conservatives have been waging a multigenerational, moral war to protect American families from the destructive impulses of feminists in general and Planned Parenthood in particular is a fiction, invented by modern conservatives who deliberately ignore this history to stoke contemporary partisan proclivities.

This consensus soon frayed, however. When *Roe v. Wade* legalized a woman's right to choose an abortion in 1973—and Planned Parenthood began providing pregnancy termination as a small part of their maternal-health and family-planning services—a new generation of Republican activists eager to court conservative Catholics and consolidate evangelical support seized upon this case as clear evidence that feminists were out to destroy families by killing unborn babies. When Reagan won the presidency in 1980, most Republicans actually supported some access to abortion as of a piece with individual liberty and privacy from government intervention. Conservatives were correct that this generation of feminists was unapologetically fighting for women's bodily autonomy and greater openness about sexuality, but they misunderstood these efforts as undermining the family, when in fact they were often intended to undergird it. In 1965 feminists hailed the Supreme Court's *Griswold v. Connecticut* decision, which allowed married couples to use birth control, a win that surely invested women with more power over their bodies, but it just as certainly only further legally encoded the special legitimacy of the family.

Deliberately named "Family Life Education"—not the more readily misinterpreted "sex education"—programs rolled out in some school districts in the late 1950s functioned similarly. Liberals struck by the open eroticism of popular culture—thanks to the Supreme Court's narrowing of the definition of *obscenity*—devised curricula to help children understand that sexual desire was a natural part of human development but that it was appropriately consummated only within heterosexual marriage. To conservatives, acknowledging and destigmatizing sexual pleasure—with children, in tax-supported schools!—not only trespassed on parental authority to broach such issues but also fundamentally attacked what they understood as the chief purpose of sex and of the family: procreation. Never mind that even the most incendiary of such curricula instructed that homosexuality was an illness and culminated in a lesson about building a happy marriage—presuming that this was students' only logical life path—conservatives successfully painted these curricula as part of a nefarious plot cooked up by feminists, communists, and other "one-worlders" and "child seducers" who were intent on subverting America, beginning with its children.[14] Hundreds of such moderate programs did the opposite, fortifying the family by arguing that a happy, heterosexual marriage was the only appropriate place for pursuing sexual pleasure.

Some feminists found political allies among a liberal policy establishment similarly invested, at times fixated, in valorizing the two-parent family. In 1965 Assistant Secretary of Labor Daniel Patrick Moynihan published a ninety-page report on the plight of "the Negro family," which he and his staffers argued was at the heart of racial inequality that persisted a full century after the close of the Civil War. Despite securing formal legal equality, greater income, and increased levels of educational attainment, "the Negro family in the urban ghettos is crumbling," Moynihan argued, and only a concerted national effort to fortify the "stable Negro family structure" could interrupt this "cycle of poverty and disadvantage."[15] This was hardly a feminist position: the first section of the report's most famous chapter, titled "The Tangle of Pathology," unsparingly vilified "matriarchy," and Black feminists were understandably enraged that the economic and social strength that Black women exhibited as heads of household was portrayed as a source of social malaise rather than of collective uplift. On the contrary, they argued to expand the notion of a functional family, in that the "rough equality which came into existence out of necessity and is now ingrained in the black life style" could provide an alternative to the hierarchical white family structure enshrined by a political culture that spanned parties and generations.

But despite these critiques, the fact remained that the major political party most sympathetic to the feminist cause, the Democrats, was reaffirming the patriarchal nuclear family as core even to the apparently unrelated policy priority of racial equality. Such "breadwinner liberalism" had long formed the basis for welfare policy, and in the polarizing 1960s it was an especially attractive position in that it built bridges with conservatives who increasingly could not ignore racial injustice but who preferred solutions that centered personal responsibility over policy intervention.[16] Similarly, some leading feminists calculated that continuing to prop up the nuclear family might advance the cause of women's liberation more effectively than promoting the radical politics amplified on college campuses and among activists increasingly resisting gradualist approaches. The year after the release of the Moynihan Report, a diverse group of feminists gathered in Betty Friedan's hotel room, each chipping in five dollars to establish the National Organization for Women (NOW). But the organization made clear that it was seeking to defend the rights of certain women: heterosexuals in traditional marriages. When one lesbian couple attempted to renew their membership at the advertised "couples' membership," they were rebuffed and told that this deal was meant to attract husbands of their ostensibly straight membership. Friedan, who had become famous for decrying the malaise of suburban wifehood in *The Feminine Mystique*, doubled down on this exclusivity and in 1969 insisted that amplifying the concerns of this "lavender menace" would only give ammunition to conservative opponents and threaten the movement's mainstream acceptance.[17]

Indeed, feminists seized the opportunity to channel the resources of Great Society federal programs to bolster women and families in less controversial ways. Head Start began in the summer of 1965 as a multi-week early-childhood-education program, soon authorized by Congress—with bipartisan support—to run all year. Providing prenatal health services and child care as well as socialization and instruction to economically disadvantaged families, Head Start proved an important resource for parents, especially mothers, as well as children. Feminist mobilization that did not center mothers and families so explicitly still advanced these realms, as in President Johnson relenting in 1967 to specifically guarantee equal employment opportunity regardless of sex, a crucial development for women supporting families. A decade later, the Pregnancy Discrimination Act of 1978 also ensured that working mothers could more reliably provide for their children. Less visible and vaunted feminist campaigns also prioritized family stability: the interracial Federally Employed Women group advocated for flexible work scheduling and part-time options that better suited mothers, and others sought a guaranteed income that would effectively compensate caregivers for domestic labor. Outside of the policy realm, feminist health advocates and a more mystical strand of the movement celebrated motherhood as important, even divine work, to which women were uniquely suited.[18]

It is true that another form of feminism that explicitly decentered motherhood and family also gained traction in this era. Women actively participated in an expansive political Left that interrogated every social institution from the military to the media, and some seized on traditional gender roles as representing the root of social injustice. "Marriage is a joke," said Australian feminist Germaine Greer, whose best-selling 1970 book *The Female Eunuch* unsparingly condemned monogamy as a "maniacal idea." *LIFE* magazine incredulously reported that Greer "even knocks motherhood," strident perspectives that made her a "star performer" globally. Her willowy frame, long hair, and unapologetic (hetero)sexual appetites contrasted with both the image of the organizer-homemaker running for the school board or registering voters *and* that of the similarly outspoken Kate Millett, whom Greer dismissed as emblematic of "that whole pants and battledress routine," but who as a queer woman also challenged the notion that heterosexual marriage and motherhood were inextricable from female identity.[19]

Millett clashed with Friedan, but NOW leadership dialed down its homophobia in 1971 and recognized lesbians as "a legitimate concern for feminism." Many activists visibly allied with the broader fight for Gay Liberation, establishing the foundation for a broader definition of family that would include gay and lesbian parents. At the time, however, this alignment was more resonant with the feminist rallying cry for female bodily autonomy as activists successfully fought for abortion rights and legal recognition of sexual violence, from stranger rape to battery at the hands of husbands and boyfriends. A growing movement for youth self-determination, arguing for rights as varied as that of boys to wear long hair to protest the Vietnam War at school, challenged the notion that children must always bend to the authority of their elders in a similar idiom to women pushing back on patriarchy ever more insistently. Contrary to popular lore, no bras were ever burned, but the attitude that the conventional constraints of femininity should be shucked off, or at least interrogated, gained power—and fueled a conservative opposition that painted these preoccupations as attacks on motherhood in particular and the family in general. In response to the *Boston Globe*'s coverage of the fight over the Equal Rights Amendment, four readers wrote to complain that even the relatively liberal newspaper perpetuated the false dichotomy that ERA opponents were "feminine homemakers" whereas supporters "are seen as divorced, radical feminists, man-haters, and/or lesbians." The four writers, "happily married homemakers and mothers" and ERA advocates, wanted to set the record straight.[20] Long-standing activism to mobilize state support for working mothers, children, and families persisted throughout this era but was often overshadowed by popular, often exaggerated, imagery of uninhibited coeds, radical lesbians, and unshaven hippies in thrall to an unrestrained political culture that privileged the self-involvement and sexual liberation above all.

Feminists were indeed shifting away from "protective" efforts that presumed women's dependency and domesticity to an activism predicated on gender equality and a forceful articulation of the state's responsibility to guarantee it. This hardly meant that they turned their attention from the home. Indeed, during the 1970s and 1980s feminists sharpened their focus on domestic violence, notably concentrating on the crime of "marital rape," which in most states had been deliberately excepted from laws governing sexual violence, based on the perverse but prevalent rationale that this was a private matter and, secondarily, that vindictive women would use it as a legal cudgel to come after their husbands. "If you can't rape your wife, who can you rape?" a California legislator allegedly joked when the measure first came across his desk.[21] Women's liberationists such as "Laura X," who had taken the name to protest women's status as the property of men, began a state-by-state campaign to heighten awareness of marital rape and date rape and to make them illegal. In 1986, thanks to collaboration with legal organizations and campus activists, and to sympathetic media portrayal, marital rape was criminalized on federal lands, and seven years later, all fifty states had laws on the books outlawing it. Inspired by this activism—which also combated incest, wife beating, and pornography—the United Nations Women's Conference soon voted to resolve that women have a right to refuse sex to their husbands. Supportive statements from religious leaders from Catholic, Presbyterian, Pentecostal, Islamic, Jewish, and Buddhist leaders—hardly predictably feminist allies—followed, arguably because such efforts strengthened the familial bonds important to all their societies and faiths.[22]

Feminist efforts outside the home during this period also cemented family relations within it. Building on successful efforts in the 1970s to ensure that employers treated pregnancy and related disabilities such as miscarriage, abortion, and recovery from childbirth like other temporary medical conditions, feminists turned their efforts to codifying federal commitments to uphold a more expansively defined "family." In 1984 they introduced the Family Employment Security Act, which called for workers to be able to take twenty-six weeks of unpaid leave in order to recover from childbirth or to care for a spouse or child suffering from a range of illnesses and disabilities. As proposed, the bill fell short of many feminists' aims in not demanding paid leave, which would have more assuredly freed workers from nondomestic labor, and before ratification as the Family and Medical Leave Act (FMLA) in 1993, it encountered substantial stalling and resistance, including two presidential vetoes. But the version of the FMLA that ultimately passed also included a provision for caregiving for elderly parents, in 2015 expanded to cover same-sex spouses, and has been crucial in keeping family care at the forefront of the national agenda, even as the United States lags behind every other Western nation in such policy protections.[23]

Such efforts sought only to strengthen American families, but the members of a growing conservative movement resisted these policies ever more energetically, claiming with unprecedented fervor that *they* were safekeepers of the "family values" that morally debased feminists—now with the help of Big Government bureaucrats—sought to destroy. It wasn't just extremists: a 1977 poll showed that 40 percent of Americans understood the institution of the family to be in decline, and feminists its key antagonists.[24] To the extent that "family values" meant shielding a patriarchal home, at all costs, from any state intervention, Schlafly and the GOP establishment that had warmed to her were correct that feminists had long strived, often with the help of government, to boost women's economic and legal status within and beyond the family. But, crucially, these efforts were intended to strengthen rather than undermine family structure. In the late Cold War, however, this conservative framing gained traction, for traditionalists posited the archetypal American family as rooted in a Christian individualism under threat by collectivist, godless Communism. Throughout the 1980s, activist Christian groups such as the Moral Majority and Focus on the Family amplified this message, pointing squarely at feminists, gay liberationists, and civil rights activists as a threat to individuals, families, and the nation.

But which families? In a polity becoming more demographically and culturally diverse, social conservatives enshrined a "family" that was narrowly defined and ever more exclusive. For example, white parents who opposed sex education or social studies curricula as anathema to the values they espoused in their home were celebrated by a growing conservative media network as bravely defending the sacred family. Yet working-class Latino immigrants who protested that the racist depictions of their culture that their children encountered at school insulted their heritage—or who requested Spanish-language communications as a matter of practicality—were often dismissed with insistence on the superiority of the "neutral," English-only civic sphere. A broader politics of austerity promoted by the self-declared party of family values slashed welfare, child care, and health care while expanding a prison system that over the next several decades came to incarcerate Black men at more than six times the rate of white men, developments that unquestionably destabilized many families.

Despite these glaring contradictions, conservatives successfully managed to sustain the fantasy that the ideal American family was white, Christian, and heterosexual, and that only GOP policies could safeguard it from destruction by feminists and their progressive allies. But as Stephanie Coontz has written, as effectively as this imagined American family taps into conservative nostalgia, it is most accurately understood as "the way we never were."[25] Family structure has always been complex and varied, but in the early decades of the twenty-first century it has become more publicly and acceptably so: "blended" families, divorced parents, and gay couples are all over popular media, reflecting substantial legal and cultural changes. Furthermore, a strand of third-wave feminism that champions women's freedom to be homemakers as an equally legitimate path to working outside the home, and that invests traditionally feminine, domestic pastimes such as cooking and knitting with new gravitas, has deflated the caricature of the childless, man-hating feminist sustained by takeout and surrounded by cats.

Embarrassing betrayals of the traditional family values that conservatives purport to uphold have not helped their case. In 1974 Christian Crusade evangelist Billy James Hargis was accused of sleeping with male and female Bible students at American Christian College, and was forced to resign his position as the institution's president. Still, he benefited from a relatively discreet media culture and the fealty of local newspapers and law enforcement that downplayed or downright ignored the accusations. Nearly a decade later, when California state senator John Schmitz, who had burnished his right-wing credentials speaking against communism, sex education, and racial minorities, was outed for a decade-long affair that bore two children, his political career effectively ended.[26] Examples of such hypocrisy among ever-higher-profile figures—from Jim Bakker to Jerry Falwell Jr. to Donald Trump—have only accumulated over the decades, making the idea of conservative guardianship of family values, now or ever, still less tenable. Since the 1990s, the GOP has halfheartedly

tried to cement its position as defender of family values by courting socially conservative Latino voters, but the images of Border Patrol agents
separating immigrant children from their parents' arms as a part of the
Trump administration's "family separation" deterrence policy will likely
prove hard to forget.

Ironically, as the GOP becomes less able to present itself as defending
a "traditional" American family from feminist siege, conservatives are
promoting a new myth in its stead: the GOP as the party of "women's
rights" ("feminism" is a bridge too far). Cracking open the door to the
boys' club only slightly, Republicans have patted themselves on the back
for elevating (white) women such as Sarah Palin, Kellyanne Conway, and
Sarah Sanders to high-ranking positions. But like Ivanka Trump's hollow
"Women Who Work" treatise, which fails to acknowledge the phalanx of
service workers and web of family connections that make her own career
possible, this desiccated version of empowerment is irrelevant to most
women, who have little in common with these individuals who deploy
their power to prop up patriarchy rather than topple it. Moreover, the
emergence of the violent "incel" movement, which supplants the chivalry
of an older conservative ethos with a men's-rights worldview that under-
stands women's bodily autonomy as an affront, reveals the shallowness of
such commitment to women's rights.

The intensity with which an increasingly intersectional feminist
movement has evolved to take on issues as varied as imperialism and
online gaming can make the concerns of families seem almost quaint.
Indeed, across the political spectrum, movements that center motherhood, from Moms Demand Action to Moms (formerly Homemakers)
for America, often aim to strike a universalist, uncontroversial tone despite taking on divisive issues such as gun violence and religion, respectively. But the pandemic—which drove more than a million women
out of the paid workforce, largely to perform unremunerated caregiving
labor—has made clear that crucial needs of mothers and children remain
unmet. Historically consistent in blaming progressives in general—and
feminists in particular—for social ills, conservatives cry that the real
problem is overzealous leftists who want to corrupt children with ideas
that will make them ashamed of their heritage, unsure of their gender,

and disrespectful of their parents. Feminists no longer need to position themselves uniquely as mothers for political strategy, but they continue to fight for policies such as family leave, pay equity, child tax credits, robust schooling, and the affordable housing and child care that more than two centuries of feminist activist labors have proved to uphold rather than undermine American families.

19

REAGAN REVOLUTION

Julian E. Zelizer

T HERE ARE FEW POLITICAL PHRASES THAT CARRY THE WEIGHT OF the "Reagan Revolution," the notion that Ronald Reagan's defeat of President Jimmy Carter in the 1980 presidential election marked a fundamental rightward shift in American politics. The term gained standing in early 1981, when two prominent journalists, Rowland Evans and Robert Novak, published a book using the phrase as their title. "We seek here to outline," they wrote, "the most self-conscious effort at revolutionary change by any American president, surpassing Franklin Roosevelt in its intent if not its scope."[1] According to the argument, in 1980 the electorate rejected the idea that a strong federal government was a positive social good.

The idea of the "Reagan Revolution" extended into the realm of foreign policy as well. Following a decade when the Democratic Party had withdrawn from supporting a robust national security state as a result of

Vietnam, the argument goes, Americans grew tired of their weak approach toward national security. Reagan's victory thus represented the end of the so-called Vietnam Syndrome: his administration pushed for ramped-up defense spending, launched military operations in Cold War hot spots like Central America, and deployed fiery rhetoric about the Soviet Union that shunned the principles of détente—the policy of easing relations with the communist superpowers that all three presidents in the 1970s had accepted. Whereas Democrats had led congressional investigations to curtail the power of intelligence agencies such as the CIA, Reagan supported covert action with gusto. Diplomacy was pushed aside for a more muscular stance toward adversaries.

Just to be sure that people remembered the term, Reagan used it in his farewell address in 1989. "They called it the Reagan Revolution. Well, I'll accept that," he said, although he also reiterated that revolution was a return to the nation's natural state, "but for me it always seemed more like the great rediscovery, a rediscovery of our values and our common sense."[2]

Claiming that President Reagan was part of a revolution was no small thing. The term elevates the decade of the 1980s into something much grander than the normal transitions we expect to take place from one presidency to the next. Stipulating that these years constituted a genuine "revolution," though bloodless, suggests the repudiation of political ideas, interests, and policies that came before.

Everyone was a Reaganite by the end of the decade, or so his supporters claimed. When Reagan finished his term, adviser Martin Anderson published *Revolution: The Reagan Legacy*. "If we accept *Webster's Third New International Dictionary* definition that revolution is a 'fundamental change in political organization; especially: the overthrow or renunciation of one government or ruler and the substitution of another by the governed,'" Anderson wrote, "then by any reasonable standard, what was happening in America was a revolution, not a violent physical revolution driven by guns, but a revolution of political thought, a revolution of ideas."[3] Even a group of historians was swept up by the moment. The victory of a president who had come of age with the modern conservative movement represented the "end of the New Deal era," they argued in a 1990 book, one that shaped the views of scholars for decades.[4]

The trope that a "Reagan Revolution" remade American politics has remained central to the national discourse. "To conservatives, 1980 is the year one," recalled the political analyst Bill Schneider.[5] Positing that there had been a clear revolution positioned liberals and progressive Democrats as being far off from the mainstream of the electorate—even when polls showed that their policy preferences matched where most Americans stood. Reagan "shifted the political center by changing the terms of the debate," wrote the right-wing pundit Dinesh D'Souza in 1997. "He made 'liberal' a term of embarrassment, so that in 1988 the Democratic presidential candidate, Michael Dukakis, fled from the 'L-word.'"[6]

Even as the Republican Party came to represent a shrinking segment of the electorate by the 2020s—rural, white male voters—and a radicalized policy agenda that did not command broad support from the public, Reagan continued to be at the core of their origins story. Rather than talking about the centrality of institutional rules such as the Electoral College that enabled a shrinking party to hold power, conservatives spoke about a mainstream revolution in values. In a number of recent confessional works from Republicans reckoning with the implications of the Trump presidency, the Reagan presidency offers a model of when the party was pure: conservatism dominated the landscape. "For almost four decades," Gerald Seib wrote in *We Should Have Seen It Coming*, "the Republican Party had been defined by a man, Ronald Reagan, and his movement, the Reagan Revolution. Reagan was the most unlikely of revolutionary figures, a modestly successful actor with a self-effacing style and no intellectual pretensions." Yet, Seib continued, "he personally had made the Republican Party into a conservative party, and his legacy continued to inspire the movement's leaders, animate its policy debates, and stir its voters' emotions long after he left the scene."[7]

The history is more complicated than the term suggests. Indeed, the argument that there was a "Reagan Revolution" was born out of an explicit political strategy. The administration wanted to cement the impression that Reagan's victory had been a mandate for conservatism.

Claims about a Reagan Revolution exaggerated the strength of conservatism and, equally important, the demise of liberalism. They also tend to conceal the deep fault lines that continued in national politics. The 1980 election conveyed a more nuanced message about the state of American politics—as did the entire Reagan presidency. Over time, a closer look at Reagan's presidency and the 1980s has revealed that liberalism remained much stronger in America's body politic than conservatives liked to think.[8]

To begin, the implications of the 1980 election were muddled. Reagan won in an Electoral College landslide (489–49), although his margin in the popular vote was narrower—50.7 percent to Carter's 41 percent and independent John Anderson's 6.6 percent. Reagan had secured just over half the vote in the election, and polls showed that a large part of that vote was as much about opposition to Carter as it was an endorsement of Reagan or his agenda. Over half of voters said they cast their ballot based on "negative views of the candidates." Four out of five of Reagan's supporters reported they made their decision in response to Carter's record as president. "The great conservative realignment of 1980 was chimerical," noted Gil Troy. "Only 28 percent of the electorate identified as 'conservative,' only 13 percent as strong Republicans, only one Reagan voter in ten identified Reagan's conservative ideology as a key motivator."[9]

It wasn't just an unpopular incumbent at work. Reagan benefited from running after three successive presidents who had been remarkably unsuccessful politically. The 1970s had become a decade that deflated public confidence in the institution of the presidency, which had been revered throughout much of the twentieth century. President Richard Nixon was forced to resign as a result of Watergate. President Gerald Ford held office for just more than two years. When Ford was unable to reverse stagflation or to restore confidence in the government, voters chose Carter to succeed him. Yet he also couldn't put together a coalition that would last beyond one term. His presidency ended with the nation frustrated about the economy, an energy crisis, and Americans being held hostage in Iran.[10]

Reagan's team worked hard to craft an optimistic and positive image of Reagan, and in turn the meaning of the 1980 election, that papered over the deeply divisive rhetoric that had been integral to Reagan's appeal and history.[11] When running for governor of California in 1966, Reagan

railed against the "minority of beatniks, radicals and filthy speech advocates" who he said were destroying the public universities, and he called
city streets "jungle paths after dark." In 1968 he would not condemn Alabama governor George Wallace, the notorious racist who was running
as an independent for president, and in the 1976 Republican presidential
primaries Reagan went after "welfare queens" for cheating taxpayers.

Turning from the White House to Capitol Hill, the picture for Republicans was not as bright. Although Republicans gained control of the
Senate for the first time since 1955 (53–46), Democrats retained a firm
grip in the House of Representatives with a 243-seat majority. Under
Speaker Tip O'Neill of Massachusetts, Democrats were determined to
check Reagan. Although Reagan was able to pressure the House into
moving forward with a major supply-side tax reduction in 1981, much
of the rest of his legislative agenda stalled. With White House officials
understanding the realities of the political landscape they faced, the president's early budgets did not aim to dismantle the welfare state. "For all
the furor they created," wrote his biographer Lou Cannon, "the first-term
Reagan budgets were mild manifestos devoid of revolutionary purpose."[12]
In 1982 the administration failed in its effort to reduce Social Security
benefits. O'Neill mobilized a coalition that caused Reagan to back down.
"They are ill advised and unacceptable," O'Neill said. "It is unconscionable to create and exploit fears about the fate of the Social Security system
so as to make deep cuts in benefit levels."[13] Approximately three-fourths
of Americans believed that Social Security needed to offer retirees an
adequate standard of living. A majority felt that government spending
on the program should increase, and there was overall opposition to cuts.
When asked to choose between reducing Social Security and reducing
defense, three-fourths chose to cut the military budget.[14]

The economic recession of 1982, which Democrats called the "Reagan
Recession," made his first midterms even harder than they normally were.
After Reagan had promised that his tax cut would turn things around from
the Carter era's stagflation, the nation watched the unemployment rate go
up, peaking at a whopping 10 percent. In 1982 Republicans like Kansas
senator Robert Dole joined Democrats to pass the Tax Equity and Fiscal
Responsibility Act, a bill that raised taxes in an effort to curb the growing

deficit. When the Democratic majority increased to 269 in the midterm elections, the legislative challenge became even greater. Reagan found that on a number of fronts, such as steep cuts to social-safety-net spending or the elimination of the Aid to Families with Dependent Children (AFDC) program, Congress could just say no.[15] "At midterms," noted one reporter, "the once dazzling political momentum of what conservatives enthusiastically called the Reagan Revolution has stalled."[16]

The realities of liberal power in Congress were not lost on Reagan's foot soldiers. Frustration drove a young Georgia Republican congressman named Newt Gingrich to promote a more aggressive and destructive form of partisan warfare. He argued that the Reagan Revolution never had a chance to succeed because Democrats retained so much power. Gingrich went after senior Republicans like Minority Leader Robert Michel of Illinois, insisting that their willingness to compromise and work with Democrats would permanently allow the opposition to entrench themselves in positions of power. Democrats used "a spirit of bipartisanship and harmony as a polite cover to attract sympathy if we disagree with their version of 'reasonable, responsible compromises'—all of which happen to be liberal and increase spending, weaken defense, increase bureaucracy and raise taxes," he wrote in a memo. Gingrich's solution was to persuade his party to eliminate the guardrails so that they could take down Democrats and ultimately regain control of both chambers. "Fired by the ideological zeal that helped carry President Reagan into the White House in 1980," reporter Steven Roberts noted, "they see their mission as confrontation, not conciliation."[17] Gingrich's smashmouth style of partisanship became the norm.[18]

But the welfare state endured. Reagan worked with Democrats in 1983 on a deal that raised Social Security taxes to shore up the program's finances. Federal spending reached 22.2 percent of GDP by 1983; it was 20.6 percent when he took office. Total welfare spending increased in the 1980s as the programs retained significant support in Congress. Means-tested programs provided higher benefits in 1990 than in 1982, including programs like Medicaid and food stamps, which didn't garner much love from the Right.[19] The federal workforce grew by more than 200,000 persons during his two terms in office. Abortion remained legal. "Mr.

Reagan is now seen as untrustworthy by many conservatives who believe he has betrayed his own principles in an effort to appease his critics," lamented the editor of the *Conservative Digest*.[20]

Throughout his first term, Reagan remained a deeply divisive figure in American politics. For most Democrats, Reaganism embodied a reactionary shift away from the basic social contract that had been created by FDR and LBJ. In their minds, Reagan had turned his back on the poor and the disadvantaged, rolling back gains from the civil rights era and redirecting public monies toward dangerous military escapades. Although recent commentators have depicted this decade as one where the president and his most ardent opponents, like O'Neill, could fight during the day and then have beer at night, feelings were anything but civil. O'Neill wrote in his memoirs that "I've known every president since Harry Truman, and there's no question in my mind that Reagan was the worst."[21]

Nor was supply-side economics working. The premise that tax breaks for wealthier Americans and businesses would eventually trickle down to the rest of the nation didn't pan out. Instead, by the mid-1980s, economic inequality had become worse, and the deficit kept growing. Conditions were certainly better than in the 1970s, but many Americans didn't feel the benefits.

In his historic keynote address to the 1984 Democratic Convention, New York governor Mario Cuomo delivered a powerful message that captured this sentiment. Referencing Charles Dickens's classic work, he spoke about a "tale of two cities" that depicted Reagan's record as harsh, punitive, and profoundly unjust: "There are more poor people than ever, more families in trouble, more and more people who need help but can't find it." Too many people were sleeping in the gutter, Cuomo added, "where the glitter doesn't show."

Reagan was able to soundly defeat Minnesota senator Walter Mondale in the 1984 election (525 to 13 Electoral College votes). The president's campaign was conscious about selling the myth of Reaganism. The slick "Morning in America" television ad showed viewers images of suburban families enjoying a rebounding economy. Mondale's less charismatic straight talk—including his admission during one of the debates that he would raise taxes on Americans—didn't excite voters.

Many parts of the country remained deeply Democratic, including the South, where the regional realignment of voters toward the GOP had not yet been completed. Reagan's sense of limitations felt that much more urgent after the 1986 elections, when Democrats regained control of the Senate. Moreover, throughout his presidency the GOP was divided, which also checked his capacity to move the agenda. There were fissures separating senior legislators whose inclination was to keep working with Democrats and who accepted the permanence of the New Deal and Great Society framework, and younger renegades who were part and parcel of the conservative movement. As a result, Senate Democrats were able to find bipartisan support for issues like voting rights and the environment that didn't easily align with the conservative revolution that Reagan's supporters claimed to be under way. In 1986 Reagan worked with Democrats on a tax-reform package that closed loopholes benefiting corporate lobbyists. He also signed a major immigration-reform bill that offered amnesty to millions of undocumented persons. This didn't come as a total surprise to people who had followed Reagan's career, for he had been willing to cut deals with the Democratic California state legislature while serving as governor in the 1960s and early 1970s.[22]

Much of Reagan's conservative agenda in the 1980s was achieved through presidential power. The president relied on a combination of executive orders—many of which undid workplace and environmental regulations from the 1960s and 1970s—as well as staffing agencies with leaders who did not support the mission of their institution (such as Clarence Thomas, who headed the Equal Employment Opportunity Commission despite opposing affirmative action). He depended on freezing the budget so that social programs suffered a death of a thousand cuts. Programs could not be updated, funding steadily shrank, and civil servants couldn't update their policies to new needs.[23] Inaction also could serve the conservative cause. As the acquired immunodeficiency syndrome (AIDS) crisis unfolded, Reagan's unwillingness to acknowledge the disease or to take any sort of action was in itself a proactive decision about what the government wouldn't do.

The impact of Reagan's executive-based decisions was certainly significant. Regardless of the situation in Congress, the administration made a sharp dent in programs that affected these areas. Through adjustments to eligibility requirements, funding, and benefit levels, for instance, he cut social-safety-net programs by about 6 to 10 percent by the end of 1988.[24] As with all executive actions, however, these changes were vulnerable. When Democratic presidents regained office in future years, they would take steps to strengthen the policies that Reagan had weakened as well as revitalize the agencies that Reagan had harmed. Reagan's policy agenda didn't find the same kind of durable legislative support as Roosevelt's or Johnson's, thus remaining on more fragile political ground.

Reagan's effort to revolutionize foreign policy was likewise contested. During his first term, Reagan's hawkish posture toward the Soviet Union didn't earn many fans across the aisle. The president was able to pressure Congress into vastly increasing defense spending, and he used blistering rhetoric when speaking about the Soviet Union. In one famous speech to a group of evangelicals in 1983, Reagan called America's adversaries "evil." He staffed key diplomatic positions with figures who had spent much of the 1970s railing against proponents of détente who supported arms negotiations with the communists.

Not everyone was on board with his militaristic mentality.[25] As the president heated up the temperature of his program, Democrats warned that the administration risked triggering a nuclear war. Reagan had stacked his foreign policy team with staunch opponents of negotiations with the Soviet Union over arms agreements and staunch promoters of major operations in Central America to fight against socialist as well as other left-wing forces. Democrats believed that his bellicose posture was dangerous, and many Americans agreed. An international nuclear-freeze movement drew massive support throughout the country in 1982 and 1983, and also around the globe, so much so that Reagan proposed an X-ray missile shield as his alternative (mockingly called "Star Wars").[26] More than half a million people turned out for a nuclear freeze rally in New York's Central Park, larger than any demonstrations during the Vietnam War. Massachusetts Democrat Ed Markey noted that what made the gathering powerful was that it demonstrated this was a "middle class movement. These are people with real clout in their communities."[27]

A 1983 television movie about the horrors of nuclear war in a small Kansas town, *The Day After*, turned into a sensation. More than 100 million viewers tuned in to watch. Public opinion also showed that there was limited support for using ground troops in El Salvador or Nicaragua, areas of conflict that served as proxies for the superpowers. From 1982 to 1984 the House passed the Boland Amendments, which prohibited the administration from sending assistance into the region. Despite such actions, the public remained nervous. A *Washington Post* poll of adults and teenagers found that in 1984 nuclear war was one of the top issues facing the nation.[28]

By his 1984 campaign, Reagan's closest advisers were admitting that much of the public was scared by his foreign policies rather than emboldened about his rejection of limitations. They urged him to show some signs to the public of his willingness to negotiate and to take down the temperature. Reagan listened. In an address to the United Nations General Assembly in September, Reagan sounded a different note from the person who had blasted détente: "We recognize there is no sane alternative to negotiations on arms control and other issues between our two nations, which have the capacity to destroy civilization as we know it."[29]

The next term would continue to be contentious. Following the 1986 midterm elections, the administration was engulfed in a major scandal that some in the administration thought could result in impeachment. High-level national security officials had run an operation to illegally send money to the Nicaraguan Contras—despite the congressional prohibition on doing so—by using revenue from secret arms sales to Iran, then considered to be the number-one terrorist state. Reagan watched his approval ratings drop faster than any other president since Gallup started tracking these numbers (16 percentage points from October to December). Reagan survived the Iran-Contra scandal, but the investigations that ensnared many high-level officials were deeply polarizing. Many Democrats believed that the president was getting away with a scandal worse than Watergate, but one in which Congress was unable to find a "smoking gun." *Saturday Night Live* aired a biting satire of Reagan, featuring the comedian Phil Hartman, who pretended to be an avuncular and kind president when in front of reporters, but as soon as they leave the room, he is a diabolical and ruthless commander in chief. "This is the part of the job I hate!" Hartman's character yells after having to stop his meeting for a photo op with Girl Scouts.

One of the greatest ironies of the presidency was that one of his most enduring achievements directly contradicted a key premise of the Reagan Revolution: after the tumult of Vietnam, the nation had embraced a muscular posture toward communism. When Mikhail Gorbachev emerged as the new leader of the Soviet Union in 1985 and called for negotiation, diplomacy, and a new era of more peaceful relations, he proved to be quite popular in the United States. Reagan, despite conservative misgivings, entered into ongoing negotiations with Gorbachev over nuclear arms. In the end, Reagan's biggest foreign policy success was to bring to fruition exactly what he spent most of his life working against—détente with the Soviet Union. Reagan and Gorbachev convened a number of high-level summits. One of the sticking points was Star Wars; Reagan insisted that the United States be allowed to continue the project. Gorbachev said it was a dangerous arms race in space. Reagan told Gorbachev that he couldn't give in on the shield because "the people who were the most outspoken critics of the Soviet Union over the years . . . the so-called right wing, and esteemed journalists . . . they're kicking my brains out."[30] When the president finally signed on to a major arms reduction agreement in 1987, the Intermediate-Range Nuclear Forces Treaty, conservatives were furious. The head of the Conservative Caucus, Howard Phillips, decried Reagan as a "useful idiot for Soviet propaganda."[31] "Reagan is a weakened president," conservative activist Paul Weyrich complained, "weakened in spirit as well as in clout, and not in a position to make judgements about Gorbachev at this time."[32]

In the coming years, Republicans would attempt to revise this history. They claimed that Reagan's insistence on "Peace from Strength" was the reason an agreement was reached. The conservative president, they said, had pressured the Soviets into an unsustainable military spending war and convinced them that he was serious about using massive military force if necessary. There have been others who emphasize the fact that Reagan had favored the abolition of nuclear weapons for decades and sought the breakthrough that happened in 1987 all along.[33] These narratives mask the true nature of Reagan's achievement. When an opportunity for diplomacy emerged in the Soviet Union, Reagan was willing to break with his own agenda and the movement that brought him to power by changing course and accepting the centrality of diplomacy with adversaries.

The idea of a Reagan Revolution made conservatism appear stronger than it really was, but the idea that there was a rightward revolution under way also helped to invigorate liberal opposition and activism. The gay rights movement that had already taken form in the late 1960s gained strength when organizations formed to pressure the government into responding to the AIDS crisis. As this deadly condition spread in the mid-1980s, hitting the homosexual community particularly hard, Reagan refused to even utter the disease's name. He started to change only in 1985 when his long-term friend, the actor Rock Hudson, died from it. But even then, there was little substantial change in policy. In 1987 the journalist and writer Larry Kramer founded an organization called ACTUP to mobilize grassroots pressure on the government to fund research and relax the drug-approval process. In October 1988, with a growing membership, ACTUP closed down the FDA when more than a thousand protesters surrounded the building, drawing international attention. The movement had significant effect. Reagan finally started to address the issue in public, authorizing Surgeon General C. Everett Koop—a staunch conservative—to undertake a massive public relations campaign that promoted condom use and safe sex. In response to grassroots pressure, the FDA would speed up its approval process and create an Office of AIDS and Special Health Issues to give patients a larger role in deliberations over new treatments.

Other progressive movements thrived as well. Feminist organizations enjoyed newfound support as Reagan's stands enraged and galvanized a new generation of supporters. The National Organization for Women increased its membership threefold from 1979 to 1982, accumulating a budget of more than $13 million during this period.[34] Hundreds of thousands of people marched in Washington in April 1989 to protest the record of his administration on women's reproductive rights. "You know what happened in the '80s," Colorado Democrat Patricia Schroeder told supporters. "Ronald Reagan got elected and said, 'Put down your picket signs and put on your little dress-for-success suits.' Well, a lot of people put down their picket signs and lost their rights."[35]

Suburbanization proved to be a breeding ground for certain strands of liberal politics. Although residential areas outside of the city accelerated racial and economic inequality, suburban communities often produced strong liberal pulses. Concerns about the quality of life were powerful in areas where parks, water, and air mattered so much. Affluent, well-educated Americans, according to Lily Geismer in her study of Massachusetts, were extremely supportive of feminism and antiwar activism. Communities mobilized to fight homelessness and to defend reproductive rights.[36] As more immigrants created vibrant communities in the suburbs, white middle-class property owners became more accustomed and open to an ethnically pluralistic understanding of the country.

Environmental organizations likewise expanded. The ferocity of the opposition to policies that were aimed to help business instead of the environment ended up strengthening the movement. The Sierra Club's membership increased to 364,000 in 1985 from 181,000 in 1980. By 1992, membership would reach 650,000.[37] None of these developments surpassed the strength of conservative forces such as the Religious Right, but the Left remained a powerful presence.

At the local level, protests took shape following incidents of racialized police violence against African Americans. When six transit police officers were acquitted in New York City in 1985 for the death of Michael Stewart, an African American who was drawing graffiti in a subway station before being beaten, bruised, and hog-tied by the police, activists demanded justice. "Blood is on all your hands!" protesters yelled outside the courtroom.[38] Civil rights protests also formed in response to the October 29, 1984, killing of Eleanor Bumpurs, an emotionally disturbed woman in her late sixties who was shot when she wielded a knife as police entered her home for a city-ordered eviction. Activists established the Eleanor Bumpurs Justice Committee, a coalition of welfare mothers, community activists, and tenant leaders, all of whom organized protests when the police were acquitted in this case as well. "We say guilty!" they chanted.

Although the protests didn't coalesce into a movement akin to #black-livesmatter, they built a foundation for later movements.

The "Reagan Revolution" did not sweep through public opinion. In 1987, 53 percent of Americans thought that the government should do more to help the needy even if that meant increasing the federal debt, 62 percent believed that the government should guarantee food and shelter for all, and 71 percent stated that the government should take care of people who couldn't take care of themselves.[39]

Though admired as an individual in many parts of the country, Reagan was not universally loved as a leader. His average approval rating was 52.8 percent, less than his successors George H. W. Bush (60.9 percent) and Bill Clinton (55.1 percent), or predecessors such as Lyndon Johnson (55.1 percent), John F. Kennedy (70.1 percent), and Dwight Eisenhower (65 percent). Reagan did beat out Nixon (49 percent), Ford (47.2 percent), and Carter (45.5 percent), hardly the stuff of revolution.[40] Before Reagan was in office, no president in recorded history had averaged over a 40-point gap in approval ratings by party during his term. Reagan's average party gap was 52 percent (Nixon's had been 41 percent, Ford's 31 percent, and Carter's 27 percent). The percentage kept rising after Reagan to over 50 percent (other than for George H. W. Bush).[41]

The coming decades would continue to see deep divisions over Reaganism. The congressional playing field would remain Democratic until the 1994 midterms, when Gingrich finally helped his party to secure victory. Despite that sea change, congressional majorities would remain narrow and competitive. Unlike most of the twentieth century, one major political party would be unable to secure control of Capitol Hill for long periods of time. The Democrats and their liberal ideas retained a strong foothold in the legislative branch, as did the GOP. Political scientist Frances Lee has documented how since 1984 narrow and unstable congressional majorities have shifted back and forth with considerable speed, a dynamic that heightened partisan incentives on Capitol Hill and halted dramatic agenda shifts.[42]

In presidential politics, Democrats remained alive and well. To be sure, progressives argued that Democrats were able to rebound by shifting toward the center and abandoning key policy commitments, such as supporting unions. But the fact that the decades after Reagan would include two two-term Democratic presidents—Bill Clinton (1993–2001) and Barack Obama (2009–2017)—as well as another Democrat in 2021 with Joe Biden, constituted a strong rebuke to arguments about a revolution in the 1980s. All three Democrats might have displayed centrist tendencies and embraced elements of Reagan's agenda—Clinton proclaiming in 1996 that the "era of big government is over"—but all were far more liberal in their domestic policies and more skeptical of a hawkish national security agenda than the Gipper. None of them were part of the coalition that Reagan had put into place.

The Reagan Revolution has been more of a political talking point than a description of reality. Although Reagan's presidency certainly marked an important moment and a major step toward a more conservative era, with a substantial push of policy and debate to the right, politics did not begin anew when President Carter left town. The 1980s, as well as the period that follows, was defined by competing ideological agendas and fractured political coalitions. It has been this way ever since. The conservative victories were powerful but not a clean sweep. As David Stockman, budget director from 1981 to 1985, wrote in his account of the presidency, "The true Reagan Revolution never had a chance. It defied all of the overwhelming forces, interests and impulses of American democracy. Our Madisonian government of checks and balances . . . and infinitely splintered power is conservative, not radical. . . . It cannot leap into revolutions without falling flat on its face."[43]

Reagan's presidency did not remake the nation, nor did it halt the powerful forces of liberalism that had evolved in the twentieth century. As a result, when pundits in current times talk about the way Reagan brought the New Deal and Great Society eras to an end, they ignore the power of liberal policies and ideas. They don't explain why Tea Party activists protesting President Barack Obama's proposed Affordable Care Act in 2009 and 2010 would hold up banners that read "Keep your government hands off my Medicare," a slam on proposed spending reductions in the program. All historical accounts that use the programmatic framing of a president and his supporters as an actual description of history overstate the level of change that occurred, but this is especially true with the Reagan Revolution, given the limited legislative agenda left behind and the fact that the period took place after many decades of huge expansions of policy under FDR and LBJ that were not easily taken apart. The narratives about a Reagan Revolution don't explain the roots of our current moment, and they overstate the dominance of conservatism. It's time to leave this flattened understanding of the 1980s in the dustbin.

20

VOTER FRAUD

Carol Anderson

THE FALLOUT FROM THE 2020 PRESIDENTIAL ELECTION SHOOK THE nation's confidence in the stability and viability of democracy.[1] Donald Trump's lie of massive, rampant voter fraud had compromised the US Department of Justice, sparked retaliation against those who refuted the lie, led to an attack on the US Capitol, homed in on urban minorities as the threat to American democracy, and served as an excuse for a new wave of voter-suppression legislation.[2] GOP stalwarts such as former House Speaker Newt Gingrich intimated that there were some Americans whose votes should not count. Not surprisingly, they lived in cities where whites were the minority.[3] On a Fox News segment shortly after the election, Gingrich identified those locales that purportedly hijacked the presidency from Donald Trump. "Steal the election in Philadelphia," he railed. "Steal the election in Atlanta," he added. "Steal the election in Milwaukee," he asserted.[4]

But Trump's claims that rampant voter fraud had stolen his electoral victory were, as one judge noted, based on "levels of hearsay" so "speculative" as to be "fantastical."[5] Attorney General William Barr, after feeding the allegations for months, was eventually more direct as he concluded that the charge of widespread, multistate voter fraud "was all bullshit."[6]

Yet, regardless of how unfounded, discredited, and thoroughly disproved—Georgia Republican Alan Powell admitted that "widespread voter fraud . . . wasn't found"—the Big Lie still provided a handy excuse for Republicans in forty-eight states to propose nearly four hundred voter-suppression bills.[7] GOP attorney Benjamin Ginsberg, who had spent four decades litigating election cases for the Republicans, admitted that "proof of systematic fraud has become the Loch Ness Monster of the Republican Party. People have spent a lot of time looking for it, but it doesn't exist."[8]

This epic electoral battle in the twenty-first century was not an anomaly. It built on a long, sordid history of partisan allegations of voter fraud: attacks, in fact, that targeted racial and ethnic minorities as well as naturalized citizens from immigrant communities.[9] Because the Reconstruction-era Fifteenth Amendment bans using race to disfranchise Americans, the operatives and politicians camouflaged their discriminatory intent behind the charge of voter fraud to create the illusion that their primary concern was election integrity and democracy. And by deploying the pretense of defending a significant state interest—protecting the sanctity of free and fair elections—rather than the more distasteful power grab based on pandering to racism and xenophobia, lawmakers legitimized a number of policies to disfranchise millions of American citizens. Indeed, in the late nineteenth century, these racially targeted electoral changes were, as Alexander Keyssar notes, sanitized as attempts to "purify the ballot box," although they were "aimed largely at particular ballot boxes and particular voters."[10]

What made the nineteenth-century charges so maddening was that there was widespread fraud, just not the kind that seemingly provoked policy makers to make extensive changes to the law. The red herring often dragged before the electorate and judges was voter fraud, where individuals impersonated someone else to cast a ballot. However, the real villain attacking democracy was much more systemic and systematic: extensive election fraud, which was organized by political leaders, usually *against* African Americans, to alter the outcome of elections and weaken Black electoral power, especially in counties and states where Blacks were a sizable portion of the population. Journalist Andrew Gumbel observed that these machinations would eventually expose the United States as "a world-class laboratory for vote suppression and election-stealing techniques."[11]

The quintessential example of this was in 1890, when Mississippi lawmakers, panicked by the growing political power of a coalition of African Americans and poor whites, raised the false flag about voter fraud as the reason to redraft the state's constitution, which would, by design, disfranchise as many Black voters as possible. The Fifteenth Amendment made the traditional race-specified methods of disfranchisement unconstitutional. Southern Democrats resented mightily this addition to the Bill of Rights. Indeed, one Alabama newspaper called it "'a monstrous crime,' rife with 'evils.'"[12] Another southern newspaper wrote that the amendment "may stand forever; but we intend . . . to make [it a] dead letter . . . on the statute-book."[13] Therefore, the southern states soon figured out how to maneuver around their constitutional enemy. Masking racially targeted policies behind race-neutral language and covering that with a state's interest in ensuring free and fair elections became a masterful disguise to rob Black people of their voting rights.

Thus, although Mississippi lawmakers said they were concerned about corruption at the ballot box, Judge J. J. Chrisman, a delegate at the state's constitutional convention, admitted that it wasn't Black men who had committed fraud but rather that the Democrats, which was the party of white supremacy, had rigged every election in Mississippi since 1875.[14] As Chrisman stated, "It is no secret that there has not been a full vote and a fair count in Mississippi since 1875—that we have been preserving the ascendancy of the white people by revolutionary methods. In plain words we have been stuffing the ballot boxes, committing perjury, and . . . carrying the elections by fraud and violence until the whole machinery was about to rot down. No man can be in favor of the election methods which have prevailed . . . who is not a moral idiot."[15]

Although they framed the problem very starkly in terms of the corrosive effects of election fraud, Judge Chrisman and his colleagues argued that salvation would come by treating voter fraud as the real menace. Chrisman contended that it was the very presence of Black voters and their threat to the old antebellum order that had forced whites to commit fraud at the ballot box. Scholar Michael Fellman summarized Chrisman's viewpoint: Remove African Americans from the electorate and "it would eliminate the need to rig elections. When Black voters were banished, white voters would be able to conduct free and fair elections."[16]

This quest to dilute Black political power was born of demographics and the threat that it posed to white supremacy.[17] Law professor Gordon A. Martin Jr., a former attorney in the Civil Rights Division of the Department of Justice, laid out that in Mississippi in 1890, the "state's voting-age population . . . was 271,080: 150,469 blacks and 120,611 whites."[18] The opening salvo of the chair of the state's constitutional convention, Judge Solomon Calhoon, therefore made clear that a multiracial democracy was not only undesirable but also unacceptable. Instead, he offered, it was time for whites to write a constitution of "self-protection."[19]

That led to the Mississippi Plan, a wave of disfranchising policies using racially targeted but race-neutral and Supreme Court–approved language, such as the poll tax and the literacy test, which devastated Black voter participation.[20] The poll tax required a fee be paid, sometimes cumulative, sometimes years before the election, in order to vote. The literacy test made voters read sections of the state or US Constitution or correctly respond to any other test the registrar devised, such as "count the number of bubbles in a soap bar," to be able to access the ballot box.[21] A decade after the passage of the Mississippi Plan and the rise of Jim Crow, one newspaper editor wrote that "the negroes are as far from participating in governmental affairs in this state as though they were [in] a colony in Africa." By 1940, only 3 percent of age-eligible African Americans were registered to vote in the South. In the early 1960s, there were counties in Alabama, Mississippi, and Georgia that had single-digit percentages of African Americans on the voter rolls.[22] Those conditions, especially in a nation that billed itself as the "Leader of the Free World," were intolerable. The ongoing struggle for civil rights was designed to rectify that, overturn Jim Crow root and branch, and dismantle all the disfranchising restrictions that the 1890 Mississippi Plan had spread throughout the South.

As movement activists noted, this was "no easy walk." The movement was a direct assault on the structures of power and racism that propped up the nation's political, economic, and legal systems. Not surprisingly, the backlash included beatings, bombings, murders, mass arrests, and—more subtly but equally lethal—doubling down on the myth of voter fraud. Challenging Black electoral power on the seemingly legitimate grounds of stopping fraud was an effective way to deflect charges of racism and undermine the moral and legal power of the civil rights movement's victories.

Key in this strategy to enervate the robust expansion of Black voters was the GOP's transformation from the multiracial party of Lincoln to, as Leah Wright Rigueur recounts, "a lily white Republican Party" that deliberately siphoned away from the Democrats whites who were opposed to the civil rights movement and its resulting legislation and court decisions.[23] As laid out in *Eyes off the Prize: The United Nations and the African American Struggle for Human Rights, 1944–1955*, this realignment pulled what should have been an isolated "racist, fanatical fringe into the wholly acceptable mainstream."[24] The genesis of what would become known as the Southern Strategy was a series of electoral tremors in 1948, 1952, and 1956 that exposed major fissures in the Solid Democratic South when a bloc of states, angry about the national party's support (regardless how tepid) for civil rights and desegregation, either broke away altogether or voted for the Republican presidential candidate.[25] The possibility of demolishing the hold of the Democrats on the South convinced the Republican National Committee (RNC) that there were electoral victories in the politics of barely veiled white supremacy.[26]

That was one consideration, but there was another. It was also clear that during the 1960 elections, the Republicans had not fared well in major metropolitan areas.[27] The combination of flaccid support in the cities and strengthening white resentment about the attainment of Black people's civil rights dictated the strategy of making the myth of voter suppression seem real. It had to be focused on minorities to continue to stoke the narrative that they were stealing something valuable from honest, hardworking white Americans and that, equally important, this danger was located in the cities and had to be suppressed.

Therefore, in 1964 the RNC, while shrinking its Minorities Division to "a skeleton operation," launched a massive, almost 100,000-member voter-intimidation program called Operation Eagle Eye.[28] It was an expansion of the scheme that future Supreme Court chief justice William Rehnquist had led in Phoenix two years earlier.[29] The new project was camouflaged as protecting democracy by ferreting out voter fraud in thirty-five selected cities. The Republicans scoured voter-registration lists and compared them to postcards that the RNC had mailed with "do not forward/return to sender" instructions. In a process called "caging," the GOP used the names on the undeliverable mail in an attempt "to discover 'tombstone' and 'vacant lot' voters—those carried on the election rolls although they have died, moved, or given false addresses." After compiling the list, the next step was to flood minority precincts on Election Day with uniformed off-duty police officers, sometimes carrying weapons; a squad of nearly 100,000 armbanded "Ballot Security" forces; and printed signs plastered near polling places warning of impending arrests if residents voted and had traffic tickets, hadn't paid child support, or were wanted for questioning by the police. The goal of this plan was to challenge 1.25 million voters and cause a visible percentage to never show up or to leave the polling place. Washington, DC, Republican city chairman Carl L. Shipley said that "Republican poll watchers would keep an eye out for 'people who . . . are not the kind of people who would register and vote.'" Who those people would be was, at its core, a stereotypical racialized definition of who was not an American, whose vote was not supposed to count. Democratic vice-presidential candidate Hubert Humphrey was furious: "It should be called Operation Evil Eye."[30] And although the Republican candidate, Barry Goldwater, did not win the presidential election, Operation Eagle Eye showed great potential for manipulating the narrative of who was American enough to vote and who was so un-American that they threatened democracy and had to be "caged."

The charge of stealing an election played right into years of politicians, scholars, and media associating criminal activity with minorities and urban areas, especially as "law and order" became a campaign plank for those vying for public office.[31] Therefore, the racialized lie of voter fraud had proven so politically useful that it survived the civil rights movement, even the passage of the Voting Rights Act (1965), and thrived with the realignment of the parties as southern Democrats continued their migration into the Republican Party.[32]

In 1977, when newly elected president Jimmy Carter proposed a series of election reforms, including same-day registration and Election Day as a federal holiday, because he was troubled that the United States wasn't even in the top twenty of the world's democracies when it came to voter turnout, the response from the invigorated right wing of the Republican Party eviscerated that attempt to have greater participation in American elections. Invoking the imagery of the unworthiness of the city-dwelling un-Americans, on one hand, and protecting democracy from voter fraud, on the other, the GOP went on the attack. Ronald Reagan, former governor of California and 1976 Republican candidate for president, declared that Carter's proposals would bring the wrong people into the voting booth. Reagan surmised that what the Democrats planned to do was flood the ballot box with votes from "the bloc comprised of those who get a whole lot more from the federal government in various kinds of income distribution than they contribute to it. . . . Don't be surprised if an army of election workers—much of it supplied by labor organizations which have managed to exempt themselves from election law restrictions—sweep[s] through metropolitan areas scooping up otherwise apathetic voters and rushing them to the polls to keep the benefit-dispensers in power."[33] Given the supposed lazy urban constituency targeted by the president's proposals, the RNC repeatedly warned against "Fraud and Carter's Voter Registration Scheme." The chairman of the Republican National Committee, according to Reagan, similarly labeled President Carter's proposals "The Universal Voter Fraud Bill."[34] Carter had initially tried to short-circuit the ongoing fears but fell right into the linguistic trap with language that, as the *New York Times* reported, made "fraudulent or multiple voting a felony punishable by five years in prison, a $10,000 fine or both. Second and subsequent convictions could carry up to 10 years' imprisonment and a $25,000 fine." Although his capitulation made the possibility of massive, rampant voter fraud seem real, the bill never made it out of Congress.[35]

Paul Weyrich, who was a cofounder of the Heritage Foundation, gave a talk in 1980 where he laid out what would become the blueprint for GOP victory. He chastised the audience for believing in "Good Government" where they wanted "everybody to vote." "Well, I don't," he said, because "our leverage in the elections, quite candidly, goes up as the voting populace goes down." Culling the electorate and severely restricting it was the game plan because, Weyrich concluded, "elections are not won by the majority of people; they never have been from the beginning of our country and they are not now."[36]

The next year, in 1981, the RNC teamed up with the state Republican Party and deployed a million-dollar "Ballot Security Task Force" during the hotly contested governor's race in New Jersey. The program was designed, as one official described the effort, "to combat a tradition of urban vote fraud in the state."[37] Like Mississippi in 1890, the party conflated a history of election fraud with a voter-fraud problem and set out to block individual citizens from voting. In a reprise of the script from 1964's Operation Eagle Eye, Republicans used 45,000 pieces of returned/undeliverable mail and outdated voter-roll lists to "cage" voters. There were, once again, uniformed off-duty police officers, weapons, four-foot-high printed warnings about the strong possibility of arrests for voting, and a $1,000 reward for turning in those who were voting illegally. The voter surveillance and intimidation forces flooded nearly seventy-five Black and Latino neighborhoods and badgered poll workers, volunteers, and voters. Word spread from Newark to Vineland of the armed officers, whose uniforms, guns, and two-way walkie-talkies gave the aura of law enforcement. Many stayed away from the polls, and those who dared vote in these minority precincts faced harassment and having their legitimacy as registered voters challenged.[38]

In the end, the Republicans got just what they paid for. But it wasn't, despite the pretext, a cache of voter-fraud cases. In fact, the Ballot Security Task Force did not uncover a single instance of voter-registration fraud. Rather, the intimidators had persuaded enough voters to stay home, which allowed the Republican candidate to win the gubernatorial election by just more than 1,700 votes.[39] That was a victory, but the downside, from the Republicans' point of view, was that it also brought the RNC before a federal judge as the Democrats sued and won a consent decree banning the GOP from engaging in ballot security–intimidation tactics.[40] The court's decision did not stop the Republicans from again resorting to caging and harassing, as one RNC official said, to "keep the black vote down considerably" in 1987, 1990, and 2004.[41] Indeed, the Republican National Committee chairman in 1981, Richard Richards, deploying a false binary, asserted that "anyone opposed to ballot security obviously must be supportive of . . . [voter] fraud."[42]

The 2000 presidential election was decisive in bringing nationwide acceptance to the lie of voter fraud. Although so much attention focused on Florida, with its illegally purged voter rolls, police checkpoints near the polling places in Black neighborhoods, hanging chads, and a US Supreme Court decision that stopped the recount with George W. Bush 537 votes ahead, the other disaster happened in St. Louis, Missouri. The city's Board of Elections wrongly removed nearly fifty thousand voters from the rolls, causing chaos when many of them showed up to cast their ballot. Poll workers, unable to rectify the error on the spot, sent thousands downtown to the Board of Elections to get back on the rolls. Hours upon hours of Election Day drained away with purged voters struggling to work through the bureaucratic swamp to get back on the books. As the polls were getting ready to close, Democrats sued to keep them open. The court agreed, noting that the snafu was not the voters' fault, and ruled that the precincts had to remain operational for three additional hours, until 10 p.m. The Republicans countersued. Mark "Thor" Hearne, representing the Bush/Cheney campaign, argued that the Democrats had just pulled a stunt that would lead to "voter fraud and the casting of hundreds of illegal votes." Senator Christopher "Kit" Bond said that the decision "to keep the polls open until 10 p.m. 'represents the biggest fraud on the voters in this state and nation that we have ever seen.'" Convinced that something untoward was afoot, the judge hearing the countersuit ordered the polls to close at 7:45 p.m.[43]

With the political soil already saturated with tales about Democrats and their urban constituency's efforts to steal the election, Bond did not let up. He asserted that the attempt to "keep the polls open was a 'brazen, shocking, astonishing, and stunning' effort to commit 'voter fraud . . . with dead people registering and voting from the grave, fake names and phony addresses proliferating across the nation's voter rolls, dogs registering, and people signing up to vote from vacant lots.'" This was nothing less, the senator contended, than "a major criminal enterprise designed to defraud voters."[44]

Bond took that false narrative of a nefarious conspiracy to steal the election by voters in St. Louis, which was more than 50 percent Black, into Congress as he helped shape federal legislation that was supposed to reinstill the American public's confidence in the electoral system, especially after the debacle in Florida. The *St. Louis Post-Dispatch* painstakingly investigated each of Bond's claims and systematically dismantled virtually every one of them. Dead people had not voted. Neither had dogs. Eighty-two percent of the vacant lots actually had homes built on them. Out of the more than three million votes cast that year in Missouri, there were only four cases of something awry, and none of them could have been resolved with Bond's chief prescription, voter ID. Regardless of that reality, the myth of voter fraud seeped into federal legislation, the Help America Vote Act (HAVA). That law's policy prescriptions took the reality of addressing the electoral weaknesses exposed in Florida and put it on the same footing as the lie of voter fraud in Missouri. In fact, that lie led to federal law that allowed states to require identification to vote.[45]

Through congressional hearings, media appearances, and DOJ-driven prosecutions, Bush, Attorney General John Ashcroft, and "Thor" Hearne and his American Center for Voting Rights (ACVR) amplified this fear of the mythical beast of fraudulent voters pillaging and plundering American democracy. Key to generating the national aura of thievery at the ballot box was Hearne, who repeatedly told Congress and the media that the hot spots for voter fraud were in key cities, where, coincidentally, minorities constituted up to 95 percent of the population. The airwaves, newspapers, and legislative bodies soaked up these stories of purloined elections. However, David Iglesias, a US Attorney in New Mexico, refused to buy into the GOP-created hysteria about a zombie apocalypse of dead people voting, residents using multiple addresses from vacant lots to cast several ballots, and Lassie and other canines stuffing the ballot box. Instead, he chose to tell the truth. Iglesias stated clearly and unequivocally that there was no voter fraud. Certainly nothing that warranted federal charges. Voter fraud, he said, was a "phantom." That act of integrity cost Iglesias his job. Legal scholar Michael Waldman drew a compelling analogy: "Firing a prosecutor for failing to find voter fraud is like firing a park ranger for failing to find Sasquatch." Iglesias explained how the search for a mythical beast put him and American democracy in jeopardy: "First would come the spurious allegations of voter fraud, then unvarnished legal manipulations to sway elections, followed by a rigorous insistence on unquestioned and absolute obedience, and, finally, a phone call from out of the blue."[46]

But with a DOJ-launched nationwide hunt for voter fraud and numerous congressional hearings telling a sordid tale, the mystique was so powerful that when Indiana used the excuse of stopping voter fraud to pass the nation's first strict voter ID law, the Seventh Circuit and the US Supreme Court, though acknowledging that there had not been one documented case of voter-impersonation fraud in the state's history, ruled that the supposed burdens on minority voters to obtain those IDs could not outweigh Indiana's vested interest in thwarting voter fraud.[47] Judge Terrence T. Evans, in his dissent in the Seventh Circuit, wrote, "let's not beat around the bush: The Indiana voter photo ID law is a not-too-thinly-veiled attempt to discourage election-day turnout by certain folks believed to skew Democratic."[48] Justice John Paul Stevens, who authored the Supreme Court's majority ruling, years later called it "a fairly unfortunate decision."[49] Judge Richard Posner, of the Seventh Circuit, regretted writing the opinion that supported Indiana's voter photo ID, "a type of law now widely regarded as a means of voter suppression rather than of fraud prevention."[50] Indeed, as if channeling Paul Weyrich's mantra, a Texas Republican explained that while there might not be widespread voter fraud, "'an article of religious faith' among Republicans . . . was that an ID law 'could cause enough of a drop-off in legitimate Democratic voting to add 3 percent to the Republican vote.'"[51]

The drumbeat of voter fraud, voter fraud, voter fraud has done its damage: "Nearly half of Americans believe voter fraud happens at least somewhat often, and 70 percent think it happens at least occasionally, according to an ABC News/*Washington Post* poll released" in 2016.[52] In a 2018 survey, when asked to identify a major problem in the nation's election system, 52 percent of Republicans pointed to "people who were not eligible to vote" casting a ballot.[53] The reality is very different. Loyola law professor Justin Levitt conducted a study and found that from 2000 to 2014, out of one billion votes cast in elections in the United States, there were only thirty-one cases of voter-impersonation fraud.[54] Despite the paucity of evidence, the decades of associating Black citizens with stealing elections have succeeded. Research studies have found that the vast majority of whites who hold implicit and explicit racial biases against African Americans strongly support voter ID laws, which are the purported legislative answer to massive, rampant voter fraud. However, researchers have also found that whites who hold implicit biases are convinced that their advocacy for voter IDs is not based on racism but rather on ensuring election integrity.[55]

Thus, the language of election integrity created an acceptable post–civil rights race-neutral cover to allow the myth of massive, rampant voter fraud to continue to do damage. There was Trump's Presidential Advisory Commission on Election Integrity, which was based on his 2016 claims that he would have won the popular vote if three to five million illegal votes had not been cast. That commission collapsed with nothing but blank pages in the section on voter fraud.[56] But the air of nefarious electoral shenanigans remained. In 2019 Texas's acting secretary of state created a sensation when he said he had identified the names of 95,000 immigrants who were illegally on the voter rolls and, worse yet, that there were 58,000 of them who had already cast ballots. He triumphantly exclaimed that he had turned their names over to the state's attorney general for further investigation and possible prosecution. However, the explosive press conference, replete with cheers from Trump for confirming his contentions about rampant voter fraud, fizzled into ignominy when it became clear that the list was seriously flawed, that many who were labeled as criminal immigrants were actually naturalized citizens, and that this was a publicity stunt.[57]

Yet as long as respectable and respected members of American society, such as presidents, governors, senators, and Supreme Court justices, continue to hunt for Sasquatch, the Loch Ness Monster, and the phantom of massive, rampant voter fraud, democracy in the United States will be under the very real threat of sowing distrust in election results and blocking millions of voters from the ballot box. That distrust has led to the assault on the US Capitol and, nearly six months after the election, to 66 percent of Republicans refusing to believe that Joe Biden is the president of the United States. Voter fraud supposedly stole it from Trump.[58] Myths masquerading as reality do enormous damage.

NOTES

Introduction by Kevin M. Kruse and Julian E. Zelizer

1. "In Four Years, President Trump Made 30,573 False or Misleading Claims," *Washington Post*, January 20, 2021, www.washingtonpost.com/graphics/politics/trump-claims-database/?itid=lk_inline_manual_4.

2. "How President Trump Took 'Fake News' into the Mainstream," BBC News, November 12, 2018, www.bbc.com/news/av/world-us-canada-46175024.

3. Michelle Stoddart, "Here Are the Four Inspectors General Ousted by the Trump Administration," ABC News, May 19, 2020, https://abcnews.go.com/Politics/inspectors-general-ousted-trump-administration/story?id-70773531.

4. Libby Cathey, "With String of Attacks on Doctors and Experts, Trump Takes Aim at Science: Analysis," ABC News, August 6, 2020, https://abcnews.go.com/Politics/string-attacks-doctors-experts-trump-takes-aim-science/story?id=72170408.

5. Will Stone, "On Trump's Last Full Day, Nation Records 400,000 Covid Deaths," KHN, January 19, 2021, https://khn.org/news/nation-records-400000-covid-deaths-on-last-day-of-donald-trump-presidency.

6. David Folkenflik, "You Literally Can't Believe the Facts Tucker Carlson Tells You. So Say Fox's Lawyers," NPR, September 29, 2020, www.npr.org/2020/09/29/917747123/you-literally-cant-believe-the-facts-tucker-carlson-tells-you-so-say-fox-s-lawye.

7. H. W. Brands, *Reagan: The Life* (New York: Anchor, 2015), 3.

8. "I Miss Republicans," *Kung Fu Monkey*, December 15, 2004, http://kfmonkey.blogspot.com/2004/12/i-miss-republicans.html.

9. Ron Suskind, "Faith, Certainty, and the Presidency of George W. Bush," *New York Times Magazine*, October 17, 2004, www.nytimes.com/2004/10/17/magazine/faith-certainty-and-the-presidency-of-george-w-bush.html.

10. David Greenberg, "Creating Their Own Reality: The Bush Administration and Expertise in a Polarized Age," in *The Presidency of George W. Bush: A First Historical Assessment*, ed. Julian E. Zelizer (Princeton, NJ: Princeton University Press, 2010), 199–216.

11. Patrice Taddonio, "'A Serial Liar': How Sarah Palin Ushered in the 'Post-truth' Political Era in Which Trump Has Thrived," *PBS Frontline*, January 10, 2020, www .pbs.org/wgbh/frontline/article/a-serial-liar-how-sarah-palin-ushered-in-the-post -truth-political-era-in-which-trump-has-thrived.

12. Don Gonyea, "From the Start, Obama Struggled with Fallout from a Kind of Fake News," NPR, January 10, 2017, www.npr.org/2017/01/10/509164679 /from-the-start-obama-struggled-with-fallout-from-a-kind-of-fake-news.

13. Kevin M. Kruse and Julian E. Zelizer, *Fault Lines: A History of the United States Since 1974* (New York: W. W. Norton, 2019), 305–306.

14. Kevin M. Kruse, "The Real Loser: Truth," *New York Times*, November 5, 2012, www.nytimes.com/2012/11/06/opinion/the-real-loser-truth.html.

15. Sam Youngman, "Trump Birther Remarks Overshadow Romney Appearance," Reuters, May 30, 2012, www.reuters.com/article/us-usa-campaign/trump-birther -remarks-overshadow-romney-appearance-idUKBRE84S19O20120530.

16. "How President Trump Took 'Fake News' into the Mainstream."

17. George Orwell, *1984* (Boston: Houghton Mifflin, 1983 [1949]), 33.

18. Richard E. Neustadt and Ernest R. May, *Thinking in Time: The Uses of History for Decision-Makers* (New York: Free Press, 1988).

19. Sarah Maza, *Thinking About History* (Chicago: University of Chicago Press, 2017), 7.

20. Michel-Rolph Trouillot, *Silencing the Past: Power and the Production of History* (Boston: Beacon, 1995), xxii.

21. Elle Hunt, "Trump's Inauguration Crowd: Sean Spicer's Claims Versus the Evidence," *Guardian*, January 22, 2017, www.theguardian.com/us-news/2017/jan/22 /trump-inauguration-crowd-sean-spicers-claims-versus-the-evidence.

22. Gillian Brockell, "'A Hack Job,' 'Outright Lies': Trump Commission's '1776 Report' Outrages Historians," *Washington Post*, January 20, 2021, www.washingtonpost .com/history/2021/01/19/1776-report-historians-trump.

23. Caitlin O'Kane, "Nearly a Dozen States Want to Ban Critical Race Theory in Schools," CBS News, May 20, 2021, www.cbsnews.com/news/critical-race-theory -state-bans.

24. Maza, *Thinking About History*, 5; Lynne Cheney, "The End of History," *Wall Street Journal*, October 20, 1994; Karen Diegmueller, "Playing Games with History," *Education Week*, November 15, 1995; Gary Nash, Charlotte Crabtree, and Ross Dunn, *History on Trial: Culture Wars and the Teaching of the Past* (New York: Knopf, 1997).

25. Maza, *Thinking About History*, 134–135; David Thelen, "History After the *Enola Gay* Controversy: An Introduction," *Journal of American History* 82, no. 3 (December 1995): 1029–1035. For detailed responses to the controversy from several prominent historians, see "History and the Public: What Can We Handle? A Roundtable About History After the *Enola Gay* Controversy," *Journal of American History* 82, no. 3 (December 1995): 1029–1135; Edward T. Linenthal and Tom Engelhardt, eds., *History Wars: The Enola Gay and Other Battles for the American Past* (New York: Henry Holt, 1996).

26. Joyce Appleby, Lynn Hunt, and Margaret Jacob, *Telling the Truth About History* (New York: W. W. Norton, 1994).

27. Carl L. Becker, "Everyman His Own Historian," American Historical Association, www.historians.org/about-aha-and-membership/aha-history-and-archives /presidential-addresses/carl-l-becker.

Chapter 1: American Exceptionalism by David A. Bell

1. The literature on "American exceptionalism" is immense. I have found the following titles particularly helpful: Greg Grandin, *The End of the Myth: From the Frontier to the Border Wall in the Mind of America* (New York: Metropolitan, 2019); Steve Lagerfeld, "America, the Exception?," *Hedgehog Review* 22, no. 3 (2020): 92–102; Daniel Rodgers, *As a City on a Hill: The Story of America's Most Famous Lay Sermon* (Princeton, NJ: Princeton University Press, 2018); and Abram C. Van Engen, *City on a Hill: A History of American Exceptionalism* (New Haven, CT: Yale University Press, 2020).

2. See Emmanuel Godin and Tony Chafer, eds., *The French Exception* (New York: Berghahn, 2005); Jürgen Kocka, "Der 'deutsche Sonderweg' in der Diskussion," *German Studies Review* 5, no. 3 (1982): 365–379; Yuan-kang Wang, "The Myth of Chinese Exceptionalism: A Historical Perspective on China's Rise," in *Responding to China's Rise: US and EU Strategies*, ed. Vinod Aggarwal and Sara Newland (Heidelberg: Springer, 2014), 51–74; Veljko Vujacic, "Reexamining the 'Serbian Exceptionalism' Thesis," Berkeley Program in Soviet and Post-Soviet Studies working papers series (Spring 2004); and Max Blaisdell, "Tunisian Exceptionalism or Constitutional Timing: A Comparison of Democratic Transitions in the Middle East," *Elements* 12, no. 2 (2016): 15–26.

3. One prominent exception is Seymour Martin Lipset, *American Exceptionalism: A Double-Edged Sword* (New York: W. W. Norton, 1996).

4. See John Breuilly, ed., *The Oxford Handbook of the History of Nationalism* (New York: Oxford University Press, 2013).

5. See especially Van Engen, *City on a Hill*; and Rodgers, *As a City on a Hill*.

6. See Richard Waswo, "Our Ancestors, the Trojans: Inventing Cultural Identity in the Middle Ages," *Exemplaria* 7, no. 2 (1995): 269–290.

7. See William R. Hutchison and Hartmut Lehmann, eds., *Many Are Chosen: Divine Election and Western Nationalism* (Minneapolis: University of Minnesota Press, 1994); Eran Shalev, *American Zion: The Old Testament as a Political Text from the Revolution to the Civil War* (New Haven, CT: Yale University Press, 2013); Rodgers, *As a City on a Hill*, 3; and in general the works of Rodgers and Van Engen.

8. See Eran Shalev, *Rome Reborn on Western Shores: Historical Imagination and the Creation of the American Republic* (Charlottesville: University of Virginia Press, 2009).

9. See Jonathan Israel, *The Expanding Blaze: How the American Revolution Ignited the World, 1775–1848* (Princeton, NJ: Princeton University Press, 2017). Paz, quoted in Grandin, *The End of the Myth*, 13. See Matthew Karp, *This Vast Southern Empire: Slaveholders at the Helm of American Foreign Policy* (Cambridge, MA: Harvard University Press, 2016), esp. 51–69. Quotation from William Harper, *Memoir on Slavery* (Charleston: James S. Burges, 1838), 4.

10. Josiah Strong, *Our Country, Its Possible Future and Its Present Crisis* (New York: Baker and Taylor, 1885); "U.S. Senator Albert J. Beveridge Speaks on the Philippine Question, U.S. Senate, Washington, D.C., January 9, 1900," https://china.usc

.edu/us-senator-albert-j-beveridge-speaks-philippine-question-us-senate-washington
-dc-january-9-1900. Albright, quoted in Godfrey Hodgson, *The Myth of American Exceptionalism* (New Haven, CT: Yale University Press, 2009), 152.

11. Stalin's *исключительность* can also be translated as "exclusivity," but the American communists, thinking back to Lovestone's invocation of an American "exception,"
rendered it as "exceptionalism." See Nina E. Adamova, "The Coinage of the Term
American Exceptionalism and Its Original Meanings," *Vestnik of Saint Petersburg University: History* 62, no. 1 (2017): 106–119.

12. Lipset summed up his many previous writings on the subject in *American Ex-
ceptionalism*. For the historians, see, for example, the essays in Steve Fraser and Gary
Gerstle, eds., *The Rise and Fall of the New Deal, 1930–1980* (Princeton, NJ: Princeton
University Press, 1989); and Sean Wilentz, "Against Exceptionalism: Class Conscious-
ness and the American Labor Movement, 1790–1920," *International Labor and Working-
Class History* 26 (1984): 1–24.

13. Google Ngram Viewer, https://books.google.com/ngrams; https://advance
.lexis.com; Jerome Karabel, "'American Exceptionalism' and the Battle for the Presidency," *Huffington Post*, December 22, 2011, www.huffpost.com/entry/american
-exceptionalism-obama-gingrich_b_1161800.

14. See Newt Gingrich, "The Left's Linguistic War," AmmoLand.com, November 17, 2018, www.firearmlicense.net/the-lefts-linguistic-war.php and Newt Gingrich, quoted in "The 1994 Campaign in Their Own Words: Excerpts from Candidates'
Speeches in the Gingrich-Jones Race in Georgia," *New York Times*, November 2, 1994,
section A, p. 18.

15. Gingrich, "The Left's Linguistic War"; Newt Gingrich with Vince Haley, *A Nation Like No Other: Why American Exceptionalism Matters* (Washington, DC: Regnery,
2011). The film was released in 2011. See www.cityuponahill.com.

16. William Kristol and David Brooks, "What Ails Conservatism," *Wall Street Journal*, September 15, 1997, A22.

17. "Beyond Red vs. Blue: The Political Typology," Pew Research Center, May 4,
2011, section 5, www.pewresearch.org/politics/2011/05/04/beyond-red-vs-blue
-the-political-typology.

18. See on this subject Karabel, "'American Exceptionalism.'" On the use of the term
after 9/11; see also Harold Hongju Koh, "On American Exceptionalism," *Stanford Law
Review* 55, no. 5 (2003): 1479–1527.

19. *The Charlie Rose Show*, March 30, 2007, https://advance.lexis.com.

20. Karen Tumulty, "Conservatives' New Focus: America, the Exceptional," *Washington Post*, November 29, 2010, A1; Gingrich, *A Nation Like No Other*, 9.

21. "Transcript: Donald Trump's RNC Speech," *CNN Politics*, August 28, 2020,
www.cnn.com/2020/08/28/politics/donald-trump-speech-transcript/index.html.

22. Quoted in Greg Sargent, "Donald Trump's Revealing Quote About 'American Exceptionalism,'" *Washingtonpost.com*, June 7, 2016, www.washingtonpost
.com/blogs/plum-line/wp/2016/06/07/donald-trumps-revealing-quote-about-american
-exceptionalism.

23. Daniel White, "Read Hillary Clinton's Speech Touting 'American Exceptionalism,'" *Time*, September 1, 2016, https://time.com/4474619/read-hillary-clinton-american
-legion-speech.

24. Wade Davis, "The Unraveling of America," *Rolling Stone*, August 6, 2020, www.rollingstone.com/politics/political-commentary/covid-19-end-of-american-era-wade-davis-1038206.

25. Daniel Bell, "The End of American Exceptionalism," *Public Interest* 41 (Fall 1975): 193–224, quotation from 197. The author of the present essay is Bell's son.

Chapter 2: Founding Myths by Akhil Reed Amar

1. Letters of January 7 and 14, 1787; letter of Washington to William Gordon, July 8, 1783.

2. Max Farrand, ed., *The Records of the Federal Convention of 1787* (New Haven, CT: Yale University Press, 1966 rev. ed. [hereinafter *Farrand's Records*]), 2:666–667 (emphasis added).

3. See Douglass Adair, *Fame and the Founding Fathers: Essays by Douglass Adair*, ed. Trevor Colbourn (New York: W. W. Norton, 1974), 75–76 (reprinting "The Tenth Federalist Revisited," *WMQ* 8 [1951]: 48); Larry D. Kramer, "Madison's Audience," *Harvard Law Review* 112 (1999): 611, 664 (Madison's distinctive arguments in No. 10 were "virtually absent from the context to secure the Constitution's adoption"). The reprinting data on *Federalist* essays more generally confirm the lack of impact of No. 10; see *DHRC Digital*, 19: 540–549, app. IV ("Printings and Reprintings of *The Federalist*"). For still further confirmation, see William H. Riker, *The Strategy of Rhetoric: Campaigning for the American Constitution* (New Haven, CT: Yale University Press, 1996).

4. In the preceding *Federalist* essay (No. 9), Hamilton/Publius quoted Montesquieu by name and offered yet another response, this one emphasizing the new Constitution's formally federal structure in which states, though no longer fully sovereign, would continue to exist as important components.

5. For Wilson, see Jonathan Elliot, ed., *The Debates in the Several State Conventions on the Adoption of the Federal Constitution as Recommended by the General Convention at Philadelphia in 1787* (New York: Burt Franklin, reprint ed. 1888), 2:422, 2:433–434, 2:478, 2:482, 2:523 (emphasis altered). For Pinckney, see 4:328 (emphasis added); for Marshall, see 3:322 (emphasis added).

6. *Farrand's Records*, 1:134–135 (emphasis added).

7. For detailed documentation, see Akhil Reed Amar, *The Words That Made Us: America's Constitutional Conversation, 1760–1840* (New York: Basic, 2021), 252–265.

8. Letter of July 20, 1788; Hamilton's first speech of July 24, 1788.

9. For more evidence and citations, see Amar, *The Words That Made Us*, 259–265.

10. Beyond Beard and neo-Beardian historians, both modern political parties have had partisan reasons to tout Madison. Today's Democrats like Madison because he and Jefferson later cofounded an early incarnation of the Democratic Party; today's Republicans embrace Madison because he said nicer things about the R-word than the D-word. By contrast, neither modern party can quite claim Washington as its own.

11. For the juicy details, see Akhil Reed Amar, *America's Constitution: A Biography* (New York: Random House, 2005), 503–505nn1–2. Full disclosure: the author of that 2005 book is also the author of the current chapter.

12. For details, see Amar, *The Words That Made Us*, 219, 741–744n38.

13. Many Americans today misunderstand why the Electoral College arose in Philadelphia in 1787 and evolved in the Twelfth Amendment a decade and a half later. The

key point is not, as neo-Beardians would have it, that the framers and early amenders distrusted ordinary voters and thus tried to substitute the judgment of wise statesmen ("electors"). In fact, and foreseeably, most electors from the beginning were potted
plants—men chosen democratically who did as instructed by their democratic masters,
exercising little independent judgment. The better explanation of why the framers and
early amenders eschewed direct popular election of presidents is not neo-Beardian but
neo-Garrisonian: as Madison made clear at Philadelphia, any system of direct popular
election would overwhelmingly empower the free-soil North, giving the South no credit
for its slaves, who of course could not vote. The Electoral College system crafted at Philadelphia and revised by the Twelfth Amendment finessed this sectional issue by giving
the South partial—three-fifths—credit for its slaves. The big winner of this pro-slavery
presidential election system was Washington's Virginia, a large state with an enormous
slave population. In the early 1800s, Virginia had fewer actual voters than did Pennsylvania but more electoral votes, thanks to the Three Fifths Clause. Eight of the first nine
presidential elections crowned a plantation-owning Virginian. In 1800–1801, the Three
Fifths Clause gave Virginia's Jefferson more than a dozen extra and unjustified electoral
votes—far more than his margin of victory over northerner John Adams. As northern
newspapers emphasized at every turn, Jefferson was in effect elected on the backs of
slaves. Northern congressmen urged that any constitutional amendment aiming to fix
other glitches of the Electoral College that came to light in this election should also fix
this glaring pro-slavery tilt, but the Twelfth Amendment as adopted ignored these pleas,
instead knowingly ratifying and strengthening the system's pro-slavery skew. See generally Amar, *America's Constitution*, and Amar, *The Words That Made Us*.

Chapter 3: Vanishing Indians by Ari Kelman

1. The Young America's Foundation mission statement can be found at www.yaf
.org/about. The full transcript of Santorum's remarks can be found at www.newsweek
.com/what-did-rick-santorum-say-about-native-americans-transcript-full-speech
-1586628. See also www.mediamatters.org/rick-santorum/cnns-rick-santorum-there
-isnt-much-native-american-culture-american-culture.

2. Dee Brown, *Bury My Heart at Wounded Knee: An Indian History of the American West*
(New York: Holt, Rinehart & Winston, 1970), 418.

3. Jean M. O'Brien, *Firsting and Lasting: Writing Indians out of Existence in New
England* (Minneapolis: University of Minnesota Press, 2010), xi–xxii, 26, 55, 106,
134, 145.

4. Joseph Story, *Discourse Produced at the Request of the Essex Historical Society, on the
18th of September, 1828, In Commemoration of the First Settlement of Salem, in the State
of Massachusetts* (Boston: Hilliard, Gray, Little, and Wilkins, 1828), 74–75. See also
Thomas Jefferson to Benjamin Hawkins, February 18, 1803, in Paul Leicester Ford, ed.,
The Works of Thomas Jefferson, www.loc.gov/resource/mtj1.027_1066_1069.

5. Alan Taylor, *The Civil War of 1812: American Citizens, British Subjects, Irish Rebels &
Indian Allies* (New York: Vintage, 2011), 4–9, 127–144, 203–233, 412–451.

6. *Addresses and Messages of the Presidents of the United States, from Washington to Ty-
ler, Embracing the Executive Proclamations, Recommendations, Protests, and Vetoes, from
1780–1843, Together with the Declaration of Independence of the United States* (New York:
Edward Walker, 1843), 399–400.

7. J. C. Nott and George R. Gliddon, *Types of Mankind; or, Ethnological Researches, Based upon the Ancient Monuments, Paintings, Sculptures, and Crania of Races, and upon Their Natural, Geographical, Philological, and Biblical History* (London: Trubner & Co., 1854), 69, 77. See also Ann Fabian, *The Skull Collectors: Race, Science, and America's Unburied Dead* (Chicago: University of Chicago Press, 2010), 3–7, 11–86.

8. James McPherson, *Battle Cry of Freedom: The Civil War Era* (Oxford: Oxford University Press, 1988), 193–196; Annie Heloise Abel, *The American Indian as Participant in the Civil War* (Cleveland: Arthur H. Clark, 1919), 13–29; Scott W. Berg, *38 Nooses: Lincoln, Little Crow, and the Beginnings of the Frontier's End* (New York: Vintage, 2013), 187–243; Ari Kelman, *A Misplaced Massacre: Struggling over the Memory of Sand Creek* (Cambridge, MA: Harvard University Press, 2013), 3–41.

9. T. J. Styles, *Custer's Trials: A Life on the Frontier* (New York: Alfred A. Knopf, 2015), 161–178, 304–318, 447; C. Joseph Genetin Pilawa, *Crooked Paths to Allotment: The Fight over Federal Indian Policy After the Civil War* (Chapel Hill: University of North Carolina Press, 2014), 53–98; Louis Warren, *God's Red Son: The Ghost Dance Religion and the Making of Modern America* (New York: Basic, 2017), 21–53, 271–363.

10. Helen Hunt Jackson, *A Century of Dishonor: A Sketch of the United States Government's Dealings with Some of the Indian Tribes* (New York: Harper & Brothers, 1881), 27–29.

11. Franz Boas, "Ethnological Problems," in *Congrès International des Américanistes, XVe Session, Tenue à Québec en 1906* (Quebec: Dussault & Proulx, Imprimeurs, 1907), 152. See also Frederick Jackson Turner, *The Frontier in American History* (New York: Henry Holt, 1921), 1–38; Andrew C. Isenberg, *The Destruction of the Bison: An Environmental History, 1750–1920* (Cambridge: Cambridge University Press, 2020), 2–9, 127–152; Miles A. Powell, *Vanishing America: Species Extinction, Racial Peril, and the Origins of Conservation* (Cambridge, MA: Harvard University Press, 2016), 3–11, 49–52, 87–104.

12. Timothy Egan, *Short Nights of the Shadow Catcher: The Epic Life and Immortal Photography of Edward Curtis* (Boston: Houghton Mifflin Harcourt, 2012), 147; Zane Grey, *The Vanishing American* (New York: Harper & Brothers, 1925), 116–124; Brian Dippie, *The Vanishing American: White Attitudes & U.S. Indian Policy* (Lawrence: University Press of Kansas, 1982), 210.

13. Frank Ernest Hill, "A New Pattern of Life for the Indian," *New York Times Magazine*, July 14, 1935, 10; John Collier, "Office of Indian Affairs," *Annual Report to the Secretary of the Interior, 1938* (Washington, DC: Government Printing Office, 1938), 209.

14. "The Angry American Indian: Starting down the Protest Trail," *Time*, February 9, 1970, 15.

15. Dale L. Walker, "A Talk with Dee Brown," https://web.archive.org/web/20031018170600/http://www.readwest.com/deebrown.html. See also Keith H. Basso, *Wisdom Sits in Places: Landscape and Language Among the Western Apache* (Albuquerque: University of New Mexico Press, 1996), 3–151.

16. Tom Phillips, "Bury My Heart at Wounded Knee: An Indian History of the American West, by Dee Brown," *Wisconsin Magazine of History* 55 (Spring 1972): 249. See also Kent Blansett, *Journey to Freedom: Richard Oakes, Alcatraz, and the Red Power Movement* (New Haven, CT: Yale University Press, 2020), 1–9, 166–270.

17. Gerald Vizenor, *Manifest Manners: Narratives on Postindian Survivance* (Lincoln: University of Nebraska Press, 1999), vii. See also Tiffany Midge, *Bury My Heart*

at Chuck E. Cheese's (Lincoln: University of Nebraska Press Bison Books, 2019), 3–6, 81–90, 97–104; David Treuer, *The Heartbeat of Wounded Knee: Native America from 1890 to the Present* (New York: Riverhead, 2019), 1–17.

18. Treuer, *The Heartbeat of Wounded Knee*, 15, 17, 451.

19. Simon Moya-Smith, "Rick Santorum's 'Native American Culture' Crack Was Racist. But Here's Why He Thought It Was Okay," NBC News, April 27, 2021, www.nbcnews.com/think/opinion/rick-santorum-s-native-american -culture-crack-was-racist-here-ncna1265548; Richard Luscombe, "CNN Urged to Fire Rick Santorum After Racist Comments on Native Americans," *Guardian*, April 26, 2021, www.theguardian.com/us-news/2021/apr/26/rick-santorum-native -americans-comments-outrage-cnn. See also Mark Kennedy, "CNN Ousts Rick Santorum over Disparaging Comments About Native American Culture," *Los Angeles Times*, May 23, 2021, www.latimes.com/entertainment-arts/business/story/2021-05-23 /cnn-ousts-rick-santorum-over-disparaging-comments-about-native-american-culture.

20. Brian Stetler, "Rick Santorum Departs CNN After Criticism of Native American Comments," *CNN Business*, May 22, 2021, www.cnn.com/2021/05/22/media /rick-santorum-cnn-departure-native-american-criticism/index.html; Jesus Jiménez, "CNN Drops Rick Santorum After Dismissive Comments About Native Americans," *New York Times*, May 22, 2021, www.nytimes.com/2021/05/22/business/media/rick -santorum-cnn.html; Daniel Polti, "CNN Gets Rid of Rick Santorum After Comments on Native Americans," *Slate*, May 22, 2021, https://slate.com/news-and-politics/2021/05 /cnn-drops-rick-santorum-comments-native-americans.html.

Chapter 4: Immigration by Erika Lee

1. "Pete Wilson 1994 Campaign Ad on Illegal Immigration," YouTube, February 15, 2010, www.youtube.com/watch?time_continue=8&v=lLIzzs2HHgY.

2. Leo Chavez, *Covering Immigration: Popular Images and the Politics of the Nation* (Berkeley: University of California Press, 2001), 90–127.

3. Erika Lee, *America for Americans: A History of Xenophobia in the United States* (New York: Basic, 2021 [2019]).

4. Benjamin Franklin, *Observations Concerning the Increase of Mankind* (Boston: S. Kneeland, 1755), 10; Benjamin Franklin to James Parker, March 20, 1751, collected in American Philosophical Society and Yale University, *The Papers of Benjamin Franklin*, franklinpapers.org.

5. Sally Schwartz, *"A Mixed Multitude": The Struggle for Toleration in Colonial Pennsylvania* (New York: New York University Press, 1987), 23–24.

6. Lyman Beecher, *A Plea for the West* (Cincinnati: Truman & Smith, 1835), 70, 15–16, 59, 49, 54; Hidetaka Hirota, *Expelling the Poor: Atlantic Seaboard States and the Nineteenth-Century Origins of American Immigration Policy* (New York: Oxford University Press, 2017), 127.

7. John R. Mulkern, *The Know Nothing Party in Massachusetts: The Rise and Fall of the People's Movement* (Boston: Northeastern University Press, 1990), 65; Kevin Kenny, "Diaspora and Comparison: The Global Irish as a Case Study," *Journal of American History* 90, no. 1 (June 2003): 43–44.

8. California Senate, Committee on Chinese Immigration, *Chinese Immigration: The Social, Moral, and Political Effect of Chinese Immigration. Report of the California State*

Senate of the Special Committee on Chinese Immigration (Sacramento: State Printing Office, 1878), 275, 9, 55.

9. Erika Lee, *At America's Gates: Chinese Immigration During the Exclusion Era, 1882–1943* (Chapel Hill: University of North Carolina Press, 2003).

10. Roger Daniels, *Guarding the Golden Door: American Immigration Policy and Immigrants Since 1882* (New York: Hill and Wang, 2004), 45; Madison Grant, *The Passing of the Great Race or The Racial Basis of European History*, 4th rev. ed. (New York: Scribner, 1921), 32, 91, xxxi.

11. James Murphy Ward, *The Immigration Problem, or America First* (n.p., 1917); Theodore Roosevelt, "America for Americans, Afternoon Speech of Theodore Roosevelt at St. Louis, May 31, 1916," in *The Progressive Party, Its Record from January to July, 1916* (New York: Mail and Express Job Print, 1916); Ku Klux Klan, "America for Americans," 1920–1929, Item No. 214406, Kansas Historical Society, www.kansasmemory.org/item/display.php?item_id=214406&f=00734445. See also Sarah Churchwell, *Behold, America: The Entangled History of "America First" and "the American Dream"* (New York: Basic, 2018).

12. Francisco E. Balderrama and Raymond Rodríguez, *Decade of Betrayal: Mexican Repatriation in the 1930s* (Albuquerque: University of New Mexico Press, 2006), 9.

13. David G. Gutiérrez, *Walls and Mirrors: Mexican Americans, Mexican Immigrants, and the Politics of Ethnicity* (Berkeley: University of California Press, 1995), 54; Roy L. Garis, "Report on Mexican Immigration" submitted to House Committee on Immigration and Naturalization, in House Committee on Immigration, *Immigration from Countries of the Western Hemisphere: Hearings*, 1930, 424–428, 436; California Department of Industrial Relations, Department of Agriculture, and Department of Social Welfare, *Mexicans in California: Report of Governor C. C. Young's Mexican Fact-Finding Committee* (San Francisco: California State Printing Office, 1930), 206.

14. Balderrama and Rodríguez, *Decade of Betrayal*, 151, 330; Mac M. Ngai, *Impossible Subjects: Illegal Aliens and the Making of Modern America* (Princeton: Princeton University Press, 2004), 75.

15. John M. Hart, *Empire and Revolution: The Americans in Mexico Since the Civil War* (Berkeley: University of California Press, 2001), 73, 121–122.

16. Lawrence A. Cardoso, *Mexican Emigration to the United States, 1897–1931: Socio-Economic Patterns* (Tucson: University of Arizona Press, 1980), 71; Mireya Loza, *Defiant Braceros: How Migrant Workers Fought for Racial, Sexual, and Political Freedom* (Chapel Hill: University of North Carolina Press, 2016), 100–103; Adam Goodman, *The Deportation Machine: America's Long History of Expelling Immigrants* (Princeton, NJ: Princeton University Press, 2020), 47; Kelly Lytle Hernández, *Migra! A History of the U.S. Border Patrol* (Berkeley: University of California Press, 2010), 110–127.

17. Lytle Hernández, *Migra!*, 184.

18. William G. Hartley, "United States Immigration Policy: The Case of the Western Hemisphere," *World Affairs* 135, no. 1 (1972): 58.

19. Kevin R. Johnson, "The Beginning of the End: The Immigration Act of 1965 and the Emergence of the Modern U.S.-Mexico Border State," in *The Immigration and Nationality Act of 1965: Legislating a New America*, ed. Gabriel J. Chin and Rose Cuison Villazor (New York: Cambridge University Press, 2015), 116–170, 139.

20. US Department of Homeland Security, Office of Immigration Statistics, *2019 Yearbook of Immigration Statistics* (Washington, DC, 2020), 5.

21. Sarah Coleman, *The Walls Within: The Politics of Immigration in Modern America* (Princeton, NJ: Princeton University Press, 2021).

22. Peter Brimelow, *Alien Nation: Common Sense About America's Immigration Disaster* (New York: HarperPerennial, 1996); Patrick J. Buchanan, *The Death of the West: How Dying Populations and Immigrant Invasions Imperil Our Country and Civilization* (New York: Thomas Dunne, 2002); Samuel P. Huntington, "The Hispanic Challenge," *Foreign Policy* (March–April 2004): 29–45.

23. Joseph Nevins, *Operation Gatekeeper: The Rise of the "Illegal Alien" and the Remaking of the U.S.-Mexico Boundary* (New York: Routledge, 2001), 4.

24. Muzaffar Chishti, Sarah Pierce, and Jessica Bolter, "The Obama Record on Deportations: Deporter in Chief or Not?," Migration Policy Institute, January 26, 2017, www.migrationpolicy.org/article/obama-record-deportations-deporter-chief -or-not; Alfonso Gonzales, *Reform Without Justice: Latino Migrant Politics and the Homeland Security State* (Oxford: Oxford University Press, 2014), 147–149; Ted Robbins, "Little-Known Immigration Mandate Keeps Detention Beds Full," NPR, November 19, 2013, www.npr.org/2013/11/19/245968601/little-known-immigration -mandate-keeps-detention-beds-full.

25. Donald Trump's Presidential Announcement Speech, *Time*, June 16, 2016, https://time.com/3923128/donald-trump-announcement-speech.

26. Woodrow Wilson International Center for Scholars and the Migration Policy Institute, *The Hispanic Challenge? What We Know About Latino Immigration* (Washington, DC: Woodrow Wilson International Center for Scholars and the Migration Policy Institute, 2004), 7, 12, 14; Ana Gonzalez-Barrera, "More Mexicans Leaving Than Coming to the U.S.," Pew Hispanic Center, November 19, 2015, www.pewresearch.org /hispanic/2015/11/19/more-mexicans-leaving-than-coming-to-the-u-s.

27. Immigration Policy Tracking Project database, January 31, 2021, https://imm policytracking.org/home.

Chapter 5: America First by Sarah Churchwell

1. Michael Barone, "'America First' Is Not a Threat but a Promise," *Washington Examiner*, January 26, 2017, www.washingtonexaminer.com/author/michael-barone/21.

2. Michael Anton, "The Trump Doctrine," *Foreign Policy*, April 20, 2019, https:// foreignpolicy.com/2019/04/20/the-trump-doctrine-big-think-america-first-nationalism.

3. Louis Vitale, "Nativism Afoot in Our Politics Once Again," *Asheville (NC) Citizen-Times*, June 8, 2016, https://citizen-times.com/story/opinion/contributors /2016/06/07/guest-columnist-nativism-afoot-politics/85546184.

4. For origins in the AFC, see Eric Rauchway, "Donald Trump's New Favorite Slogan Was Invented for Nazi Sympathizers," *Washington Post*, June 14, 2016, www .washingtonpost.com/posteverything/wp/2016/06/14/donald-trumps-new-favorite -slogan-has-a-nazi-friendly-history; Eli Lake, "Trump's New Slogan Has Old Baggage from Nazi Era," Bloomberg.com, April 27, 2016, www.bloomberg.com/opinion /articles/2016-04-27/trump-s-america-first-slogan-has-nazi-era-baggage; Louisa Thomas, "America First, for Charles Lindbergh and Donald Trump," *New Yorker*, July 24, 2016, www.newyorker.com/news/news-desk/america-first-for-charles-lindbergh -and-donald-trump. For origins in the Klan, see "Christian Nationalism, 2020,"

Rutland (VT) Daily Herald, July 14, 2018, www.rutlandherald.com/opinion/perspective /christian-nationalism-2020/article_becfe145-4cc8-5632-8e21-9d3347bf20f9.html.

5. In my 2018 book *Behold, America: The Entangled History of America First and the American Dream*, I traced "America First" back to the 1880s while noting that there might yet prove earlier instances of the phrase in a political context. Having found such occurrences, I am glad to have the opportunity to extend the record here.

6. *New York Daily Herald*, June 18, 1855, 1.

7. "Romanism in America," *Buffalo (NY) Commercial*, January 22, 1876, 2.

8. "Beside Blaine, Who?," *Daily Northwestern* (Oshkosh, WI), August 13, 1888, 2.

9. *Carolina Watchman* (Salisbury, NC), September 24, 1896, 1.

10. See Marc-William Palen, *The "Conspiracy" of Free Trade: The Anglo-American Struggle over Empire and Economic Globalisation, 1846–1896* (Cambridge: Cambridge University Press, 2016).

11. "Hazing the Hyphenates," *New York Times*, October 13, 1915, 14.

12. "Plead for Patriotism," *Washington Post*, April 26, 1916, 4.

13. "He'd Rid America of Foes," *Wichita (KS) Eagle*, November 28, 1915, 6.

14. "President Vouches for Authenticity of German Plot," *El Paso (TX) Times*, March 2, 1916, 1.

15. "'I'm an Undiluted American,' Says Hughes," *Salt Lake (UT) Tribune*, August 6, 1916, 1.

16. "'America First, Last and Always and No "Hyphens,"' Says Hughes," *Altoona (PA) Tribune*, October 25, 1916, 1.

17. "Pussy-Footing Not on Program If Teddy Runs," *Owensboro (KY) Inquirer*, April 6, 1916, 1.

18. "America First, and How to Maintain That Position," *Washington Post*, May 12, 1915, 6.

19. "Americanism vs. the World," *Los Angeles Times*, January 2, 1916, 7.

20. "'America First' Plea of Beveridge," *Evening Times-Republican* (Marshalltown, IA), October 6, 1916, 12.

21. "Stand with George Washington for America First, Writes 'Americanus,'" *San Francisco Examiner*, June 24, 1917, 8.

22. "Wobblies" was the popular nickname for members of the Industrial Workers of the World, an international labor union established in Chicago in 1905. See "Tar and Feather I.W.W.'s," *Sun* (Pittsburg, KS), November 10, 1917, 1.

23. "Spies, Traitors, Etc.," *Green Bay (WI) Press-Gazette*, April 23, 1918, 4.

24. "This Austrian Asserts He's for America First, Last and All the Time," *Escanaba (MI) Morning Press*, March 14, 1918, 2.

25. "Citizens, You Must Fight Another Battle for America Right Now," *San Francisco Examiner*, January 5, 1920, 16.

26. "Defence Society Fights Bolsheviki," *New York Sun*, December 30, 1918, 6.

27. "300 More Reds Nabbed in New York Raid on Hall," *San Francisco Examiner*, November 9, 1919, 1; "Democrat to Vote Against Japan's Grab," *San Francisco Examiner*, October 16, 1919, 1.

28. "Harding Advocates 'America First' in Japanese Question," *Philadelphia Inquirer*, September 15, 1920, 19.

29. "International Bankers and the League," *Albany (OR) Democrat-Herald*, September 2, 1920, 2.

30. "Hiram Johnson Becomes the Logical Nominee," *Sacramento (CA) Bee*, May 30, 1923, 28.

31. "Abolish Money Interest, Ford Plan for World," *New York Tribune*, October 29, 1922, 7.

32. "Ritchie Agrees to Make Changes," *News and Observer* (Raleigh, NC), July 5, 1919, 7.

33. "They Say They're Here: Ku Klux Creed," *Indiana (PA) Weekly Messenger*, June 1, 1922, 1.

34. "Ku Klux Night Assemblage Dispersed by One City Cop," *Evening Journal* (Wilmington, DE), September 23, 1921, 18.

35. "Cold Facts Laid Before an Illinois Audience About 'Invisible Empire,'" *Oklahoma Herald* (Muskogee, OK), December 12, 1922, 1.

36. "Klan Is Not Anti; It Is Pro-American," *Waterloo (IN) Press*, March 1, 1923, 4.

37. "Near Riot Ensues in Chase After Citizen Who Upholds Klan," *Press and Sun-Bulletin* (Binghamton, NY), August 28, 1923, 11.

38. "America Last," *Saturday Evening Post*, March 4, 1922, 22.

39. "American Cement Has Had About All the Sand Put in It Will Stand," *Fulton Democrat* (McConnellsburg, PA), April 21, 1921, 6.

40. "Land Law Proposed to Halt All Aliens," *San Francisco Examiner*, December 31, 1920, 1.

41. "Ban on Japanese Passed by House Despite Protest," *Philadelphia Inquirer*, April 13, 1924, 13.

42. "America Right," *Sioux City (IA) Journal*, March 11, 1924, 6.

43. "Senate Votes in Anger Says Doctor Franklin," *Times Herald* (Port Huron, MI), April 17, 1924, 1.

44. "Thompson Now Ready to Put Spirit of 'America First' in National Affairs," *Dayton (OH) Daily News*, April 6, 1927, 2.

45. "Great Exit of Gunmen Promised by Thompson When He Takes Office," *Tampa (FL) Tribune*, April 8, 1927, 23.

46. "Coolidge Halts U.S. Action in Chicago Fight," *Press and Sun Bulletin* (Binghamton, NY), April 5, 1928, 7.

47. "Illinois G.O.P. Factions Hurl Klan Accusations," *State* (Columbia, SC), April 5, 1928, 1.

48. "Dies Committee Prober Called Anti-Semitic," *Wisconsin Jewish Chronicle* (Milwaukee, WI), September 2, 1938, 1.

49. "Nationalism Seen Pointing Way to War," *Hartford (CT) Courant*, May 18, 1936, 7; "New Jersey G.O.P. Engaged in Hard Delegate Battle," *Morning Post* (Camden, NJ), April 11, 1936, 8.

50. "Editor's Mail Bag," *Globe-Gazette* (Mason City, IA), June 2, 1936, 4.

51. Advertisement: "Hon. Senator Henry Cabot Lodge Speaks Tonight on 'Defend America First,'" *Salt Lake Tribune* (Salt Lake City, UT), September 25, 1940, 18.

52. "Hitler's Megaphones," *Charlotte (NC) Observer*, March 13, 1941, 14.

53. "Col. Charles A. Lindbergh's Radio Address, September 15, 1939," *World Affairs* 102, no. 3 (1939): 164–166, www.jstor.org/stable/20663305.

54. "German Newspaper Lauds Lindbergh," *Bangor (ME) Daily News*, April 25, 1941, 12.

55. "Cheers and Jeers Greet Lindbergh as He Takes Stage," *Des Moines (IA) Tribune*, September 12, 1941, 7.

56. Leo P. Ribuffo, *The Old Christian Right: The Protestant Far Right from the Great Depression to the Cold War* (Philadelphia: Temple University Press, 1983), 141, 175.

57. "Survey Reveals Native Fascists Worked for GOP Victory," *California Eagle* (Los Angeles, CA), November 14, 1946, 5.

58. "A Rose by Any Other Name," *Wisconsin Jewish Chronicle* (Milwaukee, WI), August 8, 1947, 8.

59. "The 'Least Liberal' Will Get His Vote," *Minneapolis (MN) Star Tribune*, April 25, 1960, 6.

60. "Kennedy Drops Two to Nixon," *Decatur (AL) Daily*, May 4, 1960, 1.

61. "Coming Campaign Offers Excitement," *Minneapolis (MN) Star Tribune*, July 13, 1964, 6.

62. "Let's Again Teach 'America First.'" *Miami (FL) Herald*, October 18, 1964, 153.

63. "Real Republican," *Indianapolis (IN) Star*, July 29, 1964, 18.

64. Dolph Honicker, "In 1920, GOP Picked Man Who Had Failed," *Tennessean* (Nashville, TN), July 8, 1964, 6.

65. "Several for Wallace," *Bradenton (FL) Herald*, November 2, 1968, 4.

66. George Brimmell, "Klan Puts on New Face, but It's Still 'Colored' White," *Calgary (Alberta) Herald*, March 12, 1976, 7.

67. Edwin M. Yoder, "'America First' Neo-isolationism Is the Worst Idea Since Slavery," *Atlanta (GA) Constitution*, December 17, 1991, 25.

68. "Put America First, Buchanan Declares in Presidential Kickoff," *Miami Herald*, December 11, 1991, 6.

69. Francis X. Clines, "Trump Quits Grand Old Party for New," *New York Times*, October 25, 1999, A28.

70. Adam Nagourney, "Reform Bid Said to Be a No-Go for Trump," *New York Times*, February 14, 2000, https://archive.nytimes.com/www.nytimes.com/library/politics/camp/021400wh-ref-trump.html.

71. "David Duke, Former Ku Klux Klan Leader, to Run for Congress," BBC News, July 22, 2016, www.bbc.co.uk/news/election-us-2016-36870438.

72. "State of the Union Interview with Presidential Candidate Donald Trump," CNN, February 28, 2016, http://edition.cnn.com/TRANSCRIPTS/1602/28/sotu.01.html.

73. David Duke, "White Revolution and America First," Stormfront.org, January 25, 2017, archived at https://davidduke.com/hail-to-the-chief-and-mark-colletts-new-book.

74. Amy B. Wang, "Reps. Greene, Gaetz Push Trump's Grievances, 'America First' Message at Florida Rally," *Washington Post*, May 8, 2021, www.washingtonpost.com/politics/2021/05/07/reps-greene-gaetz-push-trumps-grievances-america-first-message-florida-rally.

75. Jonathan Chait, "Congressman Recruits Holocaust Deniers into the Republican Party," *New York*, June 29, 2021, https://nymag.com/intelligencer/2021/06/paul-gosar-nick-fuentes-white-nationalist-holocaust-denier-republican-groyper.html.

76. "America First Caucus Policy Platform," https://punchbowl.news/wp-content/uploads/America-First-Caucus-Policy-Platform-FINAL-2.pdf.

77. Laurie Roberts, "Rep. Paul Gosar Finally Reveals Himself with His America First Caucus Nonsense," AZ Central.com, April 16, 2021, https://eu.azcentral.com/story/opinion/op-ed/laurieroberts/2021/04/16/rep-paul-gosar-american-first-caucus-platform-4-words/7260875002.

78. Em Steck and Andrew Kaczynski, "Marjorie Taylor Greene's History of Dangerous Conspiracy Theories and Comments," CNN, February 5, 2021, https://edition.cnn.com/2021/02/04/politics/kfile-marjorie-taylor-greene-history-of-conspiracies/index.html.

79. Luke Mogelson, "Among the Insurrectionists," *New Yorker*, January 25, 2021, www.newyorker.com/magazine/2021/01/25/among-the-insurrectionists.

Chapter 6: The United States Is an Empire by Daniel Immerwahr

1. George W. Bush, "A Distinctly American Internationalism," November 19, 1999, www.mtholyoke.edu/acad/intrel/bush/wspeech.htm.

2. Richard Milhous Nixon, *Beyond Peace* (New York: Random House, 1994), 30; Bill Clinton, Remarks at Memorial Day Celebration, May 29, 2000; Gerhard Peters and John T. Woolley, *American Presidency Project*, www.presidency.ucsb.edu (hereafter *APP*).

3. Robert M. Gates, *Exercise of Power: American Failures, Successes, and a New Path Forward in the Post–Cold War World* (New York: Alfred A. Knopf, 2020), 47.

4. My book, *How to Hide an Empire: A History of the Greater United States* (New York: Farrar, Straus and Giroux, 2019), documents many of this chapter's claims.

5. Donald Fixico, "Federal and State Policies and American Indians," in *A Companion to American Indian History*, ed. Philip J. Deloria and Neal Salisbury (Malden, MA: Blackwell, 2002), 381; US Department of the Interior, *Report on Indians Taxed and Indians Not Taxed in the United States (Except Alaska) at the Eleventh Census: 1890* (Washington, DC: Government Printing Office, 1894), 643; Russell Thornton, *American Indian Holocaust and Survival: A Population History Since 1492* (Norman: University of Oklahoma Press, 1987), 43.

6. Ken De Bevoise, *Agents of Apocalypse: Epidemic Disease in the Colonial Philippines* (Princeton, NJ: Princeton University Press, 1995), 13.

7. Quoted in Immerwahr, *How to Hide an Empire*, 13.

8. *Downes v. Bidwell*, 182 U.S. 244, 279, and 287 (1901).

9. John Gallagher and Ronald Robinson, "The Imperialism of Free Trade," *Economic History Review* 6 (1953): 13.

10. William Appleman Williams, *The Tragedy of American Diplomacy* (Cleveland: World Publishing, 1959), 45.

11. Louis A. Pérez, *The War of 1898: The United States and Cuba in History and Historiography* (Chapel Hill: University of North Carolina Press, 1998), 32.

12. Woodrow Wilson, address before the Southern Commercial Congress, October 27, 1913, *APP*.

13. Foreign Policy and National Security Team Announcement, November 23, 2020, *APP*.

14. Geir Lundestad, "Empire by Invitation? The United States and Western Europe, 1945–52," *Journal of Peace Research* 23 (1986): 263–277; Victoria de Grazia, *Irresistible*

Empire: America's Advance Through Twentieth-Century Europe (Cambridge, MA: Harvard University Press, 2005).

15. National Security Council meeting, March 10, 1955, in *Foreign Relations of the United States, 1955–57, American Republics: Multilateral; Mexico; Caribbean* (Washington, DC: US Government Printing Office, 1987), 6:618.

16. Lindsey A. O'Rourke, *Covert Regime Change: America's Secret Cold War* (Ithaca, NY: Cornell University Press, 2018), 2, 7.

17. David Vine, *The United States of War: A Global History of America's Endless Conflicts, from Columbus to the Islamic State* (Oakland: University of California Press, 2020), 348n7.

18. Quoted in J. L. Granatstein and Robert Bothwell, *Pirouette: Pierre Trudeau and Canadian Foreign Policy* (Toronto: University of Toronto Press, 1990), 51.

19. Vine, *United States of War*, 2.

20. Quoted in John Lewis Gaddis, *We Now Know: Rethinking Cold War History* (New York: Oxford University Press, 1997), 264.

21. Lawrence Wright, *The Looming Tower: Al-Qaeda and the Road to 9/11* (New York: Alfred A. Knopf, 2007), 209–210; Bruce Lawrence, ed., *Messages to the World: The Statements of Osama bin Laden,* trans. James Howarth (London: Verso, 2005), 119.

Chapter 7: The Border by Geraldo Cadava

1. Benjamin Fernandez, quoted in Geraldo Cadava, *The Hispanic Republican: The Shaping of an American Political Identity, from Nixon to Trump* (New York: Ecco, 2020).

2. Brian DeLay, *War of a Thousand Deserts: Indian Raids and the U.S. Mexican War* (New Haven, CT: Yale University Press, 2009); Alice Baumgartner, *South to Freedom: Runaway Slaves to Mexico and the Road to the Civil War* (New York: Basic, 2020).

3. Alexis McCrossen, ed., *Land of Necessity: Consumer Culture in the United States— Mexico Borderlands* (Durham, NC: Duke University Press, 2009).

4. Ramón Gutiérrez, *When Jesus Came, the Corn Mothers Went Away: Marriage, Sexuality, and Power in New Mexico, 1500–1846* (Stanford, CA: Stanford University Press, 1991); James Brooks, *Captives & Cousins: Slavery, Kinship, and Community in the Southwest Borderlands* (Chapel Hill: University of North Carolina Press, 2002).

5. DeLay, *War of a Thousand Deserts*; Pekka Hämäläinen, *The Comanche Empire* (New Haven, CT: Yale University Press, 2008); Karl Jacoby, *Shadows at Dawn: A Borderlands Massacre and the Violence of History* (New York: Penguin, 2008).

6. Andrew Torget, *Seeds of Empire: Cotton, Slavery, and the Transformation of the Texas Borderlands, 1800–1850* (Chapel Hill: University of North Carolina Press, 2015); David Montejano, *Anglos and Mexicans in the Making of Texas, 1836–1986* (Austin: University of Texas Press, 1987).

7. Rachel St. John, *Line in the Sand: A History of the Western U.S.–Mexico Border* (Princeton, NJ: Princeton University Press, 2011), Chapter 1.

8. Jeffrey M. Schulze, *Are We Not Foreigners Here? Indigenous Nationalism in the U.S.-Mexico Borderlands* (Chapel Hill: University of North Carolina Press, 2018); Geraldo Cadava, "Borderlands of Modernity and Abandonment: The Lines Within Ambos Nogales and the Tohono O'odham Nation," *Journal of American History* 98, no. 2 (September 2011): 362–383.

9. Elliott Young, *Alien Nation: Chinese Migration in the Americas from the Coolie Era Through World War II* (Chapel Hill: University of North Carolina Press, 2014).

10. Linda Gordon, *The Great Arizona Orphan Abduction* (Cambridge, MA: Harvard University Press, 2001), Chapters 1 and 2; Samuel Truett, *Fugitive Landscapes: The Forgotten History of the U.S.-Mexico Borderlands* (New Haven, CT: Yale University Press, 2005).

11. Ashley Johnson Bavery, *Bootlegged Aliens: Immigration Politics on America's Northern Border* (Philadelphia: University of Pennsylvania Press, 2020); Matthew Frye Jacobson, *Barbarian Virtues: The United States Encounters Foreign Peoples at Home and Abroad* (New York: Hill and Wang, 2001); David Dorado Romo, *Ringside Seat to a Revolution: An Underground and Cultural History of El Paso and Juárez, 1893–1923* (El Paso, TX: Cinco Puntos, 2005).

12. Mae Ngai, *Impossible Subjects: Illegal Aliens and the Making of Modern America* (Princeton, NJ: Princeton University Press, 2001); Kelly Lytle Hernández, *Migra! A History of the U.S. Border Patrol* (Berkeley: University of California Press, 2010); Bavery, *Bootlegged Aliens.*

13. Abraham Hoffman, *Unwanted Mexican Americans in the Great Depression: Repatriation Pressures, 1929–1939* (Tucson: University of Arizona Press, 1974); Francisco Balderrama and Raymond Rodriguez, *Decade of Betrayal: Mexican Repatriation in the 1930s*, rev. ed. (Albuquerque: University of New Mexico Press, 2006).

14. Kelly Lytle Hernández, "The Crimes and Consequences of Illegal Immigration: A Cross-Border Examination of Operation Wetback, 1943 to 1954," *Western Historical Quarterly* 37, no. 4 (December 2006): 421–443.

15. Ngai, *Impossible Subjects*, Chapter 7.

16. On David Duke and the Klan border patrol, see Kathleen Belew, *Bring the War Home: The White Power Movement and Paramilitary America* (Cambridge, MA: Harvard University Press, 2018).

17. Geraldo Cadava, *Standing on Common Ground: The Making of a Sunbelt Borderland* (Cambridge, MA: Harvard University Press, 2013), Chapter 2.

18. Samuel Truett, *Fugitive Landscapes: The Forgotten History of the U.S.-Mexico Border* (New Haven, CT: Yale University Press, 2006).

19. Geraldo Cadava, "The Other Migrants: Mexican Shoppers in American Borderlands," in *Race and Retail: Consumption Across the Color Line*, ed. Mia Bay and Ann Fabian (New Brunswick, NJ: Rutgers University Press, 2015), 57–76.

20. Eileen Guo, "The Border Commuters," *TheOutline.com*, September 8, 2017, https://theoutline.com/post/2219/the-border-commuters.

21. Cadava, *Standing on Common Ground*, Chapter 4.

22. See C. J. Alvarez, *Border Land, Border Water: A History of Construction on the U.S.-Mexico Divide* (Austin: University of Texas Press, 2019), especially Chapter 3; Mary E. Mendoza, "Treacherous Terrain: Racial Exclusion and Environmental Control at the U.S.-Mexico Border," *Environmental History* 23, no. 1 (January 2018): 117–126; Sean Parulian Harvey, "Assembly Lines: Maquiladoras, Poverty, and the Environment in the U.S.-Mexico Borderlands, 1966–1972," PhD diss., Northwestern University, 2020.

23. Paul Kramer, "A Border Crosses," *New Yorker*, September 21, 2014, www.newyorker.com/news/news-desk/moving-mexican-border.

24. Ana Minian, "Offshoring Migration Control: Guatemalan Transmigrants and the Construction of Mexico as a Buffer Zone," *American Historical Review* (February 2020): 92.

25. Guillermo Gómez-Peña, *The New World Border: Prophecies, Poems, and Loqueras for the End of the Century* (San Francisco: City Lights, 1996).

26. William L. Hamilton, "A Fence with More Beauty, Fewer Barbs," *New York Times*, June 18, 2006, www.nytimes.com/2006/06/18/weekinreview/18hamilton.html.

27. @realDonaldTrump, October 19, 2016, https://twitter.com/realdonaldtrump /status/788913202474000384.

28. Miriam Jordan, "The Overlooked Undocumented Immigrants: From India, China, Brazil," *New York Times*, December 1, 2019, www.nytimes.com/2019/12/01/us /undocumented-visa-overstays.html.

29. Wendy Brown, *Walled States, Waning Sovereignty* (New York: Zone, 2010).

30. Perla Trevizo and Jeremy Schwartz, "Records Show Trump's Border Wall Is Costing Taxpayers Billions More Than Initial Contracts," *Texas Tribune*, October 27, 2020, www.texastribune.org/2020/10/27/border-wall-texas-cost-rising-trump.

31. For most recent budget information, see www.epa.gov/planandbudget/budget; www.commerce.gov/about/budget-and-performance; www.nasa.gov/content/previous -years-budget-requests; www.ed.gov/news/press-releases/statement-miguel-cardona -secretary-education-us-department-education-fiscal-year-2022-budget-request; www .hud.gov/budget.

32. Ana Campoy, "The People Trump's Border Wall Is Supposed to Protect the Most Say They Don't Want It," *Quartz*, July 26, 2016, https://qz.com/741259/the-people -trumps-border-wall-is-supposed-to-protect-the-most-say-they-dont-want-it/.

33. Michael Dear, *Why Walls Won't Work: Repairing the U.S.-Mexico Divide* (New York: Oxford University Press, 2013).

34. US Census Bureau, "Top Trading Partners—July 2020," www.census.gov/ foreign-trade/statistics/highlights/top/top2007cm.html.

35. Fernando Romero, *Hyperborder: The Contemporary U.S.-Mexico Border and Its Future* (Princeton, NJ: Princeton Architectural Press, 2007). US exports to Mexico in 2019: accessed April 5, 2022, https://ustr.gov/countries-regions/americas/mexico# :~:text=U.S.%20goods%20exports%20to%20Mexico,overall%20U.S.%20exports%20 in%202019.

36. Monica Campbell, "70% of This El Paso School's Students Live in Mexico and Cross the U.S.-Mexico Border Every Day for Class," *BusinessInsider.com*, April 5, 2019; Charlotte West, "Thousands of Students Cross the U.S.-Mexico Border Every Day to Go to College," *Hechinger Report*, July 19, 2019, https://hechingerreport.org /thousands-of-students-cross-the-southern-border-every-day-to-go-to-college.

Chapter 8: American Socialism by Michael Kazin

1. I have adapted some parts of this essay from Michael Kazin, *American Dreamers: How the Left Changed a Nation* (New York: Alfred A. Knopf, 2011), and from Peter Dreier and Michael Kazin, "How Socialists Changed America," in *We Own the Future: Democratic Socialism, American Style*, ed. Kate Aronoff, Peter Dreier, and Michael Kazin (New York: New Press, 2020), 15–45. Thanks to Peter for giving me permission to do that. Donald Trump, 2019 State of the Union address, quoted in Jacob Pramuk, "Expect Trump to Make More 'Socialism' Jabs as He Faces Tough 2020 Re-election Fight," CNBC, February 6, 2019, www.cnbc.com/2019/02/06/trump-warns-of-socialism-in -state-of-the-union-as-2020-election-starts.html.

2. Robert Owen, "First Discourse on a New System of Society," in *Socialism in America: From the Shakers to the Third International, A Documentary History*, ed. Albert Fried (Garden City, NY: Anchor, 1970), 94–111.

3. On the presidents who heard Owen speak and/or spoke to him, see Elizabeth Johnson, "A Welcome Attack on American Values: How the Doctrines of Robert Owen Attracted American Society," *Constructing the Past* 8, no. 1, article 9 (2007), https://digitalcommons.iwu.edu/constructing/vol8/iss1/9.

4. Tom Cole, "Socialism Is Un-American," April 30, 2019, https://cole.house.gov/media-center/weekly-columns/socialism-un-american.

5. Quoted in Kazin, *American Dreamers*, 116.

6. Albert Einstein, "Why Socialism?," *Monthly Review*, May 1949, https://monthlyreview.org/2009/05/01/why-socialism.

7. Adam Howard, "Don't Let Politicians Use MLK's Name in Vain," *Grio*, January 17, 2022, https://thegrio.com/2022/01/17/dont-let-politicians-use-mlks-name-in-vain.

8. Irving Howe, *Socialism and America* (New York: Harcourt Brace Jovanovich, 1985), 5. On the electoral fortunes of socialists in Europe, Australia, and New Zealand, see Seymour Martin Lipset and Gary Marks, *It Didn't Happen Here: Why Socialism Failed in the United States* (New York: W. W. Norton, 2000), 188. For a list of where Socialist Party members won local office in the United States, see James Weinstein, *The Decline of Socialism in America, 1912–1925* (New York: Alfred A. Knopf, 1967), 116–118. Socialists also occupied 150 seats in state legislatures at some time from 1910 to 1920. See Weinstein, *The Decline of Socialism in America*, 118.

9. For references to these quotations, see my article "The Agony and Romance of the American Left," *American Historical Review* 100 (December 1995): 1488–1512. The best summary and analysis of the question is Lipset and Marks, *It Didn't Happen Here*. But also see Eric Foner, "Why Is There No Socialism in the United States?," in Foner, *Who Owns History? Rethinking the Past in a Changing World* (New York: Hill and Wang, 2002), 110–145.

10. Quoted in Kazin, "Agony and Romance."

11. Bryan, quoted in Michael Kazin, *A Godly Hero: The Life of William Jennings Bryan* (New York: Alfred A. Knopf, 2006), 128; Roosevelt, speech at Osawatomie, quoted in Martin J. Sklar, *The Corporate Reconstruction of American Capitalism, 1890–1916: The Market, the Law, and Politics* (Cambridge: Cambridge University Press, 1988), 359; Wilson, quoted in Sklar, *Corporate Reconstruction of American Capitalism*, 407.

12. Ronald Reagan, "Radio Address on Socialized Medicine," circa 1961, www.americanrhetoric.com/speeches/ronaldreagansocializedmedicine.htm; "On the Record: Text of 1960 Reagan Letter," *New York Times*, October 27, 1984, www.nytimes.com/1984/10/27/us/on-the-record-text-of-1960-reagan-letter.html.

13. Michael Harrington, quoted in Dreier and Kazin, "How Socialists Changed America," 38, 39.

14. Dreier and Kazin, "How Socialists Changed America," 39.

15. Karlyn Bowman, "Socialism, Capitalism, and Candidates: Updating Attitudes," *Forbes*, July 1, 2021, www.forbes.com/sites/bowmanmarsico/2021/07/01/socialism-capitalism-and-candidates-updating-attitudes/?sh=66a1a4dc6c41; Peter Dreier, "The Number of Democratic Socialists in the House Will Soon Double. But the

Movement Scored Its Biggest Victories Down Ballot," *Talking Points Memo*, December 11, 2020, talkingpointsmemo.com/cafe/number-democratic-socialists-congress-soon -double-down-ballot-movement-scored-biggest-victories.

16. Quoted in Dreier and Kazin, "How Socialists Changed America," 39.

Chapter 9: The Magic of the Marketplace by Naomi Oreskes and Erik M. Conway

1. Nicholas Stern, Richard T. Ely Lecture: "The Economics of Climate Change," *American Economic Review: Papers & Proceedings* 98, no. 2 (2008): 1–37; William D. Nordhaus, *The Climate Casino: Risk, Uncertainty, and Economics for a Warming World* (New Haven, CT: Yale University Press, 2013). Stern was referring here specifically to greenhouse gas emissions; elsewhere it has been framed as climate change being the "greatest market failure" the world has seen.

2. Naomi Oreskes and Erik M. Conway, *Merchants of Doubt: How a Handful of Scientists Obscured the Truth on Issues from Tobacco Smoke to Global Warming* (New York: Bloomsbury, 2011).

3. For example, NYU professor Jonathan Haight has said: "You're not crazy to worship markets. Markets really are amazing things." Quoted in James Hoggan and Grania Litwin, *I'm Right and You're an Idiot: The Toxic State of Public Discourse and How to Clean It Up* (Gabriola Island, BC: New Society, 2016). See also Harvey Cox, *The Market as God* (Cambridge, MA: Harvard University Press, 2016); Ronald Reagan, "Opening Remarks," 1983 Annual Meetings of the Boards of Governors, International Bank for Reconstruction and Development, International Finance Corporation, and International Development Association, Washington, DC, September 27–30, 1983, 2, http:// documents.worldbank.org/curated/en/306871468331792401/pdf/534190BR0board 1Official0Use0Only100.pdf.

4. Emma Rothschild, "Adam Smith and Conservative Economics," *Economic Historical Review* 45, no. 1 (1992): 74–96; Amartya Sen, "Uses and Abuses of Adam Smith," *History of Political Economy* 43, no. 2 (Summer 2011): 257–271. See also Naomi Oreskes and Erik Conway, *The Big Myth: How American Business Taught Us to Loathe Government and Love the Free Market* (New York: Bloomsbury, forthcoming), Chapter 9. One of the most common tropes of climate-change denial is to claim that it is natural variability—in effect, that it will just go away on its own. Donald Trump also claimed that COVID-19 would "magically" disappear. See "40 Times Trump Said the Coronavirus Would Go Away," *Washington Post*, November 2, 2020, www.washingtonpost .com/video/politics/40-times-trump-said-the-coronavirus-would-go-away/2020/04/30 /d2593312-9593-4ec2-aff7-72c1438fca0e_video.html.

5. Richard S. Tedlow, "The National Association of Manufacturers and Public Relations During the New Deal," *Business History Review* 50, no. 1 (Spring 1976): 28.

6. Wendy Wall, *Inventing the American Way: The Politics of Consensus from the New Deal to the Civil Rights Movement* (New York: Oxford University Press, 2009), 49.

7. J. Howard Pew to Lane, Dec. 30, 1948, box 17, J. Howard Pew Papers, acc. 1634, Hagley Museum and Library, Wilmington, DE, 19807.

8. "Declaration of Principles Relating to the Conduct of American Industry Adopted by the Congress of American Industry," December 8, 1939, Folder National Association of Manufacturers 1939–40, Box 2, J. Howard Pew Papers, acc. 1634, Hagley Museum

and Library, Wilmington, DE 19807. On the NAM promotion of the term *free enterprise*, see Wall, *Inventing the American Way*, 48–62.

9. Wall, *Inventing the American Way*, 59.

10. Gary Gerstle, *Liberty and Coercion: The Paradox of American Government from the Founding to the Present*, rev. ed. (Princeton, NJ: Princeton University Press, 2015), 63.

11. Gerstle, *Liberty and Coercion*, 63, citing L. Ray Gunn, *The Decline of Authority: Public Economic Policy and Political Development in New York: 1800–1860* (Ithaca, NY: Cornell University Press). See also William G. Roy, *Socializing Capital: The Rise of the Large Industrial Corporation in America* (Princeton, NJ: Princeton University Press, 1999), who discusses state uses of corporations in the nineteenth century, and David I. Spanagel, *DeWitt Clinton and Amos Eaton: Geology and Power in Early New York* (Baltimore: Johns Hopkins University Press, 2014).

12. "U.S. Constitution and Acts—The Abolition of the Slave Trade," accessed April 2, 2021, https://wayback.archive-it.org/13235/20200727205120/http://abolition.nypl .org/essays/us_constitution. Further statutes were passed in 1818, 1819, and 1820. The first weakened the law—reducing penalties—but the second two added enforcement mechanisms. It was also legal to murder fugitives who had fled enslavement—a rare example of the law sanctioning the destruction of "property" (although the owner would have to be compensated). See Paul Finkelman, "Slavery in the United States: Persons or Property?," in *The Legal Understanding of Slavery: From the Historical to the Contemporary*, ed. Jean Allain (Oxford: Oxford University Press, 2012), 114. See also Ken Alder, *Engineering the Revolution: Arms and Enlightenment in France, 1763–1815* (Princeton, NJ: Princeton University Press, 1997); David Hounshell, *From the American System to Mass Production* (Baltimore: Johns Hopkins University Press, 1984); Gerstle, *Liberty and Coercion*; and Richard White, *Railroaded: The Transcontinentals and the Making of Modern America* (New York: W. W. Norton, 2011).

13. Item: NIIC slide show May 11, 1944, Folder NIIC objectives 1943–45 (2/2) labeled 1943–45 but materials are 1944, Box 845, Series III NIIC Records, National Association of Manufacturers Records, accession 1411, Hagley Museum and Library, Wilmington, DE 19807.

14. Lawrence B. Glickman, *Free Enterprise: An American History*, illustrated edition (New Haven, CT: Yale University Press, 2019), 3.

15. "NAM Finds 11 Fallacies," 1941, quoted in Burton St. John III and Robert Arnett, "The National Association of Manufacturers' Community Relations Short Film *Your Town*: Parable, Propaganda, and Big Individualism," *Journal of Public Relations Research* 26, no. 2 (2014): 103–116. See also Burton St. John III, "A View That's Fit to Print: The National Association of Manufacturers' Free Enterprise Rhetoric as Integration Propaganda in *The New York Times*, 1937–1939," *Journalism Studies* 11, no. 3 (June 1, 2010): 377–392.

16. Wall, *Inventing the American Way*, 18.

17. Glenn Beck, *The Road to Serfdom*, June 8, 2010, Fox News, www.youtube.com /watch?v=CMk5_4pBlfM&ab_channel=AllThingsBeck; Glenn Beck, "The Road to Serfdom," Fox News, January 1, 2009, updated March 25, 2015, www.foxnews.com /story/the-road-to-serfdom; Daniel Hannan, *The New Road to Serfdom: A Letter of*

Warning to America (New York: Harper, 2010); Bernard Harcourt, "How Paul Ryan Enslaves Friedrich Hayek's 'The Road to Serfdom,'" *Guardian*, September 12, 2012, www .theguardian.com/commentisfree/2012/sep/12/paul-ryan-enslaves-friedrich-hayek -road-serfdom; Rush Limbaugh, "Rush Limbaugh on Brooks, Hayek & Obama," *Taking Hayek Seriously* (blog), February 25, 2009, http://hayekcenter.org/?p=360.

18. Richard M. Ebeling, "The Life and Works of Ludwig von Mises," *Independent Review* 13, no. 1 (Summer 2008), 107, www.independent.org/publications/tir/article .asp?id=692.

19. Bettina Bien Greaves, "Remembering Henry Hazlitt," Mises Institute, July 27, 2007, https://mises.org/library/remembering-henry-hazlitt. See also Gregory Teddy Eow, "Fighting a New Deal: Intellectual Origins of the Reagan Revolution, 1932–1952," PhD diss., Rice University, 2007, 135–142; Jörg Guido Hulsmann, *Mises: The Last Knight of Liberalism* (Auburn, AL: Ludwig von Mises Institute, 2007), 822–823. For Hazlitt's relationship to Mises, see Peter J. Boettke, "The Significance of Mises's Socialism," *Foundation for Economic Education*, September 1, 2016, https://fee.org/articles /the-significance-of-misess-socialism.

20. George H. Nash, *The Conservative Intellectual Movement in America Since 1945*, 30th anniversary edition (Wilmington, DE: Intercollegiate Studies Institute, 2006), 13, 351; Charles H. Hamilton, "The Freeman: The Early Years," in *The Conservative Press in Twentieth-Century America*, ed. Ronald Lora and William Henry Longton (London: Greenwood, 1999), 321–323; Karen I. Vaughan, *Austrian Economics in America: The Migration of a Tradition* (Cambridge: Cambridge University Press, 1994), 64

21. F. A. Hayek, *The Road to Serfdom* (Chicago: University of Chicago Press, 1956), 50.

22. Kim Phillips-Fein, *Invisible Hands: The Businessman's Crusade Against the New Deal* (New York: Norton, 2010), Chapter 8. She is referring generally to free market philosophy in the late 1940s, but Hayek's book was the most notable expression of that philosophy at that time.

23. Quoted in Phillips-Fein, *Invisible Hands*, 29.

24. Bruce Caldwell, "Hayek's *The Road to Serfdom:* A Brief Introduction," in *The Road to Serfdom: Text and Documents*, by Friedrich A. Hayek, Caldwell edition (Chicago: University of Chicago Press, 2003), 19.

25. Robert Van Horn and Philip Mirowski, "The Rise of the Chicago School of Economics and the Birth of Neoliberalism," in *The Road from Mont Pèlerin: The Making of the Neoliberal Thought Collective*, ed. Philip Mirowski and Dieter Plehwe (Cambridge, MA: Harvard University Press, 2009), 164–165.

26. Hayek, *Road to Serfdom*, 84.

27. For details, see Oreskes and Conway, *Big Myth*, Chapter 5.

28. Quoted in Van Horn and Mirowski, "Rise," 285. See also Phillips-Fein, *Invisible Hands*, 30; and Eow, "Fighting," 9.

29. Eow, "Fighting," 96–98; Van Horn and Mirowski, "Rise," 166–167.

30. Milton Friedman, *Capitalism and Freedom* (Chicago: University of Chicago Press, 1962), preface to the original edition, xv; see also Plehwe, "Introduction," in *The Road from Mont Pèlerin*, 1–42.

31. Friedman, *Capitalism and Freedom*, 17.

32. Hayek, *Road to Serfdom*, xi.

33. On patronage in science, see Naomi Oreskes, *Science on a Mission: How Military Funding Shaped What We Do and Don't Know About the Ocean* (Chicago: University of Chicago Press, 2020).

34. Peter Lewin, "Rediscovering Friedman's Capitalism and Freedom," *Foundation for Economic Education*, December 11, 2017, https://fee.org/articles/rediscovering -friedman-s-capitalism-and-freedom/; Friedman, *Capitalism and Freedom*, 2.

35. Rainer Zitelmann, "Bob Chitester: The Champion of Freedom Who Made Milton Friedman a Household Name," *Foundation for Economic Education*, June 6, 2017, https://fee.org/articles/bob-chitester-the-champion-of-freedom-who-made-milton -friedman-a-household-name; Free to Choose Network, "Tribute to Our Founder, Bob Chitester," accessed July 17, 2021, www.freetochoosenetwork.org; Oreskes and Conway, *Big Myth*, Chapter 10; *"Free to Choose*—The Original 1980 TV Series," accessed July 17, 2021, www.amazon.com/Free-Choose-Original-1980-TV/dp /B07FSV4Y8T.

36. Ronald Reagan, "What Ever Happened to Free Enterprise?," November 10, 1977, www.americanrhetoric.com/speeches/ronaldreaganhillsdalecollege.htm. See also Reagan, "Opening Remarks."

37. Naomi Klein, *The Shock Doctrine: The Rise of Disaster Capitalism* (New York: Henry Holt, 2008); Janine R. Wedel, *Shadow Elite: How the World's New Power Brokers Undermine Democracy, Government, and the Free Market* (New York: Basic, 2009); Teresa Wright, *Accepting Authoritarianism: State-Society Relations in China's Reform Era* (Palo Alto, CA: Stanford University Press, 2010).

38. Anatole France, *The Red Lily* (Paris: 1894). See also Johann J. Go, "Structure, Choice and Responsibility," *Ethics and Behavior* 30 (2019): 230–246, www.tandfonline.com/doi/abs /10.1080/10508422.2019.1620610.

Chapter 10: The New Deal by Eric Rauchway

1. 165 Cong. Rec. S1635 (daily ed., March 5, 2019). For the Green New Deal, see "Recognizing the Duty of the Federal Government to Create a Green New Deal," House Resolution 109, February 7, 2019, www.congress.gov/bill/116th-congress /house-resolution/109?q=%7B%22search%22%3A%5B%22green+new+deal%22%5D% 7D&s=1&r=5; "Recognizing the Duty of the Federal Government to Create a Green New Deal," Senate Resolution 59, February 7, 2019, www.congress.gov/bill/116th -congress/senate-resolution/59/text?q=%7B%22search%22%3A%5B%22green+new +deal%22%5D%7D&r=2&s=1.

2. "Senator Grassley Says the New Deal Didn't Work; Historians Have Other Ideas," *Checkered History*, May 2, 2019, http://historychecked.com/senator-grassley -says-the-new-deal-didnt-work-historians-have-other-ideas.

3. 155 Cong. Rec. H310 (daily ed., January 14, 2009).

4. Harry G. Frankfurt, *On Bullshit* (Princeton, NJ: Princeton University Press, 2005), 47, 56.

5. Claude Lévi-Strauss, "The Structural Study of Myth," *Journal of American Folklore* 68, no. 270 (October–December 1955): 428–444, esp. 430.

6. Quoted in Eric Rauchway, *Winter War: Hoover, Roosevelt, and the First Clash over the New Deal* (New York: Basic, 2018), 75.

7. See Peter Fearon, *The Origins and Nature of the Great Slump, 1929–1932* (London: Macmillan, 1979); and Barry Eichengreen, "The Origins and Nature of the Great Slump Revisited," *Economic History Review* 45, no. 2 (May 1992): 213–239. For an alternative business-cycle dating, see Christina D. Romer, "Remeasuring Business Cycles," *Journal of Economic History* 54, no. 3 (September 1994): 573–609, esp. 598n47. Those estimates put the trough in July 1932, but Romer elsewhere uses March 1933. See Christina D. Romer, "What Ended the Great Depression?," *Journal of Economic History* 52, no. 4 (December 1992): 757–784; and Christina D. Romer, "Lessons from the Great Depression," teach-in on the Great Depression and World War II, University of Oklahoma, March 11, 2013, https://eml.berkeley.edu/~cromer/Lectures/Lessons%20from%20the%20Great%20Depression%20for%20Policy%20Today%20Written.pdf.

8. Gauti B. Eggertsson, "Great Expectations and the End of the Depression," *American Economic Review* 98, no. 4 (September 2008): 1476–1516, esp. 1477.

9. Romer, "What Ended the Great Depression?," 757.

10. This was Hoover's description of the dam at Muscle Shoals, the basis for the Tennessee Valley Authority. Herbert Hoover, "Statement on Muscle Shoals Legislation," February 28, 1931, and "Veto of the Muscle Shoals Resolution," March 3, 1931, in *Public Papers of the Presidents of the United States, 1931* (Washington, DC: Government Printing Office, 1976), 115–116 and 120–129. Hoover believed that the New Deal as a whole was even worse. See Eric Rauchway, "The New Deal Was on the Ballot in 1932," *Modern American History* 2, no. 2 (July 2019): 201–213.

11. Gauti B. Eggertsson, "Was the New Deal Contractionary?," *American Economic Review* 102, no. 1 (February 2012): 524–555; Price Fishback, "How Successful Was the New Deal? The Microeconomic Impact of New Deal Spending and Lending Policies in the 1930s," *Journal of Economic Literature* 55, no. 4 (December 2017): 1435–1485.

12. William E. Leuchtenburg, "The Election of 1936," in *The FDR Years: On Roosevelt and His Legacy* (New York: Columbia University Press, 1995), 101–158; see also Eric Schickler, *Racial Realignment: The Transformation of American Liberalism, 1932–1965* (Princeton, NJ: Princeton University Press, 2016).

13. Christopher H. Achen and Larry M. Bartels, *Democracy for Realists: Why Elections Do Not Produce Responsive Government* (Princeton, NJ: Princeton University Press, 2017), 184–189.

14. Quoted in Studs Terkel, *Hard Times: An Oral History of the Great Depression* (New York: Pantheon, 1970), 442–443.

15. Studs Terkel, *The Good War: An Oral History of World War II* (New York: New Press, 1984), 9.

16. Stanley Lebergott, *Manpower in Economic Growth: The American Record Since 1800* (New York: McGraw-Hill, 1964), 184–185.

17. Nikolaus Wachsmann, *KL: A History of the Nazi Concentration Camps* (New York: Farrar, Straus and Giroux, 2015), 163–166, 412; Kiran Klaus Patel, *Soldiers of Labor: Labor Service in Nazi Germany and New Deal America, 1933–1945* (Cambridge: Cambridge University Press, 2005), 97–100.

18. Federal Works Agency, *Final Report on the WPA Program, 1935–1943* (Washington, DC: Government Printing Office, 1946), 19–26.

19. Alexander J. Field, *A Great Leap Forward: 1930s Depression and U.S. Economic Growth* (New Haven, CT: Yale University Press, 2011), 40; see also the "first national road network," 72.

20. "Emergency workers" in *Historical Statistics of the United States* include other New Deal workers, such as those employed by the Civilian Conservation Corps, but the WPA accounts for the bulk of them.

21. Elna C. Green, "Relief from Relief: The Tampa Sewing-Room Strike of 1937 and the Right to Welfare," *Journal of American History* 95, no. 4 (March 2009): 1012–1037; Chad Alan Goldberg, "Contesting the Status of Relief Workers During the New Deal: The Workers Alliance of America and the Works Progress Administration, 1935–1941," *Social Science History* 29, no. 3 (Fall 2005): 337–371; Matt Perry, *Bread and Work: The Experience of Unemployment, 1918–1939* (London: Pluto, 2000), 155–158.

22. David R. Weir, "A Century of U.S. Unemployment, 1890–1990: Revised Estimates and Evidence for Stabilization," *Research in Economic History* 14 (1992): 301–346, esp. 322.

23. Ole Bjørn Rekdal, "Academic Urban Legends," *Social Studies of Science* 44, no. 4 (2014): 638–654, esp. 641.

24. Amity Shlaes, *The Forgotten Man: A New History of the Great Depression* (New York: HarperCollins, 2007), 397.

25. "Senator Grassley Says the New Deal Didn't Work."

26. Andrew B. Wilson, "Five Myths About the Great Depression," *Wall Street Journal*, November 4, 2008, A19.

27. Frankfurt, *On Bullshit*, 51.

28. Wilson, "Five Myths About the Great Depression," A19. Some economists prefer not to look at GDP or jobs. The economists Harold L. Cole and Lee E. Ohanian set aside unemployment and GDP and instead look at hours worked. As the economist J. Bradford DeLong says, "You don't want to maintain that the interwar decline in hours worked tells us about cycle and not trend"—that is, hours worked did drop during the 1930s, but that was an expression of worker preference enabled by unionization, not an indication of a business slump. If you misuse hours worked this way, you must believe (as DeLong says) that "the economy was even more depressed in the 1950s than it was in 1939," which it was not. Using hours worked as a measure of cycle without attending to trend is neither myth nor bullshit; it is—to borrow the physicist Wolfgang Pauli's mournful assessment of an off-point analysis—"not even wrong." Moreover, the Cole and Ohanian model presumes no involuntary unemployment—an assumption at odds with what we know of the 1930s—and an absence of monopoly power in the Coolidge era—an assumption at odds with what we know of the 1920s. See "Lessons from the New Deal," Senate Hearing 111-140, March 31, 2009 (Washington, DC: Government Printing Office, 2009), 27; Greg Hannsgen and Dimitri Papadimitriou, "Did the New Deal Prolong or Worsen the Great Depression?," *Challenge* 53, no. 1 (January–February 2010): 63–86; R. E. Peierls, "Wolfgang Ernst Pauli, 1900–1958," *Biographical Memoirs of Fellows of the Royal Society* 5 (February 1960): 174–192, esp. 186.

29. John Maynard Keynes, "Sees Need for $400,000,000 Monthly to Speed Recovery," *New York Times*, June 10, 1934, E1. Some scholars believe that Keynes found Roosevelt uncomprehending. I suspect the failure of their minds to meet had more to do with Roosevelt's belief that Keynes was attending more to the arithmetic than to the

politics of the situation. Eric Rauchway, *The Money Makers: How Roosevelt and Keynes Ended the Depression, Defeated Fascism, and Secured a Prosperous Peace* (New York: Basic, 2015), 95–101.

30. Roosevelt cut fiscal stimulus at the same time as the Treasury cut monetary stimulus and the Fed instituted a contractionary policy, so it is not easy to distinguish the recession-inducing effects. Gauti B. Eggertsson and Benjamin Pugsley, "The Mistake of 1937: A General Equilibrium Analysis," *Monetary and Economic Studies* (2006): 151–207; Douglas A. Irwin, "Gold Sterilization and the Recession of 1937–1938," *Financial History Review* 19, no. 3 (December 2012): 249–267.

31. William J. Barber, *Designs Within Disorder: Franklin D. Roosevelt, the Economists, and the Shaping of American Economic Policy, 1933–1945* (Cambridge: Cambridge University Press, 1996), esp. 112–131; Alan Brinkley, *The End of Reform: New Deal Liberalism in Recession and War* (New York: Alfred A. Knopf, 1995).

32. Franklin D. Roosevelt, "Report to Congress on Lend Lease Operations, for Year Ended March 11, 1942," 8.

33. A corollary myth holds that war employment was led by private employment and business, in contrast to the New Deal; this myth is comprehensively debunked in Mark R. Wilson, *Destructive Creation: American Business and the Winning of World War II* (Philadelphia: University of Pennsylvania Press, 2016).

34. Franklin D. Roosevelt, *Government—Not Politics* (New York: Covici Friede, 1932), 29.

35. Franklin D. Roosevelt, "Address on Election of Liberals," November 4, 1938, in *The Public Papers and Addresses of Franklin D. Roosevelt*, vol. 7, *The Continuing Struggle for Liberalism* (New York: Macmillan, 1941), 584–593; Franklin D. Roosevelt, "Annual Message to the Legislature," January 6, 1932, in *The Public Papers and Addresses of Franklin D. Roosevelt*, vol. 1, *The Genesis of the New Deal, 1928–1932* (New York: Random House, 1938), 111–126; Franklin D. Roosevelt, "Annual Message to the Congress," January 3, 1934, *The Public Papers and Addresses of Franklin D. Roosevelt*, vol. 3, *The Advance of Recovery and Reform* (New York: Random House, 1938), 8–14.

36. Franklin D. Roosevelt, "Unless There Is Security Here at Home, There Cannot Be Lasting Peace in the World," January 11, 1944, in *The Public Papers and Addresses of Franklin D. Roosevelt*, vol. 13, *Victory and the Threshold of Peace* (New York: Harper and Brothers, 1950), 32–44. On these promises and the campaign, see Stephen K. Bailey, *Congress Makes a Law: The Story Behind the Full Employment Act of 1946* (New York: Columbia University Press, 1950).

Chapter 11: Confederate Monuments by Karen L. Cox

1. Edward A. Pollard, *The Lost Cause: A New Southern History of the War of the Confederates* (New York: E. B. Treat, 1866).

2. Jack P. Maddex Jr., *The Reconstruction of Edward A. Pollard: A Rebel's Conversion to Postbellum Unionism* (Chapel Hill: University of North Carolina Press, 2011), 40–42.

3. *Ceremonies in Augusta, Georgia, Laying the Cornerstone of the Confederate Monument and the Unveiling and Dedication of the Monument* (Augusta, GA: Chronicle and Constitution Job Printing Establishment, 1878), 21.

4. *Ceremonies in Augusta*, 21.

5. *Ceremonies in Augusta*, 22.

338 *Notes to Chapter 11*

6. *Address of Justice Heriot Clarkson at the Memorial Day Exercises of the Johnston Petti-grew Chapter, United Daughters of the Confederacy, May 10, 1933, Raleigh, NC* (typescript, n.p.), 4.

7. "The Dixie Volunteers," Harmony Sheet Music, accessed January 20, 2020, http://webapp1.dlib.indiana.edu/metsnav/inharmony/navigate.do?oid=http://fedora.dlib.indiana.edu/fedora/get/iudl:290803/METADATA.

8. "Bombast," *New National Era* (Washington, DC), November 10, 1870.

9. David W. Blight, "For Something Beyond the Battlefield: Frederick Douglass and the Struggle for the Memory of the Civil War," *Journal of American History* 75, no. 4 (March 1989): 1169.

10. "The Lee Monument Unveiled," *Richmond (VA) Planet*, May 31, 1890.

11. "Tear the Spirit of the Confederacy from the South," *Chicago Defender*, July 16, 1921.

12. "Tear the Spirit of the Confederacy from the South."

13. "What Do You Say About It," *Chicago Defender*, September 10, 1932.

14. "What Do You Say About It."

15. "Executive Order on Protecting American Monuments, Memorials, and Statues and Combating Recent Criminal Violence," accessed July 26, 2020, www.whitehouse.gov/presidential-actions/executive-order-protecting-american-monuments-memorials-statues-combating-recent-criminal-violence.

Chapter 12: The Southern Strategy by Kevin M. Kruse

1. Carol Swain, "Why Did the Democratic South Become Republican?," PragerU, July 24, 2017, www.prageru.com/video/why-did-the-democratic-south-become-republican. For early works on realignment, see Walter Dean Burnham, *Critical Elections and the Mainsprings of American Politics* (New York: W. W. Norton, 1970); James L. Sundquist, *Dynamics of the Party System: Alignment and Realignment of Political Parties in the United States* (Washington, DC: Brookings Institution, 1973); and Jerome M. Chubb, William H. Flanigan, and Nancy H. Zingale, *Partisan Realignment: Voters, Parties, and Government in American History* (Beverly Hills, CA: Avalon, 1980).

2. Carol M. Swain, *The New White Nationalism in America: Its Challenge to Integration* (Cambridge: Cambridge University Press, 2002), 150.

3. Eric Foner, *Reconstruction: America's Unfinished Revolution, 1863–1877* (New York: Harper, 1988).

4. Williamjames Hoffer, *Plessy v. Ferguson: Race and Inequality in Jim Crow America* (Lawrence: University Press of Kansas, 2012).

5. Arthur M. Schlesinger, ed., *History of U.S. Political Parties* (New York: Chelsea House, 1973), 2262, 2555; Boris Heersink, *Republican Party Politics and the American South, 1865–1968* (Cambridge: Cambridge University Press, 2020), 13; Donald J. Lisio, *Hoover, Blacks, & Lily-Whites: A Study of Southern Strategies* (Chapel Hill: University of North Carolina Press, 1985); Samuel O'Dell, "Blacks, the Democratic Party, and the Presidential Election of 1928: A Mild Rejoinder," *Phylon* (1987): 2–3; Hanes Walton, *Black Republicans: The Politics of the Black and Tans* (Lanham, MD: Scarecrow, 1975).

6. Michael C. Dawson, "African-American Partisanship and the American Party System," in *Behind the Mule: Race and Class in African-American Politics* (Princeton, NJ:

Princeton University Press, 1994), 96–129; Paul Frymer, *Uneasy Alliances: Race and Party Competition in America* (Princeton, NJ: Princeton University Press, 2010); Glenda E. Gilmore, "False Friends and Avowed Enemies: Southern African Americans and Party Allegiances in the 1920s," in *Jumpin' Jim Crow: Southern Politics from Civil War to Civil Rights*, ed. Glenda E. Gilmore, Jane Dailey, and Bryant Simon (Princeton, NJ: Princeton University Press, 2000), 219–238; Linda Gordon, *The Second Coming of the KKK: The Ku Klux Klan of the 1920s and the American Political Tradition* (New York: Liveright, 2017).

7. Ira Katznelson, *Fear Itself: The New Deal and the Origins of Our Time* (New York: Liveright, 2013): 156–194; Arthur M. Schlesinger Jr., *The Age of Roosevelt: The Politics of Upheaval: 1935–1936* (Boston: Houghton Mifflin, 1966), 430; Nancy J. Weiss, *Farewell to the Party of Lincoln: Black Politics in the Age of FDR* (Princeton, NJ: Princeton University Press, 1983); Keneshia Nicole Grant, *The Great Migration and the Democratic Party: Black Voters and the Realignment of American Politics in the 20th Century* (Philadelphia: Temple University Press, 2020).

8. Leah Wright Rigueur, *The Loneliness of the Black Republican: Pragmatic Politics in the Pursuit of Power* (Princeton, NJ: Princeton University Press, 2016), 15–16.

9. Quoted in James T. Patterson, "The Failure of Party Realignment in the South, 1937–1939," *Journal of Politics* 27, no. 3 (August 1965): 603.

10. "Dixie Rebellion at Majority Rule Quelled by Reapportionment Pledge," *Hackensack (NJ) Record*, June 26, 1936, 2.

11. Susan Dunn, *Roosevelt's Purge: How FDR Fought to Change the Democratic Party* (Cambridge, MA: Harvard University Press, 2010).

12. Quoted in Patterson, "Failure of Party Realignment in the South," 602.

13. John Robert Moore, "Senator Josiah W. Bailey and the 'Conservative Manifesto' of 1937," *Journal of Southern History* 31, no. 1 (February 1965): 30, 39; Vandenberg, quoted in Patterson, "Failure of Party Realignment in the South," 605.

14. Quoted in Kari Frederickson, *The Dixiecrat Revolt and the End of the Solid South, 1932–1968* (Chapel Hill: University of North Carolina Press, 2001), 129.

15. Quoted in Harvard Sitkoff, "Harry Truman and the Election of 1948: The Coming of Age of Civil Rights in American Politics," *Journal of Southern History* 37, no. 4 (November 1971): 611.

16. Quoted in Frederickson, *Dixiecrat Revolt*, 140.

17. Frederickson, *Dixiecrat Revolt*,184–186.

18. Sitkoff, "Harry Truman and the Election of 1948," 613–614.

19. V. O. Key, *Southern Politics in State and Nation* (New York: Alfred A. Knopf, 1949), 277.

20. Quoted in "Republicans, Dixiecrats Plot to Control Congress," *Sioux Falls (SD) Argus Leader*, August 17, 1950, 6; Samuel Rosenfeld, *The Polarizers* (Chicago: University of Chicago Press, 2017), 70.

21. Quoted in "Republican-Dixiecrat Scheme?," *Charlotte (NC) News*, December 20, 1949, 12.

22. Quoted in "Sen. Humphrey Urges Realignment of Parties," *Kenosha (WI) Evening News*, June 1, 1950, 2.

23. Rosenfeld, *Polarizers*, 70.

24. "Unity from Discord," *St. Louis Globe-Democrat*, August 5, 1951, 51.

25. *Jackson (MS) Daily News* editorial, reprinted in "Mundt's Coalition Plan Stirs South," *Sioux Falls (SD) Argus Leader*, April 14, 1951, 4.

26. Karl E. Mundt, "Should the G.O.P. Merge with the Dixiecrats?," *Collier's*, July 28, 1951, 20, 45–46; Clifford P. Case, "Should the G.O.P. Merge with the Dixiecrats?," *Collier's*, July 28, 1951, 54, 56.

27. Quoted in Frederickson, *Dixiecrat Revolt*, 227.

28. "States' Rights Position on Civil Rights in GOP Platform," *Atlanta Daily World*, June 10, 1952, 1; "Democratic Party Nails Down Strong Civil Rights Plank," *Atlanta Daily World*, June 24, 1952, 1.

29. Frederickson, *Dixiecrat Revolt*, 228, 230; Joseph E. Lowndes, *From the New Deal to the New Right: Race and the Southern Origins of Modern Conservatism* (New Haven, CT: Yale University Press, 2008): 38; "Dixiecrat Says Eisenhower Could Do Well in South," *Sacramento (CA) Bee*, January 19, 1951, 29.

30. "Sillers to Vote for GOP Ticket," *Monroe (LA) Morning World*, October 26, 1952, 13.

31. "Ike and Adlai Await Voters' Choice," *Orangeburg (SC) Times and Democrat*, November 4, 1952, 1.

32. "Eisenhower Jubilant at Reaction to Speeches in Southern Cities," *Baltimore Sun*, September 4, 1952, 1–2; "Miami GOP Man Hits Selection of Democrat to Introduce Ike," *Tampa Tribune*, September 3, 1952, 7.

33. Frederickson, *Dixiecrat Revolt*, 231.

34. Earl Black and Merle Black, *The Rise of the Southern Republicans* (Cambridge, MA: Belknap, 2002), 61–65.

35. "Talladega's Tom Abernethy Likely GOP Choice to Vie with Folsom in November," *Birmingham News*, May 19, 1954, 34; "Abernethy's Success," *Anniston (AL) Star*, November 8, 1954, 4; "He Quits a Sinking Ship," *Tampa Tribune*, September 14, 1948, 6; "One Man's Lake County," *Orlando Sentinel*, June 24, 1954, 1; "Hard Fighting J. Tom Watson Dies in Tampa," *Tallahassee Democrat*, October 25, 1954, 1; "State by State Returns from Tuesday's Elections," *Des Moines (IA) Tribune*, November 3, 1954, 10.

36. Quoted in William E. Leuchtenburg, *A Troubled Feast: American Society Since 1945* (Boston: Little, Brown, 1979), 99; Harvard Sitkoff, *The Struggle for Black Equality* (New York: Farrar, Straus and Giroux, 2008), 24.

37. Roy Wilkins and Tom Mathews, *Standing Fast: The Autobiography of Roy Wilkins* (New York: Viking, 1982), 222.

38. Stuart Gerry Brown, "Civil Rights and National Leadership: Eisenhower and Stevenson in the 1950s," *Ethics* (January 1960): 118–134.

39. M. V. Hood III, Quentin Kidd, and Irwin L. Thomas, *The Rational Southerner: Black Mobilization, Republican Growth and the Partisan Transformation of the American South* (Oxford: Oxford University Press, 2012), 77.

40. "Broyhill Seeks Ike Troop Parley," *Washington Post*, October 11, 1957, B5.

41. Edward H. Miller, *Nut Country: Right-Wing Dallas and the Birth of the Southern Strategy* (Chicago: University of Chicago Press, 2015), 9, 82.

42. Neil R. McMillen, "Perry W. Howard, Boss of Black-and-Tan Republicanism in Mississippi, 1924–1960," *Journal of Southern History* 48, no. 2 (1982): 205–224; Michael Bowen, "The First Southern Strategy: Taft and the Dewey/Eisenhower Factions in the GOP," in *Painting Dixie Red: When, Where, Why and How the South Became Republican,*

ed. Glenn Feldman (Gainesville: University Press of Florida, 2011), 231–232; Boris Heersink and Jeffrey A. Jenkins, *Republican Party Politics and the American South, 1865–1968* (Cambridge: Cambridge University Press, 2020), 175–176; Eric Schickler, *Racial Realignment: The Transformation of American Liberalism* (Princeton, NJ: Princeton University Press, 2016), 253.

43. "Nixon Scores Rights Victory," *Chicago Defender*, July 27, 1960, A1; "Rights Platform Stiffened," *Newsday*, July 27, 1960, 1.

44. Miller, *Nut Country*, 122–123.

45. Quoted in Angie Maxwell and Todd Shields, *The Long Southern Strategy: How Chasing White Voters in the South Changed American Politics* (Oxford: Oxford University Press, 2019), 41.

46. Quoted in Schickler, *Racial Realignment*, 256.

47. Transcript, Citizens Council Radio Forum, 1959, Special Collections Department, Manuscripts Division, Mississippi State University Libraries, https://cdm16631 .contentdm.oclc.org/digital/api/collection/p16631coll22/id/481/page/0/inline /p16631coll22_481_0.

48. Quoted in D. Sunshine Hillygus and Todd G. Shields, *The Persuadable Voter: Wedge Issues in Presidential Campaigns* (Princeton, NJ: Princeton University Press, 2008), 119–120.

49. Quoted in Schickler, *Racial Realignment*, 254.

50. William Loeb, "Thinks GOP Can Win as 'White Man's Party,'" *Shreveport (LA) Journal*, June 9, 1961, 6.

51. "Barry Seeking Segregationist Backing," *(Tucson) Arizona Daily Star*, November 19, 1961, A6; Hillygus and Shields, *Persuadable Voter*, 117; E. M. Schreiber, "'Where the Ducks Are': Southern Strategy Versus Fourth Party," *Public Opinion Quarterly* (Summer 1971): 157–167.

52. Miller, *Nut Country*, 117–118.

53. Quoted in Lowndes, *From the New Deal to the New Right*, 63; Joseph Crespino, "Goldwater in Dixie: Race, Region and the Rise of the Right," in *Barry Goldwater and the Remaking of the American Political Landscape*, ed. Elizabeth Tandy Shermer (Tucson: University of Arizona Press, 2013): 156; "For Martin," *Montgomery (AL) Advertiser*, November 4, 1962, 12; Schickler, *Racial Realignment*, 254; Philip A. Klinkner, *The Losing Parties: Out-Party National Committees, 1956–1993* (New Haven, CT: Yale University Press, 1994), 56.

54. Quoted in "GOP Ponders Election Gains in South," *Richmond (VA) Times-Dispatch*, November 11, 1962, 16A.

55. Joseph Crespino, *In Search of Another Country: Mississippi and the Conservative Counterrevolution* (Princeton, NJ: Princeton University Press, 2007), 89; Jere Nash and Andy Taggart, *Mississippi Politics: The Struggle for Power, 1976–2008* (Jackson: University Press of Mississippi, 2009), 43; "Mississippi Sees First Real Fight Between Democrats, GOP," *Daily Advertiser* (Lafayette, LA), November 4, 1963, 8; Lowndes, *From the New Deal to the New Right*, 61.

56. Joseph Alsop, "The Southern Strategy Is Segregationist Strategy," *Hartford (CT) Courant*, December 7, 1962, 18.

57. Robert D. Novak, *The Agony of the G.O.P. 1964* (New York: Macmillan, 1965), 176–179.

58. "Wallace Wanted Job as Goldwater Veep," *Austin (TX) American Statesman*, April 30, 1976, A9.

59. Quoted in Lowndes, *From the New Deal to the New Right*, 72.

60. Rowland Evans and Robert Novak, "Backlash to Civil Rights Measures to Make GOP 'White Man's Party'?," *Daily Oklahoman* (Oklahoma City, OK), July 18, 1964, 10.

61. "Republican Party Platform of 1960," American Presidency Project, July 25, 1960, www.presidency.ucsb.edu/documents/republican-party-platform-1960; "Republican Party Platform of 1964," American Presidency Project, July 13, 1964, www .presidency.ucsb.edu/documents/republican-party-platform-1964; "The Platform Challenge," *Philadelphia Inquirer*, July 15, 1964, 18.

62. Lowndes, *From the New Deal to the New Right*, 72.

63. Evans and Novak, "Backlash to Civil Rights Measures?"

64. Quoted in Wright Rigueur, *Loneliness of the Black Republican*, 37.

65. Quoted in Matthew Delmont, "When Jackie Robinson Confronted a Trump-Like Candidate," *Atlantic*, March 19, 2016, www.theatlantic.com/politics/archive/2016/03 /goldwater-jackie-robinson/474498.

66. Quoted in Tim Galsworthy, "Carpetbaggers, Confederates, and Richard Nixon: The 1960 Presidential Election, Historical Memory, and the Republican Southern Strategy," *Presidential Studies Quarterly* (June 2022): 22.

67. "A Party Switch That's No Surprise," *Courier-Post* (Camden, NJ), September 22, 1964, 12.

68. Quoted in Crespino, "Goldwater in Dixie," 163.

69. Harry S. Dent, *The Prodigal South Returns to Power* (New York: Wiley, 1978), 68.

70. William F. Buckley Jr., "Who Will Follow Thurmond?," *Boston Globe*, September 18, 1964, 15.

71. "Switches to GOP Applauded," *Orlando Sentinel*, November 17, 1963, 3; "GOP Precinct Chief Joins Johnson Group," *Chicago Herald*, September 24, 1964, 154.

72. Nash and Taggart, *Mississippi Politics*, 45–46.

73. *Birmingham News*, reprinted in "Some Wallace Allies Are Bitter in Defeat," *Charlotte (NC) Observer*, November 8, 1964.

74. "Prentiss Walker Now Congressman," *Jackson (MS) Clarion-Ledger*, November 4, 1964, 18; "Prentiss Walker to Be Speaker," *Jackson (MS) Clarion-Ledger*, November 22, 1964, 13; "Civil Rights Groups Hit by Walker," *Washington Post*, January 17, 1966, A3.

75. Quoted in "Democrats & Republicans Line Up for County Battle," *Geneva (AL) County Reaper*, September 10, 1964, 1.

76. Quoted in "Dixie Victory: A Republican Illusion?," *Tampa Bay Times*, November 8, 1964, 59.

77. "Callaway to Seek Third District Seat," *Atlanta Constitution*, July 30, 1964, 15; "Georgia No Longer 'Safe State,'" *Kingsport (TN) Times*, November 4, 1964, 3; Jason W. Gilliland, "The Calculus of Realignment: The Rise of Republicanism in Georgia," *Georgia Historical Quarterly* (Winter 2012): 413–452.

78. Jack Bass and W. Scott Poole, *The Palmetto State: The Making of South Carolina* (Columbia: University of South Carolina Press, 2009), 114; "New GOP Congressman," *Globe-Gazette* (Mason City, IA), June 26, 1965, 4.

79. "Southern Republican Solons Talk as the Dixiecrats Did," *Atlanta Journal-Constitution*, February 14, 1965, 6B.

80. Thomas Byrne Edsall with Mary D. Edsall, *Chain Reaction: The Impact of Race, Rights and Taxes on American Politics* (New York: W. W. Norton, 1992), 35–36.

81. Wright Rigueur, *Loneliness of the Black Republican*, 52.

82. "Negro Voters Doubled in 5 States of South," *New York Times*, October 21, 1966, 26.

83. "'White Backlash' Seen Slowing Civil Rights," *Hartford (CT) Courant*, October 31, 1966, 13A.

84. Harris Survey, October 1, 1966, Roper Study #31107550, Roper Center for Public Opinion Research.

85. Godfrey Hodgson, *The World Turned Right Side Up: A History of the Conservative Ascendancy in America* (Boston: Houghton Mifflin, 1996), 119.

86. "Measuring the 'White Backlash,'" *Los Angeles Times*, November 11, 1966, B4.

87. Quoted in Lowndes, *From the New Deal to the New Right*, 108–109.

88. Quoted in "Nixon Campaigns Once More," *Camden (NJ) Courier-Post*, May 18, 1966, 16.

89. "Harry Dent, the President's Political Coordinator, Says: 'I Gave Thurmond 100% Loyalty and Now I Give Mr. Nixon 100%,'" *New York Times*, February 1, 1970, SM7.

90. "When LBJ Was No Help Whatsoever," *Daily Press* (Newport News, VA), June 17, 1966, 4.

91. Joseph Crespino, *Strom Thurmond's America* (New York: Hill and Wang, 2012), 194–195.

92. Quoted in Lowndes, *From the New Deal to the New Right*, 109.

93. Dent, *Prodigal South Returns to Power*, 68.

94. Lowndes, *From the New Deal to the New Right*, 111–112.

95. Quoted in Hillygus and Shields, *Persuadable Voter*, 120–121; "Nixon's Selection of Agnew for No. 2 Spot Astounds Politicians," *Los Angeles Times*, August 9, 1968, 1; "Agnew in No. 2 Spot Called Political Risk to Get Dixie Votes," *Philadelphia Inquirer*, August 11, 1968, 10.

96. Joseph Alsop, "Nixon's Southern Strategy," *Los Angeles Times*, August 13, 1968, A5.

97. Quoted in Dan T. Carter, *The Politics of Rage: George Wallace, the Origins of the New Conservatism, and the Transformation of American Politics* (Baton Rouge: Louisiana State University Press, 2000), 326; Crespino, *In Search of Another Country*, 205.

98. Hillygus and Shields, *Persuadable Voter*, 120–121.

99. Rick Perlstein, *Nixonland: The Rise of a President and the Fracturing of America* (New York: Scribner, 2008), 341.

100. Quoted in Lowndes, *From the New Deal to the New Right*, 116.

101. Crespino, *In Search of Another Country*, 205.

102. Quoted in Nash and Taggart, *Mississippi Politics*, 49.

103. John Ehrlichman, *Witness to Power: The Nixon Years* (New York: Simon and Schuster, 1982), 217.

104. Hodgson, *World Turned Right Side Up*, 122; "Haynsworth Latest Nixon Debt to South," *Boston Globe*, August 24, 1969, A33.

105. Quoted in Hillygus and Shields, *Persuadable Voter*, 121.

106. Quoted in Dov Grohsgal and Kevin M. Kruse, "How the Republican Majority Emerged," *Atlantic*, August 6, 2019, www.theatlantic.com/ideas/archive/2019/08/emerging-republican-majority/595504.

107. Quoted in "Nixon's Southern Strategy," *New York Times*, May 17, 1970, 215.

108. Edsall with Edsall, *Chain Reaction*, 81.

109. Quoted in Grohsgal and Kruse, "How the Republican Majority Emerged."

110. William Safire to John Ehrlichman, Internal Memorandum, "Avoiding an Imposed 'Nixon Philosophy,'" July 17, 1969, Box 1, Harry S. Dent Papers, White House Special Files, Nixon Presidential Library and Museum, Yorba Linda, CA; "'Southern Strategy' Exists?," *Atlanta Constitution*, March 8, 1970, 1A; "Shift to the Right Misleading?," *Asheville (NC) Times-Citizen*, August 13, 1970, 4; "President Joins in Muzzling Author of Book on GOP's 'Southern Strategy,'" *Daily Press* (Newport News, VA), September 30, 1969, 4.

111. Harry S. Dent, Memorandum for the President, "Re: 'Southern strategy' and the Northeast," December 11, 1969, Box 5, Contested Materials: White House Special Files, Nixon Presidential Library and Museum.

112. Quoted in Jerry Greene, "Getting Rid of a Sticky Label," *(Spokane, WA) Spokesman Review*, December 21, 1969, 4.

113. Harry S. Dent, Memorandum for the President, "Wallace TV Appearance," January 19, 1970, Box 30, John D. Ehrlichman Papers, White House Special Files, Nixon Presidential Library and Museum.

114. William Safire, *Safire's Political Dictionary* (Oxford: Oxford University Press, 2008), 683.

115. Quoted in Kenneth O'Reilly, *Nixon's Piano: Presidents and Racial Politics from Washington to Clinton* (New York: Free Press, 1995), 6.

116. Quoted in "Racial Theme Dominates South Carolina Campaign," *New York Times*, October 24, 1970, 13.

117. Matthew D. Lassiter, *The Silent Majority: Sunbelt Politics in the Suburban South* (Princeton, NJ: Princeton University Press, 2006), 251–275; Randy Sanders, "Rassling a Governor: Defiance, Desegregation, Claude Kirk and the Politics of Richard Nixon's Southern Strategy," *Florida Historical Quarterly* (Winter 2002): 332–359; Horance G. Davis Jr., "Do You, Governor Kirk?," *Gainesville (FL) Sun*, August 3, 1970, 4.

118. Quoted in David W. Reinhard, *The Republican Right Since 1945* (Lexington: University of Kentucky Press, 1983), 222.

119. "Text of President Nixon's Address in Atlanta," *Atlanta Constitution*, October 13, 1972, 8A.

120. Timothy N. Thurber, *Republicans and Race: The GOP's Frayed Relationship with African Americans* (Lawrence: University Press of Kansas, 2013), 358; Lowndes, *From the New Deal to the New Right*, 137.

121. Quoted in Kevin P. Phillips, "Political Parties Exchanging Regional Strengths," *Orlando Sentinel*, December 3, 1972, 15.

122. Quoted in Thurber, *Republicans and Race*, 358.

123. Harry S. Dent, Memorandum for the President, November 17, 1969, Box 5, Contested Materials: White House Special Files, Nixon Presidential Library and Museum.

124. "5 Georgia Officials Switch to Republicans, Back Nixon," *Los Angeles Times*, September 20, 1968, 1.

125. Perlstein, *Nixonland*, 466; "Former Governor Switches to GOP," *Atlanta Constitution*, July 22, 1973, 6A.

126. Kevin P. Phillips, "GOP Southern Strategy Now Rolling Along," *Lawton (OK) Constitution*, July 21, 1973, 6.

127. Robert Mason, "'I Was Going to Build a New Republican Party and a New Majority': Richard Nixon as Party Leader, 1969–1973," *Journal of American Studies* (December 2005): 475; Robert Mason, *Richard Nixon and the Quest for a New Majority* (Chapel Hill: University of North Carolina Press, 2004), 175–176.

128. William A. Rusher, *The Rise of the Right* (New York: William Morrow, 1984), 251.

129. American Conservative Union ratings database, Senate, 1972, http://ratings .conservative.org/people?chamber=S&limit=50&orderBy=rating&party&state=US& year=1972.

130. "Sen. Byrd Mum on Rumors He May Join GOP in Virginia," *Washington Post*, November 14, 1972, B2; "Senators Reported Set to Switch Parties," *Christian Science Monitor*, November 20, 1972, 3.

131. Hodgson, *World Turned Right Side Up*, 123–127; Black and Black, *Rise of the Southern Republicans*, 165–166.

132. "What's Philadelphia Got That We Haven't Got?," *Birmingham (AL) News*, July 17, 1948, 2; "Colmer Calls for a Party Realignment," *Hattiesburg (MS) American*, November 11, 1966, 8; "Colmer Retiring from Congress," *Hattiesburg (MS) American*, March 6, 1972, 1; "Lott to Run as Republican," *Clarion-Ledger* (Jackson, MS), April 1, 1972, 15; "Colmer Endorses Lott; GOP Committeeman Quits," *Enterprise-Journal* (McComb, MS), November 2, 1972.

133. "Republican Came in on Changing Tide," *Atlanta Constitution*, November 12, 1978, 25C.

134. "Treen Victory Caps Political Comeback," *New York Times*, December 13, 1979, A23.

135. William A. Link, *Righteous Warrior: Jesse Helms and the Rise of Modern Conservatism* (New York: St. Martin's, 2008), 113–114; "Nixon Victory Boosts GOP Strength in the South," *News and Observer* (Raleigh, NC), November 12, 1972, 9.

136. Quoted in Phillips, "GOP Southern Strategy," 6.

137. Quoted in "Shift to Republican Ticket Seen as Anti-Carter Votes," *Anniston (AL) Star*, November 5, 1980, 9.

138. Quoted in Black and Black, *Rise of the Southern Republicans*, 212.

139. Warren E. Miller, "Party Identification, Realignment and Party Voting: Back to the Basics," *American Political Science Review* (June 1991): 562.

140. Quoted in Crespino, *In Search of Another Country*, 1.

141. Quoted in Black and Black, *Rise of the Southern Republicans*, 217.

142. "GOP Plots Southern Strategy," *Greenwood (MS) Commonwealth*, August 19, 1980, 10.

143. "Over 3,000 Visit Governor to Protest," *Orangeburg (SC) Times and Democrat*, January 26, 1970, 1; *Orangeburg (SC) Times and Democrat*, May 20, 1970, 1.

144. Rick Perlstein, "Exclusive: Lee Atwater's Infamous 1981 Interview on the Southern Strategy," *Nation*, November 13, 2012, www.thenation.com/article/archive /exclusive-lee-atwaters-infamous-1981-interview-southern-strategy; transcript of audio:

www.bradford-delong.com/2017/03/lee-atwater-interview-with-alexander-p-lamis
-rough-transcript-weekend-reading.html.

145. Quoted in Jack W. Germond and Jules Witcover, "Don't Stop Reagan If You've Heard That One," *Miami News*, February 20, 1980, 14.

146. Maxwell and Shields, *The Long Southern Strategy*, 7–8.

147. Quoted in "Divisive Words: Rebukes and Records," *New York Times*, December 13, 2002, A36.

148. Joseph Aistrup, *The Southern Strategy Revisited: Republican Top-Down Advancement in the South* (Lexington: University Press of Kentucky, 1996), 244.

149. Christopher A. Cooper and H. Gibbs Knotts, "Partisan Changes in Southern State Legislatures, 1953–2013," *Southern Cultures* (Summer 2014): 77, 82, 87.

150. James M. Glaser, *The Hand of the Past in Contemporary Southern Politics* (New Haven, CT: Yale University Press, 2013), 179.

151. Gary Gerstle, "Minorities, Multiculturalism and the Presidency of George W. Bush," in *The Presidency of George W. Bush: A First Historical Assessment*, ed. Julian E. Zelizer (Princeton, NJ: Princeton University Press, 2010), 252–281.

152. Quoted in "RNC Chief to Say It Was 'Wrong' to Exploit Racial Conflict for Votes," *Washington Post*, July 14, 2005, A4.

153. Quoted in "GOP's Southern Strategy Lives On," *Baltimore Sun*, March 9, 2016, www.baltimoresun.com/opinion/op-ed/bs-ed-gop-racism-20160309-story.html.

154. Quoted in Corey D. Fields, *Black Elephants in the Room: The Unexpected Politics of African American Republicans* (Berkeley: University of California Press, 2016), 178.

Chapter 13: The Good Protest by Glenda Gilmore

1. David Brooks, "What Will You Do If Trump Doesn't Leave?," *New York Times*, September 4, 2020, www.nytimes.com/2020/09/03/opinion/trump-election-2020.html.

2. Brandon M. Terry, "Revolution in Values," September 10, 2018, http://boston review.net/forum/mlk-now/brandon-m-terry-revolution-values.

3. Keith Medley, *We as Freemen:* Plessy v. Ferguson (New Orleans: Pelican, 2003); Glenn Rifkin, "Overlooked No More: Homer Plessy, Who Sat on a Train and Stood Up for Civil Rights," *New York Times*, January 31, 2020, www.nytimes.com/2020/01/31 /obituaries/homer-plessy-overlooked-black-history-month.html.

4. August Meier and Elliott Rudwick, "The Boycott Movement Against Jim Crow Streetcars in the South, 1900–1906," *Journal of American History* 55 (March 1969): 756; Blair L. M. Kelley, *Right to Ride: Streetcar Boycotts and African American Citizenship in the Era of* Plessy v. Ferguson (Chapel Hill: University of North Carolina Press, 2010), 1–3.

5. Kelley, *Right to Ride*, 1.

6. Exceptions are Meier and Rudwick, "The Boycott Movement," 770–771, and Walter Elijah Campbell, "The Corporate Hand in an Urban Jim Crow Journey," PhD diss., University of North Carolina at Chapel Hill, 1991. On Savannah, see Walter Elijah Campbell, "Profit, Prejudice, and Protest: Utility Competition and the Generation of Jim Crow Streetcars in Savannah, 1905–1907," *Georgia Historical Quarterly* 70 (Summer 1986): 197–231; and Kelley, *Right to Ride*, 4–5.

7. Barbara Welke, "When All the Women Are White, and All the Blacks Are Men: Gender, Class, and Race on the Road to *Plessy*, 1855–1914," *Law and History Review* 13

(1955): 261–316; Barbara Welke, *Recasting American Liberty: Gender, Race, Law, and the Railroad Revolution, 1865–1920* (New York: Cambridge University Press, 2001).

8. Robin D. G. Kelley, "Congested Terrain: Resistance on Public Transportation," in *Race Rebels: Culture, Politics, and the Black Working Class* (New York: Free Press, 1996), 55–76.

9. Glenda Elizabeth Gilmore, *Defying Dixie: The Radical Roots of Civil Rights, 1919–1950* (New York: W. W. Norton, 2008), 315–329.

10. Craig Simpson, "Origins of the Civil Rights Sit In—U.S. Capitol: 1934," *Washington Area Spark*, February 26, 2018, https://washingtonareaspark.com/2018/02/26/origins-of-the-civil-rights-sit-in-u-s-capitol-1934.

11. Gilmore, *Defying Dixie*, 384–393.

12. Jeanne Theoharis, "Don't Forget That Martin Luther King Jr. Was Once Denounced as an Extremist," *Time*, January 12, 2018, https://time.com/5099513/martin-luther-king-day-myths/#:~:text=Nationally%2C%20white%20people's%20support%20of,King%20was%20helping%20the%20cause; Jeanne Theoharis, *A More Beautiful and Terrible History: The Uses and Misuses of Civil Rights History* (Boston: Beacon, 2018), 21–25.

13. David Garrow, *Bearing the Cross: Martin Luther King, Jr., and the Southern Leadership Conference* (New York: William Morrow, 2004), 322, 321, 468–469; see also 117, 134, 200, 222, 223, 235, 272, 280, 310, and 426.

14. "Communism," *The Martin Luther King, Jr. Encyclopedia* (Stanford, CA: Martin Luther King, Jr. Research and Education Institute, n.d.), https://kinginstitute.stanford.edu/encyclopedia/communism. For an outstanding historiographical essay on the civil rights movement, see Charles M. Payne, "Bibliographic Essay: The Social Construction of History," in *I've Got the Light of Freedom: The Organizing Tradition and the Mississippi Freedom Struggle*, 2nd ed. (Berkeley: University of California Press, 2007), 413–432.

15. Some 70 percent of the students were white. Sam Wineburg, "Goodbye, Columbus," *Smithsonian*, May 2008, www.smithsonianmag.com/history/goodbye-columbus-38785157.

16. Ronald Reagan, "Radio Address to the Nation," June 15, 1985, www.reaganlibrary.gov/archives/speech/radio-address-nation-civil-rights; Martin Luther King, Jr., "I Have a Dream," NPR, August 8, 1963, www.npr.org/2010/01/18/122701268/i-have-a-dream-speech-in-its-entirety.

17. "Alex Haley Interviews Martin Luther King, Jr.," *Playboy*, January 1965, https://alexhaley.com/2020/07/26/alex-haley-interviews-martin-luther-king-jr.

18. Ernest Owens, "Republicans, Keep Dr. Martin Luther King Jr.'s Name out of Your Mouths," *Daily Beast*, January 18, 2021, www.thedailybeast.com/republicans-keep-dr-martin-luther-king-jrs-name-out-of-your-mouths.

19. King, Jr., "I Have a Dream."

20. Thomas R. Brooks, *Walls Come Tumbling Down: A History of the Civil Rights Movement, 1940–1970* (Englewood, NJ: Prentice Hall, 1974), 19–20; Herbert Garfinkel, *When Negroes March* (New York: Free Press, 1959), 42–60; Paula F. Pfeffer, *A. Philip Randolph: Pioneer of the Civil Rights Movement* (Baton Rouge: Louisiana State University Press, 1990), 48–49; Harvard Sitkoff, *A New Deal for Blacks: The Emergence of Civil Rights as a National Issue* (New York: Oxford University Press, 1978), 314–335.

21. Brooks, *Walls Come Tumbling Down*, 19–20.

22. Lucius C. Harper, "Roosevelt Gives Only 'Lip Service' to Aid Negroes," *Chicago Defender*, June 25, 1941, 15.

23. "47 Branches Picket," *Afro-American*, May 3, 1941, 6.

24. Pauline E. Myers, *March on Washington Movement Mobilizes a Gigantic Crusade for Freedom* (Washington, DC: March on Washington Movement, n.d.), 3; "Roosevelt Orders End," *Chicago Defender*, June 28, 1941, 1.

25. Ella Baker, "Bigger Than a Hamburger," *Southern Patriot*, June 1960, www .cliohistory.org/fileadmin/files/click/Classroom/Ella_Baker/Click_Ella_Baker _Hamburger.pdf; "The Founding of SNCC," www.crmvet.org/info/snccfoun.htm.

26. Lauren Pearlman ties the Poor People's Campaign to Nixon's victory and a law-and-order turn against demonstrations in Chapter 3 of *Democracy's Capital; Black Political Power in Washington, D.C., 1960s–1970s* (Chapel Hill: University of North Carolina Press, 2019).

27. Keeanga-Yamahtta Taylor, "Pivot to Class," September 10, 2018, http://boston review.net/forum/mlk-now/keeanga-yamahtta-taylor-pivot-class.

28. Martin Luther King Jr., "Letter from a Birmingham Jail," April 16, 1963, https:// swap.stanford.edu/20141218230016/http://mlk-kpp01.stanford.edu/kingweb/popular _requests/frequentdocs/birmingham.pdf.

29. Martin Luther King Jr., quoted in Terry, "Revolution in Values."

30. Terry, "Revolution in Values."

31. Langston Hughes, "Let America Be America Again," in *The Collected Poems of Langston Hughes*, ed. Arnold Rampersad (New York: Vintage Classics, 1995), 190–191.

32. Jackie Robinson, *I Never Had It Made* (New York: HarperCollins, 1995 [1972]), xxiv; Steve Gardner, "Colin Kaepernick Tweets Jackie Robinson on the National Anthem," *USA Today*, https://eu.usatoday.com/story/sports/nfl/2018/04/15 /colin-kaepernick-jackie-robinson-national-anthem-racial-inequality/519354002.

33. Thomas Sugrue, "Stop Comparing Today's Protests to 1968," *Washington Post*, June 11, 2020, www.washingtonpost.com/outlook/2020/06/11/protests-1968-george-floyd.

34. Alondra Nelson, "The *Longue Durée* of Black Lives Matter," *American Journal of Public Health*, September 16, 2020, doi:10.2105/AJPH.2016.3034222.

35. Giovanni Russonelle, "Americans See Their Rights to Protest Threatened, a Poll Finds, and Some Republicans Are Less Troubled by That," *New York Times*, September 2, 2020, www.nytimes.com/2020/09/02/us/elections/americans-see-their-rights -to-protest-threatened-a-poll-finds-and-some-republicans-are-less-troubled-by-that .html.

36. Sophie Quinton, "Eight States Enact Anti-protest Laws," Pew, June 21, 2021, www.pewtrusts.org/en/research-and-analysis/blogs/stateline/2021/06/21 /eight-states-enact-anti-protest-laws.

37. International Center for Not for Profit Law, "US Protest Law Tracker," www .icnl.org/usprotestlawtracker/?location=&status=enacted&issue=&date=12&type =legislative.

38. Quoted in Daniel Q. Gillion, "Protest and Congressional Behavior: Assessing Racial and Ethnic Minority Protest in the District," *Journal of Politics* 74, no. 4 (October 2012): 950–962, esp. 950.

39. Cheryl Lynn Greenburg, *Troubling the Waters: Black Jewish Relations in the American Century* (Princeton, NJ: Princeton University Press 2006), 60; Cheryl Lynn Greenburg,

"Or Does It Explode?" Black Harlem in the Great Depression (New York: Oxford University Press, 1991), 113–139; Ralph J. Bunche, "Negroes in the Depression: Ralph J. Bunche Describes a Direct-Action Approach to Jobs," in *Black Protest Thought in the Twentieth Century*, 2nd ed., ed. August Meier, Elliott Rudwick, and Frances L. Broderick (New York: Collier MacMillan, 1985), 122–131; Jonah Engel Bromwich, "Why 'Cancel Culture' Is a Distraction," *New York Times*, August 14, 2020, www.nytimes.com/2020/08/14/podcasts/daily-newsletter-cancel-culture-beirut-protest.html.

40. Maya Rhodan, "This Photo of MLK Kneeling Has New Power amid the NFL Protests," *Time*, September 25, 2017, https://time.com/4955717/trump-protests-mlk-martin-luther-king-kneeling.

41. Theoharis, *A More Beautiful and Terrible History*, xv.

42. Theoharis, *A More Beautiful and Terrible History*; Martha Jones, *Vanguard: How Black Women Broke Barriers, Won the Vote, and Insisted on Equality for All* (New York: Basic, 2020); Hasan Kwame Jeffries, *Understanding and Teaching the Civil Rights Movement* (Madison: University of Wisconsin Press, 2019).

43. Quoted in Heather Cox Richardson, "Letters from an American," August 31, 2020, https://heathercoxrichardson.substack.com.

44. Charles P. Pierce, @CharlesPPierce, September 1, 2020, tweet.

45. Rick Maese and Emily Guskin, "Most Americans Support Athletes Speaking Out," *Washington Post*, September 10, 2020, www.washingtonpost.com/sports/2020/09/10/poll-nfl-anthem-protests/?hpid=hp_hp-top-table-low_nflanthempoll-12a%3Ahomepage%2Fstory-ans.

46. Kenneth Clark, quoted in Simpson, "Origins of the Civil Rights Sit In."

47. "A Revealing Experiment: *Brown v. Board* and 'The Doll Test,'" NAACP Legal Defense Fund, www.naacpldf.org/ldf-celebrates-60th-anniversary-brown-v-board-education/significance-doll-test; Richard Kluger, *Simple Justice: The History of Brown v. Board of Education and Black America's Struggle for Equality* (New York: Random House, 1975).

Chapter 14: White Backlash by Lawrence B. Glickman

1. I'd like to thank Jill Frank, Paul Friedland, and the editors of this volume for careful reading and helpful suggestions. "Black Power–White Backlash," *CBS Reports*, September 27, 1966.

2. Martin F. Nolan, "Few Dare Fight White Backlash," *Boston Globe*, October 4, 1966, 13; Rowland Evans and Robert Novak, "Backlash Will Be Felt On and On in Politics," *Fort Worth (TX) Star-Telegram*, October 25, 1966, 26; Charles Stafford, "'Black Power' Phrase Seen as Harmful," *Tampa Tribune*, October 16, 1966, 26; Stokely Carmichael and Charles V. Hamilton, *Black Power: The Politics of Liberation in America* (New York: Random House, 1967).

3. George Gallup, "More Saying That Kennedy Pushes Integration 'Too Fast,'" *Jackson (MS) Clarion-Ledger*, August 11, 1963, 53; Gallup, "Rights Issue Hits Hard at JFK's Popularity Rating," *Capital Times* (Madison, WI), October 12, 1963, 5; "Gallup: Too Fast," *Canonsburg (PA) Daily Notes*, August 2, 1963, 4.

4. John B. Judis, "What Happened to Wisconsin?," *Nation*, April 1, 2019, 35–37. For similar framing, see Michael J. Klarman, "How *Brown* Changed Race Relations: The Backlash Thesis," *Journal of American History* 81 (June 1994): 81–118.

5. Relman Morin, "Phenomenon of Backlash," *Lebanon (PA) Daily News*, November 7, 1966, 22.

6. "Johnson Feels Backlash on Civil Rights Efforts," *New Castle (PA) News*, February 29, 1960, 1; Rowland Evans and Robert Novak, "Why House Rejected Depressed Areas Plan," *Los Angeles Times*, June 24, 1963, 33; Charles McDowell, "Political Words of '64: Backlash and Variations," *Ogden (UT) Standard-Examiner*, August 4, 1964, 4; Tom Wicker, "In the Nation: Frontlash and Backlash," *New York Times*, October 5, 1967, 36.

7. Martin Luther King, Jr., "Racism and the White Backlash," in *Where Do We Go from Here? Chaos or Community* (Boston: Beacon, 1968), 72; Lerone Bennett Jr., "The First White Backlash," *Ebony*, December 1966, 146–150, 152, 154, 156, 158. Cosell's comments from October 18, 1968, can be seen at www.youtube.com/watch?v=fEg3uNqsTYQ.

8. Dick Nolan, "The Arithmetic of the Campaign," *San Francisco Examiner*, October 31, 1963, 35.

9. Lawrence Goodwyn, *The Populist Moment: A Short History of the Agrarian Revolt in America* (New York: Oxford University Press, 1978), x; "Virginia's Election Picture," *Newport News (VA) Daily Press*, November 8, 1968, 4.

10. Lisa McGirr, *Suburban Warriors: The Origins of the New American Right* (Princeton, NJ: Princeton University Press, 2001), 54–110.

11. "Reconstructing Reconstruction," *Ravenna (OH) Democratic Press*, May 5, 1870, 1.

12. Hans Trefousse, *Andrew Johnson: A Biography* (New York: W. W. Norton, 1989), 236; "Remarks of President Johnson," *Staunton (VA) Spectator*, January 28, 1868, 2.

13. "The Political Issues," *Detroit Free Press*, October 17, 1868, 3.

14. Claire R. Gerould, "Says Bill Would Force Citizens into Revolution," *Shreveport (LA) Journal*, February 13, 1964, 6.

15. "JFK Tries Persuasion in Civil Rights Matters," *Atlanta Constitution*, March 25, 1961, 4; "Something Like Prohibition," *Portage (WI) Daily Register*, July 27, 1964, 4; "The 'Now' Outlook on Illinois Election," *Moline (IL) Dispatch*, August 1, 1968, 1; "House Judiciary Committee Expected to Offer Tougher Civil Rights Package," *Magee (MS) Courier*, October 3, 1963, 2; Tom Ethridge, "Mississippi Notebook: Could Provoke a 'White Revolution,'" *Jackson (MS) Clarion-Ledger*, June 30, 1966, 20.

16. See, for example, Jonathan Rieder, *Canarsie: The Jews and Italians of Brooklyn Against Liberalism* (Cambridge, MA: Harvard University Press, 1987); Katherine J. Cramer, *The Politics of Resentment: Rural Consciousness in Wisconsin and the Rise of Scott Walker* (Chicago: University of Chicago Press, 2016); Arlie Hochschild, *Strangers in Their Own Land: Anger and Mourning on the American Right* (New York: New Press, 2016); Allen J. Matusow, *The Unraveling of America: A History of Liberalism in the 1960s* (New York: Harper & Row, 1984), xv; and Gordon Turtle, "Sixties Explained Perceptively at Last," *Edmonton (Alberta) Journal*, March 25, 1985, 24.

17. Dan Balz, "The Politics of Race Are Shifting, and Politicians Are Struggling to Keep Pace," *Washington Post*, July 5, 2020, www.washingtonpost.com/graphics/2020/politics/race-reckoning; Jim Tankersley and Jason DeParle, "Stimulus Signals Shifting Politics of Poverty Fight," *New York Times*, March 14, 2021, 1, 20. Inglehart is quoted in Thomas B. Edsall, "Red and Blue Voters Live in Different Economies," *New York Times*, September 25, 2019, www.nytimes.com/2019/09/25/opinion/trump-economy.html.

18. E. H. Carr, *What Is History?* (New York: Cambridge University Press, 1961), 87, 89, 103.

19. Carr, *What Is History?*, 104–105.

20. "Revolution and Counter Revolution," *Lincoln (NE) Journal Star*, October 24, 1963, 4.

21. Robert David Johnson, *All the Way with LBJ: The 1964 Presidential Election* (New York: Cambridge University Press, 2009), 191.

22. Norman Lockman, "Republicans' New Revolution Is the Same Old White Backlash," *Salinas Californian*, January 13, 1995, 6.

23. A. Philip Randolph, "Freedom Is Not Free," *New York Age*, May 24, 1958, 17. See also John S. Huntington and Lawrence B. Glickman, "America's Most Destructive Habit," *Atlantic*, November 7, 2021, www.theatlantic.com/ideas/archive/2021/11/conservative-backlash-progress/620607.

24. King, Jr., "Racism and the White Backlash," 72.

25. King, Jr., "Racism and the White Backlash," 72, 96; King, "The Dilemma of Negro Americans," in *Where Do We Go from Here?*, 125; Alan Stang, "Lest We Forget," *Review of the News*, April 24, 1968, 20. Thanks to David A. Walsh for this citation.

Chapter 15: The Great Society by Joshua Zeitz

1. Ronald Reagan, "Remarks at a Fundraising Dinner Honoring Former Representative John M. Ashbrook in Ashland, Ohio," May 9, 1983, Reagan Library, www.reaganlibrary.gov/archives/speech/remarks-fundraising-dinner-honoring-former-representative-john-m-ashbrook-ashland; "Reagan Blames 'Great Society' for Economic Woes," *New York Times*, May 10, 1983, A19.

2. "Ryan: Stop 'Dependency' Culture," *Politico*, October 24, 2012, www.politico.com/story/2012/10/ryan-stop-debilitating-culture-of-dependency-082834; "Paul Ryan: War on Poverty Failed," *Politico*, January 9, 2014, www.politico.com/story/2014/01/paul-ryan-war-on-poverty-failed-102001.

3. See Amity Shlaes, *Great Society: A New History* (New York: Harper, 2019), and "An Argument That Lyndon Johnson's Great Society Wasn't So Great," *New York Times*, December 3, 2019, www.nytimes.com/2019/12/03/books/review/great-society-amity-shlaes.html.

4. Quoted in Robert M. Collins, *More: The Politics of Economic Growth in Postwar America* (New York: Oxford University Press, 2000), 1–16; Alvin Hansen, "Economic Progress and Declining Population Growth," *American Economic Review* 29 (March 1939): 4; Robert Dallek, *Flawed Giant: Lyndon Johnson and His Times, 1961–1973* (New York: Oxford University Press, 1998), 75.

5. Irwin Unger, *The Best of Intentions: The Triumphs and Failures of the Great Society Under Kennedy, Johnson, and Nixon* (New York: Doubleday, 1996), 28, 92–93; Allen J. Matusow, *The Unraveling of America: A History of Liberalism in the 1960s* (New York: Harper & Row, 1984), 239.

6. Matusow, *The Unraveling of America*, 239; James T. Patterson, *America's Struggle Against Poverty, 1900–1994* (Cambridge, MA: Harvard University Press, 1994 [1981]), 192–194; Joan Hoff, *Nixon Reconsidered* (New York: Basic, 1994), 115–119; Dominic Sandbrook, *Eugene McCarthy and the Rise and Fall of Postwar American Liberalism* (New York: Random House, 2004), 233.

7. Unger, *Best of Intentions*, 195; Gareth Davies, *From Opportunity to Entitlement: The Transformation and Decline of Great Society Liberalism* (Lawrence: University of Kansas Press, 1996), 97–102.

8. Edward D. Berkowitz, *Mr. Social Security: The Life of Wilbur J. Cohen* (Lawrence: University Press of Kansas, 1995), 167; James L. Sundquist, *Politics and Policy: The Eisenhower, Kennedy, and Johnson Years* (Washington, DC: Brookings Institution, 1968), 290, 298.

9. Unger, *Best of Intentions*, 35.

10. Randall B. Woods, *Prisoners of Hope: Lyndon Johnson, the Great Society, and the Limits of Liberalism* (New York: Basic, 2016), 153–154.

11. F. Peter Libassi to Cater, Califano, and Nicholas Katzenbach, May 13, 1966, and F. Peter Libassi to Cater, Califano, and Nicholas Katzenbach, July 15, 1966, "Material on Title VI, Civil Rights Bill," Box 52, Office Files of Douglass Cater, LBJ Library.

12. "Guidelines for Compliance with Title VI of the Civil Rights Act of 1964," n.d., "Material on Title VI, Civil Rights Bill," Box 52, Office Files of Douglass Cater, LBJ Library.

13. Francis Keppel OH, April 21, 1969, 17–19, 26, LBJ Library; Transcript, undated, "School Desegregation," Box 8, Office Files of Joseph Califano, LBJ Library.

14. J. Michael Ross, "Trends in Black Student Racial Isolation, 1968–1992," Office of Educational Research and Improvement, US Department of Education, 1995.

15. Joshua Zeitz, *Building the Great Society: Inside Lyndon Johnson's White House* (New York: Viking, 2018), 191–192.

16. "Consumer Price Index, 1913–," Federal Reserve Bank of Minneapolis, www.minneapolisfed.org/about-us/monetary-policy/inflation-calculator/consumer-price-index-1913-; "Labor Force Statistics from the Current Population Survey," Bureau of Labor Statistics, Department of Labor, www.bls.gov/cps.

17. Annual GDP growth in the United States, 1961–1969: 2.3 percent, 6.1 percent, 4.4 percent, 5.8 percent, 6.4 percent, 6.5 percent, 2.5 percent, 4.8 percent, 3.1 percent, respectively. See "World Bank Open Data," https://data.worldbank.org.

18. See United States Census Bureau, "Historical Income Levels: Households," www.census.gov/data/tables/time-series/demo/income-poverty/historical-income-households.html.

19. Frank Levy, *The New Dollars and Dreams: American Incomes and Economic Change* (New York: Russell Sage Foundation, 1998), 102.

20. United States Census Bureau, "Historical Living Arrangements of Children," www.census.gov/data/tables/time-series/demo/families/children.html; Alana Semuels, "How Poor Single Moms Survive," *Atlantic*, December 1, 2015, www.theatlantic.com/business/archive/2015/12/how-poor-single-moms-survive/418158.

21. "More and More Americans Are Outside the Labor Force Entirely. Who Are They?," Pew Research Center, November 14, 2014, www.pewresearch.org/fact-tank/2014/11/14/more-and-more-americans-are-outside-the-labor-force-entirely-who-are-they.

22. US Bureau of Labor Statistics, "Union Membership in the United States (September 2016), 2, 4, www.bls.gov/spotlight/2016/union-membership-in-the-united-states/home.htm; Jacob Hacker, "Failing the Middle Class: The Real Dangers to the American Middle Class," *Challenge* 50, no. 3 (May/June 2007): 26–42.

23. US Department of Agriculture, SNAP Data Tables, www.fns.usda.gov/pd/supplemental-nutrition-assistance-program-snap; Centers for Medicare & Medicaid Services, "Latest Enrollment Figures," December 21, 2021, www.cms.gov/newsroom/news-alert/cms-releases-latest-enrollment-figures-medicare-medicaid-and-childrens-health-insurance-program-chip; USDA Economic Research Service, "National School Lunch Program," www.ers.usda.gov/topics/food-nutrition-assistance/child-nutrition-programs/national-school-lunch-program; US Department of Health and Human Services, "CMS Fast Facts," www.cms.gov/Research-Statistics-Data-and-Systems/Statistics-Trends-and-Reports/CMS-Fast-Facts.

24. Jane Waldfogel, "The Safety Net for Families with Children," in *Legacies of the War on Poverty*, ed. Martha J. Bailey and Sheldon Danziger (New York: Russell Sage Foundation, 2013), 155–158.

25. Martha J. Bailey and Sheldon Danziger, eds., *Legacies of the War on Poverty* (New York: Russell Sage Foundation, 2013), 12–14.

26. Mark K. Updegrove, *Indomitable Will: LBJ in the Presidency* (New York: Crown, 2012), 153.

27. United States Census Bureau, "Historical Poverty Tables: People and Families, 1959–2019," www.census.gov/data/tables/time-series/demo/income-poverty/historical-poverty-people.html.

28. Elizabeth Cascio and Sarah Reber, "The K–12 Education Battle," in *Legacies of the War on Poverty*, 73.

29. Patrick McGuinn and Frederick Hess, "Freedom from Ignorance? The Great Society and the Evolution of the Elementary and Secondary Education Act of 1965," in *The Great Society and the High Tide of American Liberalism*, ed. Sidney M. Milkis and Jerome M. Mileur (Amherst: University of Massachusetts Press, 2005), 302–303.

30. Chris Weller, "Hillary Clinton Nearly Ran for President on a Policy of Giving People Unconditional Free Money," *Business Insider*, September 12, 2017, www.businessinsider.in/hillary-clinton-nearly-ran-for-president-on-a-policy-of-giving-people-unconditional-free-money/articleshow/60487639.cms.

31. Christopher Pulliam and Richard V. Reeves, "New Child Tax Credit Could Slash Child Poverty Now and Push Social Mobility Later," Brookings Institution, March 11, 2021, www.brookings.edu/blog/up-front/2021/03/11/new-child-tax-credit-could-slash-poverty-now-and-boost-social-mobility-later.

32. "Biden Administration Prompts Largest Permanent Increase in Food Stamps," *New York Times*, August 15, 2021, www.nytimes.com/2021/08/15/us/politics/biden-food-stamps.html.

33. Quoted in Vaughn Davis Bornet, *The Presidency of Lyndon B. Johnson* (Lawrence: University Press of Kansas, 1983), 9.

Chapter 16: Police Violence by Elizabeth Hinton

1. Tom Cotton, "Send in the Troops," *New York Times*, June 3, 2020, www.nytimes.com/2020/06/03/opinion/tom-cotton-protests-military.html.

2. St. Paul sources include "Unrest Hits St. Paul; Several Hurt," *Ann Arbor (MI) News*, August 31, 1968 (no page number given), Folder "Minnesota—St. Paul August 30–31, 1968," Box 9, Lemberg Center for the Study of Violence Collection (hereafter "LCSVC"); "12 Officers Hurt in St. Paul Riot," *Baltimore Sun*, September 1, 1968, 4;

"St. Paul Quiet After Violence," *Norfolk Virginian*, September 2, 1968, 4; "St. Paul Quiet Again," *Ann Arbor (MI) News*, September 2, 1968, 8; "St. Paul Quiet," *New York Times*, September 2, 1968 (no page number given), in LCSVC; Nick Woltman, "50 Years Ago, St. Paul Police Tear Gassed a Barricaded Dance Hall," *Twin Cities (MN) Pioneer Press*, August 31, 2018, www.twincities.com/2018/08/31/stem-hall-race-riots-st-paul-labor-day-weekend-1968-50-years-ago-police-civil-rights-investigation; "Minneapolis Calls Guard to End Riots," *Chicago Tribune*, July 22, 1967, 6.

3. "Timeline of Black Rebellions," in Elizabeth Hinton, *America on Fire: The Untold History of Police Violence and Black Rebellion Since the 1960s* (New York: Liveright, 2021); Michael W. Flamm, *In the Heat of the Summer: The New York Riots of 1964 and the War on Crime* (Philadelphia: University of Pennsylvania Press, 2016).

4. Elizabeth Hinton, "Policing Unrest and Collective Violence," *Science* 374, no. 6565 (2021): 272–274; Stuart Schrader, *Badges Without Borders: How Global Counterinsurgency Transformed American Policing* (Berkeley: University of California Press, 2019).

5. "West Side Violence Subsides," *Akron (OH) Beacon Journal*, September 14, 1970, A1.

6. On "potential delinquency" see Elizabeth Hinton, *From the War on Poverty to the War on Crime* (Cambridge, MA: Harvard University Press, 2016).

7. Quoted in Woltman, "50 Years Ago."

8. Michael O. Zahn, "Racine Unrest Flares Again," *Milwaukee Journal*, August 5, 1968, 1; "12 Arrested, Man Shot as Disorders Continue," *Racine (WI) Journal-Times*, August 5, 1968, 1; Joseph R. McClure, "A City's Centennial: Harrisburg's 1960 Celebration as a Pivotal Event," MA thesis, American Studies, Pennsylvania State University at Harrisburg, 2015.

9. Woltman, "50 Years Ago"; Ehsan Alam, "Before It Was Cut in Half by I-94, St. Paul's Rondo Was a Thriving African-American Cultural Center," *MinnPost*, June 19, 2017, www.minnpost.com/mnopedia/2017/06/it-was-cut-half-i-94-st-paul-s-rondo-was-thriving-african-american-cultural-center.

10. Woltman, "50 Years Ago."

11. Woltman, "50 Years Ago."

12. Woltman, "50 Years Ago."

13. "12 Officers Hurt in St. Paul Riot"; "St. Paul Quiet After Violence"; "St. Paul Quiet Again"; "St. Paul Quiet"; Woltman, "50 Years Ago."

14. Woltman, "50 Years Ago."

15. Federal Bureau of Investigation, *The Prevention and Control of Mobs and Riots* (Washington, DC: US Government Printing Office, 1967), 82; *To Establish Justice, to Insure Domestic Tranquility* (Washington, DC: US Government Printing Office, 1969), 71.

16. *National Advisory Commission on Civil Disorders, Report* (Washington, DC: US Government Printing Office, 1968), 9; see also Chapter 12, "Control of Disorder"; Schrader, *Badges Without Borders*, 197; Anna Feigenbaum, *Tear Gas: From the Battlefields of World War I to the Streets of Today* (Brooklyn: Verso, 2017), 2; Howard Hu, "Tear Gas—Harassing Agent or Toxic Chemical Weapon?," *Journal of the American Medical Association* 262, no. 5 (1989): 660–663.

17. Feigenbaum, *Tear Gas*, 69.

18. Quoted in Seymour M. Hersh, "Poison Gas in Vietnam," *New York Review of Books*, May 9, 1968; Maryland State Police, *Manual on Civil Disturbances*, no date given (after 1971); Hu, "Tear Gas," 660–663.

19.. Feigenbaum, *Tear Gas*, 74; Hersh, "Poison Gas in Vietnam"; Schrader, *Badges Without Borders*, 197.

20. Rohini J. Haar et al., "Death, Injury and Disability from Kinetic Impact Projectiles in Crowd-Control Settings: A Systematic Review," *British Medical Journal* 7, no. 12 (2017), https://bmjopen.bmj.com/content/7/12/e018154.

21. K. K. Rebecca Lai, Bill Marsh, and Anjali Singhvi, "Here Are the 100 U.S. Cities Where Protesters Were Tear Gassed," *New York Times*, June 18, 2020, www.nytimes.com/interactive/2020/06/16/us/george-floyd-protests-police-tear-gas.html; Colby Itkowitz and John Wagner, "Trump Calls Use of Tear Gas, Other Force on Minneapolis Protestors 'a Beautiful Scene,'" *Washington Post*, June 12, 2020, www.inquirer.com/politics/nation/trump-george-floyd-protests-beautiful-scene-tear-gas-force-minneapolis-20200612.html; Tom Jackman and Carol D. Leonnig, "National Guard Officer Says Police Suddenly Moved on Lafayette Square Protestors, Used 'Excessive Force' Before Trump Visit," *Washington Post*, July 27, 2020, www.washingtonpost.com/nation/2020/07/27/national-guard-commander-says-police-suddenly-moved-lafayette-square-protesters-used-excessive-force-clear-path-trump.

22. "Demonstrations & Political Violence in America: New Data for Summer 2020," Armed Conflict Location & Event Data Project (ACLED), September 2020, https://acleddata.com/2020/09/03/demonstrations-political-violence-in-america-new-data-for-summer-2020; Samantha Campbell, "Scenes of Chaos Unfold After a Peaceful Vigil in Ferguson," *New York Times*, August 12, 2014, www.nytimes.com/2014/08/13/us/after-a-peaceful-vigil-in-ferguson-scenes-of-chaos-unfold.html; Kim Barker, Mike Baker, and Ali Watkins, "In City After City, Police Mishandled Black Lives Matter Protests," *New York Times*, March 20, 2021, 1.

Chapter 17: Insurrection by Kathleen Belew

1. This chapter represents a synthesis of research in a large number of archival collections of materials written by and about the white power movement. These include more than two dozen white power periodicals, newsletters, and autobiographies; court records; documents obtained from the FBI, ATF, and DOJ; and contemporary journalistic accounts in and beyond the United States. For an itemized bibliography, please see Kathleen Belew, *Bring the War Home: The White Power Movement and Paramilitary America* (Cambridge, MA: Harvard University Press, 2018), 319–332. For reactions to the events of 1/6, see Lindsay Crouse, Adam Westbrook, and Sanya Dosani, "Stop Pretending 'This Is Not Who We Are,'" *New York Times*, January 8, 2021, www.nytimes.com/video/opinion/100000007538961/capitol-riot-america.html.

2. PolitiFact, "Andrew Clyde," May 12, 2021, www.politifact.com/factchecks/2021/may/13/andrew-clyde/ridiculous-claim-those-capitol-jan-6-resembled-nor/; "Inside the Capitol Riot: An Exclusive Video Investigation," *New York Times*, June 30, 2021; Caroline Vakil, "Stefanik in Ad Says Democrats Want 'Permanent Election Insurrection,'" *The Hill*, September 16, 2021; on refusal of subpoenas by the US House of Representatives January 6 Committee, see for instance David Smith, "Steve Bannon Indicted for Refusal to Comply with Capitol Attack Subpoena," *Guardian*, November 12, 2021.

3. Kathleen Belew, "Lynching and Power in the United States: Southern, Western, and National Vigilante Violence from Early America to the Present," *History Compass* 12, no. 1 (January 2014), https://doi.org/10.1111/hic3.12121; Lisa Arellano, *Vigilantes*

and Lynch Mobs: Narratives of Community and Nation (Philadelphia: Temple University Press, 2012); Christopher Waldrep, *The Many Faces of Judge Lynch: Punishment and Extralegal Violence in America* (New York: Palgrave Macmillan, 2002); Richard Maxwell Brown, *Strain of Violence: Historical Studies of American Violence and Vigilantism* (New York: Oxford University Press, 1975); W. Fitzhugh Brundage, *Lynching in the New South: Georgia and Virginia, 1880–1930* (Urbana and Chicago: University of Illinois Press, 1993); Catherine McNicol Stock, *Rural Radicals: Righteous Rage in the American Grain* (Ithaca, NY: Cornell University Press, 1996); Linda Gordon, *The Great Arizona Orphan Abduction* (Cambridge: Harvard University Press, 2001).

4. Belew, "Lynching and Power in the United States," 84–99.

5. Department of Homeland Security, "Homeland Threat Assessment October 2020," www.dhs.gov/sites/default/files/publications/2020_10_06_homeland-threat -assessment.pdf; quoted in Leah Sottile, "The Chaos Agents: Inside the Boogaloo," *New York Times Magazine*, August 19, 2020, www.nytimes.com/interactive/2020/08 /19/magazine/boogaloo.html.

6. Belew, *Bring the War Home*.

7. Belew, *Bring the War Home*.

8. Although the leftist demonstrators did have weapons, these were uniformly inferior in quality and capacity; also, many of the weapons were in locked cars when the shooting began.

9. Belew, *Bring the War Home*, 55–76. Accounts of the shooting appear in *Greensboro Truth and Reconciliation Commission Final Report* (Greensboro, NC: Greensboro Truth and Reconciliation Commission, 2006); Max Elbaum, *Revolution in the Air: Sixties Radicals Turn to Lenin, Mao, and Che* (New York: Verso, 2002); David Cunningham, *There's Something Happening Here: The New Left, the Klan, and FBI Counter-intelligence* (Berkeley: University of California Press, 2004); Signe Waller, *Love and Revolution* (Lanham, MD: Rowman and Littlefield, 2002); Sally Avery Bermanzohn, *Through Survivor's Eyes: From the Sixties to the Greensboro Massacre* (Nashville, TN: Vanderbilt University Press, 2003); Elizabeth Wheaton, *Codename: GREENKILL: The 1979 Greensboro Massacre* (Athens: University of Georgia Press, 1987); and Mab Segrest, *Memoir of a Race Traitor* (Boston: South End, 1999). On racism and anticommunism, see, for instance, Jane Dailey, "Sex, Segregation, and the Sacred After *Brown*," *Journal of American History* 91, no. 119 (2004): 119–144; Robin D. G. Kelley, *Hammer and Hoe: Alabama Communists During the Great Depression* (Chapel Hill: University of North Carolina Press, 1990); and Peggy Pascoe, *What Comes Naturally: Miscegenation Law and the Making of Race in America* (Oxford: Oxford University Press, 2009), 287–306.

10. Belew, *Bring the War Home*, 51.

11. On the declaration of war, see Belew, *Bring the War Home*, 104. Although Leaderless Resistance is similar in structure to leftist guerilla warfare, the leaders of the movement took pains to say that they took the strategy not from activists of color but from the US military, specifically from a 1962 tract by Colonel Ulius Louis Amoss, which laid out hopes that an army of communist exiles would one day take up arms against the Soviet Union in alliance with the West, led not by orders but by "leading ideas." Ulius Louis Amoss, "Leaderless Resistance," *Inform* 6205 (April 17, 1962), Wisconsin Historical Society. Within the white power movement, see Louis R. Beam, "Leaderless Resistance," *Seditionist* 12 (February 1992), Intelligence Project Holdings, Southern Poverty Law

Center. Beam's other writings on Leaderless Resistance include Louis R. Beam, *Essays of a Klansman*, (Hayden Lake, ID: A.K.I.A., 1983); Louis Beam, Estes Park speech, October 23, 1992, video recording, Southern Poverty Law Center. Many otherwise excellent accounts have portrayed Leaderless Resistance as a strategy that emerged in the 1990s, rather than a decade earlier. See, for instance, Kathleen M. Blee, *Inside Organized Racism: Women in the Hate Movement* (Berkeley: University of California Press, 2002); Morris Dees with James Corcoran, *Gathering Storm: America's Militia Threat* (New York: HarperCollins, 1996); Betty A. Dobratz and Stephanie L. Shanks-Meile, *The White Separatist Movement in the United States: "White Power, White Pride!"* (New York: Twayne, 1997); Andrew Gumbel and Roger G. Charles, *Oklahoma City: What the Investigation Missed—and Why It Still Matters* (New York: William Morrow, 2012); and Stock, *Rural Radicals*.

12. On civil cases that rendered effective actions, see especially *Vietnamese Fishermen's Association, et al., v. The Knights of the Ku Klux Klan, et al.*, no. H-81-895, 518 F. Supp. 198 (1982); 34 Fed. R. Serv. 2d (Callaghan) 875; June 3, 1982; and *Donald, et al. v. United Klans of America, et al.*, no. 84-0725-CS (1984). See also below, *Bring the War Home*, 148–150.

13. This phrase was used within the movement to describe white power activism and was increasingly used for domestic terror, rather than criminal violence, from the 1980s onward. Belew, *Bring the War Home*, 127.

14. On the concept of Leaderless Resistance changing movement attitudes toward recruitment as a measure of success, see Dobratz and Shanks-Meile, *The White Separatist Movement in the United States*.

15. Belew, *Bring the War Home*, 120–121, 127, 133, 144, 172.

16. Belew, *Bring the War Home: Liberty Net*, 104–134; assassination of Alan Berg, 122–124, 132–133, 180; other targets, 104; cyanide, 134.

17. These numbers, drawn from Southern Poverty Law Center and Center for Democratic Renewal estimates, appear in Dobratz and Shanks-Meile, *The White Separatist Movement in the United States*; Raphael S. Ezekiel, *The Racist Mind: Portraits of American Neo-Nazis and Klansmen* (New York: Penguin, 1995); and Abby L. Ferber and Michael Kimmel, "Reading Right: The Western Tradition in White Supremacist Discourse," *Sociological Focus* 33, no. 2 (May 2000): 193–213. Examples of social movement activity in each circle appear in Belew, *Bring the War Home*.

18. Sara Diamond, *Roads to Dominion: Right-Wing Movements and Political Power in the United States* (New York: Guilford, 1995). See also Michael Zatarain, *David Duke: Evolution of a Klansman* (Gretna, LA: Pelican, 1990); and Leonard Zeskind, *Blood and Politics: The History of the White Nationalist Movement from the Margins to the Mainstream* (New York: Farrar, Straus and Giroux, 2009).

19. On targeted recruitment, see Belew, *Bring the War Home*: prisoners, 25, 67, 113–114; veterans, 52, 113; active-duty troops, 24, 32, 34, 52, 75, 113, 136, 141, 194.

20. Kathleen M. Blee, *Women of the Klan: Racism and Gender in the 1920s* (Berkeley: University of California Press, 1991), and Blee, *Inside Organized Racism*.

21. Belew, *Bring the War Home*, 196.

22. Kathleen Belew, "'A Model Aryan Wife and Mother': Women in the White Power Movement," *Journal of American History*, in revision.

23. See, for instance, Belew, *Bring the War Home*, 201–208.

24. *The Turner Diaries* was first printed in serial in National Alliance, *Attack!*, 1974–1976, SC, Box 31, Folder 9, and then published as Andrew Macdonald, *The Turner Diaries* (Hillsboro, WV: National Vanguard, 1978). See Belew, *Bring the War Home*: Leaderless Resistance in *The Turner Diaries*, 112–113; *Turner Diaries* and the Oklahoma City bombing, 210, 221–223, 226; the Order modeled on *Turner Diaries*, 116, 118, 126; plot and message of *Turner Diaries*, 110–111; read by the Order, 115; reissued call for Leaderless Resistance, 205; unity in white power movement, 11; white victory in, 281–282n43; white women's activism in, 165. See also Belew, "'A War for the Survival of Our People': Conspiracy and Combat in the White Power Movement, 1983–1995," in *Conspiracy/Theory*, ed. Joseph Masco and Lisa Wedeen (Princeton, NJ: Princeton University Press, forthcoming).

25. The Branch Davidians, a multiracial religious sect, were nevertheless understood within the movement as a white power–affiliated community.

26. Quoted from FBI internal documents. See Gumbel and Charles, *Oklahoma City*, 262. On the use of similar tactics in communities of color, see Kimberley L. Phillips, *War! What Is It Good For? Black Freedom Struggles and the U.S. Military from World War II to Iraq* (Chapel Hill: University of North Carolina Press, 2012); and Leslie Gill, *The School of the Americas: Military Training and Political Violence in the Americas* (Durham, NC: Duke University Press, 2004).

27. Belew, *Bring the War Home*.

28. Belew, *Bring the War Home*, 207–239.

29. Donald J. Trump, press conference, August 15, 2017, MSNBC, www.youtube.com/watch?v=JmaZR8E12bs.

30. Sheryl Gay Stolberg, "Hurt and Angry, Charlottesville Tries to Regroup from Violence," *New York Times*, August 13, 2017, A1. Additional fact-checking from snopes.com verifies that Virginia governor Terry McAuliffe's assessment of the militias as being better equipped than police was correct: Bethania Palma, "Were Police 'Outgunned' by White Supremacists Who Stashed Weapons Around Charlottesville?," snopes.com, August 19, 2017, www.snopes.com/news/2017/08/19/were-police-outgunned-by-white-supremacists.

31. Steve Contorno, "Memo Reveals a House Republican Strategy on Shootings: Downplay White Nationalism, Blame Left," *Tampa Bay Times*, August 16, 2019, www.tampabay.com/florida-politics/buzz/2019/08/16/memo-reveals-a-house-republican-strategy-on-shootings-downplay-white-nationalism-blame-left.

32. Sottile, "Chaos Agents"; Nick Visser, "FBI Director Says Domestic Extremism 'Metastasizing' Around the Country," *Huffington Post*, March 3, 2021.

33. Robert A. Pape, "New Survey Shows Mainstream Community Support for Violence to Restore Trump Remains Strong," CPost, January 2, 2022.

Chapter 18: Family Values Feminism by Natalia Mehlman Petrzela

1. Elisabeth Bumiller, "Schlafly's Gala Goodbye to ERA," *Washington Post*, July 1, 1982, C1, C6.

2. Lynn Rosellini, "Victory Is Bittersweet for Architect of Amendment's Downfall," *New York Times*, July 1, 1982, A12.

3. Megan Rosenfeld, "Sic Transit, Gloria: Phyllis Schlafly and Company Mark the End of an ERA," *Washington Post*, March 23, 1979, C1, C3.

4. Nancy A. Hewitt, *Women's Activism and Social Change: Rochester, New York, 1822–1872* (Ithaca, NY: Cornell University Press, 1984), 103.

5. Quoted in Louise Michele Newman, *White Women's Rights: The Racial Origins of Feminism in the United States* (New York: Oxford University Press, 1999), 68.

6. Martha S. Jones, *Vanguard: How Black Women Broke Barriers, Won the Vote, and Insisted on Equality for All* (New York: Basic, 2020).

7. Linda Gordon, *Pitied but Not Entitled: Single Mothers and the History of Welfare, 1890–1935* (Cambridge: Cambridge University Press, 1998), 91.

8. Christine Stansell, *The Feminist Promise: 1792 to the Present* (New York: Modern Library, 2010).

9. "Age of Consent Raised to 16," *Wilmington (NC) Morning Star-News*, February 7, 1995, 3B.

10. Mary E. Odem, *Delinquent Daughters: Protecting and Policing Adolescent Sexuality in the United States, 1885–1920* (Chapel Hill: University of North Carolina Press, 1994).

11. Notably, it was Black conservative Herman Cain who spread this myth as part of a 2010 GOP effort to defund Planned Parenthood. Peter Dreier, "The GOP's Attacks on Margaret Sanger and Planned Parenthood," *Dissent*, November 30, 2011, www.dissentmagazine.org/online_articles/the-gops-attacks-on-margaret-sanger-and-planned-parenthood.

12. "Eisenhower Backs Birth-Curb Aids," *New York Times*, November 10, 1964, 19.

13. Amelia Thomson-DeVeaux, "The Strange Bedfellows of the Anti-contraception Alliance," *American Prospect*, March 17, 2014, https://prospect.org/power/strange-bedfellows-anti-contraception-alliance.

14. John Steinbacher, *The Child Seducers* (San Marino, CA: Educator Publications, 1969).

15. US Department of Labor, "The Negro Family: The Case for National Action," March 1965, 3, https://liberalarts.utexas.edu/coretexts/_files/resources/texts/1965%20Moynihan%20Report.pdf.

16. Serena Mayeri, "Historicizing the 'End of Men': The Politics of Reaction(s)," *Boston University Law Review* 93 (2013): 729–744; Robert O. Self, "Breadwinner Liberalism and Its Discontents in the American Welfare State," in *Democracy and the Welfare State: The Two Wests in the Age of Austerity*, ed. Alice Kessler-Harris and Maurizio Vaudagna (New York: Columbia University Press, 2018), 273–294.

17. Stephanie Gilmore and Elizabeth Kaminski, "A Part and Apart: Lesbian and Straight Activists Negotiate Identity in a Second-Wave Organization," *Journal of the History of Sexuality* 16, no. 1 (January 2007): 95–113.

18. Kirsten Swinth, *Feminism's Forgotten Fight: The Unfinished Struggle for Work and Family* (Cambridge, MA: Harvard University Press, 2018); Boston Women's Health Collective, *Our Bodies, Ourselves* (Boston: New England Free Press, 1970); Jeannine O'Brien Medvin, *Prenatal Yoga and Natural Childbirth* (Mendocino, CA: Freestone, 1974).

19. Jordan Bonfante, "Germaine Greer," *LIFE*, May 7, 1971, 30–32.

20. Linda Feeney, Patricia Boyd, and two others, letter to the editor, *Boston Globe*, April 6, 1976, 20.

21. Pauline B. Bart, "Seeking Justice for Victims of Marital Rape," *Philadelphia Inquirer*, December 22, 1985, 7.

22. Jennifer A. Bennice and Patricia Resick, "Marital Rape: History, Research, and Practice," *Trauma, Violence & Abuse* 4, no. 3 (2003): 228–246, www.jstor.org /stable/26636357.

23. Megan A. Sholar, *Getting Paid While Taking Time: The Women's Movement and the Development of Paid Family Leave Policies in the United States* (Philadelphia: Temple University Press, 2016).

24. Catherine R. Stimpson, "Family, Feminism, Both Misunderstood," *Berkeley Gazette*, October 20, 1980, 12.

25. Stephanie Coontz, *The Way We Never Were: American Families and the Nostalgia Trap* (New York: Basic, 1993).

26. Pamela Warrick, "The Fall from Spyglass Hill," *Los Angeles Times*, April 29, 1998, E1, E6.

Chapter 19: Reagan Revolution by Julian E. Zelizer

1. Rowland Evans and Robert Novak, *The Reagan Revolution* (New York: Dutton, 1981), xiv.

2. Ronald Reagan, "Farewell Address," January 11, 1989, American Rhetoric Project, www.americanrhetoric.com/speeches/ronaldreaganfarewelladdress.html.

3. Martin Anderson, *Revolution: The Reagan Legacy* (Stanford, CA: Hoover Institution, 1988), 6.

4. Steve Fraser and Gary Gerstle, eds., *The Rise and Fall of the New Deal Order, 1930–1980* (Princeton, NJ: Princeton University Press, 1989).

5. Quoted in Gil Troy, *Morning in America: How Ronald Reagan Invented the 1980s* (Princeton, NJ: Princeton University Press, 2005), 17.

6. Dinesh D'Souza, *Ronald Reagan: How an Ordinary Man Became an Extraordinary Leader* (New York: Touchstone, 1999), 254.

7. Gerald F. Seib, *We Should Have Seen It Coming: From Reagan to Trump—A Front-Row Seat to a Political Revolution* (New York: Random House, 2020), vii.

8. For a series of essays challenging this volume, including my own work on Reagan, see Gary Gerstle, Nelson Lichtenstein, and Alice O'Connor, eds., *Beyond the New Deal Order: U.S. Politics from the Great Depression to the Great Recession* (Philadelphia: University of Pennsylvania Press, 2019).

9. Gil Troy, *The Reagan Revolution: A Very Short Introduction* (New York: Oxford University Press, 2009), 52.

10. Laura Kalman, *Right Star Rising: A New Politics, 1974–1980* (New York: W. W. Norton, 2010).

11. Sean Wilentz, *The Age of Reagan: A History, 1974–2008* (New York: Harper, 2008). See also Rick Perlstein, *Reaganland: America's Right Turn, 1976–1980* (New York: Simon & Schuster, 2020).

12. Lou Cannon, *President Reagan: The Role of a Lifetime* (New York: PublicAffairs, 1991), 203.

13. Helen Dewar, "Reagan Attacks Democrats on Social Security," *Washington Post*, July 21, 1982, www.washingtonpost.com/archive/politics/1981/07/21 /reagan-attacks-democrats-on-social-security/dcfce33d-39e9-4114-ac69-d5e42dcfd1bb.

14. Sally R. Sherman, "Public Attitudes Toward Social Security," *Social Security Bulletin* 52, no. 12 (December 1989): 10–12.

15. Paul Pierson, *Dismantling the Welfare State? Reagan, Thatcher and the Politics of Retrenchment* (Cambridge: Cambridge University Press, 1994).

16. Hedrick Smith, "Reagan at Midterm," *New York Times*, December 29, 1982, www .nytimes.com/1982/12/29/us/reagan-at-midterm-news-analysis.html.

17. Steven Roberts, "New Conflict a Threat to Old Ways," *New York Times*, May 19, 1984, 7.

18. Julian E. Zelizer, *Burning Down the House: Newt Gingrich, the Fall of a Speaker and the Rise of the New Republican Party* (New York: Penguin, 2020), 60.

19. Hedrick Smith, "Reagan's Effort to Change Course of Government," *New York Times*, October 23, 1984, www.nytimes.com/1984/10/23/us/reagan-s-effort-to-change -course-of-government.html; Bruce Schulman, *The Seventies: The Great Shift in American Culture, Society and Politics* (New York: Free Press, 2001), 235; James T. Patterson, *Restless Giant: The United States from Watergate to Bush v. Gore* (New York: Oxford University Press, 2005), 165.

20. Robert Pear, "Conservatives Disappointed with 'Shift' by Reagan," *New York Times*, June 26, 1983, www.nytimes.com/1983/06/26/us/conservatives-disappointed -with-shift-by-reagan.html.

21. Tip O'Neill and William Novak, "Former House Speaker Tip O'Neill Calls the President Amiable but Short on Details," *South Florida Sun Sentinel* (Fort Lauderdale, FL), September 13, 1987, www.sun-sentinel.com/news/fl-xpm-1987-09-13 -8703130479-story.html. See also Chris Matthews, *Tip and the Gipper: When Politics Worked* (New York: Simon & Schuster, 2013).

22. Lou Cannon, *Governor Reagan: His Rise to Power* (New York: PublicAffairs, 2003).

23. Jacob Hacker, "Privatizing Risk Without Privatizing the Welfare State: The Hidden Politics of Social Policy Retrenchment in the United States," *American Political Science Review* 98, no. 2 (May 2004): 243–260; Nolan M. McCarty, "The Policy Effects of Political Polarization," in *The Transformation of American Politics*, ed. Paul Pierson and Theda Skocpol (Princeton, NJ: Princeton University Press, 2007), 223–256.

24. Spencer Rich, "'Safety Net' Strands Thinner Under Reagan," *Washington Post*, November 27, 1988, www.washingtonpost.com/archive/politics/1988/11/27 /safety-net-strands-thinner-under-reagan/74e881aa-072a-4e41-96a2-0e2f3744689c.

25. Julian E. Zelizer, *Arsenal of Democracy: The Politics of National Security—From World War II to the War on Terrorism* (New York: Basic, 2010), 300–354.

26. Lawrence S. Wittner, *Toward Nuclear Abolition: A History of the World Nuclear Disarmament Movement, 1971 to the Present* (Stanford, CA: Stanford University Press, 2003); Frances Fitzgerald, *Way Out There in the Blue: Reagan, Star Wars, and the End of the Cold War* (New York: Simon & Schuster, 2000).

27. Joyce Wadler and Merrill Brown, "New York Rally Draws Half a Million," *Washington Post*, June 13, 1982, www.washingtonpost.com/archive/politics/1982/06/13 /new-york-rally-draws-half-million/2a1258be-a17f-4e41-bf12-9368766b32cf.

28. Abigail Trafford, "How Americans Deal with Their Nuclear Anxiety," *Washington Post*, December 8, 1987, www.washingtonpost.com/archive/lifestyle /wellness/1987/12/08/how-americans-deal-with-their-nuclear-anxiety/4e659edd-73cb -4911-b519-cedac15d7af3.

29. Quoted in David Hoffman, "President's Address at U.N. Conciliatory Toward Soviets," *Washington Post*, September 25, 1984, www.washingtonpost.com/archive /politics/1984/09/25/presidents-address-at-un-conciliatory-toward-soviets/837d5bf9 -d6b8-4643-a1b9-18210617ed64.

30. Quoted in Meg Jacobs and Julian Zelizer, *Conservatives in Power: The Reagan Years, 1981–1989* (Boston: Bedford, 2010), 53.

31. Quoted in James Gerstenzang and Robert Shogan, "Conservatives Hit Reagan on Treaty," *Los Angeles Times*, December 5, 1987, www.latimes.com/archives/la-xpm-1987 -12-05-mn-6395-story.html.

32. Quoted in Zelizer, *Arsenal of Democracy*, 351.

33. Paul Lettow, *Ronald Reagan and His Quest to Abolish Nuclear Weapons* (New York: Random House, 2005).

34. Joe J. Ryan-Hume, "The National Organization for Women and the Democratic Party in Reagan's America," *Historical Journal* 64, no. 2 (March 2021): 454–476.

35. Quoted in Robin Toner, "Right to Abortion Draws Thousands to Capital Rally," *New York Times*, April 10, 1989, www.nytimes.com/1989/04/10/us/right-to-abortion -draws-thousands-to-capital-rally.html.

36. Samuel Hays, *Beauty, Health and Permanence: Environmental Politics in the United States 1955–1985* (New York: Cambridge University Press, 1987); Lily Geismer, *Don't Blame Us: Suburban Liberals and the Transformation of the Democratic Party* (Princeton, NJ: Princeton University Press, 2014); Neil Foley, *Front Porch Politics: The Forgotten Heyday of American Activism in the 1970s and 1980s* (New York: Hill & Wang, 2013).

37. Samuel Kernell and Gary C. Jacobson, *The Logic of American Politics*, 9th ed. (Washington, DC: CQ Press, 2019), 482.

38. Quoted in Isabel Wilkerson, "Jury Acquits All Transit Officers in 1983 Death of Michael Stewart," *New York Times*, November 25, 1985, www.nytimes.com/1985/11/25 /nyregion/jury-acquits-all-transit-officers-in-1983-death-of-michael-stewart.html.

39. Tom Rosenstiel, "Surge in Support for Social Safety Net," Pew Research Center, May 2, 2007, www.pewresearch.org/2007/05/02/surge-in-support-for-social-safety-net.

40. "Presidential Approval Ratings—Gallup Historical Statistics and Trends," 2020, https://news.gallup.com/poll/116677/presidential-approval-ratings-gallup-historical -statistics-trends.aspx.

41. Jeffrey M. Jones, "Obama Job Approval Ratings Most Politically Polarized by Far," Gallup, January 25, 2017, https://news.gallup.com/poll/203006/obama-job -approval-ratings-politically-polarized-far.aspx.

42. Frances Lee, *Insecure Majorities: Congress and the Perpetual Campaign* (Chicago: University of Chicago Press, 2016). See also Ezra Klein, *Why We're Polarized* (New York: Avid, 2020).

43. David Stockman, *The Triumph of Politics: Why the Reagan Revolution Failed* (New York: Harper and Row, 1986), 9.

Chapter 20: Voter Fraud by Carol Anderson

1. Courtney Vinopal, "2 out of 3 Americans Believe U.S. Democracy Is Under Threat," *PBS Newshour*, July 2, 2021, www.pbs.org/newshour/politics/2-out -of-3-americans-believe-u-s-democracy-is-under-threat.

2. Katie Benner and Adam Goldman, "Federal Prosecutors Push Back on Barr Memo on Voter Fraud Claims," *New York Times*, November 13, 2020, www.nytimes

.com/2020/11/13/us/politics/justice-department-voter-fraud.html?searchResult Position=2; Ed Pilkington, "DOJ Officials Condemn Barr's Approval of Voter Fraud Inquiries Without Evidence," *Guardian*, November 10, 2020, www.theguardian.com /us-news/2020/nov/10/william-barr-voter-fraud-inquiries-justice-department; "Trump and Barr Say Mail-In Voting Will Lead to Fraud. Experts Say That's Not True," CBS News, June 24, 2020, www.cbsnews.com/news/mail-in-voting-ballot-election-fraud -claims; Katie Benner, "Meadows Pressed Justice Dept. to Investigate Election Fraud Claims," *New York Times*, June 5, 2021, www.nytimes.com/2021/06/05/us/politics /mark-meadows-justice-department-election.html; Katie Benner, "Trump Pressed Official to Wield Justice Dept. to Back Election Claims," *New York Times*, June 15, 2021, www.nytimes.com/2021/06/15/us/politics/trump-justice-department-election.html.

3. United States Census Bureau, "Atlanta, Philadelphia, Milwaukee Quick Facts," accessed July 6, 2021, www.census.gov/quickfacts/fact/table/philadelphiacitypennsylvania ,milwaukeecitywisconsin,atlantacitygeorgia/PST045219.

4. Dmitriy Khavin et al., "Day of Rage: An In-Depth Look at How a Mob Stormed the Capitol," *New York Times*, July 3, 2021, www.nytimes.com/video/us/politics /100000007606996/capitol-riot-trump-supporters.html.

5. Alison Durkee, "'Kraken' Sanctions Hearing: Lin Wood Blames Sidney Powell in Attempt to Evade Punishment as Judge Expresses Skepticism," *Forbes*, July 12, 2021, www.forbes.com/sites/alisondurkee/2021/07/12/kraken-sanctions-hearing-lin-wood -blames-sidney-powell-in-attempt-to-evade-punishment-as-judge-expresses-skepticism /?sh=2d6d9553194a. The judge's assessment of the voter-fraud claims deals with Michigan.

6. Jonathan D. Karl, "Inside William Barr's Breakup with Trump," *Atlantic*, June 2021, www.theatlantic.com/politics/archive/2021-06/william-barrs-trump -administration-attorney-general/619298/?s=03.

7. "State Voting Bills Tracker 2021," Brennan Center for Justice, May 28, 2021, www.brennancenter.org/our-work/research-reports/state-voting-bills-tracker-2021; Sue Halpern, "The Republicans' Wild Assault on Voting Rights in Texas and Arizona," *New Yorker*, June 6, 2021, www.newyorker.com/magazine/2021/06/14/the-republicans-wild -assault-on-voting-rights-in-texas-and-arizona; Alex Ebert, "Sparse Voter-Fraud Cases Undercut Claims of Widespread Abuses," *Bloomberg*, July 21, 2021, https://news.bgov .com/ballots-and-boundaries/sparse-voter-fraud-cases-undercut-claims-of-widespread -abuses-1; Nolan D. McCaskill, "Trump's False Election Fraud Claims Fuel Michigan GOP Meltdown," *Politico*, July 30, 2021, www.politico.com/news/2021/07/30 /michigan-gop-trump-election-fraud-501701?cid=apn&s=03; FairFightAction, Twitter, February 19, 2021, https://t.co/5ipHJIAPjg.

8. Benjamin Ginsberg, "My Party Is Destroying Itself on the Altar of Trump," *Washington Post*, November 2, 2020, www.washingtonpost.com/opinions/2020/11/01 /ben-ginsberg-voter-suppression-republicans.

9. R. Volney Riser, "Disfranchisement, the U.S. Constitution, and the Federal Courts: Alabama's 1901 Constitutional Convention Debates the Grandfather Clause," *American Journal of Legal History* 48, no. 3 (July 2006): 237–279; Andrew Gumbel, "Election Fraud and the Myths of American Democracy," *Social Research* 75, no. 4 (Winter 2008): 1115; David Litt, "Claims of 'Voter Fraud' Have a Long History in America. And They Are False," *Guardian*, December 4, 2020, www.theguardian.com/commentisfree/2020 /dec/04/trump-voter-fraud-america-false; E. J. Dionne, "The GOP's Past Election Lies

Led to Trump's Big One," *Washington Post*, May 12, 2021, www.washingtonpost.com /opinions/the-gops-past-election-lies-led-to-trumps-big-one/2021/05/12/83ff231e -b359-11eb-9059-d8176b9e3798_story.html; Tova Wang, *The Politics of Voter Suppression: Defending and Expanding Americans' Right to Vote* (Ithaca, NY: Cornell University Press, 2012), 19.

10. Alexander Keyssar, *The Right to Vote: The Contested History of Democracy in the United States* (New York: Basic, 2009 [2000]), 157.

11. Gael Graham, "'The Lexington of White Supremacy': School and Local Politics in Late-Nineteenth-Century Laurinburg, North Carolina," *North Carolina Historical Review* 89, no. 1 (January 2012): 28; George E. Cunningham, "Constitutional Disenfranchisement of the Negro in Louisiana, 1898," *Negro History Bulletin* 29, no. 7 (April 1966): 147–148; John Wertheimer, *Law and Society in the South: A History of North Carolina Court Cases* (Lexington: University Press of Kentucky, 2009), 139–140; Gumbel, "Election Fraud and the Myths of American Democracy," 1115.

12. Quoted in Riser, "Disfranchisement, the U.S. Constitution, and the Federal Courts," 244.

13. Quoted in Eric Foner, *Reconstruction: America's Unfinished Revolution, 1863–1877* (New York: HarperPerennial, 2014), 775.

14. William Alexander Mabry, "Disfranchisement of the Negro in Mississippi," *Journal of Southern History* 4, no. 3 (August 1938): 319.

15. Quoted in US Commission on Civil Rights, "Racial and Ethnic Tensions in American Communities: Poverty, Inequality, and Discrimination—Volume VII: The Mississippi Delta Report: Chapter 3, Voting Rights and Political Representation in the Mississippi Delta," accessed November 27, 2020, www.usccr.gov/pubs/msdelta/ch3.htm.

16. Quoted in Michael Fellman, *In the Name of God and Country: Reconsidering Terrorism in American History* (New Haven, CT: Yale University Press, 2010), 139.

17. Lawrence B. Glickman, "Three Tropes of White Victimhood," *Atlantic*, July 20, 2021, www.theatlantic.com/ideas/archive/2021/07/three-tropes-white -victimhood/619463.

18. Gordon A. Martin Jr., *Count Them One by One: Black Mississippians Fighting for the Right to Vote* (Jackson: University Press of Mississippi, 2010), 7.

19. Mabry, "Disfranchisement of the Negro in Mississippi," 324.

20. *Williams v. Mississippi*, 170 U.S. 213 (1898); *Lassiter v. Northampton County Bd. of Elections*, 360 U.S. 45 (1959).

21. Michael Waldman, *The Fight to Vote* (New York: Simon & Schuster, 2016), 145.

22. Quoted in Martin Jr., *Count Them One by One*, 8; Waldman, *The Fight to Vote*, 142; "Alabama Black Belt Counties Registered Voters: 1960," Black Freedom Struggle in the 20th Century: Federal Government Records, "Black and White Voter Registrations Statistics and Voter Registration Programs" (January 1, 1961, to December 31, 1965 [accession number 001351-019-0492]), found in Civil Rights during the Kennedy Administration, 1961–1963, Part 2: The Papers of Burke Marshall, Assistant Attorney General for Civil Rights, accessed July 3, 2015, www.teachingforchang.org/wp-content /uploads/2014/12/1960registeredvoters.pdf; Charles S. Bullock and Ronald Keith Gaddie, "Voting Rights Progress in Georgia," *Legislation and Public Policy* 10, no. 1 (Fall 2006), 5.

23. Leah Wright Rigueur, *The Loneliness of the Black Republican* (Princeton, NJ: Princeton University Press, 2015), 59; Angie Maxwell and Todd Shields, *The Long*

Southern Strategy: How Chasing White Voters in the South Changed American Politics (New York: Oxford University Press, 2019), 19.

24. Carol Anderson, *Eyes off the Prize: The United Nations and the African American Struggle for Human Rights, 1944–1955* (New York: Cambridge University Press, 2003), 122.

25. Anderson, *Eyes off the Prize*, 122–125, 210–213; "Presidential Election: 1956," American Presidency Project, accessed July 30, 2021, www.presidency.ucsb.edu /statistics/elections/1956.

26. Rick Perlstein, "Exclusive: Lee Atwater's Infamous 1981 Interview on the Southern Strategy," *Nation*, November 13, 2012, www.thenation.com/article/archive /exclusive-lee-atwaters-infamous-1981-interview-southern-strategy; Kevin Phillips, *The Emerging Republican Majority* (New Rochelle, NY: Arlington House, 1969).

27. John R. Williams, "Aspects of the American Presidential Election of 1960," *Australian Quarterly* 33, no. 1 (March 1961): 25–36.

28. Timothy N. Thurber, *Republicans and Race: The GOP's Frayed Relationship with African Americans, 1945–1974* (Lawrence: University Press of Kansas, 2013), 176.

29. Carol Anderson, *White Rage: The Unspoken Truth of Our Racial Divide* (New York: Bloomsbury, 2017), 143.

30. Quoted in "Democrats Charge G.O.P. Poll Watch Today Will Harass the Negroes and the Poor; Republicans Say Honesty Is Goal; Assert 100,000 Sentinels in 35 Cities Will Seek Only to Avert Voting Fraud," *New York Times*, November 3, 1964, www.nytimes.com/1964/11/03/archives/democrats-charge-gop-poll-watch-today-will -harass-the-negroes-and.html.

31. Khalil Gibran Muhammad, *The Condemnation of Blackness: Race, Crime, and the Making of Modern Urban America* (Cambridge, MA: Harvard University Press, 2010); Kali N. Gross, *Colored Amazons: Crime, Violence, and Black Women in the City of Brotherly Love, 1880–1910* (Durham, NC: Duke University Press, 2006); Elizabeth K. Hinton, *From the War on Poverty to the War on Crime: The Making of Mass Incarceration in America* (Cambridge, MA: Harvard University Press, 2016); Jonathan Simon, *Governing Through Crime: How the War on Crime Transformed American Democracy and Created a Culture of Fear* (New York: Oxford University Press, 2006).

32. Maxwell and Shields, *The Long Southern Strategy*.

33. Quoted in Rick Perlstein, "Jimmy Carter Tried to Make It Easier to Vote in 1977. The Right Stopped Him with the Same Arguments It's Using Today," *Time*, August 20, 2020, https://time.com/5881305/president-carter-election-reform.

34. Waldman, *The Fight to Vote*, 185; Perlstein, "Jimmy Carter Tried to Make It Easier to Vote in 1977."

35. Warren Weaver Jr., "Carter Proposes End of Electoral College in Presidential Votes," *New York Times*, March 23, 1977, www.nytimes.com/1977/03/23/archives /carter-proposes-end-of-electoral-college-in-presidential-votes.html.

36. Paul Weyrich, "'I Don't Want Everybody to Vote' (Goo Goo)," YouTube, www .youtube.com/watch?v=8GBAsFwPglw.

37. Quoted in Robert Joffee, "Democrats Accuse GOP of Intimidating Minorities in N.J. Voting," *Washington Post*, November 8, 1981, www.washingtonpost.com/archive /politics/1981/11/08/democrats-accuse-gop-of-intimidating-minorities-in-nj-voting /9cfb873d-7c3e-44ea-beb9-4c9b5d9ab5a1.

38. Matt Katz, "Armed Men Once Patrolled the Polls. Will They Reappear in November?," WNYC, September 1, 2016, www.wnyc.org/story/armed-men-once -patrolled-polls-will-they-reappear-november; Ari Berman, *Give Us the Ballot: The Modern Struggle for Voting Rights in America* (New York: Picador, 2015), 219; Joffee, "Democrats Accuse GOP of Intimidating Minorities in N.J. Voting"; Michael Wines, "Freed by Court Ruling, Republicans Step Up Effort to Patrol Voting," *New York Times*, May 18, 2020, www.nytimes.com/2020/05/18/us/Voting-republicans-trump .html.

39. Vann R. Newkirk II, "The Republican Party Emerges from Decades of Court Supervision," *Atlantic*, January 9, 2018, www.theatlantic.com/politics/archive/2018/01 /the-gop-just-received-another-tool-for-suppressing-votes/550052; Katz, "Armed Men Once Patrolled the Polls."

40. *Democratic National Committee v. Republican National Committee* (1981), Case 2:81-cv-03876-DRD-MAS, accessed May 23, 2021, www.brennancenter.org/sites /default/files/legacy/Democracy/dnc.v.rnc/1981%20complaint.pdf.

41. Quoted in Newkirk, "The Republican Party Emerges from Decades of Court Supervision."

42. Quoted in Joffee, "Democrats Accuse GOP of Intimidating Minorities in N.J. Voting."

43. Carol Anderson, *One Person, No Vote: How Voter Suppression Is Destroying Our De- mocracy* (New York: Bloomsbury, 2019), 45–47.

44. Quoted in Anderson, *One Person, No Vote*, 47.

45. Anderson, *One Person, No Vote*, 50–52.

46. Robert F. Bauer to Michael B. Mukasey and Nora R. Dannehy, letter, October 17, 2008, https://media.npr.org/documents/2008/oct/donations.pdf; Waldman, *The Fight to Vote*, 187, 193; Anderson, *One Person, No Vote*, 50–51, 54–55.

47. Anderson, *One Person, No Vote*, 52–60.

48. Wang, *The Politics of Voter Suppression*, 79.

49. Robert Barnes, "Stevens Says Supreme Court Decision on Voter ID Was Cor- rect but Maybe Not Right," *Washington Post*, May 15, 2016, www.washingtonpost .com/politics/courts_law/stevens-says-supreme-court-decision-on-voter-id-was-correct -but-maybe-not-right/2016/05/15/9683c51c-193f-11e6-9e16-2e5a123aac62_story .html?utm_term=.4c92ef515545.

50. Richard A. Posner, *Reflections on Judging* (Cambridge, MA: Harvard University Press, 2013), 84–85.

51. Quoted in Wang, *The Politics of Voter Suppression*, 79.

52. Michael Wines, "How Charges of Voter Fraud Became a Political Strategy," *New York Times*, October 21, 2016, www.nytimes.com/2016/10/22/us/how-charges-of-voter -fraud-became-a-political-strategy.html.

53. Alex Vandermaas-Peeler, Daniel Cox, Molly Fisch-Friedman, Rob Griffin, and Robert P. Jones, "American Democracy in Crisis: The Challenges of Voter Knowl- edge, Participation, and Polarization," PRRI, July 17, 2018, www.prri.org/research /american-democracy-in-crisis-voters-midterms-trump-election-2018.

54. Justin Levitt, "A Comprehensive Investigation of Voter Impersonation Finds 31 Credible Incidents out of One Billion Ballots Cast," *Washington Post*, August 6, 2014, www.washingtonpost.com/news/wonk/wp/2014/08/06/a-comprehensive-investigation

-of-voter-impersonation-finds-31-credible-incidents-out-of-one-billion-ballots
-cast.

55. Antoine J. Banks and Heather M. Hicks, "Fear and Implicit Racism: Whites' Support for Voter ID Laws," *Political Psychology* 37, no. 5 (October 2016): 641–658; David C. Wilson and Paul R. Brewer, "The Foundations of Public Opinion on Voter ID Laws: Political Predispositions, Racial Resentment, and Information Effects," *Public Opinion Quarterly* 77, no. 4 (Winter 2013): 962–984.

56. Anderson, *One Person, No Vote*, 88–92; Eli Rosenberg, "'The Most Bizarre Thing I've Ever Been a Part Of': Trump Panel Found No Widespread Voter Fraud, Ex-member Says," *Washington Post*, August 3, 2018, www.washingtonpost.com/news/politics/wp/2018/08/03/the-most-bizarre-thing-ive-ever-been-a-part-of-trump-panel-found-no-voter-fraud-ex-member-says.

57. Anderson, *One Person, No Vote*, 191–195.

58. "US Capitol and DC Police Testify on January 6 Attack," C-SPAN, July 27, 2021, www.youtube.com/watch?v=801J3ohEIW0; Dominick Mastrangelo, "Two-Thirds of Republicans Think Biden's Victory Was Not Legitimate: Poll," *The Hill*, May 26, 2021, https://thehill.com/homenews/administration/555584-two-thirds-or-republicans-think-bidens-victory-was-not-legitimate.

CONTRIBUTOR BIOS

Akhil Reed Amar is Sterling Professor of Law and Political Science at Yale University. He has been cited by Supreme Court justices in more than forty cases—tops in his generation. His latest and most ambitious book is *The Words That Made Us: America's Constitutional Conversation, 1760–1840*. Twitter: @AkhilReedAmar

Carol Anderson is the Charles Howard Candler Professor of African American Studies at Emory University and a historian of African Americans' civil and human rights struggles. She is the author of five books, including *One Person, No Vote: How Voter Suppression Is Destroying Our Democracy*. Twitter: @ProfCAnderson

Kathleen Belew is an associate professor of history at Northwestern University and a leading expert on the white power movement, vigilante violence, and political extremism. Her first book, *Bring the War Home*, has been discussed on *Fresh Air*, *Newshour*, and *Frontline*, and in the *New York Times*. Twitter: @kathleen_belew

David A. Bell is Sidney and Ruth Lapidus Professor in the Department of History at Princeton University. Trained as a historian of France, he teaches and writes on the age of revolution in the Atlantic world. His most recent book is *Men on Horseback: The Power of Charisma in the Age of Revolution*. Twitter: @DavidAvromBell

Geraldo Cadava is the Wender-Lewis Teaching and Research Professor of History and Latina and Latino Studies at Northwestern University. He is the author of *The Hispanic Republican: The Shaping of an American Political Identity, from Nixon to Trump* (Ecco, 2020), and *Standing on Common Ground: The Making of a Sunbelt Borderland* (Harvard University Press, 2013). Twitter: @gerry_cadava

Sarah Churchwell is a professor of American literature and the chair of Public Understanding of the Humanities at the School of Advanced Study, University of London. Her books include *Careless People: Murder, Mayhem and the Invention of* The Great Gatsby; *Behold, America: The Entangled History of America First and the American Dream*; and *The Wrath to Come:* Gone with the Wind *and the Myth of the Lost Cause*. Twitter: @sarahchurchwell

Erik M. Conway is a historian of technology living in Altadena, California. He is coauthor, with Naomi Oreskes, of the best-selling *Merchants of Doubt: How a Handful of Scientists Obscured the Truth on Issues from Tobacco Smoke to Global Warming*. His most recent book is *Exploration and Engineering: The Jet Propulsion Laboratory and the Quest for Mars*. Twitter: @ErikMConway

Karen L. Cox is a professor of history at the University of North Carolina at Charlotte. She is the leading national expert on the topic of Confederate monuments and has written op-eds for the *New York Times, Washington Post, TIME*, CNN, and *Smithsonian* magazine. She is also an award-winning author of four books, including *No Common Ground: Confederate Monuments and the Ongoing Fight for Racial Justice*. Twitter: @DrKarenLCox

Glenda Gilmore is the Peter V. and C. Vann Woodward Professor of History Emerita at Yale University. Her books include *Gender and Jim Crow: Women and the Politics of White Supremacy in North Carolina, 1898–1920; Defying Dixie: The Radical Roots of Civil Rights, 1920–1950; These United States: The Making of a Nation, 1890 to the Present*; and *Romare Bearden in the Homeland of His Imagination: An Artist's Reckoning with the South.* Twitter: @GilmoreGlenda

Lawrence B. Glickman is the Stephen and Evalyn Milman Professor in the Departments of History and American Studies at Cornell University. He is the author, most recently, of *Free Enterprise: An American History.* He has written frequently for public audiences in the *Atlantic, Boston Review, Slate*, the *Washington Post*, and other publications. Twitter: @larryglickman

Elizabeth Hinton is a professor of history, African American studies, and law at Yale. She is the author of *America on Fire: The Untold History of Police Violence and Black Rebellion Since the 1960s* and *From the War on Poverty to the War on Crime: The Making of Mass Incarceration in America.* Twitter: @elizabhinton

Daniel Immerwahr is a professor of history, specializing in US foreign relations, at Northwestern University. He is the author of *How to Hide an Empire: A History of the Greater United States.* Twitter: @dimmerwahr

Michael Kazin is a professor of history at Georgetown University and editor emeritus of *Dissent.* His most recent book is *What It Took to Win: A History of the Democratic Party.* Twitter: @mkazin

Ari Kelman is Chancellor's Leadership Professor of History at the University of California, Davis. His books include *Battle Lines: A Graphic History of the Civil War* and *A Misplaced Massacre: Struggling Over the Memory of Sand Creek.* Twitter: @AriKelman

Kevin M. Kruse is a professor of history at Princeton University. His books include *White Flight: Atlanta and the Making of Modern Conservatism*, *One Nation Under God: How Corporate America Invented Christian America*, and *Fault Lines: A History of the United States Since World War II* (coauthored with Julian E. Zelizer). Twitter: @KevinMKruse

Erika Lee is the author of several award-winning books, including *America for Americans: A History of Xenophobia in the United States* and *The Making of Asian America*. A Regents Professor and the director of the Immigration History Research Center at the University of Minnesota, she also serves as the president of the Organization of American Historians. Twitter: @prof_erikalee

Natalia Mehlman Petrzela is an associate professor of history at the New School in New York City. She is the author of *Classroom Wars: Language, Sex, and the Making of Modern Political Culture* and the forthcoming book *Fit Nation: The Gains and Pains of America's Exercise Obsession*. Twitter: @nataliapetrzela

Naomi Oreskes is the Henry Charles Lea Professor of the history of science and affiliated professor of Earth and planetary sciences at Harvard University. She is the author of numerous books on science and society, including, most recently, *Science on a Mission: How Military Funding Shaped What We Do and Don't Know About the Ocean*. Twitter: @NaomiOreskes

Eric Rauchway is Distinguished Professor of History at the University of California, Davis, and the author of seven books on US history, including *Winter War: Hoover, Roosevelt, and the First Clash Over the New Deal* and *Why the New Deal Matters*. Twitter: @rauchway

Joshua Zeitz is a contributing editor at *Politico* magazine. He earned his PhD at Brown University and BA at Swarthmore College, and held faculty positions at Cambridge University and Harvard University. He is the author of *Building the Great Society: Inside Lyndon Johnson's White House*. Twitter: @JoshuaMZeitz

Julian E. Zelizer is the Malcolm Stevenson Forbes, Class of 1941 Professor of History and Public Affairs at Princeton. He is also a political analyst for CNN and NPR. He is the author or editor of twenty-four books on American history. Twitter: @julianzelizer

INDEX

Kevin M. Kruse is a professor of history at Princeton University and the author or coeditor of five books, including *Fault Lines* and the award-winning *White Flight*. He lives in Princeton, New Jersey.

Julian E. Zelizer is the Malcolm Stevenson Forbes, Class of 1941 Professor of History and Public Affairs at Princeton University and the author or editor of twenty-four books on American political history, including *Fault Lines* and *Burning Down the House*. He has received fellowships from the New-York Historical Society, the Russell Sage Foundation, the Guggenheim Foundation, and New America. He lives in Princeton, New Jersey.